Reforming Africa's institutions

UNU World Institute for Development Economics Research (UNU/WIDER)

was established by the United Nations University as its first research and training centre and started work in Helsinki, Finland, in 1985. The purpose of the institute is to undertake applied research and policy analysis on structural changes affecting developing and transitional economies, to provide a forum for the advocacy of policies leading to robust, equitable, and environmentally sustainable growth, and to promote capacity strengthening and training in the field of economic and social policy making. Its work is carried out by staff researchers and visiting scholars in Helsinki and via networks of collaborating scholars and institutions around the world.

United Nations University World Institute for Development Economics Research (UNU/WIDER)
Katajanokanlaituri 6 B, FIN-00160 Helsinki, Finland
www.wider.unu.edu

Reforming Africa's institutions: Ownership, incentives and capabilities

Edited by Steve Kayizzi-Mugerwa

United Nations
University Press

TOKYO · NEW YORK · PARIS

United Nations
University
WIDER

World Institute for Development
Economics Research

United Nations University Press
The United Nations University, 53-70, Jingumae 5-chome,
Shibuya-ku, Tokyo, 150-8925, Japan
Tel: +81-3-3499-2811   Fax: +81-3-3406-7345
E-mail: sales@hq.unu.edu (general enquiries): press@hq.unu.edu
http://www.unu.edu

United Nations University Office in North America
2 United Nations Plaza, Room DC2-2062, New York, NY 10017, USA
Tel: +1-212-963-6387   Fax: +1-212-371-9454
E-mail: unuona@ony.unu.edu

United Nations University Press is the publishing division of the United Nations University.

United Nations University World Institute for Development Economics Research (UNU/WIDER)
Katajanokanlaituri 6 B, FIN-00160, Helsinki, Finland
Tel: +358-9-6159911   Fax +358-9-61599333
E-mail: wider@wider.unu.edu
http://www.wider.unu.edu

Cover design by Joyce C. Weston

Printed in the United States of America

UNUP-1082
ISBN 92-808-1082-0

Library of Congress Cataloging-in-Publication Data

Reforming Africa's institutions : ownership, incentives, and capabilities / edited by Steve Kayizzi-Mugerwa.
    p.   cm.
Includes bibliographical references and index.
ISBN 92-808-1082-0
1. Administrative agencies—Africa, Sub-Saharan—Management. 2. Civil service reform—Africa, Sub-Saharan. 3. Democratization—Africa, Sub-Saharan.
4. Africa, Sub-Saharan—Politics and government—1960- 5. Privatization—Africa, Sub-Saharan. 6. Economic assistance—Africa, Sub-Saharan. I. Kayizzi-Mugerwa, Steve.
JQ1876 .R44 2003
320′.6′0967—dc21
                                                    2002151435

Contents

Foreword

The issues addressed in the UNU/WIDER project 'Institutional Capabilities, Reform Ownership and Development in Sub-Saharan Africa' include the extent to which reforms undertaken in sub-Saharan Africa (SSA) in recent years have enhanced institutional capabilities across the breadth of government. The project also specifically examined the impact of public sector reforms on economic development in SSA. Past policies, an erroneous approach to adjustment and 'geography' are repeatedly cited as explanations for Africa's poor performance. *Reforming Africa's Institutions* addresses the weaknesses in the institutional capacity of the African state, which may be as important.

Looking at the evolution of public sector reforms in the past decade, it is relatively easy, with the benefit of hindsight, to criticize African governments for poor implementation strategies and for lack of commitment. However, in light of the nature of the reform tasks, African countries were probably more overwhelmed than uncommitted. Thus, although the failure of reforms to improve policy implementation and generate growth has been blamed on the intransigence of African governments, the donor community shares some of the blame. Both sides clearly underestimated the serious lack of capacities in individual countries as well as the time required for completing the reform process. These issues also relate to transparency and accountability, whose lack has been blamed on poor remuneration in the civil services. However, since corruption continues to be a problem even in the new agencies where wages and other benefits are far superior to those in the normal public sector, the causes of corruption are much more deep seated.

Perhaps more serious is the lack of a relevant body of law to ensure that corrupt officials are punished in a manner bound to be a deterrent. It is not surprising to find cases of corrupt officers punished under statutes from the 1960s. Thus, as well as modernizing the financial and accounting systems and raising the technical capacities for budgeting and financial analysis, it is necessary to upgrade laws relating to public sector functions. In addition, governments have weak budgeting systems. In recent years, attempts have been made to relate budgeting procedures to program targets. Much hope currently rests on the donor-supported medium-term expenditure framework, which it is believed will help countries to target their resources to poverty reduction. This is a daunting agenda, nevertheless.

Ultimately, successful reform demands strong political leadership. However, where influential bureaucrats remain largely indifferent or even cynical, reforms will make little headway. In *Reforming Africa's Institutions* examples of successful institutional reforms are characterized by enthusiasm across the board and not just at the top.

Matti Pohjola
Director of UNU/WIDER, a.i.
when project commenced

Acknowledgements

This volume is the outcome of a project on African institutions and re-form ownership undertaken at WIDER in Helsinki, Finland, during 2000–2001. UNU/WIDER gratefully acknowledges the financial contribution to its research on sub-Saharan Africa by the Government of Italy.

I would like to thank WIDER for providing the resources that made it possible for me to spend much of the above period based in Helsinki as project director for the study.

The study brought on board a number of academics from Africa, Europe and the United States. Many were drawn from universities and policy institutes, and a number were active in international organizations – I would like to thank all of them for the collaboration.

I also thank the director and staff of WIDER for creating a very con-ducive environment for the project and for taking exceptionally good care of the project participants on their visit to Helsinki. The entire project was managed efficiently by Lorraine Telfer-Taivainen. I also thank the University of Gothenburg for allowing me to spend time in Helsinki.

Steve Kayizzi-Mugerwa

Contributors

Tony Addison is deputy director of UNU/WIDER. He was previously on the faculty of the department of economics, University of Warwick, UK, as well as the School of Oriental and African Studies (University of London). He began his career as an Overseas Development Institute fellow in Tanzania's trade ministry. He is presently researching on issues of fiscal policy, debt management and reconstruction from conflict.

Arne Bigsten is professor of development economics at the University of Gothenburg, Sweden. He has done extensive research on African economic development with regard to income distribution and poverty, industrial and rural development, trade, aid and economic policy.

Anders Danielson is an associate professor of economics at the University of Lund, Sweden. His principal research interests are public sector reforms, external debt, foreign aid and poverty reduction. He has published widely on these issues, particularly in relation to field research in East Africa and the Caribbean.

Dick Durevall is a senior lecturer in economics at the University of Gothenburg, Sweden. He has undertaken research on the macroeconomics of developing countries, with a focus on inflation, money demand and international trade. He has published studies on Brazil, Kenya, Malawi, and Zimbabwe and undertaken consultancies for the Swedish Agency for International Development Cooperation (Sida).

Moses L. Golola is a former Fulbright fellow and is currently with the Inter-University Council for East

Africa where he is deputy executive secretary. He was principal and vice chancellor of Bugema University, Uganda, 1991–2000. He has undertaken research in Malawi and Uganda on issues related to governance, local-level politics and economic history.

Abdalla Hamdok is with the United Nations Economic Commission for Africa in Addis Ababa, Ethiopia. He was formerly at the African Development Bank, where he led the governance initiative, and worked as project manager and lead researcher in Zimbabwe.

Hendrik van der Heijden is economic adviser to the Government of the Solomon Islands. During 2000–1 he wrote a book for the Norwegian Agency for Development Co-operation (NORAD) and the Swedish Agency for International Development Cooperation (Sida) entitled *Economic Reform, Foreign Aid and External Debt Relief in Zambia* which reflects his work as external financing and policy adviser in Zambia's finance ministry in the 1990s. He worked as a senior economist during his twenty-year career in the World Bank.

Steve Kayizzi-Mugerwa, the editor of this book, is with the IMF's Independent Evaluation Office in Washington DC, USA. He was an associate professor of economics at the University of Gothenburg, Sweden, from 1994. He has undertaken research on many African countries and published widely on issues related to growth, economic adjustment and poverty reduction. During 2000–1, he directed the project on Institutional

Capabilities, Reform Ownership and Development in Sub-Saharan Africa at WIDER in Helsinki, Finland.

Damiano Kulundu Manda is a lecturer in economics at the University of Nairobi and a policy analyst at the Kenya Institute of Public Policy Analysis and Research (KIPPRA). He is also a researcher at the African Economic Research Consortium (AERC) network. His research focuses on labor markets, as well as education, health and poverty policy issues.

Mohammed Salisu is a lecturer in economics at Lancaster University Management School, UK. He specializes in international trade, foreign direct investment and economic growth, and has published widely on these areas. He has a forthcoming publication on the political economy of oil in Nigeria, based on his longstanding interest in rent seeking in relation to the exploitation of natural resources.

José A. Sulemane is with the finance ministry in Maputo, Mozambique, where he has held various positions. He participated in this project while finishing his doctorate in economics at Notre Dame University, South Bend, Indiana.

Aili Mari Tripp is an associate professor of political science and women's studies at the University of Wisconsin-Madison, USA, and director of the Women's Studies Research Center. She has published extensively on women's issues and politics in Africa; women's responses to economic reform in Africa; and transformations of associational life in Africa. Currently she is working on a co-authored book on the political impact of women's movements in Africa.

Yvonne M. Tsikata is a senior economist with the World Bank, Washington DC, USA, where she has worked since 1991, focusing most recently on international trade issues. Between 1998 and 2001 she was a senior research fellow at the Economic and Social Research Foundation in Dar es Salaam, Tanzania. She contributed to the World Bank's study on aid and reform in Africa and worked on the effects of globalization and the political economy of reform for the OECD Development Center in Paris.

Clas Wihlborg is a professor of finance at the Copenhagen Business School, Denmark. He has also held a similar position at the University of Gothenburg in Sweden. He has taught and done research at various universities in the United States, and is the author of many articles and books on issues of corporate finance and, more recently, on corporate governance. With colleagues, he has also studied financial issues in transition economies as well as developing countries.

Figures

Tables

Abbreviations

ACB	Anti-Corruption Bureau (Malawi)
ADB	African Development Bank
CDF	Comprehensive Development Framework
CFA	Communauté financière africaine
CGZ	Consultative Group for Zambia
CIDA	Canadian International Development Agency
COMESA	Common Market for Eastern and Southern Africa
CSAP	civil service action plan (Malawi)
DANIDA	Danish International Development Agency
DEA	data envelopment analysis
DFID	Department for International Development (UK)
DRC	Democratic Republic of the Congo
ECOWAS	Economic Community of West African States
ESAF	Enhanced Structural Adjustment Facility
FSU	former Soviet Union
GDP	gross domestic product
GNP	gross national product
HIPC	Heavily Indebted Poor Countries
IDA	International Development Association
ILO	International Labour Organization
IMF	International Monetary Fund
MIMIC	Multiple Indicators/Multiple Causes
MMD	Movement for Multiparty Democracy (Zambia)
MTEF	medium-term expenditure framework (Malawi)
NGO	non-governmental organization

NORAD	Norwegian Agency for Development Co-operation
NRM	National Resistance Movement (Uganda)
OECD	Organisation for Economic Co-operation and Development
PAMSCAD	Programme of Action to Mitigate the Social Costs of Adjustment (Ghana)
PER	public expenditure review
PFP	policy framework paper
PNDC	Provisional National Defence Council (Ghana)
ROSCA	rotating savings and credit association
SIDA	Swedish Agency for International Development Cooperation
SOE	state-owned enterprise
SSA	sub-Saharan Africa
UNDP	United Nations Development Programme
UNIP	United National Independence Party (Zambia)
USAID	United States Agency for International Development
VAT	value added tax
WAEMU	West African Economic and Monetary Union
ZCCM	Zambia Consolidated Copper Mines

Introduction

Steve Kayizzi-Mugerwa

African governments have pursued political and economic reforms since the late 1980s in a bid to promote economic growth, reduce poverty and encourage popular participation and good governance. Financial support from bilateral and multilateral donors has been crucial for the implementation of these reforms. Recent assessments indicate, however, that outcomes have been far from satisfactory. Where better results have been observed there remain serious questions of sustainability. The poor outcomes have been blamed on the weaknesses of the public sectors in Africa. According to their critics, African bureaucracies play a contradictory and conflict-ridden role, being at once part of the problem and the cure. Weak public institutions have implied loose operational guidelines for public service work, while on the other hand poor finances have reduced incentives and morale among employees (Lienert, 1998; Lienert and Modi, 1997; Olowu et al., 1997; Klitgaard, 1989).

For African countries to benefit from economic reforms demands a new modus operandi for the public sector. Distortions in its core functions must be eradicated by altering the incentive and induction systems for public employees and by changing the operation of the civil service. Furthermore, African governments need to care about their reputations and credibility, not only with respect to their domestic constituencies but also in relation to the donor community. Past experience has shown that, when governments cannot be taken at their word, their policy effectiveness, in fighting poverty for instance, becomes seriously eroded (Kayizzi-Mugerwa, 2001; DFID, 1997).

1

The chapters presented in this book have three areas of emphasis, all related to the public sector's capacity to internalize reforms in the pursuit of growth and poverty reduction. The first area is reform ownership, which relates to the ability of policymakers to define and implement policies and to manage recipient–donor relations. The second area relates to incentives in the public service and how they influence public sector efficiency and productivity. The third area is concerned with the development of institutional capabilities in the public sector and thus with the public sector's reputation and credibility.

Part I: The political economy of reform ownership

When policymakers are responsible for the formulation and implementation of their reforms, they are apt to defend them before their domestic constituencies and the donor community – they are said to 'own' their reforms. However, the concept of ownership has been used in so many contexts in recent years that its operational usefulness has diminished considerably as a result. In this volume, ownership will be taken to mean that governments have internalized reforms to such an extent that they are prepared to defend them before their domestic constituencies.

Although the donor community has emphasized the importance of ownership for reform success, few African countries have been able to establish an institutional culture that is supportive of domestic reforms. The failure of economic reforms to have lasting impact in Africa has, thus, been blamed on the lack of ownership by governments. In return, policies continue to be imposed from 'above' by donors or multilateral agencies, and domestically by the governments themselves, without the participation of the population. This lack of ownership can be blamed on the crisis-ridden nature of the African economies. In many of them 'fire brigade' operations, supported by donors, were necessary to prevent further decline, but failed to provide scope for ownership by domestic leaders. Africa has also lacked structures for consensus building, with political exclusion more the norm than the exception. The political environment has not supported the evolution of good governance (Aron, 1997; Coolidge and Rose-Ackerman, 1997).

The failure of policymakers to undertake measures for better public management and accountability has negatively affected their relations with donors. On the other hand, donor bureaucracies and those of the multilateral agencies have exhibited a lag in adapting to the new thinking which emphasizes partnership (van der Heijden, 2000; Asian Development Bank, 1999). The threat of aid embargo is still used by donors as a disciplining device, although experiences from Kenya, Zambia and Malawi indicate that this tends to hit the poor and vulnerable groups harder than the more affluent ones, and without pushing governments towards improved accountability (Bigsten and Kayizzi-Mugerwa, 2000).

In a review of the African experience, which sets the tone for the chapters in this section, Abdalla Hamdok argues that good governance is a prerequisite for sustainable development. Growth and development demand law and order, the creation of transparent administrative structures, the extension of social infrastructure to the rural areas, the protection of poor and vulnerable groups and their inclusion in the decision-making process, and the preservation of peace and security. The complex informational and financial demands of globalization also dictate that African countries should strive for more efficient and transparent governments. He concludes, however, that ultimately it is politics that determine the nature of governance. It is thus important for African countries to open up their political space and exercise more inclusive politics. The best way of nurturing good governance is to let citizens participate in decisions that affect them. This is best done via devolution of power and by strengthening domestic institutions.

Yvonne Tsikata discusses the ownership debate, closely related to governance, with a comparative study of Ghana and Tanzania. Ghana embarked on reforms as early as the 1980s, whereas Tanzania came on board much later. She argues, however, that conditionality by donors masked domestic efforts at reform ownership in both countries, stifling debate and making it difficult for domestic groups to participate meaningfully. She also notes that political legitimacy is not the only basis for economic reform. Rather, successful reforms generate growth and improve living standards, making it possible for initially illegitimate regimes to garner support. The experience of Ghana, Korea and Uganda suggests that, in the face of tangible economic results, political illegitimacy can be tolerated for a while. In the long run, however, reforms generate demands for political change, and governments eventually have to address political reforms as well.

Tsikata concludes that domestic politics, the aid relationship and public sector accountability are important determinants of reform ownership. In most African countries, public discourse on economic development and reform remains inadequate and the means of sanctioning poor government performance are equally meager. Ownership should also imply that, when citizens are dissatisfied with public policy, they are able to hold the government accountable. On the other hand, donor assistance, by helping to deliver growth and reduce poverty, strengthens the hand of government. Related to this is the need for a strong institutional mechanism for accountability. In a sense, accountability buys the recipient country implementation space. On donor–recipient relations, Tsikata argues that, for true partnership to emerge, both sides need to let go of old conceptions and focus on strengthening institutions that can facilitate domestic ownership.

Do donors matter for institutional reform in Africa? In responding to the question, Tony Addison argues that, in spite of over twenty years of debate on institutional development in Africa, in terms of results there is still precious little to show for the effort. Addison argues that part of the problem is that policymakers have failed to transcend the 'partial equilibrium' outcome of the earlier policies. African governments need to write a new social contract with their populations, based on the creation of democratic institutions and the expansion of the private sector, as opposed to one that emphasizes expansive government and public sector employment. He notes, however, that in implementing reforms it has been difficult to move ahead on issues such as the privatization of utilities and infrastructure and better public management. Democratic reforms have also been slow. Addison concludes that helping African policymakers to reform public management, the security sector and their revenue generation capacities should be a major task for donors. Improvements in these areas might help convince a skeptical population and business sector of the merits of economic reforms, thereby helping governments to exit the partial equilibrium.

In a chapter on donors and policy making in Zambia, Hendrik van der Heijden argues that, even where policymakers seem to be genuinely interested in reform, the process could still be derailed by domestic politics. In the early 1990s, a new Zambian government was elected under President Chiluba, promising political and economic reforms. It was soon engulfed in corruption and policy failure: the economy contracted and the privatization of the mines and measures to improve governance and accountability were delayed. However, donors continued to support the country, hoping that its fledgling democratic institutions and its earlier enthusiasm for reforms could still be salvaged. Van der Heijden concludes that, when the national commitment to development wanes, aid cannot fully substitute for it. Conversely, where there is national commitment, conditionalities are not needed. To address socioeconomic challenges of the decade, Zambia needs to adopt a fundamentally different approach, one that does not attempt to achieve economic development by maximizing access to external assistance and debt relief, but rather one that aims at maximizing internal development efforts to achieve growth. Transposing Zambian experience to Africa as a whole, van der Heijden argues that donors are willing to support policies and programs that are genuinely owned by policymakers. They should refrain from imposing intrusive conditionalities.

Part II: Incentive structures and performance in the public service

The public sector reforms pursued in Africa for much of the 1990s belong to two generations (Lienert, 1998; Lienert and Modi, 1997). The first generation focused on improvement of incentives in the public sector by first reducing the size of the civil service and then raising remuneration for those remaining in the system. This also included ridding central registries and payrolls of ghost workers. The second generation of reforms focused on the improvement of management systems and raising accountability in the service. There was also need for the creation of non-monetary incentives, including promotion, the assignment of more challenging tasks and training. Related to training was the general concern that a mismatch existed between the skills acquired during earlier regimes and those required by the new tasks of government: to create an enabling environment for growth, poverty reduction and private sector development (Schiavo-Campo, 1996; Van Rijckeghem and Weder, 1997). The chapters in this section look at incentive structures and performance in the public service, covering the subjects of wage structures, mechanisms for professional advancement, as well as public sector efficiency.

In his essay on economic and institutional reforms in French-speaking West Africa, Anders Danielson notes that reforms in this region were mainly triggered by national crises, hence the abrupt manner in which they were implemented. For example, a rapidly deteriorating economy or political turmoil forced governments in Benin, Mali and Côte d'Ivoire to embark on reforms, although these were often shallow and characterized by reversals. With respect to civil service reform, Danielson argues that, as in other African countries, the process has been politically difficult. The easier reforms, such as the elimination of ghost workers, needed to be accompanied by retrenchment of the labor force. However, governments have tended to undertake retrenchment only when forced to do so by donors and to rehire at the earliest opportunity. Moreover, wage restructuring was made difficult by the wage compression caused by the 50 percent devaluation of the CFA (Communauté financière africaine) franc in 1994. Danielson concludes that although the countries of the West African Economic and Monetary Union (WAEMU) are somewhat distinct from the rest of sub-Saharan Africa – notably with respect to their shared institutions and common currency and monetary policy – they have performed much like the rest of the continent in the past decade. Their close economic cooperation has not helped them to evolve a stronger institutional culture for policy implementation or to attain better levels of economic performance.

Dick Durevall's chapter looks at how Malawi has addressed the questions of incentives, governance and accountability in its public sector reform. For decades the country was ruled by an autocratic leader and a system of governance that demanded full subservience to the center. Ironically, government officials exhibited a high level of accountability at this time, also partly thanks to a well-functioning economy and reasonably high wages in the public sector. During the 1990s, however, incentives were seriously eroded. Inflation as well as the effects of the various salary reviews led to wage compression. Policymakers were forced to embark on public sector reforms. Durevall concludes that the degree to which the bureaucracy and the rest of the population have embraced the changes can be questioned. The country's president remains the driving force behind public sector reform and it will take time before the changes are accepted as part and parcel of government machinery. To succeed, reforms require champions within the public sector, not just at the top. It is only when accountability is internalized within the civil service that it will be felt elsewhere in the country.

Damiano Kulundu Manda paints a similar portrait of the Kenyan civil service. The factors affecting performance include poor remuneration, lack of supplies and equipment, absence of career development prospects and poor delegation of responsibility. As in other African countries, policymakers are keen to improve the performance of the public service but are constrained by lack of finances and by politics. Raising public sector wages to a competitive level, even after a substantial number of employees have been retrenched, will still demand substantial resources. On the other hand, large-scale retrenchment of the civil service is not popular among influential groups. Kulundu Manda concludes that the Kenyan government has no choice but to embark on an effective reform program to ensure that the public sector increases its efficiency, especially in tackling the complex social issues that have arisen in the past decade. It should also be possible for young people to make a career in the civil service. For this to happen, however, the government needs to raise the public sector's profile by improving recruitment and promotion procedures and by paying civil servants competitive wages.

In a chapter on the Nigerian civil service, Mohammed Salisu argues that Nigerians had every reason to expect their public sector to be efficient and well attuned to the development needs of the country. With one of the largest pools of human capital on the continent and endowed with vast oil wealth, the country was, on the face of it, not subject to the resource constraints experienced by other African countries. Still, its civil service has performed poorly in recent decades. The abundance of oil resources has in retrospect subverted concerns for increased efficiency in government, while also expanding the public sector beyond sustainable levels. But the perhaps most important outcome of the combination of oil riches and ineffective government was the emergence of a 'hidden' economy in Nigeria. Corruption has become an endemic feature of public sector activities. Salisu argues that corruption has led to a partiality for capital-intensive projects, because these are best suited to the culture of bribery. The productivity of the public sector has declined as a result, while the effects of industrial policy on investment have been distorted. Salisu concludes that to turn the tide of public sector inefficiency and corruption in Nigeria will demand the creation of efficiency-based incentive schemes linking reward to performance. Also, political interference in the daily operations of the civil service should be minimized if the public's confidence in the public service is to be restored.

In their chapter on Mozambique, José Sulemane and Steve Kayizzi-Mugerwa indicate that the poor state of the country's public institutions is partly a legacy of its conflict-ridden colonial history, aggravated after independence by civil war, malnutrition and mass poverty. In recent years the government has embarked on institutional reform with measures to improve wages for public workers, and has also undertaken far-reaching social reforms helping to revive service provision in the districts most affected by the civil war. However, paucity of resources has made it difficult to implement reforms fully. Still, Mozambique has demonstrated that, given political will, even poor African countries can begin to reform their public sectors. The authors conclude that, owing to shortage of financial and human resources in Mozambique, the influence of the donor community in public sector reform has become disproportionately large. There is, thus, a question of sustainability. However, given Mozambique's recent history of civil war and weather shocks, policy autonomy and financial independence are not the goals to strive for at the moment. More important is the improvement of capacities in the public sector in general and the civil service in particular to ensure that future reforms are driven from within.

Part III: Developing institutional capabilities

The chapters in this section portray a complex picture of the challenges facing African bureaucracies in their efforts at institution building at both center and local levels, establishing legal frameworks to ensure orderly insolvency and debt recovery procedures, as well as private sector development. In order to reach specific targets in reform efforts, African governments have sought to 'fence off' some projects and programs from the rest of the public service. Besides reducing political interference and bureaucratic 'overload,' the goal has also been to instill a more business-like approach to public sector management (Munene, 1995; Rose-Ackerman, 1986).

This section on institutional capabilities begins with a chapter on the political economy of privatization. Although the issue of making development policies more inclusive also relates to private sector development, Steve Kayizzi-Mugerwa argues that the process of privatization has varied from country to country depending on institutional constraints and donor leverage. He notes that, although formal explanations emphasize the normative benefits of privatization, including higher efficiency and increased investment, the process has been driven by politics as well. A review of the laws setting up privatization agencies in the various countries shows that policymakers sought to ensure that their supporters were on board. In no African country were the voucher-based privatizations – used earlier in Eastern Europe – attempted, most likely because African populations were not in a position to demand a stake in the companies as their constitutional right. In some countries, however, there were attempts at affirmative action. Some firm sizes were reserved for indigenous Africans, and in other cases funds were set aside to enable Africans to acquire businesses.

Kayizzi-Mugerwa concludes that privatization should not be seen as a static process. It soon acquires its own dynamics and support groups. After a decade of privatization, many governments in Africa are now privatizing with less domestic opposition than a decade ago. Although privatization has not made governments richer, it has shown that companies can function efficiently outside the ambit of the public sector.

On the theme of inclusive policies, Moses Golola argues that decentralization in Uganda was accorded a dual mandate: enhancing the process of democratization (that is, encouraging participatory democracy via self-determination, self-governance and social justice), and the mobilization of the people for production. To be meaningful, however, political decentralization must be accompanied by financial decentralization. A notable difficulty in Uganda has been how to devise a policy for revenue sharing so that the poorer districts, with little of their own local revenue, also benefit. Direct handouts from the center make policymakers at the local level beholden to the central bureaucracies, and the intended positive impacts of decentralization on local self-determination fail to be realized. Golola concludes that, in spite of continuing tension between center and locality, decentralization has brought tangible benefits to districts in Uganda. Populations are able to influence decisions that affect them, and political consultation has become simpler and less formal. He warns, however, that a high level of accountability is required if decentralization is to lead to local development. The corruption and malfeasance evident at the center should not be 'decentralized' to the local level.

Laws and regulations are crucial to the development of the private sector in Africa. However, in his discussion of the role of insolvency law in institutional development, Clas Wihlborg argues that, although concerns over administrative and economic management structures have tended to dominate the debate, the promotion of the private sector demands that issues of debt recovery and insolvency be put on the agenda. In countries where procedures for debt resolution and for orderly insolvency are missing, business risk increases markedly and few investors will want to engage in new but risky ventures, because failure would lead to long-term indebtedness. Wihlborg concludes that all economic actors stand to gain from the reduction of the risks that emanate from a poor business environment. However, insolvency touches on the very fundamentals of the political and economic system of the country; enforcement of an insolvency law can thus be problematic. Powerful domestic groups need to be convinced that the law does not threaten them.

Discussions of reform ownership tend to focus on the modern sector of the economy. However, Aili Mari Tripp argues that informality does not imply lack of form; rather, the activities engaged in lack formalization. This makes them more adaptable and resilient. Thus, whereas formal institutions, both private and public, have responded poorly to economic crisis in Africa, informal institutions have responded dynamically, providing livelihoods to the population. Savings clubs, engaged in by many groups, have been crucial in generating savings for investment. Relations in the informal sector are based on mutuality, reciprocity and fairness. These provide the flexibility and public spirit needed to overcome crisis. Tripp concludes that government policies harm the informal sector more than they help. Informal operators continue to have poor access to services and credit, their property rights are poorly respected and they are subjected to harassment from the police and other authorities. It is necessary to change this official attitude if the interests of the poorest groups in Africa are to be protected.

In the last chapter of the volume, Arne Bigsten looks at the relevance of the Nordic model to African development. Whereas Nordic countries were still a poor agrarian outpost at the European periphery at the turn of the twentieth century, roughly sixty years later they were among the most affluent countries in the world. Furthermore, they had managed to achieve rapid growth while preserving a high degree of social compassion. To what extent could African countries benefit from the Nordic experience? Bigsten argues that, although institutions evolve from particular country and regional circumstances, there are still a number of areas where Africa could draw lessons. Political inclusion has been a key ingredient in the maintenance of political stability in the Nordic countries. African governments also need to build on a much broader political base than is currently the case in order to ensure stability. Another issue is social compassion. Nordic countries have striven to minimize welfare gaps among their citizens and to care for the poor and vulnerable. This has been made possible by focusing on the provision of social services such as health and education. However, the provision of social services requires financing, which can lead to high rates of taxation. African countries have so far had low tax income and donors have funded a substantial amount of their social expenditure. If the problem of improving social provision is to be tackled, African countries need to find a more sustainable revenue base. Bigsten concludes that a high degree of public accountability is crucial for reform success. Populations soon withdraw support from unaccountable governments, thereby derailing their programs.

REFERENCES

Aron, J. (1997) 'Political, Economic and Social Institutions: A Review of Growth Evidence,' CSAE Working Papers 98/4, Centre for the Study of African Economies, Oxford.

Asian Development Bank (1999) *Governance in Thailand: Challenges, Issues and Prospects*, ADB: Manila.

Bigsten, A. and S. Kayizzi-Mugerwa (2000) 'The Political Economy of Policy Failure in Zambia,' Working Papers in Economics No. 23, Göteborg University, Department of Economics.

Coolidge, J. and S. Rose-Ackerman (1997) 'High Level Rent Seeking and Corruption in African Regimes: Theory and Causes,' World Bank Working Paper No. 1780, World Bank, Washington, DC.

DFID (Department for International Development) (1997) *Eliminating World Poverty: A Challenge for the 21st Century*, The Stationery Office: London.

Heijden, H. van der (2000) 'The Effectiveness of Economic Policy Reform, Foreign Aid and External Debt Relief in Zambia,' book draft presented at Sida (Swedish Agency for International Development Cooperation), Stockholm.

Kayizzi-Mugerwa, S. (2001) 'Africa and the Donor Community: In Search of a Partnership for Development,' in L. Rikkilä and K. Sehm-Patomäki (eds.) *Democracy and Globalization. Promoting a North South Dialogue*, Department for International Development Cooperation, Ministry of Foreign Affairs: Helsinki.

Klitgaard, R. (1989) 'Incentive Myopia,' *World Development* 17(4):447–59.

Lienert, I. (1998) 'Civil Service Reform in Africa: Mixed Results after 10 Years,' *Finance and Development* 35(2).

Lienert, I. and J. Modi (1997) 'A Decade of Civil Service Reform in Sub-Saharan Africa,' IMF Working Paper 97/179.

Munene, J. C. (1995) 'The Institutional Environment and Managerial Innovations: A Qualitative Study of Selected Nigerian Firms,' *Journal of Occupational and Organizational Psychology* 68(4).

Olowu, D., E. Otobo and M. Okotoni (1997) 'The Role of the Civil Service in Enhancing Development and Democracy: An Evaluation of the Nigerian Experience,' paper presented at a conference on Civil Service Systems in a Comparative Perspective, School of Public and Environmental Affairs, Indiana University.

Rose-Ackerman, S. (1986) 'Reforming Public Bureaucracy through Economic Incentives?' *Journal of Law, Economics and Organization* 2(1):131–61.

Schiavo-Campo, S. (1996) 'Reforming the Civil Service,' *Finance and Development* 33(3).

Van Rijckeghem, C. and B. Weder (1997) 'Corruption and the Rate of Temptation: Do Low Wages in the Civil Service Cause Corruption?' IMF Working Paper 97/73.

Part I

The political economy of reform ownership

1

Governance and policy in Africa: Recent experiences

Abdalla Hamdok

1 Introduction

The promotion of 'good governance' has been an important focus and key ingredient in development efforts for African governments and the donor community since the early 1990s. Whereas the first and second generations of economic reforms emphasized stabilization and structural adjustment – in order for markets to play a greater role in the economies – the current emphasis on governance issues is an admission that the nature of domestic institutions also matters for outcomes. For Africa as a whole, more than a decade of economic reforms has produced only scattered examples of renewed growth and optimism. But, even in countries where growth had resumed, the continued weakness of institutions, marked by civil strife and the absence of political pluralism, puts the sustainability of recovery into question. Increasingly, good governance, also implying participatory and inclusive politics, has been identified as the missing ingredient in the reform efforts undertaken thus far.

The focus on governance has also highlighted the broad-ranging obligations of governments to their constituencies, hitherto overshadowed by the economic crisis management role that governments have had to play in recent years. These include:

• the establishment and maintenance of law and order
• creating transparent administrative structures
• extending social infrastructure to rural areas

- protecting poor and vulnerable groups and including them in the decisionmaking process
- the preservation of peace.

The complex informational and financial demands of globalization also dictate that African countries strive for more efficient and transparent governments.

This chapter reviews the issue of governance in the context of Africa's recent experience with economic and political reforms. The point of departure is that good governance is a prerequisite for sustainable development in Africa. Growth and development require a predictable regulatory framework, an effective and transparent public administration, and an independent judiciary where civilian, business and other legal issues can be resolved. Apart from ensuring the development of a growth-supporting economic and political environment, the above elements are also necessary for securing the legitimacy of the state. However, although it is important for the state to strive to (re)create a growth- and development-enhancing environment, it should be realized that the attainment of good governance is a process that cannot be obtained by the stroke of the pen, like, for example, adjustments in the exchange rate.

The chapter proceeds as follows. Section 2 presents a conceptual framework for analyzing good governance. Section 3 provides a brief historical background of Africa's governance problems, linking them to the growth challenge of more recent decades. Section 4 discusses the policy implications of good governance and the constraints facing African governments in attempting to achieve it. Section 5 concludes the chapter.

2   Conceptual issues

Governance can be defined as the science of government behavior and performance, including the exercise of economic, political and administrative authority to manage a country's affairs at all levels (Dethier, 1999). It provides the framework through which citizens and groups exercise their rights, meet their obligations and articulate their interests. Governance systems of various types have been elucidated at various periods in the past, but the recent emphasis on governance as an essential ingredient of Africa's reform process is unique in that it was initiated by donors and not by domestic leaders under pressure from their constituencies (Doornbos, 2001).[1] The first extensive discussion of the link between economic performance and governance was undertaken by the World Bank (1989) in its report on economic crisis and growth in sub-Saharan Africa at the end of the 1980s. The report marked a turning point from an almost exclusive concern with issues of economic structure and market behavior to issues of reforming public administrations, giving voice to the population and enhancing the credibility of governments.

As a policy framework, 'good governance' imposes demands on policymakers in their exercise of power. It encompasses:[2]

- An effective state – i.e. one that possesses an enabling political and legal environment for economic growth and equitable distribution.
- Civil societies and communities that are represented in the policymaking process, with the state facilitating political and social interaction and fostering societal cohesion and stability.
- A private sector that is allowed to play an independent and productive role in the economy.

All three elements, singly and in combination, together with sound economic management, are essential for sustained development as emphasized in recent assessments by the African Development Bank (1993, 1998, 1999a,b). However, although 'good governance' is an attractive concept, it also implies value judgments that might shift between communities and countries. To achieve many of the precepts of good governance, such as increased public sector efficiency or reduced poverty, necessarily implies a loss to some groups. For example, increased efficiency in public service delivery implies that the activities of rentseekers have to be minimized. On the other hand, reducing poverty might call for income redistribution measures, which could hurt the interests of richer groups. Good governance can thus not be achieved in a vacuum and is the product of a bargaining process between the various interest groups in the country. The underlying assumption is that the will of the majority, as expressed via an electoral process based on pluralist political systems for example, is cardinal (de Mello and Barenstein, 2001).

Good governance presupposes the existence of effective domestic institutions. These are generally few, and those that exist are bound to address complex agency problems. What makes government institutions particularly complex is the hierarchical nature of the political power structures, each level being at once principal and agent. For example, although line ministries at the center are principals for local governments they also are agents of the cabinet, which in turn is an agent of the prime minister or president. The government as a whole has parliament as its principal, at least in representative democracies. Implied is that the people have the ultimate authority in the political process.

Such power structures as presented above would pose few problems if the various relationships between agents and principals were governed by complete contracts; that is, contracts made on the basis of perfect information. At each level, the bureaucracy agents would do exactly as prescribed in the contract. In the real world, however, contracts are incomplete because information is imperfect and agents have discretionary power. At each level, agents will have information that they do not share with the layer above them in the hierarchy. Principals cannot be sure that, once reached, contracts will be honored – facing as a result moral hazard.

In a review of governance issues, Dethier (1999:6) notes that good development policy involves the design of appropriate incentive schemes and institutions such that agents can precommit to good behavior. Without this, agents will continue to maximize their own utility or that of interest groups to which they belong. In this latter case, public administrations at the various levels will run the risk of being captured by those interest groups. In light of these problems, principals are forced to design incentive-compatible contracts that reduce the gap between expected output and the effort expended by the agents.

In this regard, four interrelated approaches could help reduce the conflicts between principals and agents that arise from the information asymmetries highlighted above (Bardhan, 1997; Singh, 1999). First, governments should be able to commit with credibility. Good governance is thus closely related to the credibility that governments can establish with their populations. For example, a government with a reputation for corruption will find it difficult to convince the population that the policies it is advocating, however good they might appear to be, will in fact be implemented. The low credibility of the government thus exerts high costs of implementation. Failure then becomes self-fulfilling as resistance to the new policies forces the government to abandon them, only to try to implement the same policies somewhat later in a different guise (see Bigsten and Kayizzi-Mugerwa, 2000). To gain reputation, governments sometimes need to break away entirely from past practices, as for example when a new government comes to power after an election (as in Nigeria and Senegal) or the guerrilla side wins a civil war (as in Ethiopia, Uganda and Rwanda). Governments might also improve their reputations and gain credibility by agreeing to regional arrangements, which imply the ceding of some sovereignty to a regional authority, as in the case of currency arrangements or trade policies. Such arrangements tie the hands of the government, enabling the populations to infer that there will be no policy shift in the future. The earlier fear of a policy shift thus dissipates and the government is able to raise its credibility with the public.

Second, administrative systems should be accountable. In recent years, accountability – domestically to program beneficiaries and other stakeholders and externally to donors with respect to their financial support – has come to comprise a key element of aid conditionality. Donors believe that accountability increases public sector credibility, especially in the implementation of programs. Governments have sought to enhance institutional accountability by increasing administrative transparency. Proffering institutional autonomy on key institutions such as the judiciary, the central bank and the revenue collection agencies has been important in attempts to raise public sector accountability. Accountability also calls for legal and institutional structures to ensure that proper accounting procedures are maintained and verifiable standards are set (Collier, 1999).

Third, the political and economic environment should minimize risk, thereby elongating the time horizon of the economic actors. One of the most important tasks of the government is thus the provision of a stable and orderly macroeconomic environment. This enables economic actors to invest long term, which is crucial for economic development. However, markets in many African countries are distorted or, owing to earlier regulations, do not yet exist. There is clearly a need for an effective regulatory framework since the recent opening up of economies has led to various monopolies. Along with the creation of effective regulation, governments should make every effort to improve the efficiency with which they provide public services, including education, communications and security.

Fourth, it is important that domestic politics encompass most interest groups and that the political system is open to contestation. Ultimately, domestic politics will dictate the speed with which countries can move towards more transparency and increased accountability. Although the donor community has encouraged African countries to adopt more pluralistic systems of government, it also acknowledges that sustainable political systems can be achieved only over a long period of learning by doing. Still, few political systems that ignored political participation were able to deliver 'development.' It is important to point out, however, that involvement in public affairs need not be confined to elections or to membership in political parties. It can also take the form of engagement in voluntary organizations. For many of these civil society activities to take place unhindered, governments need to minimize the risk of conflict.

3 How governance appeared on the agenda

At the end of the 1980s, after close to a decade of structural adjustment, and with many African countries in economic distress and deep indebtedness, the governance debate began to feature in policy statements. In her paper on the role of government in economic development, Irma Adelman (1999) has traced the debate on the role of the government in economic development from after the Second World War. In the postwar era of reconstruction, the role of the government was never ambiguous.

The state was widely seen as the prime mover. In response to the problems of investment lumpiness, poor infrastructure provision and missing markets, government intervention would ensure that resources were moved from low- to high-productivity sectors (also known as the commanding heights of the economy), thereby leading to rapid growth.[3]

There are three explanations for the rise of governance to the top of Africa's political agenda in the 1990s. The first impulse came from within Africa itself. Over three decades after the attainment of independence, many of the hopes that had characterized the 1960s had not been realized. Authoritarian regimes had become the order of the day, and very little development had taken place. The strongarm tactics that many leaders believed would ensure national unity had in many cases led to economic decline, fractionalization and civil war. Many African countries saw peasants withdrawing from the modern market economy and returning to subsistence. There was growing recognition that weaknesses in governance were limiting the payoffs to economic reform (Anyang' Nyong'o, 1997, 1999). Second, the fall of the Berlin Wall and subsequent end of the Cold War and collapse of the totalitarian regimes of the Soviet bloc caused advocates of Soviet-type regimes in Africa suddenly to lose a strong moral and material backer. The third reason relates closely to the first two, as a result of which African leaders ran out of easy options for funding their development programs and armies. As an outcome of diminished geopolitical competition between the West and East, donors were less inclined to support 'trusted allies' irrespective of their governance record. As a group, the donor community conditioned its lending to improvements in governance, that is to reduction in corruption and to increased domestic political participation. Donors have been willing to support only countries that were demonstrating movement towards more democratic rule, which explains the recent interplay between economic reforms and political liberalization.

The role of donors in the debate and in the implementation of governance is often contradictory, however (Brautigam, 2000; Therkildsen, 2001). Although donor governments have reached the conclusion that project-based aid is injurious to the domestic bureaucratic process, the alternative of sector-based aid or budget support is yet to take firm root. Much effort still goes towards implementing projects in which domestic governments have little input (DFID, 2000). This is probably a reflection of the political constraints on donor agencies back home. Voters in donor countries still need to know what impact their aid is having in the recipient countries. On their own, outcomes from budgetary support cannot be differentiated by donor input. Even more serious for domestic capacity development is the tendency, marked in the early 1990s, for donors to bypass government in disbursing resources to projects. However, in countries where efforts to improve accountability have been made, donors have been willing to support central budgets directly and to undertake ex post evaluations of their own afterwards.[4]

African countries have responded variously to domestic and external demands for increased governance, but a number of key features have emerged in the past decade to indicate a commonality of experience. The responses can be divided into three categories. The first comprises a limited group of countries that quickly embarked on economic liberalization, but which now need to undertake deeper reforms, including public sector reforms as well as political reforms, to remain on track. Since the early 1990s, many African countries have held multiparty elections, with average voter turnout exceeding 76 percent (Chege, 1999). In many of these, the incumbent regimes have been defeated, while in others the opposition parties have increased their representation in parliament. This marks a sharp departure from past practice where incumbent regimes typically never lost elections and military coups and assassinations were the only means of changing the leadership. The second group comprises countries that may have embarked on economic reforms but that have made little progress in the area of governance. In this case, the government finds it difficult to establish a solid domestic coalition for improved governance. The third group comprises countries where little or no progress has been made. Governments are distracted by other concerns such as civil war, with the state machinery all but broken. In this case, the re-establishment of peace and law and order takes precedence over governance issues.

Globalization is another source of pressure on African governments to improve their governance image. With developing countries competing with each other for international investment, experience has shown that funds tend to flow to countries that already have an economic environment considered conducive by domestic entrepreneurs. For example, an economic environment riddled with corruption and characterized by a history of capital flight, owing to poor economic policies and controls, will not be attractive to foreign investors. Concerns here include the management of intellectual property rights, investor protection and the setting of labor and environmental standards. Related to globalization is the issue of neighboring or contagion effects. The experience of Africa's Great Lakes region has demonstrated that adverse events in one country tend to affect the investment patterns and general economic performance of its neighbors.

Since many African countries are similarly vulnerable, it might be necessary to set up organizations to ensure and preserve regional governance. National attempts at improving governance will then stop fluctuating with the whims of the government and the reaction of neighbors. Recently, African leaders have been engaged in attempts to coordinate development efforts, but outside the strictures of formal organization. Thus, the annual Smart Partnerships meetings of leaders, organized by developing countries to discuss business issues, now attract several African leaders. In 2001, a number of countries belonging to the Common Market for Eastern and Southern Africa (COMESA) created an agency (Africa Trade Insurance Agency) to insure firms against political risk. It is important to note that the sums paid out by the insurance agency to cover injury from political disturbances will in turn be reimbursed by the country where this happens. Thus countries will be penalized for being risky political environments and there will be an incentive to lower that risk.

4   Governance and policy in Africa: A cross-section of experiences

Whereas the beginning of the 1990s witnessed a positive turnaround in Africa's economic performance, with positive spillover effects on the region's politics, by the end of the decade the bulk of the economic gains had been reversed. Not only had a combination of poor weather, external shocks and civil wars reduced growth in the bulk of African countries, but declining total investments indicated that growth would remain low in the medium term. However, in spite of the growth setback, the movement towards pluralistic systems of government in many African countries has continued, although the degree of political commitment has varied from country to country (see *Freedom House*, various issues; Gelb, 1999; Levy, 1999).

The major political change in Africa in the 1990s was the reintroduction of multiparty systems of government. This included the holding of multiparty elections, adoption of new pluralist constitutions and the legalization of opposition party activities. It is noteworthy that the changes have not been confined to particular regions of Africa. Multiparty elections have been held in Benin, Ghana, Mali and Senegal in West Africa and in Botswana, Kenya, Tanzania, Malawi, Mozambique and Zambia in Eastern and Southern Africa. The latter group of countries has held at least two rounds of multiparty elections in the past decade. In many other countries, there have been significant improvements in the rule of law, and civil liberties have been steadily gaining ground.

However, a close look at the experience of individual countries indicates a diversity of experience. Botswana and Mauritius have demonstrated, for example, a capacity to build effective institutions on the basis of democracy and the rule of law. Although the Botswana Democratic Party has dominated the country's politics since independence in 1965, wide political latitude has been given to the opposition. Mauritius has demonstrated, on the other hand, that ethnic heterogeneity need not lead to divisive politics and conflict. It has been possible to include Hindus, Muslims, Creoles, Africans and Europeans in the political process and thus to defy the view that ethnolinguistic diversity leads to fractionalization and lowers development potential. This has been achieved first through the holding of regular multiparty elections, where political competition cuts across the ethnic divide; and secondly through the country's constitution ensuring a balance of ethnic representation at the top levels of government, regardless of the victorious party. Similarly, political tolerance and inclusive politics have characterized South Africa's transition since 1994 when the black majority assumed power (Chege, 1999).

Evidence from elsewhere in Africa overwhelms the few democratic achievements listed above, however. In the course of the 1990s, many states and regions in Africa seemed to disintegrate into civil war and collapse of the rule of law. These cases are also well represented in all regions of the continent. In Somalia, the clan rivalries following the overthrow of the government in the early 1990s brought the country to the verge of implosion. Liberia, on the other hand, experienced close to a decade of civil war (1989–97), which seriously destabilized many neighboring countries, notably Guinea-Bissau and Sierra Leone. Since 1992, Sierra Leone has undergone a bitter civil war, whose effects have spilled over its borders into neighboring countries. Civil wars have raged in other areas of Africa as well, confining the space for institution building and introduction of the rule of law. Though potentially rich countries, Angola and the Democratic Republic of the Congo (DRC) have been severely affected by civil war, the former case raging for a quarter of a century. Populations have been displaced and, especially in the case of the DRC, the spillover into the politics of neighboring countries has been large and negative. The problems of the DRC can in turn be traced to the genocide in Rwanda and the civil war in Burundi. The problems of the Great Lakes region demonstrate clearly how interdependent countries in the region have become. A concept of regional governance that would ensure a more uniform code of government behavior could be a useful tool in the search for peace in the region.

Why have African countries, even those that were not directly affected by civil war, such as Côte d'Ivoire, Kenya, Tanzania, Malawi and Zambia, failed to generate sufficient growth and to strengthen institutions in the past decade? Although in many countries the poor performance was blamed on adverse weather patterns and international commodity price shocks, there is little doubt that domestic factors such as declining levels of efficiency in the civil service, corruption and the politics of exclusion share some of the blame.

In Côte d'Ivoire, for example, the government resisted adjustment for far too long, partly in deference to its aging president, who had been the architect of the earlier prosperity. For a commodity-exporting country, the maintenance of an overvalued exchange rate was the equivalent of a punitive tax on the countryside.[5] For a considerable time the government was able to fund its programs thanks to commercial loans and to some support from the multilateral institutions. However, by the end of the 1980s there were increasing signs of serious poverty, notably in the urban areas. In the countryside, peasants were restive, accusing immigrants of taking their land. There were also increasing demands for multiparty political activity. In retrospect, Ivorian policymakers adjusted slowly to domestic demands for democracy. They also failed to perceive the threats inherent in the failure to address the growing poverty. Indeed the coup d'état of December 1999 and associated social disturbances emanated directly from the sharp decline of the economy and the uneven nature of the recovery when adjustment policies were embarked on in the mid-1990s. The government's failure to promote more inclusive politics added to the social disruption.

Kenya and Zimbabwe shared Côte d'Ivoire's capitalist-oriented economic structure, with substantial foreign investments. The three countries had relatively high levels of income inequality, partly thanks to the presence of settlers and other groups who operated estates that contrasted sharply in productivity with the smaller peasant holdings. In both Kenya and Zimbabwe, an entrenched leadership was reluctant to cede power to younger leaders or opposition groups. Economic reforms became politically difficult to implement, especially when the donor community linked them to democratic reforms. Countries experienced off/on relationships with donors, with financial support becoming intermittent as well.

Of countries that earlier had professed a socialist approach to development, Ethiopia, Tanzania, Mozambique and Zambia provide interesting contrasts. Tanzania and Zambia are neighboring countries that experimented with African socialism from the 1960s and have so far been spared serious social cleavages. However, decades of government control of the economy led to a sharp decline in economic performance. In both countries, governments nationalized private companies and subsidies became a key element of government control. This commandist approach to development policy was also evident in politics, where leaders favored single parties which exercised influence on all facets of economic life. When the multiparty era was introduced, the opposition party in Zambia won the elections in the early 1990s and it embarked on policies that were lauded as launching good governance in Africa. There was emphasis on human rights, inclusive politics and a free press. The powers of the presidency were also to be curtailed. Few of these promises were realized. Zambia's experience provides a good example of how difficult it can be to transform the political and thus governance culture of countries. In Zambia an added difficulty was that the bulk of the 'new' political leaders had merely switched sides from the previous establishment. As Bigsten and Kayizzi-Mugerwa (2000) have argued in an analysis of the political economy of reform failure in Zambia, policy statements mean little in countries where the administrative and political elite can see few benefits in altering their ways (see also Chapter 4 on Zambia and the donor community). Tanzania, on the other hand, adopted a more gradualist approach to political reform. A decade after introducing multiparty elections, the political structures are becoming more responsive to the needs of the population, without the country experiencing the fractious politics of its neighbors.

Ethiopia and Mozambique experienced fully fledged civil wars, which eventually ended but not before seriously damaging the infrastructure and weakening society at all levels. In the 1990s, both countries embarked on the twofold task of economic adjustment and reconstruction. The nature of the earlier armed struggles dictated that, whereas the economic policies would be similar, the political configurations and outcomes would be radically different. With respect to economic reforms, including some of the more drastic ones related to privatization and retrenchment, the two countries implemented them at a faster pace than their neighbors. The extent of the economic decline in Ethiopia and Mozambique was probably such that policies which promised aid inflows and economic recovery were more effective there than in countries that had not experienced civil war. In politics, the approaches differed markedly. In Ethiopia, the war ended in victory for the guerrillas, whereas in Mozambique the government reached a negotiated settlement with its opponents. Mozambique opted for a multiparty form of government with parties free to recruit supporters and to engage in active politics, whereas Ethiopia settled for a policy that potentially allowed self-determination for the various nationalities but without embracing competitive politics. In subsequent years, both countries have attracted considerable donor support and their growth rates were above the African average in the 1990s. Still, Ethiopia was once again engulfed in a bitter war, this time with Eritrea, whereas Mozambique has been able to undertake a process of national reconciliation and averted the risk of descent into civil war.

In the early 1960s, Rwanda and Somalia were counted among the African countries most likely to succeed. They had, at least on the face of it, a homogeneous population, sharing a common language and with no serious religious cleavages. However, they were the only two countries in Africa that imploded.[6] Again, the root causes of their instability differed, as well as the pace of their reconstruction. In Rwanda, five years after the genocide of 1994, the government had returned the country to normalcy, with many state institutions, including the parliament, functioning once again. In Somalia, parts of the country have declared independence unilaterally, while the portion of the country that includes the capital is under a transitional government that has promised to reunite the country. With the state broken into bits in Somalia, the issues of accountability and governance have been clearly superseded by those of national unity. Still, it is important for the Somali leaders to assure their citizens that the structures they are trying to put in place are credible and can elicit the support of the international community.

5   Policy discussion and conclusion

A number of lessons derive from this overview of the governance challenge in Africa. First, political leaders have been forced by domestic circumstances and external donor pressure to rethink the role of the state and that of its support structures in development. Redefining the role of the state demands the creation of domestic institutions, including the public sector, that are facilitators and not impediments to growth. Since bureaucrats take or implement many policies and decisions in government, they must have the necessary training and skills to do so. Thus, creation of an enabling environment for growth and development entails the attraction of high-calibre workers to the public sector and putting in place facilities for training and skills upgrading. However, the government also needs to restructure the bureaucracy, including its size, not only to contain costs but also to enable the government to pay meaningful wages to those remaining behind.

Second, proper financial management lies at the center of good governance and accountability. However, in many African countries financial controls within the public sector have been weak, leading to serious abuse and outright corruption. The modernization of the financial system is thus crucial, especially in the light of decentralization efforts currently under way in many African countries. Even here, there is a need to raise the technical capacities for budgeting and financial analysis in the public sector.

Third, governments will never be able to meet all of society's social and development needs. It is thus necessary to encourage the participation of civil society in the formulation of policies. This, in turn, demands the decentralization of power to increase proximity to policymakers and to make it possible for citizens to monitor the performance of local leaders. However, mere proximity is not enough to ensure that citizens will be empowered at the local level. They need to be encouraged to participate in decisions that affect them. Decentralization demands financial and human resources at the local level, along with the power for local leaders to manage and allocate resources on the basis of local decisions and needs. The center's partiality for control cannot be eradicated via legislation alone, however. Local governments need to raise their legitimacy by being more efficient at dealing with local issues and at prioritizing development needs.

Fourth, the role of the public sector is bound to change, with the main tasks being to enforce policies, ensure that markets function properly and undertake requisite regulatory measures. The public sector should also be supportive of private sector activities and not be an impediment, as so often in the past. To make the public sector more efficient, governments have created independent agencies that manage key tasks such as tax collection, regulation of key sectors such as communications, and the management of monetary policy or investment promotion. These agencies are allowed to determine their own wage structures and other incentives. However, although service delivery increases as a result, there has been a tendency for the positive effects to level off, often necessitating the 'unclogging' of the systems by laying off workers and employing new ones. 'Atomization' might thus not necessarily be the solution to the problem of low productivity and poor accountability in the public service. It will also be necessary to undertake more holistic measures in order to raise productivity in the rest of the public sector.

Fifth, governance is part and parcel of the political process. Good governance cannot be sustained in an environment that is characterized by exclusive politics. In many African countries the opening up of the political space – including the introduction of multiparty politics and allowing a free press to operate – has raised the level of political accountability, as well as of political competition. However, the success achieved falls far short of the hopes raised in the early 1990s, when the process began. The behavior of the political elite has not changed by much.

Notes

1. The UK's Department for International Development (DFID, 2000:2) has, for example, listed seven key capabilities that governments in developing countries need to develop in order to meet the International Development Targets, which revolve around the eradication of poverty. These touch on many of the governance issues discussed in this chapter, including inclusive politics and political and financial accountability.
2. See also Hamdok (2000); Hamdok and Kifle (2000).
3. Adelman (1999:1) states that it was argued in the postwar years that 'uncoordinated investments would not permit the realization of the inherent increasing returns to scale ...

Hence the need for government action to propel the economy from uncoordinated, low-income, no-long-run-growth static equilibrium to the coordinated, high-income, dynamic equilibrium, golden-growth path.'
4. For example, DFID supports Rwanda's education sector directly via the budget, with the audit done afterwards by Crown agents (see Bigsten and Kayizzi-Mugerwa, 2001).
5. Although the parity of the CFA franc was determined by the regional central bank based in Dakar, the devaluation of the currency was strongly opposed by the Ivorian government.
6. It is possible to include Liberia and Sierra Leone, although the two countries never quite reached total collapse.

REFERENCES

Adelman, I. (1999) 'The Role of Government in Economic Development,' Department of Agricultural and Resource Economics and Policy Working Paper No. 890, University of California, Berkeley, CA.

African Development Bank (1993) *Governance and Development: Issues and the Role of the African Development Bank and other Multilateral Institutions*, African Development Bank: Abidjan.

—— (1998) *African Development Report*, Oxford University Press: Oxford.

—— (1999a) 'Country Policy and Institutional Assessment,' unpublished report, Abidjan.

—— (1999b) 'Bank Group Policy on Good Governance,' unpublished report, Abidjan.

Anyang' Nyong'o, P. (1997) 'Institutionalization of Democratic Governance in Sub-Saharan Africa,' ECDPM Working Paper No. 36, ECDPM, Maastricht.

—— (1999) 'The State of Governance in Africa,' paper presented at a conference on Good Governance and Sustainable Development in Africa, African Development Bank, Abidjan.

Bardhan, P. (1997) 'The Role of Governance in Economic Development: A Political Economy Approach,' paper for the OECD Development Center, Paris.

Bigsten A. and S. Kayizzi-Mugerwa (2000) 'The Political Economy of Policy Failure in Zambia,' Working Papers in Economics No. 23, Department of Economics, Gothenburg University.

—— (2001) 'Towards Peace, Growth and Poverty Reduction in Rwanda,' *Country Economic Report*, Sida: Stockholm.

Brautigam, D. (2000) *Aid Dependence and Governance*, Expert Group on Development Issues: Stockholm.

Chege, M. (1999) 'Politics of Development: Institutions and Governance,' paper presented at the workshop on Can Africa Claim the 21st Century?, Abidjan.

Collier, P. (1999) 'How to Reduce Corruption,' paper presented at a conference on Good Governance and Sustainable Development in Africa, African Development Bank, Abidjan.

Dethier, J.-J. (1999) 'Governance and Economic Performance: A Survey,' Discussion Papers on Development Policy No. 5, Center for Development Research, Universität Bonn.

DFID (Department for International Development) (2000) 'Making Government Work for the Poor,' DFID Consultation Document, DFID Information Department, London.

Doornbos, M. (2001) 'Good Governance: The Rise and Decline of a Policy Metaphor,' *Journal of Development Studies* 37(6).

Gelb, A. (1999) 'Where Are We Now? Reforms, Performance and Country Groups in Africa,' paper presented at the workshop on Can Africa Claim the 21st Century?, African Development Bank, Abidjan.

Hamdok, A. (2000) 'Good Governance and the Policy Challenge: The African Development Bank Perspective,' paper presented at the Workshop on Evaluation Capacity Development in Africa, Johannesburg.

Hamdok, A. and H. Kifle (2000) 'Governance, Economic Reform, and Sustainable Growth: The Policy Challenge for International Development Organizations,' paper presented at the First International Forum on African Perspectives on Emerging Africa, organized by the African Development Bank, Abidjan, and the OECD Development Center, Paris.

Levy, B. (1999) 'Improving Governance in Sub-Saharan Africa: From "Best Practice" to "Good Fit",' paper presented at the workshop on Can Africa Claim the 21st Century?, African Development Bank, Abidjan.

Mello, L. de and M. Barenstein (2001) 'Fiscal Decentralization and Governance: A Cross-Country Analysis,' IMF Working Paper WP/01/71, Washington, DC.

Singh, S. (1999) 'The Political Underpinnings of Economic Governance,' paper presented at the workshop on Indicators for Monitoring Progress towards Good Governance in Africa, United Nations Economic Commission for Africa, Addis Ababa.

Therkildsen, O. (2001) *Efficiency, Accountability and Implementation, Public Sector Reform in East and Southern Africa*, United Nations Research Institute for Social Development: Geneva.

World Bank (1989) *Sub-Saharan Africa: From Crisis to Sustained Growth*, World Bank: Washington, DC.

2

Owning economic reforms: A comparative study of Ghana and Tanzania

Yvonne M. Tsikata

1   Introduction

Ghana and Tanzania provide interesting contrasts of sub-Saharan Africa's reform experience. Though situated in politically volatile regions of the continent, they have so far managed to steer clear of political destabilization and have been able to introduce and maintain political pluralism. Reform ownership by policymakers and institutions and participation in policy making by the population are key ingredients of reform success. Both countries have tried to address these issues in recent years. Ghana was an early reformer, starting in the 1980s, whereas Tanzania was a much later convert to the reform process. In the latter part of the 1990s Ghana experienced significant backsliding in its reform efforts, partly owing to the policy diversion implied by the introduction of political pluralism. Although Tanzania, whose policy of state-led development was for several years supported by a number of bilateral donors, was ostensibly slow to reform and slower still in committing to market liberalization, it is now seen as making tangible progress. Comparing the experiences of Ghana and Tanzania is thus useful in trying to understand how reform ownership affects economic performance in sub-Saharan Africa.

Reform ownership is an important determinant of policy success for several reasons. Typically, economic reforms involve difficult decisions that, at least initially, have negative impacts on important segments of the population. Devaluation and trade liberalization, for example, affect not only the activities of exporters and importers but also those of manufacturers and, in the countryside, commodity producers. On the other hand, fiscal adjustment, civil service reforms and privatization impact variously on the welfare of groups engaged within and outside the public sector and in the different geographic regions. There are thus bound to be winners and losers during the reform process, and net gainers are often difficult to pinpoint a priori. Where potential losers are plentiful and well connected, reforms will be resisted. Since the benefits of the reforms accrue only in the medium to long run, it is necessary for the government to be committed. In the absence of commitment, reforms cannot to be sustained, and reversal is likely in the face of political opposition.

This chapter looks at the subject of reform ownership in sub-Saharan Africa, with Ghana and Tanzania as case studies. It identifies the factors, including institutions and policies, that determine the countries' capacity to formulate, implement and sustain economic reforms. Section 2 reviews evidence on the links between ownership and reform, and section 3 provides a chronology of the reform process in both countries, including the role of domestic institutions as well as that of donors. Section 4 summarizes the determinants of reform ownership and concludes the chapter.

2 Linking ownership to reform outcomes

Since reform ownership touches on a wide range of policy and institutional issues, it tends to defy simple characterization and definition. Johnson and Wasty (1993) have suggested four contexts in which reform ownership can be demonstrated:
- at the level of initiation
- during the process of refinement, when broad consensus among policy-makers is required to move ahead
- with respect to expressible political support for reform
- the extent of public support and participation.

In the case of initiation, for example, ownership is considered high when the government initiates and implements the program, as opposed to the program being prepared by the World Bank itself.

Research on reform ownership has focused on two main areas, corresponding roughly to the role of donors and multilateral agencies in the process and the response of recipient governments. To the first set of studies belong those that have looked at the effectiveness of policy conditionality in bringing about reform (Burnside and Dollar, 1997; Collier, 1997; International Monetary Fund, 2001; Killick, 1997; White and Morrissey, 1997; Killick et al., 1998). The second set of studies examines more directly the link between ownership and policy implementation and outcomes (Devarajan et al., 2001; Dollar and Svensson, 1997; World Bank, 1998).

Policy conditionality relates closely to the political economy of reform ownership. It is instructive that the authors of the external evaluation of the Enhanced Structural Adjustment Facility (ESAF) noted that 'a common theme that runs through perceptions of ESAF at the country level is a feeling of loss of control over the policy content and the pace of implementation of reform programs' (International Monetary Fund, 1998:36). The recipient country's ability to influence its reform ownership depends on the size of its financial resources, its human capacities and its strategic importance. In a context where one party is perceived to be weak, with little technical competence to propose options or to implement programs, ownership will be difficult to achieve. There are several examples of this in the World Bank's negotiations with its member countries. Those with greater bureaucratic and policy management expertise, such as Argentina and Chile, are not only better prepared for negotiations but also more likely to get their points of view incorporated in the programs.

African case studies in Devarajan et al. (2001) strongly suggest that, although conditionality may, in a period of rapid reform, be helpful in establishing a country's credibility, its usefulness is often short lived.[1] This is because the continued use of conditionality by donors masks efforts at reform ownership, even in environments where it is beginning to take root. Moreover, the arduous process of confirming whether the conditions have been fulfilled gives the impression that reforms are imposed from outside. It is also likely that numerous conditionalities complicate the policy debate, as was partly the case in Ghana in the late 1980s, making it difficult for domestic groups to participate meaningfully. The studies in Devarajan et al. (2001) reached a number of conclusions on ownership and economic reform in Africa.

First, implementation aside, the success of reforms is a result of the extent to which governments have been able to undertake broad domestic consultation. However, the latter need not necessarily follow any predetermined pattern. In Uganda, for example, the government used its umbrella-type political structure, which because it excludes individual political parties from power is not seen as democratic in the Western sense, to enable a fair amount of consultation during the reform process. 'President Museveni established the Presidential National Forum to debate reform issues in 1987. Uganda's Manufacturers' Association sponsored seminars and discussion papers in the 1987–9 period. The Presidential Economic Council had open debates on reform and sponsored a December 1989 conference on trade liberalization that has been described as a turning point in public opinion' (Devarajan et al., 2001:11).

Also crucial for reform ownership is the institutional capacity of governments. Since ownership means both that political commitment exists and that there are 'able technocrats who can work out the details of reform' (Devarajan et al., 2001:29), technical assistance that provides training and policy advice to ensure this can be useful in strengthening and broadening the foundation of ownership. Aid during reforms, by increasing their benefits or reducing their disruptive impacts, could also strengthen commitment and increase the likelihood that reforms are sustained. The case studies find, however, that complex reforms, such as privatization and civil service reform, that directly threaten vested interests are difficult to champion, whereas macroeconomic reforms, being less discriminating in their impacts, are associated with greater ownership.

In the Johnson and Wasty study cited above, based on a sample of eighty-one World Bank adjustment credits approved in thirty-eight countries between 1980 and 1988, a positive correlation is found between ownership and how satisfactorily the programs met their objectives.[2] They also found that ownership was strongly predictive of program success in 73 percent of all cases. Notably, the commitment of the country's political leadership was found to be the most important determinant of success. Similar findings are cited in Kahler (1992) and Killick et al. (1998). They indicate that, in reform programs considered well implemented, the government's prior commitment was a crucial factor. By contrast, the majority of the poorly implemented ones took place in environments of low commitment.

Political legitimacy and credibility are thus key ingredients. Johnson (1994) observes, with respect to the poor implementation of International Monetary Fund (IMF) programs, that lack of legitimacy means that the government will 'attain only a rather modest degree of implementation in the face of sabotage, indifference, non participation, and minimum effort and compliance from the general population.' However, the experience of countries such as Ghana, Korea and Uganda suggests that in the short to medium run it might be possible to pursue reform relatively well even where political legitimacy is lacking. This is because reforms that generate growth and improve the standards of living are likely to find support, in spite of the perceived illegitimacy of the governments implementing them. In the long run, however, reforms nurture their own demands for political change, and governments eventually have to address political reforms as well.

The empirical analyses of reform ownership reviewed above have two important weaknesses. First, efforts are often biased towards assessing government, thereby ignoring beneficiary ownership. Second, the 'measurement' of ownership is often done ex post and not when it is happening, raising the possibility that evaluators could be biased by their perception of developments in the country.

Ignoring beneficiary ownership can be a costly oversight. For example, Ndulu (2001:6) argues that, in enforcing accountability and ensuring aid effectiveness, strengthening the voice of the citizens is crucial. This can be ensured only by their increased participation in the design and implementation of the programs. However, although evidence from the aid effectiveness literature highlights the importance of beneficiary participation for performance, this is easier to do at the project level than at the macroeconomic level. Furthermore, the fact that 'ownership' tends to be 'measured' after the fact is problematic. In conjunction with the subjectivity of the term itself, there is the risk of the evaluation being biased by perceptions of developments in the country at a given moment. In a sense, we are 'predicting' after the event. Haggard and Kaufman (1992:7) argue that what is important in assessing ownership is not so much the progress made with respect to some 'variables' but rather the extent to which reforms have become 'consolidated'; that is, 'that they have been institutionalized within the policy system.' This is important because it ensures the existence of stable coalitions of political support.

Of perhaps more serious concern are the queries raised by Killick et al. (1998) and Lancaster (1999) about the desirability of ownership for reform success. Using a principal–agent framework, Killick argues that ownership is really a proxy for the extent to which the reforms are perceived to be in the interest of the government and the population. In other words, the degree of government ownership that is demonstrated is a function of the extent to which its objectives dominate those of the donors. Ownership is thus an indicator of 'interest conflict.' Under domestic ownership, the government is in the driver's seat as far as identifying priorities and changes are concerned, whereas in its absence the donors' objectives and priorities dominate, increasing the possibility of interest conflict. In Killick's view, there is unlikely to be convergence between the objectives and interests of donors and recipients. The reasons he gives are that the two parties

are conditioned by different historical and institutional backgrounds; they are answerable to different constituencies; they each have their own internal management imperatives; there may be differences in attitude to the role of the supporting finance offered by donors (the moral hazard issue); there are asymmetries in the incidence of adjustment costs, including the costs of mistakes, and these lead to differing attitudes to risk and the desirable speed of change; nationalistic resentment of 'donor interference' and of inequities in the treatment of countries is apt to give rise to generalized suspicion of externally recommended policy reforms. (Killick et al., 1998:98–9)

The existence of interest conflict helps to explain why ownership may not be sufficient to generate the desired economic outcomes.

Finally, ownership is a dynamic and endogenous concept. Generally, good economic outcomes will tend to support greater ownership. In Botswana, for example, diamonds and the benefits of a well-managed economy not only led to steady economic growth, but also reduced the economic importance of aid, giving the government an advantage in its negotiations with donors (Maipose et al., 1997). Even governments that might initially be lukewarm about reforms are likely to change their tactics when they perceive that the reforms are enhancing their political capital. On the other hand, no amount of ownership can prop up a program that fails to yield tangible benefits over time. As the saying goes, 'success has many parents, but failure is an orphan.'

3   Economic reforms in Ghana and Tanzania

In both Ghana and Tanzania, economic crisis was an important impetus for reform. However, the initiation and sequencing of reforms and political change, and their implications for economic policy, differed, influenced by the historical context of each country. Thus in both cases it is important to understand the economic quandary that had to be addressed as well as the nature of the ensuing reform process.

In Ghana, a democratically elected government was overthrown in 1981 in a coup d'état. On seizing power, Flight Lieutenant Jerry Rawlings and his populist Provisional National Defence Council (PNDC) inherited a bankrupt economy. Economic mismanagement during previous governments, as well as adverse terms of trade, had led to economic stagnation, economic imbalances characterized by severe shortages, ineffective controls and corruption. By 1977, inflation had reached 77 percent and production had shrunk in every sector of the economy.[3]

Although the PNDC recognized the severity of the problems it faced, internal dissent meant that an economic reform program could not be adopted until towards the end of the military regime's first year in power (1982),[4] when it felt more secure. By then, it had become clear to the PNDC how few alternatives were available. Ideological supporters of the regime, not only influential leftist intellectuals but also the governments of Libya and the Soviet Union, indicated that the PNDC had little choice but to turn to the Bretton Woods institutions for assistance. A number of exogenous shocks in 1983, including a severe drought, bush fires that decimated the cocoa crop and the deportation of over 1 million Ghanaian workers from neighboring Nigeria, as well as a number of counter-coup attempts in the earlier part of the PNDC rule, compounded the sense of crisis.

What then gave the PNDC the political space to undertake economic reforms initially? The 1981 coup marked a significant break from the past. Rawlings was not beholden to the established interest groups (parastatal managers, holders of import licenses or former politicians) and could afford to undertake politically difficult reforms such as currency devaluation. The political sphere was implicitly demarcated into the beneficiaries of the earlier system of controls and import licensing, that is former politicians and their associates, and its own supporters, including labor unions, workers, the armed forces, farmers and students (Tsikata, 2000). The former were kept out of the new government's initial reforms while the empowerment of the latter was said to be the PNDC's raison d'être. That the leadership was convinced that the reforms would help the poor was also an important factor in consolidating reform in the initial years of the PNDC (Herbst, 1993; Jeffries, 1991).

With the advent of multiparty democracy and the elections of 1992, the reform process became more complex, however. By their nature, second-generation reforms, such as privatization and civil service reforms, went well beyond core ministries, requiring the involvement of both sector ministries and subnational governments. The difficulty of economic reform in a budding democracy was brought into stark relief by the value added tax (VAT) fiasco of 1995. The government had attempted to introduce VAT with little prior information or consultation. However, the resulting civil disturbances forced the government to withdraw the tax and to undertake consultations (see Pereira et al., 2000:38). The VAT was reintroduced three years later after a much broader public information campaign and down from the originally proposed 15 percent to 10 percent.

Although economic decline was equally dramatic in Tanzania in the 1970s, recognizing the need for reform and acting on it appear to have taken much longer than in Ghana. With support from like-minded bilateral donors (mostly the Nordic countries of Denmark, Finland, Norway and Sweden), Tanzania was able – even though the country's relationship with the IMF and the World Bank had virtually collapsed by 1981 – to attempt to extricate itself from the economic crisis by relying on national experts. Between 1981 and 1983, it introduced 'homegrown' initiatives such as the national economic survival program of 1981–2. These, however, failed to address the core weaknesses of the economy and were subsequently abandoned (Stein 1991:93–4).

The decade that followed the introduction of economic reforms in the early 1980s saw many initiatives and programs whose implementation was complicated by lack of a broad-based domestic consensus for reform.[5] The slow pace of implementation also reflected the difficulty of undoing the country's socialist legacy. An important landmark of the socialist past was the Arusha Declaration of 1967, which led to the nationalization of businesses as well as the collectivization of rural activities including farming. It had also strengthened control over the economy of the sole political party – Chama Cha Mapinduzi (CCM) – under the leadership of Nyerere. Thus, in the early 1980s, socialism was much more embedded in Tanzanian society when reforms began than was Rawlings' leftist populism in Ghana. The Tanzanian tradition of consensus building and participatory decision making also reduced the space for dramatic reform action by the leadership. Above all, Nyerere's influence as president, head of CCM and elder statesman meant that little could be done without his consent. Since reforms implied the undoing of his legacy, reformers had to tread carefully. Indeed the pace of reform accelerated markedly and gained momentum after he stepped down from the presidency in 1985.

The shifting fortunes of groups supporting limited and guided liberalization and those supporting a more open approach were reflected in policy inconsistencies in Tanzania in the mid-1980s. For instance, towards the end of 1987, when elements in the government continued to advocate further liberalization, the agriculture and livestock ministries and local governments and cooperatives banned private businesspeople from buying produce directly from farmers, with only cooperative unions and primary societies allowed to do so (Kiondo, 1991:31). Among the two groups vying for influence over economic policy, the first included the bulk of the party elite and business groups connected to them, while the second comprised mainly Asian business families. Political sensitivities, it has been argued, precluded the latter from overt declaration of support for the reforms (Kiondo, 1991:39). Moreover, the reforms were perceived as secretive even by highly placed party officials.

3.1 Adjustment programs

In 1983, the PNDC introduced a four-year economic recovery program in Ghana which, together with its follow-up in 1987–91, received substantial assistance from donors and multilateral agencies. Reform objectives included movement toward market-based prices and exchange rates and demonstrable fiscal discipline. A discrete devaluation of the cedi was followed by the introduction of a fully fledged auction-based exchange rate system. In 1988, Ghana became the first country in sub-Saharan Africa to introduce foreign exchange bureaux, where foreign exchange was traded with 'no questions asked.' The rehabilitation of the country's deteriorated ports, roads and railways was given priority early in the program, as was the liberalization of input and producer markets, notably in the cocoa sector. However, the impact of reforms was not uniformly positive. Thus in 1988 the PNDC adopted a Programme of Action to Mitigate the Social Costs of Adjustment (PAMSCAD), one of the first of its type in sub-Saharan Africa. It was a short-term measure with a focus on employment creation, supporting those retrenched from the public sector, meeting the basic needs of the poor and encouraging community participation. However, not entirely unexpectedly, the impact of PAMSCAD on poverty reduction was limited by poor implementation, political interference and lack of capacities at the lower levels, where interventions were to be concentrated (Batse et al., 1999).

In the area of institutional reforms, the government embarked on the restructuring of the civil service in 1987. The main objective was to reduce overstaffing and make civil service wages competitive, while decompressing the wage structure. The reforms faced considerable internal resistance, especially from older cohorts of workers. Moreover, the pay reform, by raising wages only modestly, did not significantly enhance incentives within the service. It has been argued that the relatively modest outcomes of the civil service reform are partly to be blamed on the proliferation of reforms, often competing, in the late 1980s and early 1990s, which stretched the government's implementation capacities to the limit (Pereira et al., 2000:43). Privatization was, for example, undertaken at this time with equally unsatisfactory results. Between 1988 and 1992, its pace was erratic; it then accelerated between 1994 and 1996, losing momentum thereafter. As in many other sub-Saharan African countries, state divestiture was subject to pressure from vested interests and politicians. A lack of technical capacity for evaluating companies, writing contracts and undertaking due diligence was, however, often the main impediment. Membership of the divestiture implementation committee was dominated by political appointees chosen from supporters of the PNDC, who had little experience in the private sector.

In the early 1990s, with the onset of multiparty democracy, there was a noticeable slowdown in reforms. The loss of fiscal discipline, including sharp increases in civil service wages, in the run-up to the parliamentary and presidential elections of 1992 meant a breakdown in macroeconomic stabilization. A political business cycle of sorts had thus emerged in Ghana. Although the government launched a National Institutional Renewal Programme in late 1994, in a bid to better coordinate public sector reforms, the earlier momentum was not regained. Still, there is no doubt that the reforms enabled Ghana to return to steady growth, albeit from a narrow base. In a matter of three years (1983–6), macroeconomic reforms helped lower inflation by 90 percentage points to 33 percent. Traditional exports improved rapidly as producers responded to higher producer prices and the removal of marketing impediments, although re-maining confined to a few products. In addition to the positive macro-economic gains in Ghana, poverty and inequality were reduced over the reform period. The incidence of extreme poverty declined from 36 per-cent of the population at the beginning of the 1990s to 29 percent at the end of the decade, although with sharp variation across regions. In Accra, the capital, extreme poverty declined over the same period from 11.5 percent to 2.5 percent (Armstrong, 1996; Aryeetey et al., 2000), whereas improvement in the poorer north was slight. Also notable was the im-provement in income distribution during the reform period. The Gini coefficient declined from 35.9 in 1988 to 32.7 ten years later (Tsikata, 2000). These gains are closely linked to the nature of Ghana's economic reforms. They had focused on the resuscitation of the agricultural sector by, inter alia, offering better producer prices to farmers and improving social service provision in the rural areas. The rehabilitation of the in-frastructure created additional job opportunities (Ahiakpor, 1991). The economic recovery was made possible by financial assistance from the donor community; thus the policymakers' ability to win the latter's con-fidence was also crucial to success.

As a commentary on the fragility of the achievements of the initial reforms, the macroeconomic stability of the late 1980s in Ghana was rapidly reversed with the introduction of multiparty democracy in the early 1990s. Subsequently, growth became uneven, fiscal indiscipline re-emerged, as did inflation. It is clear that the rapid implementation of the earlier reforms was partly the result of a more streamlined 'command' structure of a dedicated, if non-pluralist, government. With the entry of democracy and competitive politics, the policy agenda was no longer straightforward, necessitating bargaining and compromise over party boundaries.

As noted earlier, Tanzania's initial conditions differed from those of Ghana. Importantly, Ghana's military government was not constrained by political commitments from the past. However, the countries shared rundown economies as well as the desperate need for financial resources. As in Ghana, foreign supporters and isolated but influential domestic groups made the case that Tanzania needed to approach the IMF and the World Bank for advice and funding. Thus, between 1982 and 1986, the government undertook to implement reform.[6] Notably, on the basis of a report by an independent Tanzania Advisory Group, a structural ad-justment program was introduced in 1982. It is noteworthy, however, that the team was funded by a technical assistance credit from the Inter-national Development Association (IDA) and its members had to be cleared by both the Tanzanian government and the World Bank.[7] Be-sides the devaluation of the shilling to boost exports, prices, including those for producers, were partially liberalized and government expenditure and money supply were reduced. Measures were also taken to improve the efficiency of the parastatal sector.

In 1986, a fully fledged IMF-supported economic recovery program was introduced during the first year of the presidency of Ali Hassan Mwinyi, who had replaced Julius Nyerere in 1985. There was further devaluation of the shilling and a gradual movement towards a more market-determined exchange rate system. These were accompanied by further price liberalization and monetary tightening in a bid to eliminate the inflation overhang. To consolidate these reforms, as well as mitigate their social costs, an economic and social action program was introduced in 1989.

The transition from macroeconomic stability to structural reforms in the civil service and the parastatal sector was equally difficult in Tanzania. The first phase of the civil service reform program (1993–6) focused on retrenchment, whereas the second, which began in early 1996, addressed institutional issues, including the strengthening of managerial capacity in government. With respect to state divestiture, the Presidential Parastatal Sector Reform Commission was set up in 1993, following the amendment of the Public Corporations Act of 1992, to handle privatization. According to the commission, as of January 2000 close to 50 percent of a total portfolio of 383 state-owned companies had been privatized.[8] However, as in other sub-Saharan African countries, it was easier to privatize the smaller companies than the monopolies in the utilities sector, notably those supplying water and electric power. Difficulties have ranged from the latent distrust of private sector activities in Tanzania to failure to raise sufficient funds to compensate workers who have been laid off, to the existence of bad debts in virtually all the companies offered for sale, making negotiations for their divestiture intractable (Bigsten and Danielson, 1999:86–7).

However, it is illusory to think that Tanzania's socialist legacy had been put to rest (Baregu, 1994). The policy reversals experienced in the 1990s were the direct results of the unresolved debate between the 'nationalistic liberalizers,' that is, those who felt that reform could build on the earlier collectivist premises, and the 'free marketeers,' those who wanted a complete break with the controls of the past. Recent political statements have, however, advocated placing restraints on the activities of foreign businesses in certain sectors of the economy, suggesting that the latter group has not quite taken the day. A reason why this tug of war seems to go on without resolution is that the Tanzanian political leadership places enormous importance on the 'politics of accommodation.' Cabinet members enjoy a degree of autonomy, whose lack would probably drive them to the opposition. Therkildsen (2000:66) has noted that in

Tanzania 'policy decisions ... do not necessarily reflect collectively binding political compromises nor genuine political support for the reform
package as a whole. Rather, such decisions are often influenced by larger
political aims (which may not be relevant to the reform *per se*) or by accommodation to perceived or real donor pressures, or to individual ministries' resource-mobilizing strategy vis-à-vis donors.'

As in Ghana, growth in Tanzania rebounded after the introduction of
reforms, but was much lower and with a more modest impact on poverty.
Between 1987 and 1992, real GDP growth averaged 3.5 percent, double
the average growth of the previous decade. The last half of the 1990s
noted only a modest increase in growth to an average of 3.7 percent.
Thus, in terms of welfare, Tanzania's picture is mixed. The gains made in
education and health during the socialist era, and eroded during the crisis
years, have not been restored. Furthermore, preliminary results from an
ongoing household budget survey suggest that poverty may have increased in the 1990s. Gross and net enrolment ratios have been stagnant
at best, while, despite rising costs borne by Tanzanian households, the
quality of primary education and healthcare is deteriorating (Cooksey
and Mmuya, 1997; Cooksey et al., 1997).

3.2   The institutional framework

In both Ghana and Tanzania, initial economic reforms focused on macroeconomic stabilization and primarily involved the technical staff of the
ministries of finance, the central banks and the planning commissions.
Thus, in both countries, a relatively small group of people was involved
in the initial analysis. However, the composition of the groups differed in
each country, as did the extent to which final program designs incorporated their views.

In Ghana, a core group of technical staff, mostly from the finance ministry, worked with an experienced former finance minister and the new
finance secretary to put together a program in the early 1980s. A Ghanaian World Bank staff member visited Ghana at regular intervals and
also met with the government's team in Washington before the negotiations and advised its members. Those involved in this process have indicated that the programs that were ultimately negotiated with the Bretton Woods institutions were very much Ghanaian products. However,
given the departure from its populist rhetoric, the PNDC government
was compelled to explain its change of tactics to its key constituencies
(students and workers in particular), especially regarding the nature of
the reform program and why it was necessary.

In retrospect, the stability of the core decisionmaking team was crucial
to the success of Ghana's early reforms because it provided continuity.

Although up to 1986 three teams – an economic management committee, a structural adjustment team and a budget task force – were involved, their somewhat overlapping membership was merged in 1989 to form an economic review committee.[9] The new team combined technocrats and PNDC functionaries who mostly knew each other well. The committee met bi-annually, including the so-called 'external examiners' (Ghanaians living overseas). However, although by all accounts this new arrangement strengthened coordination, its institutional foundation was weak. To function properly, the new arrangement relied heavily on personal relationships and did not draw sufficiently on the know-how and experience of the civil servants in the ministries involved in the reform process.

In Ghana, the reform program and its success became strongly identified with the long-serving finance minister Dr. Kwesi Botchwey. In conjunction with changes in the core economic team, ownership of the program became increasingly personalized and associated with him and a small team around him. With his departure in the mid-1990s, the earlier cohesiveness in Ghanaian reform was lost and a new modus operandi had to be found. Ghana illustrates that reform ownership becomes more complex as the need for reform shifts to sector levels, requiring a variety of microeconomic interventions. Moreover, early success is no guarantee of future progress. In Ghana, initial success and a paucity of similarly promising performers on the continent attracted much donor support, completely overwhelming officials in the line ministries. It has been estimated that by the early 1990s 'senior officials were spending an estimated 44 weeks a year facilitating or participating in donor supervision missions, time they were unable to devote to their "own" work' (Sawyerr, 1997:7). Thus, ironically, early success did not make it easier for the government to own reforms or to embark on further reforms.

In Tanzania, given the initial resistance within the party and government to reforms, the core analytical work was borne by academicians at the University of Dar es Salaam and technical staff from the Bank of Tanzania and the finance ministry. They were, for example, largely responsible for the design of the abortive homegrown reform efforts, mentioned earlier, and for providing advice during subsequent negotiations with the IMF and World Bank. However, in contrast with Ghana, the Tanzanian side was unable to gain much from its negotiations with the IMF and the World Bank at the outset. Mutalemwa et al. (1999:31) have argued that 'even when potential centers of ... intellectual capacity existed, they were either bypassed for lack of a consultative mechanism for interacting with non-decision making bodies, or their comments would be ignored because of the kasumba[10] habit of listening only to foreigners.' In Tanzania, the apparent lack of influence on policy implementation led to the disintegration of the core group of technocrats mentioned earlier.

A series of personnel changes in the economic ministries prevented continuity.

Finally, in contrasting the institutional responses in the two countries, the case of the public expenditure reviews (PERs) is illustrative. Since 1993, the Ghanaian government has conducted its own public expenditure reviews, with the finance ministry using inputs from the sector ministries and the planning commission to do so. In addition to the overall review of expenditures each year, the PER also focuses on an issue of particular concern with respect to expenditure and fiscal balance. In Tanzania, on the other hand, the PER working group, comprising government, donors and academics, was first established in 1997. Although the PER process is driven by mechanisms set up in Tanzania, the country's traditional aid dependence nevertheless tends to elevate the role of the donors in the process. The secretariat of the working group is, for example, based at the World Bank offices, although the permanent secretary of the finance ministry chairs the meetings. Comments on the reports related to the exercise are more likely to come from donors other than nationals. Moreover, although the PER is supposed to be a Tanzanian document, it still goes through the review process of the World Bank, leading to inordinate delays. This reduces the legitimacy of the Tanzanian consultative process. In the most recent cycle, the bulk of the work and consultations took place in Dar es Salaam in April–May 2000 but eleven months later the final PER report was still not available.

3.3   The role of donors

The discussion of reform ownership leads to that of the role of the donor community in the provision of financial resources and technical assistance and the nature of the attached conditionalities (Burnside and Dollar, 1997; Rowley, 2000). Lancaster and Wangwe (2000:40) have argued that

aid can strengthen organizations by expanding the technical and administrative capacity of their staffs and by increasing their activities ... but it can also weaken recipient country institutions by undercutting the planning, budgeting, administrative capacities, and general operations of recipient organizations and their political accountability and legitimacy. It can also reduce the sense of initiative and responsibility on the part of individuals in recipient organizations for achieving their goals and missions.

Whether one or the other happens depends on how aid is managed. This is in turn a function of the historical relationship with donors, their numbers, the institutional framework for aid coordination and the capacity of recipients to absorb aid. The nature and magnitude of donor support both before and during the reform episodes were different in Ghana and Tanzania. Political instability in Ghana had reduced donor interest in the country. However, the rapid withdrawal of aid began only when the Acheampong government repudiated foreign commercial loans in 1973, with the introduction of a 'we won't pay' (*yentua*) policy. Subsequent increases in corruption in the face of economic decline did not help revive donor interest. By 1981, aid per capita was US$14 or 3.4 percent of GNP, both well below the sub-Saharan African average. As already noted, the initial rhetoric of the PNDC did not endear it to the donor community, with its ties to Libya scaring off other potential donors. By 1981, Ghana's sources of external finance had narrowed down to a small number of donors (Harrigan and Younger, 2000:193). Ghana thus undertook the economic reforms of 1982–3 with limited donor support. It was only when the economic recovery program began to show good results that donors jumped onto the bandwagon. Ironically, this donor stampede had negative implications for the government's ability to manage aid flows and thus hurt aid effectiveness.

In contrast, Tanzania has always had strong support from bilateral donors, particularly from the Nordic countries. This support was partly a reflection of the respect enjoyed around the world by President Julius Nyerere. His policies of 'African socialism' had initially been effective in improving social indicators (primary school enrollment and literacy rates) and welfare in Tanzania. The dominance of donors in Tanzania presented a real challenge for government, however. Indeed, it has been argued that donor support may have delayed reform in the early 1980s. In efforts to address this dependence, recent years have seen the government putting in place institutional mechanisms to improve its management of aid inflows.

Apart from the difference in the degree of aid intensity in the two countries, Tanzania shows a marked stability of donor composition, with Sweden, Denmark, Germany and Norway consistently among the biggest donors up to the early 1990s. The Nordic countries, with their own background of social equity and democracy, were particularly enamored of Tanzania. In fact, the Nordics, as a bloc, became with time something of a donor lobby for Tanzania. This was important during the earlier phase of the economic reforms when Tanzania had to negotiate with the IMF and the World Bank in rather acrimonious circumstances. The Nordic countries continued to support Tanzania even after the multilateral agencies had cut off support in the early 1980s. This longstanding relationship has contributed to significant commitment on both sides. Close personal relationships were formed between successive Nordic ambassadors and Nyerere himself. A downside of this is that, when the donors were forced to change their approach in light of changed realities, as during the period 1993–4 when serious concerns arose regarding weak fiscal structure, poor accountability and lack of democracy, their actions were deemed to be intrusive by the Tanzanians (Helleiner et al., 1995).

The composition of aid donors to Ghana has changed markedly over the years. In the 1970s, the most important donors were Canada, the United Kingdom and the United States, whereas in the 1980s aid from Denmark, Germany, Japan and the Netherlands increased in importance. In the 1990s, Japan became the largest bilateral donor (Tsikata, 2001). Thus, historically the country has not had a dominant long-term relation with a donor or group of donors, and the associated donor leverage has accordingly been missing. However, although traditionally less intrusive in approach and not focusing on policy-based lending, Japan's eminence in providing aid to Ghana might be changing this. This was, for example, evident in Ghana's decision not to apply for HIPC (Heavily Indebted Poor Countries) relief, since Japan does not support debt forgiveness as a development and growth strategy for poor countries. Comparing the benefits of Japanese aid, which tends to be less conditional, with those of HIPC relief (with its attendant conditionalities), the Ghanaian authorities chose to keep the former. As a postscript, the UK recently successfully dissuaded the new Ghanaian government from rejection of the HIPC initiative.[11]

With economic improvement in the 1980s, aid to Ghana increased exponentially from US$9 to US$49 per capita between 1983 and 1991. Much of the support came directly from the World Bank, which saw Ghana as its showpiece for economic reform in Africa. But, as discussed above, Ghanaian policymakers were better prepared than those in other countries in the region. Martin (1991) has noted that the good economic outcomes and better preparation enabled Ghanaians to enjoy, at least for a while, a special relationship with the IMF and the World Bank, which led to flexibility on the part of the multilateral agencies and won Ghana a number of concessions. For example, between 1992 and 1997, Ghana was able to defer action on devaluation, price control, trade liberalization and privatization. In both countries, the proliferation of aid, in terms of flows and the number of donors involved, created serious aid management problems. Thus the impact of aid on the local bureaucracies has become a concern in its own right, because it impedes the quality of ownership that aid demands (Brautigam and Botchwey, 1998). In Ghana, administering the conditions associated with the different projects stretched the staff of the sectoral and line ministries to the limit.

However, although this problem was well known and governments tried to put in place mechanisms to resolve it, success was not achieved. Ghana, for example, created the international economic relations department in the finance ministry to supervise aid matters, while Tanzania set up a Tanzania assistance strategy in an effort at better coordination. In both cases, donors pledged to collaborate with these new institutional arrangements, although in practice they were flouted. Many donors continue to deal directly with project management units in the sector ministries, which they feel are more efficient than the coordination departments. Weak institutional capacities have meant that ownership continues to be shallow and the results inadequate. The poor budgeting of aid flows that results from this bypassing of the central budget makes it difficult for the governments to ensure that their priorities are met by donor funding. This further compounds the difficulty of managing aid. In Tanzania, this is especially true of the development budget, where up to 90 percent of the funds are from donor sources, with 70 percent not going through the budget (Tsikata et al., 1999). In contrast, less than 40 percent of donor aid to Ghana is channeled outside of the budget.

An ironical feature of aid to Tanzania during the reform period is that donors were increasingly worried about the apparent lack of government ownership of the programs. With respect to Danish aid, programs were plagued by a perceived decline in the administrative capacity of public institutions and in the ability of the government to contribute domestic resources as well as a rising incidence of corruption. The problems then forced Denmark to institute parallel delivery structures, notably nongovernmental organizations, under its control. However, this reduced the effectiveness of Danish aid, with the aid relationship between Tanzania and Denmark becoming increasingly unequal. Similar sentiments have arisen from reviews of Finnish (Porvali and Associates, 1995), Norwegian (Royal Norwegian Ministry of Foreign Affairs, 1999:122) and Swedish (Adam et al., 1994) aid programs. A lack of genuine dialogue is generally indicated, with Tanzania being mainly a commentator on the planned programs rather than the initiator.

In 1994, Denmark sponsored a group of eminent academics to look at the Tanzania–donor relationship. The resulting Helleiner Report (Helleiner et al., 1995) noted that donors were 'frequently ambivalent about the ownership issue: some demand that the government take greater control of their programs and at the same time resist when it attempts to do so at the expense of their own preferred projects.'[12] The report recommended a move towards greater Tanzanian ownership of aid programs and processes, with government formulating a clear development strategy for the country. The donors needed to coordinate their activities better and to harmonize their rules and procedures, while leaving overall coordination of development in the hands of Tanzanians, focused especially at the sector level. Priority was to be given to political and administrative reforms and to addressing the problems of corruption. The report suggested that, in the medium to long term, aid could be reduced, but it warned against reductions if they were to take place 'abruptly and without warning' (Helleiner et al., 1995).

In conclusion, it is notable that generous aid to Tanzania, and from a somewhat homogeneous set of donors, did not ensure better use or planning for the aid inflows. Indeed, traditional aid ties seem to have inhibited ownership at various levels. In Ghana, on the other hand, donors had fled the country with the decline of the economy and increasingly autocratic nature of the regimes. Reforms were embarked on with little aid. Still, Ghana was able to formulate a reform program that was more acceptable at home and yielded faster results in the first decade of implementation than that in Tanzania. However, the Ghanaian government was unable to withstand the political pressures that came with political liberalization in the 1990s, and the earlier policy cohesiveness collapsed (Harrigan and Younger, 2000).

4   Determinants of ownership: Summary and conclusions

This chapter has focused on the subject of reform ownership in sub-Saharan Africa, with Ghana and Tanzania as case studies. In Ghana, economic reform had sprung from the revolutionary zeal of young military officers and left-leaning academics. Although Bretton Woods type reforms were not their initial focus, a general lack of resources and support had forced them to approach the IMF and the World Bank. Significantly, when the decision for reform was made, the PNDC was able to bring many of its followers on board by encouraging a broad debate, which contributed to the success of the early reforms, generating rapid growth, macroeconomic stabilization and increased donor assistance.

In Tanzania, on the other hand, the initial conditions were radically different. The government had enjoyed a long period of uninterrupted donor support, and many donors continued to deliver aid even when the economic performance deteriorated. Continued aid inflows helped the government to resist drastic reforms and to attempt to introduce its 'home-made' versions. As the crisis deepened, and with donors becoming more willing to withdraw aid, the government had no option but to embark on reforms. These were implemented in an environment not marked by a clear break with the past and where groups within the government and the private sector wrestled for control of the reform agenda. Most recently, however, Tanzania seems to have made more tangible progress, with the government making efforts to influence the reform agenda positively. This has been rewarded with improved economic performance and higher aid inflows. Ghana, on the other hand, seems to have regressed. The economic performance of the 1990s was clearly undistinguished and the onset of political pluralism seems to have introduced a political business cycle characterized by worsening macroeconomic aggregates at the onset of elections.

A set of six interrelated lessons can be derived from the above comparison of Ghana and Tanzania. The first is that, in both countries, historical antecedents to reform are important determinants of subsequent progress. Also, although reform can sprout from many political environments, what is important is political commitment. In Tanzania, both within government and among the population, reforms were popularly seen as 'imposed' from outside. This perception was reinforced by the fact that Tanzania's homegrown efforts, rolled out with fanfare as alternatives to structural adjustment, failed to garner foreign support. By contrast, Ghana's sense of commitment was reinforced by the fact that its economic program (drawn up domestically but patterned on those of the Bretton Woods institutions) was largely accepted and opened the way for resource inflows.

Secondly, the nature of the aid relationship and how it evolves are important determinants of reform ownership. This relates to the number of donors relative to the country's coordination capacity and the type of technical assistance it receives. In Tanzania and Ghana (from the late 1980s onwards), the sheer number of donors and the volume of aid overwhelmed staff in the key economic ministries, leaving them little time to formulate strategies or simply think. The failure of governments to articulate their priorities and the absence of institutional capacities led to loss of control over programs. Donors took to bypassing the government by constructing parallel mechanisms for aid delivery. The absence of a well-established institutional framework for managing aid thus led to a lack of selectivity and to the proliferation of projects.

The third lesson is that analytical capacity among implementing institutions is crucial to the ownership of policies and programs. The differing experiences of Ghana and Tanzania are partly linked to varying capacities within the countries and the use to which they were put. Analytical capacity appears to have been stronger in Ghana than in Tanzania, although the latter had a very strong economics department at the University of Dar es Salaam. Yet, as discussed earlier, the Tanzanian government failed to draw on this technical expertise effectively or consistently.

The fourth lesson is that reform ownership is a dynamic concept, evolving with changes in the economy. In Ghana, the first decade of reform saw good economic outcomes, reduced poverty in rural areas and improving socioeconomic indicators. These strengthened the government's hand and increased its commitment to reform. In Tanzania, where macroeconomic improvements have not been matched by social sector improvements, it was harder to find champions for broader reforms. Nostalgia for the socialist days, when social services were provided almost free, was palpable, and political anxiety regarding the benefits of reform remained high until only recently. Good macroeconomic performance and improving government revenues are also important in helping the government to attract skilled professionals and to remunerate its employees. Poor economic outcomes have the insidious effect of encouraging the most qualified civil servants to leave for the private sector.

The fifth lesson is that a strong institutional mechanism for accountability is the foundation on which mutual trust is built between recipient and donor. In a sense, accountability buys the recipient country some implementation space. A loss of trust following perceived mismanagement (whether through incompetence or corruption), such as in Tanzania in 1993–4, or in Ghana during the 1992 presidential and parliamentary elections, can set a vicious cycle of events in motion. Aside from withdrawing, a typical reaction of donors can be to try to micromanage projects by introducing parallel management units with expatriate staff. This intrusiveness rarely leads to trust between recipient and donor or to reform ownership by the recipient.

The last lesson is that the political context matters in several ways for ownership. The emergence of winners and losers in the reform process can strengthen or weaken ownership depending on their ability to shift the political balance. Where the gains tend to be enjoyed by groups with which the government is aligned, there will be open official acceptance of the reforms (for example, Ghana during the first five years of reform). However, if the political costs of associating with the reforms and alienating support groups exceed the benefits, then the government is unlikely to be a vocal champion of the process (as in Tanzania). The political context also establishes the degree of accountability to which government is held. In most African countries, public discourse on economic development and reform remains inadequate and the means of sanctioning poor government performance are equally meager. Thus a democratic system, whereby the government can be voted out peacefully if the citizens are dissatisfied with it, is necessary if governments are to be held accountable to citizens for the policies pursued.

An important implication of the above lessons is that both donors and aid recipients need to work much harder at creating conditions that will ensure that reform policies are properly defined, articulated and implemented. The donor community's desire to control aid, in order to ensure full accountability to the home electorate, must be balanced against the need to allow sufficient space for recipients to refine their bureaucratic systems and evolve their own procedures for aid management. For a true partnership to emerge, both sides need to let go of the old conceptions and focus on strengthening institutions that can facilitate greater recipient ownership. This will demand not only higher levels of accountability in recipient countries but also measures to establish mutual trust as well as respect for each community's need to respond with credibility to the demands of its political constituency.

Notes

1. Côte d'Ivoire, Democratic Republic of Congo, Ethiopia, Ghana, Kenya, Mali, Nigeria, Tanzania, Uganda and Zambia.
2. Assessed by looking at four indicators: (i) who initiated reforms; (ii) political leadership's commitment; (iii) technocrats' intellectual conviction; and (iv) how broad based the support for reforms is. Each of these indicators was rated according to a four-level scale depending on the degree of ownership. So for example, in the case of the first indicator, if the government initiated and implemented the program then ownership was highest. On the other hand, if the program was prepared by the World Bank and implemented despite serious disagreements, then ownership was ranked at the lowest level.
3. There is a voluminous literature on economic reform in Ghana. See, for example, Aryeetey et al. (2000), Herbst (1993) and Pereira et al. (2000). This chapter extends the literature by focusing on reform ownership in a comparative perspective.
4. However, the underlying ideological battles and power struggles within the inner circle were not over. Between 1982 and 1985, several unsuccessful coup attempts occurred. By the mid-1980s, however, a political stability of sorts had been established.
5. Bigsten et al. (2001) provide a good flavor of the internal debate of the time.
6. The discussion of events is based on Kiondo (1991) and on interviews with important participants who were advisers, academics or government officials at the time.
7. The Tanzania Advisory Group was established in late 1981 as a result of an understanding between the former Tanzanian president Julius Nyerere and former World Bank president McNamara. An IDA technical assistance credit financed it. The members agreed upon by both Tanzania and the World Bank were M. Head, C. Pratt and G. K. Helleiner. In the secretariat were B. van Arkadie and J. Loxley.
8. See the Presidential Parastatal Sector Reform Commission's *Impact of Privatization in Tanzania*, January 2000:10.
9. The committee was chaired by Kojo Tsikata and included the finance secretary, two deputy finance secretaries, the governor of the central bank, a former governor of the Bank of Ghana then at UNCTAD, a Ghanaian World Bank manager, the Ghanaian ambassador to the USA (a former finance secretary himself) and four close advisers (some of whom held secretary positions). With regard to earlier reforms, see World Bank (1993a,b).
10. 'Kasumba' is a Kiswahili word that translates loosely as 'having a complex.'
11. In April 2001, following a visit by the UK Minister for Overseas Cooperation, the Ghanaian government announced that it was applying for HIPC relief.
12. In a later paper (Helleiner, 2000), based on interviews conducted in Tanzania, Helleiner elaborated on this point, adding to examples in the initial report. When asked to define what they understood by ownership, donor representatives variously answered (i) 'We have to pressure the government to take ownership of ...'; (ii) 'Ownership exists when they do what we want them to do but they do it voluntarily'; and (iii) 'We want them to

take ownership. Of course they must do what we want. If not, they should get their money elsewhere.'

REFERENCES

Adam, C., A. Bigsten, P. Collier, E. Julin and S. O'Connell (1994) *Evaluation of Swedish Development Cooperation with Tanzania*, a report for the Secretariat for Analysis of Swedish Development Assistance, SIDA: Stockholm.

Ahiakpor, J. A. (1991) 'Rawlings, Economic Policy Reform, and the Poor: Consistency or Betrayal?' *Journal of Modern Africa Studies* 28(4):583–600.

Armstrong, R. P. (1996) *Ghana Country Assistance Review: A Study in Development Effectiveness*, A World Bank Operations Evaluation Study, World Bank: Washington, DC.

Aryeetey, E., J. Harrigan and M. Nissanke (eds.) (2000) *Economic Reforms in Ghana: The Miracle and the Mirage*, James Currey: Oxford.

Baregu, M. (1994) 'The Rise and Fall of the One-Party State in Tanzania,' in J. A. Widener (ed.) *Economic Change and Political Liberalization in sub-Saharan Africa*, Johns Hopkins University Press: Baltimore, MD.

Batse, Z. K. M., G. Botschie and N. Agyemang-Mensah (1999) 'Integrating Capacity Building within the Context of Social Policies for Poverty Reduction in Ghana,' *IDRC: Social Development Networks*, Regional Office for West and Central Africa, March.

Bigsten, A. and A. Danielson (1999) 'Is Tanzania an Emerging Economy?' a report for the OECD Project, *Emerging Africa*, OECD Development Centre: Paris.

Bigsten, A., D. Mutalemwa, Y. Tsikata and S. Wangwe (2001) 'Tanzania,' in S. Devarajan et al. (eds.) *Aid and Reform in Africa: A Report from 10 Countries*, World Bank: Washington, DC.

Brautigam, D. and K. Botchwey (1998) 'The Institutional Impact of Aid Dependence on Recipients in Africa,' paper prepared for the AERC/ODC Joint Collaborative Project on Managing the Transition from Aid Dependency in sub-Saharan Africa, Washington and Nairobi.

Burnside, C. and D. Dollar (1997) 'Aid, Policies, and Growth,' Policy Research Working Paper No. 1777, World Bank, Washington, DC.

Collier, P. (1997) 'The Failure of Conditionality,' in Catherine Gwin and Joan Nelson (eds.) *Perspectives on Aid and Development*, Overseas Development Council: Washington, DC.

Cooksey, B. and M. Mmuya (1997) 'The Uses and Quality of Health Service in Tanzania: Results of a Service Delivery Survey,' TADREG Working Paper Series No. 6 (August).

Cooksey, B., M. Mmuya and F. Wamura (1997) 'The Uses and Quality of Primary Schooling in Rural Tanzania: A Baseline Service Delivery Survey for Rural Tanzania,' TADREG Working Paper Series No. 7 (December).

Devarajan, S., D. Dollar and T. Holmgren (eds.) (2001) *Aid and Reform in Africa: A Report from 10 Countries*, World Bank: Washington, DC.

Dollar, D. and J. Svensson (1997) 'What Explains the Success or Failure of Structural Adjustment Programs?' Policy Research Working Paper No. 1938, World Bank, Washington, DC.

Haggard, S. and R. Kaufman (eds.) (1992) *The Politics of Economic Adjustment*, Princeton University Press: Princeton, NJ.

Harrigan, J. and S. Younger (2000) 'Aid, Debt and Growth,' in E. Aryeetey, J. Harrigan and M. Nissanke (eds.) *Economic Reforms in Ghana: The Miracle and the Mirage*, James Currey: Oxford.

Helleiner, G. K. (2000) 'External Conditionality, Local Ownership and Development,' in J. Freedman (ed.) *Transforming Development: Foreign Aid for a Changing World*, University of Toronto Press: Toronto.

Helleiner, G. K., T. Killick, N. Lipumba, B. J. Ndulu and K. E. Svendsen (1995) *Report of the Group of Independent Advisers on Development Cooperation Issues between Tanzania and Its Aid Donors*, Royal Danish Ministry of Foreign Affairs: Copenhagen.

Herbst, J. (1993) *The Politics of Reform in Ghana, 1982–91*, University of California Press: Berkeley, CA.

International Monetary Fund (1998) *External Evaluation of the ESAF: Report by a Group of Independent Experts*, IMF: Washington, DC.

——— (2001) *Review of Conditionality*, on IMF website, www.imf.org.

Jeffries, R. (1991) 'Leadership Commitment and Political Opposition to Structural Adjustment in Ghana,' in D. Rothchild (ed.) *Ghana: The Political Economy of Recovery*, Lynne Rienner Publishers: Boulder, CO.

Johnson, J. H. and S. S. Wasty (1993) 'Borrower Ownership of Adjustment Programs and the Political Economy of Reform,' World Bank Discussion Paper No. 199, World Bank, Washington, DC.

Johnson, O. E. G. (1994) 'Managing Adjustment Costs, Political Authority, and the Implementation of Structural Adjustment Programs, with Special Reference to African Countries,' *World Development* 22(3):399–411.

Kahler, M. (1992). 'External Influence, Conditionality, and the Politics of Adjustment,' in S. Haggard and R. R. Kaufman (eds.) *The Politics of Economic Adjustment*, Princeton University Press: Princeton, NJ.

Killick, T. (1997) 'Principals and Agents and the Failings of Conditionality,' *Journal of International Development* 9(4):483–95.

Killick, T. with R. Gunatilaka and A. Marr (1998) *Aid and the Political Economy of Policy Change*, Routledge: London and New York.

Kiondo, A. (1991) 'The Nature of Economic Reforms in Tanzania,' in H. Campbell and H. Stein (eds.) *The IMF and Tanzania: The Dynamics of Liberalization*, Southern Africa Political Economy Series Trust: Harare.

Lancaster, C. (1999) 'Aid Effectiveness in Africa: The Unfinished Agenda,' *Journal of African Economies* 8(4):487–503.

Lancaster, C. and S. Wangwe (2000) 'Managing a Smooth Transition from Aid Dependence in Africa,' ODC Policy Essay No. 28, Johns Hopkins University Press: Baltimore, MD.

Maipose, G., G. Somolekae and T. Johnston (1997) 'Effective Aid Management: The Case of Botswana,' in J. Carlsson, G. Somolekae and N. van de Walle (eds.) *Foreign Aid in Africa: Learning from Country Experiences*, Nordiska Afrikainstitutet: Uppsala.

Martin, M. (1991) 'Negotiating Adjustment and External Finance: Ghana and the International Community, 1982–1989,' in D. Rothchild (ed.) *Ghana: The Political Economy of Recovery*, Lynne Rienner Publishers: Boulder, CO.

Mutalemwa, D., P. Noni and S. Wangwe (1999) 'Managing the Transition from Aid Dependence: The Case of Tanzania,' paper prepared for the AERC/ODC Aid Dependence Project, Washington and Nairobi.

Ndulu, B. J. (2001) 'Partnership, Inclusiveness and Aid Effectiveness in Africa,' mimeo.

Pereira L., S. A. Pellechio, L. Zanforlin, G. Begashaw, S. Fabrizio and J. Harnack (2000) 'Ghana: Economic Development in a Democratic Environment,' IMF Occasional Paper No. 199, International Monetary Fund, Washington, DC.

Porvali, H. and Associates (1995) *Evaluation of the Development Cooperation between the United Republic of Tanzania*, Ministry for Foreign Affairs, Department for International Development Cooperation: Helsinki.

Rowley, C. (2000) 'Political Culture and Economic Performance in Sub-Saharan Africa,' *European Journal of Political Economy* 16(1):133–58.

Royal Norwegian Ministry of Foreign Affairs (1999) *Tanzania–Norway Development Cooperation 1994–97*, Oslo.

Sawyerr, H. (1997) *Country-led Aid Coordination in Ghana*, Association for Development of Education in Africa (ADEA): Paris.

Stein, H. (1991) 'Economic Policy and the IMF in Tanzania: Conditionality, Conflict and Convergence,' in H. Campbell and H. Stein (eds.) *The IMF and Tanzania: The Dynamics of Liberalization*, Southern Africa Political Economy Series Trust: Harare.

Therkildsen, O. (2000) 'Public Sector Reform in a Poor, Aid-Dependent Country, Tanzania,' *Public Administration and Development* 20:61–71.

Tsikata, Y. (2000) 'Globalization, Poverty and Inequality in Sub-Saharan Africa: A Political Economy Appraisal,' paper prepared for the OECD Dialogue on Poverty and Inequality, 30 November – 1 December, Paris.

—— (2001) 'Ghana,' in S. Devarajan et al. (eds.) *Aid and Reform in Africa: A Report from 10 Countries*, World Bank: Washington, DC.

Tsikata, Y., S. Wangwe, D. Mutalemwa and A. Mtowa (1999) 'Tanzania's Development Budget: Issues and Implementation,' report prepared for the PER '00 Working Group, Dar es Salaam.

White, H. and O. Morrissey (1997) 'Conditionality When Donor and Recipient Preferences Vary,' *Journal of International Development* 9(4):497–505.

World Bank (1993a) *Ghana 2000 and Beyond: Setting the Stage for Accelerated Growth and Poverty Reduction*, World Bank: Washington, DC.

—— (1993b) *Report of the Proceedings by the Chairman*, Meeting of the Consultative Group for Ghana, Paris, 24–25 June, opening statement by the minister of finance.

—— (1998) *Assessing Aid: What Works, What Doesn't and Why*, Oxford University Press: New York.

3

Do donors matter for institutional reform in Africa?

Tony Addison

Reform will only occur if it promises to offer the rulers a bundle of resources and policies that improve on the status quo. (Jean-Laurent Rosenthal, discussing the failure of the monarchy to reform in eighteenth-century France)[1]

Until the issue of the presidential succession is resolved, nothing fundamental will change in Kenya. There will be some progress with the IMF and the World Bank, and then after three months we'll be back to square one. (Gitobu Imanyara, Kenyan opposition politician and lawyer, 4 April 2001)[2]

1 Introduction

The past twenty years have seen an extensive and exhaustive debate on how to improve the institutions of African states. There is now a welcome emphasis on service delivery and accountability in the use of public money. But progress has been patchy at best. More than ever, sustained reform depends on the establishment of a domestic consensus on, and an internalization of, the need for change. 'Blaming donors and multilateral agencies for domestic policy failures, while a popular approach among some African regimes, cannot be a viable strategy in the long run' (Kayizzi-Mugerwa, 2000). Ownership is therefore crucial.

This chapter is entitled 'Do donors matter for institutional reform in Africa?' The reader can probably guess the answer: if reform is fully owned by African governments and societies, then they will devise the

54

agenda and lead the process. Aid would still be important in reducing the financial and human resource constraints, but donors would otherwise take the back seat. However, because many countries find it difficult to move the process forward, donors will remain important in devising the agenda. It is therefore crucial that donors have a clear and effective strategy. This chapter suggests that many of the problems arise from a 'partial reform equilibrium'; initial reforms are in many cases undertaken, but then strong resistance is encountered and reform is not completed. In thinking through this issue the chapter has been influenced by the literature on transition economies, which is more relevant to sub-Saharan Africa (SSA) than is often supposed. In particular, the term 'partial reform equilibrium' used by Hellman (1998) is helpful in understanding why reform may stall.

I do not attempt an evaluation of donor projects in institutional reform; to do that properly would require a comprehensive inventory of what has happened and, more fundamentally, an agreed definition of what constitutes success and failure. Rather, the chapter focuses on issues of strategy for donors in assisting institutional reform in SSA. The examples that are given are mainly drawn from the experiences of the UK's Department for International Development (DFID) – probably the most innovative of the bilateral donors presently supporting institutional reform in Africa.

The chapter begins, in section 2, by discussing the crisis in Africa's state institutions that came to a head in the 1980s. This destroyed the old contract between incumbent rulers and the populace, which rested on the expansion of public employment and public services. In its place, a new social contract is being written. This has a democratic clause, but also a clause relating to the relationship between the state and business. If this social contract is successful it will drive a process in which voters and businesses provide resources (through taxes) in return for better institutions. However, section 2 also argues that progress down this path to institutional improvement is in many countries impeded by winners from the first generation of reform who wish to preserve their rents. A partial reform equilibrium is the result. Consequently, although donors may be heartened to find governments speaking the rhetoric of private sector development, state actors may not in fact buy into many second-generation reforms (such as regulation in the public interest).

Section 3 of the chapter considers the specifics of the partial reform equilibrium as they affect the state itself; in particular, public management and public expenditure reform; security sector reform; and revenue reform. Each is an unfinished agenda. Public management reform has been driven by fiscal crisis, but this has resulted in a focus on cost cutting at the expense of improvement in the public sector's effectiveness. And distressingly little progress has been achieved in measuring the impact of public spending, particularly on the poor. This failure impedes not only poverty reduction but the process of democratization as well. In the security sector, donors are beginning to grapple realistically with the problem of conflict in Africa and therefore with the problem that military spending poses for budgetary transparency. But donors are still at an early stage and their efforts will not be effective unless collective action is taken. Lastly, revenue reform is an important foundation of the new social contract, but progress appears to have stagnated and it is difficult to justify donor support to mobilize more revenue when not enough of it is being transferred into effective development (and pro-poor) spending. Section 4 concludes the chapter by arguing that donors can influence countries that are stuck in a partial reform equilibrium, but generally only when internal political dynamics succeed in changing national leaderships, as is recently the case in Ghana.

2   Writing a new social contract

After independence, public employment expanded rapidly as new governments Africanized state administrations and nationalized key enterprises. New governments offered the populace more state jobs and better public services in exchange for acquiescence to single-party political systems. This social contract was not so different from that offered elsewhere in the developing world in the 1960s. While public employment and wages expanded, new rulers gained legitimacy – although not necessarily among all ethnic groups. Commodity windfalls in the 1970s bolstered this modus operandi; most governments (Botswana being a notable exception) viewed the windfalls as permanent, rather than temporary, and spent accordingly. Public employment growth accelerated, often reaching 10 percent or more per year (Lienert, 1998). Natural resource rents, general taxation and 'prerogative' income (from the granting of licenses, etc.) provided rulers with considerable powers of patronage, including the distribution of public jobs.[3] Urban populations benefited the most, but remittances carried some of the fruit to rural Africa as well.

By 1980, this social contract was in deep trouble. Excessive indirect taxation of agriculture led to economic contraction, thereby reducing the direct tax base as well. Rent seeking siphoned talent and resources out of the productive economy. Falling revenues and weak expenditure management led inexorably to macroeconomic disequilibrium. The post-independence social contract was finally killed off by the terms-of-trade shocks that buffeted Africa from 1980–2 onwards. Hiring stalled and real wages in the public sector collapsed; by 1985, the average Tanzanian civil servant's salary was one-fourth of its level a decade earlier (Lienert, 1998). Civil servants moonlighted to recover lost income. A sharp decline in service standards, corruption and institutional paralysis were the results (Table 3.1).

2.1 The two clauses of the new social contract

The 1980s crisis weakened the rule of incumbents. With the exception of Botswana and Mauritius, leaderships had neither the legitimacy provided by free and fair elections nor the populist support provided by fast growth (such as enjoyed by East Asia's authoritarian rulers). Donor acceptance of the post-independence contract withered as the doctrine of market liberalism took hold and as Africa's strategic importance declined with the winding down of the Cold War. Accordingly, political mobilization within civil society and political conditionality on aid initiated a transition to multiparty politics from the second half of the 1980s onwards (Crawford, 2001). By 1999, forty-five countries had multiparty constitutions compared with only eight in 1988 (Thomson, 2000:216). The first part of the new social contract is therefore a democratic one. The state promises higher living standards, better services and respect for human rights in exchange for votes (and taxes) from the populace. A second clause relates to the relationship between business and the state. The state provides public goods and protects property rights, and the private sector provides revenues in return. The literature refers to this as a 'resources for institutions' exchange (Mahon, 2000).

Both of these clauses represent ideals, of course. But both are ways of describing processes that, if they work well, yield better institutions. Simply put: the people and business demand better institutions, voting out politicians who fail to deliver and withholding resources (taxes) from states that fail to keep their side of the bargain. But, as with any contract, much of the final outcome depends on how well organized the parties are (in particular how they resolve their collective action problems) and how much information they have about each other's intentions. In particular, elections are themselves incomplete contracts; electorates can vote out bad leaders, but leaders can break promises and abuse power between elections. Institutional investments such as judicial reform, independent auditors general and legislative oversight of the public sector and its spending therefore strengthen democracy. And, to function well, democracies must be served by an active and competitive media. All of this takes considerable time and resources to build. Consequently, opinion is sharply divided over whether SSA can sustain democratization (Herbst, 2000).

Table 3.1 Sub-Saharan Africa and other developing country groups: Quality of governance, institutions and public services

	Quality of bureaucracy 1984–98	Extent of corruption 1984–98	Government stability 1984–98	Ethnic tensions 1984–98	Political violence 1984–98	Law and order 1984–98	Risk of expropriation 1984–97	Risk of contract repudiation 1984–97
Asian NIEs[a]	7.3	6.9	6.5	7.5	9.0	7.4	8.3	9.1
Asia	4.6	4.3	5.0	4.5	6.0	5.0	6.3	6.0
Advanced economies	8.7	8.3	6.5	8.2	8.7	8.7	7.9	9.2
Western hemisphere	4.2	4.6	4.9	7.1	5.8	4.8	5.7	6.0
Middle East and Europe	4.8	4.7	5.7	5.9	5.7	5.4	6.2	5.9
Sub-Saharan Africa	4.1	4.6	4.8	4.9	5.5	4.4	5.3	4.8
World	5.4	5.5	5.4	6.4	6.6	5.8	6.3	6.4
SSA countries: unweighted grouping by yearly per capita GDP growth rate in 1970–98								
High growth (top quintile)	4.3	5.9	5.5	5.7	6.4	5.1	5.6	5.3
Medium group	4.6	4.7	5.0	5.1	5.7	4.6	5.7	5.2
Low growth (bottom quintile)	3.0	3.5	3.8	3.9	4.5	3.6	4.3	3.4
Memorandum								
CFA: unweighted average[b]	4.5	4.3	4.9	5.4	6.0	4.4	5.7	5.3

Source: Reproduced from IMF, *World Economic Outlook*, Washington, DC (October 1999). Original data from International Country Risk Guide (published by Political Risk Services).

Notes: Scores are on a scale of 1–10, where higher means better quality. For regional groupings, scores are unweighted averages of countries in the dataset.

[a] Hong Kong SAR, Korea, Singapore and Taiwan Province of China.

[b] Communauté Financière Africaine and Coopération Financière en Afrique.

2.2 The state's relationship with business

The ideal for transforming the state–business relationship is to foster private investment, innovation and competition, while simultaneously protecting the public interest – constraining the abuse of market power, protecting consumers and workers and safeguarding the environment (Albouy, 1999). First-generation reforms often deviated markedly from this ideal; privatization was largely driven by fiscal pressures, efficiency (and equity) considerations taking second place despite their equal weight in donor rhetoric (Kayizzi-Mugerwa, 2001). Insider privatization was rife (Bayliss and Fine, 1998; DFID, 2000a:8), sometimes directly at the expense of the poor (Addison, 2001b; Wuyts, 2000). About 75 percent of privatizations over 1980–95 were in sectors such as manufacturing, which accounted for 52.0 percent of all state-owned enterprises (SOEs) sold (data from Bennell, 1997). These require lighter regulation than financial services (5.3 percent of SOEs sold over 1980–95) and utilities (0.8 percent), whose characteristics demand tight regulation to satisfy the public interest.[4]

But second-generation privatization is now increasingly focused on infrastructure and utilities – telecommunications, transport, water supply and sanitation, electricity, oil and gas – whose characteristics (natural monopoly, etc.) require well-designed regulation, especially to meet the needs of poor communities (Ugaz, 2001). However, little if any regulatory capacity was built up during the first generation of reforms in preparation for the more demanding second generation. A recent review for DFID summarizes the imbalance in priorities:

New forms of market-friendly regulation and support have rarely been properly instituted. The result has been that only one side of the liberal equation has been implemented,... and government is left with few effective instruments to assert the public interest ... The best performing cases are those where direct providers are accountable to users or local voters, that is where the need for regulation is reduced by effective mechanisms of (market or participatory) accountability. (Batley, 2000)

Accordingly, issues of business regulation are becoming more prominent in donor assistance, to help countries converge towards the ideal state–business relationship by overhauling competition policy, reforming business licensing and introducing post-privatization regulation that balances commercial incentives with public interests.[5] 'Transparency' and 'a level playing field' are donor watchwords. There is, however, a serious problem. First-generation reforms benefited the nascent business interests of senior state actors, who have, over the past decade, increasingly 'straddled' the private and public sectors (Bigsten and Moene, 1996). Many have replaced the economic rents that they enjoyed in SOEs and from import licensing with business profits – often derived from SOE assets that they bought cheaply. In conflict countries (for example, Angola and Liberia), state actors and rebels also capitalized their businesses using wartime profits. And political parties have developed extensive business interests (the case in Ethiopia for example) giving them more finance and hence an advantage in the new era of multiparty politics. Consequently, although donors may be heartened to find governments speaking the rhetoric of private sector development, governments may not fully buy into second-generation reform. There are parallels here with transition in the former Soviet Union (FSU) (Addison, 2001a). Several FSU countries are stuck in a 'partial reform equilibrium' (Hellman, 1998:233):

In each case the winners from an earlier stage of reform have incentives to block further advances in reform that would correct the very distortions on which their initial gains were based. In effect they seek to prolong the period of partial reforms to preserve their initial flow of rents, though at considerable social cost.

Early winners can influence the evolution of nascent regulatory frameworks to their advantage, and their opportunity is greatest when democratic institutions are newborn, and thus constraints are at their weakest. If this is so, it will have four undesirable consequences:
1. Regulatory frameworks will be unbalanced, tilted too much to commercial incentives and insufficiently to public interests. For example, land use regulation may favor commercial interests over community interests in access to valuable natural capital – already a problem in both Kenya and Mozambique – thereby undermining the donor agenda of poverty reduction (Addison, 2001b).
2. Incumbent parties and their leaders may use the regulatory framework to limit the entry of competitors to their own enterprises. In Ethiopia, businesspeople complain that the regulatory framework discriminates in favor of businesses linked to the ruling party. Likewise, the ban on entry of foreign banks favors Ethiopia's domestic banks, including one linked to the ruling party.
3. 'Big capital has big money' and can therefore influence the regulatory agenda (via party political donations, lobbying and corruption) in ways not open to smaller capital and micro-entrepreneurs (who, given their number and dispersion, find it more difficult to take collective action than does big capital). This could constrain the kind of desirable broad-based employment growth envisaged in such donor strategies as DFID's 'Making Markets Work for the Poor' (DFID, 2000b).

4. Technical assistance may help in constructing regulatory frameworks and institutions – for post-privatized utilities, for banking systems, and for environmental protection – but state actors that benefit from a partial reform equilibrium can encourage regulatory forbearance, thus undermining institutional effectiveness. Examples include Kenya, Uganda and (especially) Zambia. Regulatory forbearance in the financial sector is especially serious because financial crisis endangers macroeconomic stability – the recent insolvency of Mozambique's two largest privatized banks is a case in point (Addison et al., 2001).

In summary, the African state's relationship with business is evolving in ways that differ from the ideal model promoted by donors. In this sense it is more 'owned' than the ideal model and is therefore more likely to be implemented.

2.3   Democracy and the state–business relationship

Democracy is unlikely to sustain itself without a satisfactory state–business relationship; a faster rate of private investment is necessary to raise economic growth, and with it the increased revenues necessary for politicians to meet voters' expectations. However, the prospects for democracy are not good while Africa remains poor; Przeworski and Limongi (1997:165) find that democracies with per capita income of less than US$1,000 do not last more than eight years on average. Indeed, Herbst (2000) argues that it takes a per capita income of at least US$6,000 to secure democratization.

But is a democracy necessary for a satisfactory state–business relationship? A number of leaderships, while not repudiating democracy outright, certainly see it as less important than the deal they do with business. Thus Ottaway (1999:14) notes that the leaderships of Eritrea, Ethiopia, Rwanda and Uganda[6] 'came to power by winning a civil war, and consequently, they believe in the importance of force, strong organization, and good strategy'. She concludes:

In so far as they have a model of economic and political development, it is neither the 'African socialism' of the early days of African independence nor the Marxism–Leninism that guided them when they started their own wars. It is not even the democracy-and-free market model that multilateral and bilateral donors preach. This new generation believes in a mixture of strong political control, limited popular participation, and economic liberalization that allows for a strong state in regulating the market – South Korea, Taiwan, and even Singapore are viewed as models to be emulated.

If this model yields growth and rising living standards, then these African states will build a large measure of popular support, independently of democratization – with the new social contract resting on private, rather than public, employment growth – thereby replicating the thirty-year East Asian miracle that was constructed on a strong state–business relationship. In 'owning' this development trajectory, government would have an interest in ensuring that the relevant institutional investments occur, including the completion of first-generation reform – in particular the creation of a meritocratic bureaucracy – together with some (but not all) of the second-generation regulatory reforms favored by donors. And, as stocks of private fixed capital rise, so business would have the incentive to demand better institutions. A successful resources-for-institutions exchange would thereby ensue.

This process of successful institutional investment is least likely to occur in countries that are rich in mineral resources, at least those that now have histories of conflict. For, in these countries, private investment has been mostly in enclaves that lead an existence that is virtually independent from the rest of the economy: West African offshore oil is the classic example. Provided that their property rights remain secure (and governments largely respect them because they are the source of immense personal wealth for rulers), company operations are unhindered. And because there is little incentive for the governments concerned to set up a resources-for-institutions exchange that would embrace private investment outside the mineral sector, state institutions wither. This perhaps explains the 'paradox' of the Angolan government allowing the real wages of its civil servants to collapse in the 1990s despite rising oil wealth. In summary, institutional reform could occur without an advance in democratization, and might even withstand its reversal. But the business–state relationship that succeeded in East Asia is a difficult trick to pull off, for, as Haggard (2000:15) argues:

In the past, it was believed that the nature of business–government relations in Asia contributed to *good* policy, at least by developing country standards; even the World Bank came around to this view in its *East Asian Miracle* report ... But quite strict political requirements are required for such a 'good equilibrium' to occur, including political counterweights to private economic power, meritocratic bureaucracies, independent regulatory agencies, and transparency in business–government relations.

These requirements were never fully met in East Asia, but they existed to an extent sufficient to ensure thirty years of fast growth before cronyism finally overwhelmed the system. For African states to enter this path, they would have to move beyond the partial reform equilibrium in which many find themselves. Accordingly, I now turn to the specifics of that equilibrium as it affects state institutions.

3   Reforming the state

Rewriting Africa's social contract requires the reform of the state. This means completing an unfinished agenda that has now existed for well over twenty years – better public management and better expenditure management – as well as a 'new' agenda of security sector reform. And for all three of these to work out, more domestic revenue must be mobilized since aid is unlikely to recover its previous levels (Figure 3.1).

3.1   Public management reform and public expenditure reform

Public management reform includes 'restructuring to allow for greater decentralization of management within public services, including breaking up of large and traditional bureaucracies into autonomous and semi-autonomous agencies, and emphasis on explicit standards of measurement and performance' (Larbi, 2000). This is combined with changes in service delivery and funding, including contracting out to private and other non-government providers. These measures and others emanate from the New Public Management Model, which is in vogue – but has not in fact been systematically applied – in the OECD countries (Fozzard and Foster, 2001). In turn, this agenda is now supposed to drive another:

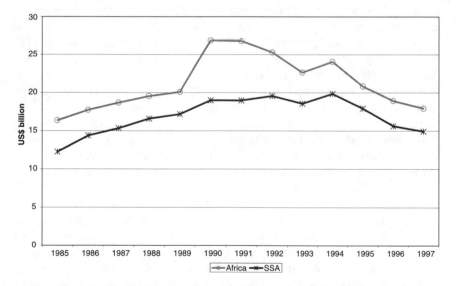

Figure 3.1 Net ODA disbursements for Africa region and sub-Saharan Africa at constant prices, 1985–97
Source: World Bank (2000b).

Changes in public expenditure management practice have followed and accommodated these broader public sector reforms, driven by a change in the perceived purpose of public expenditure management systems. Traditional administrative approaches emphasized expenditure control, assessed in terms of compliance with procedures and legislatively mandated expenditure policies, as expressed in the annual budget. Public expenditure management now emphasizes performance, assessed in relation to the goals of macroeconomic stabilization and economy, efficiency and effectiveness in the use of public funds. (Fozzard and Foster, 2001:2)

These reforms continue on their unsteady path. Civil service reform, which is central to both better management and better expenditure control, has shown only modest progress (Lienert and Modi, 1997:42; Nunberg and Nellis, 1995). The main exception is Uganda, which cut civilian government employment from 320,000 in 1989 to 148,000 in 1995 (Schiavo-Campo, 1995), and decompressed wage differentials to restore incentives to key employees. By 1996 Uganda's real wage per civil servant was over nine times its 1990 level (Lienert and Modi, 1997:42).[7] Donor support therefore contributed to better management and better expenditure control. Ghana, Mozambique and Tanzania are also moving forward, albeit hesitantly at times (Sulemane and Kayizzi-Mugerwa, 2001; Tsikata, 2001).

Elsewhere, however, most governments contained their wage bills by allowing real wages to continue their decline. By 1996 the real wage per civil servant was 88 percent of its 1990 level across SSA (and the 1990 level was often well below the 1980 level), and in some countries (for example, Cameroon) it was less than half (Lienert and Modi, 1997:42). This subverted efforts to improve management and service delivery, and in frustration donors created separate and well-paid project management units within the civil service, thereby often disabling the concept of local ownership.

Reviews of the first generation (1981–91) of civil service reforms (of which at least ninety were donor-supported programs) repeatedly conclude that expenditure control was often at the cost of improved management and service delivery: 'Civil service reforms have primarily been concerned with cost cutting and containment. The issue of productivity and the need for appropriate human capital for it have largely been secondary' (Haque and Aziz, 1998:33). Organizing the state around the ambitious New Public Management principles, worthy as they may be, therefore remains a distant mirage for much of SSA.

Accountability in service delivery is an important aspect of the democratization; people need to know how their money is being spent. Donors have moved a long way on this, from the mid-1980s when 'beneficiary assessment' was new to the World Bank (Salmen, 1987) to today, when civil society – and its assessment of service delivery – is recognized as an important participant in the Comprehensive Development Framework (CDF).[8] Yet, the reality is disappointing. Little progress has been made in establishing systems to measure the impact of public spending, and basic data on school and clinic attendance are collected only infrequently or not at all (see Durevall, 2001, on Malawi for instance). Uganda's expenditure tracking surveys are an exception, and donors are promoting these as best practice (Reinikka, 1999). In response to the survey finding that only 30 percent of non-salary funds actually reached Uganda's primary schools, and similar leakage in the health sector, '[m]onthly transfers of government funds to districts are now reported in the press and on radio. Fund transfers to schools are now displayed on public notice boards in schools and district government centers, and the government monitors compliance with this public spending' (Mackay and Gariba, 2000:7). Uganda's public accounting system for education has improved with donor support, but there is as yet no improvement in the health sector (Mackay and Gariba, 2000:7).

In summary, a partial reform equilibrium certainly exists in the areas of public management and public expenditure reform. There is no shortage of ideas as to how to improve matters, but the political process appears to be generating insufficient momentum. Donors will therefore have to continue to act as catalysts for faster progress.

3.2   Security sector reform

Twenty years ago, when SSA embarked upon first-generation reform, the Cold War was still at its height. The superpowers acted as agencies of restraint on client dictators; vicious internal conflict was less likely to spill across borders than is the case today. War is now a fact of life across the region – twenty-nine African countries have recently gone through major conflict – and civil wars increasingly have regional dimensions (DFID, 2001a). In the aggregate, military spending in SSA fell by about 25 percent in real terms over 1990–6 (Omitoogun, 2000:291). This reflected the worsening fiscal situation and demilitarization in South Africa. But military spending has been rising since 1997, and reached US$6.6 billion in 1999 (Figure 3.2).[9]

Development economists traditionally view military and security spending as an 'unproductive' expenditure that, given enough political commitment, can be cut and resources transferred into development spending. Certainly, on an accounting basis, education and health spending could be doubled in some countries if the military were simply closed down (Table 3.2). But, given the extent of regional insecurity, donors

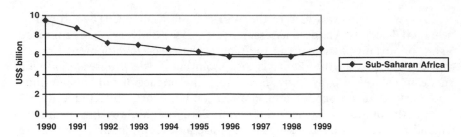

Figure 3.2 Sub-Saharan Africa military expenditure, 1990–9
Source: SIPRI data reported in Omitoogun (2000).
Notes: Figures are in US$ billion at constant 1995 prices and exchange rates.
Angola is excluded from these data.

have now come round to the view that 'there is a fundamental need and right for nations to provide for security' (DFID, 2000c:6), which must be taken into account in assessing military expenditures.[10] Thus, DFID states that:

Focusing solely on the level and composition of military spending and the degree to which defence budgets 'crowd out' development expenditures has not enabled the bilateral and multilateral actors to achieve their objectives of lower defence spending and higher outlays on development. Governments may be forced to reduce the amount of resources allocated to defence forces in their budgets, but that does not mean that fewer resources are actually being spent in the defence sector. Rather than learning to appreciate the value of good governance in the security sector, bad practices are being reinforced. Non-defence budgetary lines are used as pass-throughs to camouflage defence expenditure. Off-budget expenditure is frequently a problem of significant proportions. Profits from the sale of primary resources are skimmed to supplement defence budgets. Enterprises owned by the armed forces are used to fund defence spending. (DFID, 2000c:67)

Uganda illustrates the issue. Uganda's forces are presently engaged in the Democratic Republic of the Congo (leading to clashes with Rwanda) as well as in fighting the Lord's Resistance Army in the north. Military spending has risen accordingly, straining donor–government relations; the IMF suspended lending in 1999 because of overspending in the defense budget for 1998/99. In 1998 the Ugandan government commissioned DFID to undertake a study of the defense budget; this recommended improved auditing and the reform of procurement in order to improve transparency (DFID, 2000c:53). Nevertheless, the issue rumbles on, most lately in a public commission into irregularities in the procurement of helicopters by the Ugandan military.[11] The Rwandan government has also attempted to hide military spending (Figure 3.3):

Table 3.2 Public expenditure on health, education and the military as percentages of GNP in sub-Saharan Africa

	Expenditure on health, 1990–8	Expenditure on education, 1997	Military expenditure, 1997
Angola	3.9	–	20.5
Benin	1.6	3.2	1.5
Botswana	2.7	8.6	5.1
Burkina Faso	1.2	1.5	2.8
Burundi	0.6	4.0	6.1
Cameroon	1.0	–	3.0
Central African Republic	1.9	–	3.9
Chad	2.4	1.7	2.7
Congo, Democratic Rep.	1.2	–	5.0
Congo, Rep.	1.8	6.1	4.1
Côte d'Ivoire	1.4	5.0	1.1
Eritrea	2.9	1.8	7.8
Ethiopia	1.7	4.0	1.9
Ghana	1.8	4.2	0.7
Guinea	1.2	1.9	1.5
Kenya	2.2	6.5	2.1
Lesotho	3.7	8.4	2.5
Madagascar	1.1	1.9	1.5
Malawi	2.8	5.4	1.0
Mali	2.0	2.2	1.7
Mauritania	1.8	5.1	2.3
Mozambique	2.1	–	2.8
Namibia	3.8	9.1	2.7
Niger	1.3	2.3	1.1
Nigeria	0.2	0.7	1.4
Rwanda	2.1	–	4.4
Senegal	2.6	3.7	1.6
Sierra Leone	1.7	–	5.9
South Africa	3.2	7.9	1.8
Tanzania	1.3	–	1.3
Togo	1.1	4.5	2.0
Uganda	1.8	2.6	4.2
Zambia	2.3	2.2	1.1
Zimbabwe	3.1	–	3.8

Source: DFID (2001a:24–5).

The IMF disputed the official figure, reported by the Rwandan government in 1998, of military expenditure accounting for 4.3 percent of GDP. It is estimated that the share of GDP taken by defense in 1998 is about 8 percent, taking into account extra resources derived from incomes from semi-public companies and illegal trading in diamonds from the DRC. (Omitoogun, 2000:297)

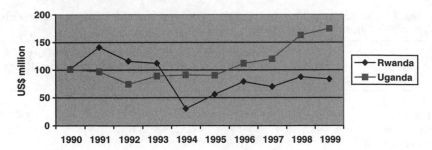

Figure 3.3 Rwanda and Uganda: Military expenditure, 1990–9
Source: SIPRI data reported in Sköns et al. (2000).
Notes: Figures are in US$ million at constant 1995 prices and exchange rates.

In July 2000, the Zimbabwean government told the IMF that it was spending US$3 million per month on the DRC war. But a leaked government memo put the cost at US$166 million between January and June 2000, and this led to the suspension of IMF loan disbursement. In August 2000, the Zimbabwean finance minister admitted that the government had spent US$200 million since entering the DRC war in 1998 (Addison and Laakso, 2000).

Again, a partial reform equilibrium exists. Can donors move the process forward? The IMF and the World Bank can collect data to assess the scale of military spending within a country's overall resource envelope, but they have no mandate – nor should they – to determine whether the level of spending is appropriate relative to a country's security objectives, or indeed whether those objectives are legitimate or not. Bilateral donors have more leeway, and DFID is one of the few bilaterals actively advancing 'security sector reform,' including its program in Sierra Leone. However, initiatives by bilateral donor countries will work only if donors pursue a consistent line, including joint action on arms sales. But some donor countries are compromised by a history of partial interests; the Angolan arms-for-oil scandal involving senior French politicians is a recent example (Africa Confidential, 2001). Donor countries certainly do matter for security sector reform, but they have not yet taken effective collective action.

3.3   Revenue reform as a foundation of the new social contract

Without more revenue (and less instability in revenues), the ambitious reform agendas in management, expenditure and security cannot be met.[12] Donors have supported revenue reforms since the first adjustment programs of the 1980s, and there was no let-up in the 1990s: DFID alone has supported over forty projects to strengthen revenue administration and collection in Africa and elsewhere since 1992. Reforms often include the creation of a single revenue authority as an executive agency, with a high level of autonomy (Delay et al., 1999).

Some success has been achieved, notably in Uganda, where the ratio of revenue to GDP rose from a low of 5 percent in the mid-1980s to 11.3 percent by 1996, with strong donor support (mainly DFID) to the semi-autonomous Uganda Revenue Authority (URA). Chen et al. (2001) find that the reform was generally pro-poor: the replacement of the sales tax by VAT did not make the poor worse off, and the reduction of export taxation was positive for rural incomes. Mozambique also raised its tariff revenues by radical institutional innovation. The UK's Crown Agents won the first three-year contract (starting in 1997 and subsequently extended) to reorganize the customs service, cut delays in customs clearance and meet higher revenue targets. Customs revenue rose to US$198 million in 1999, up from US$86 million in 1996, despite a reduction in the average tariff rate under the trade liberalization program (Crown Agents, 2000).

However, revenue mobilization has been tougher than expected. Governance problems in the URA led DFID to reduce its support, and the rise in Uganda's tax/GDP ratio tailed off to 12.1 percent in FY 1998/99. Similarly taxation reform got off to a good start in Ghana, with the tax/GDP ratio rising to 16.2 percent in 1998, up from 11.3 percent over 1984–91, and 6.5 percent over 1970–83 (Table 3.3). But tax mobilization then stagnated despite further DFID project assistance.

Early bilateral and multilateral projects paid much attention to improving management in revenue institutions and upgrading their human resources. But numerous project evaluations conclude that donors need to give more attention to the governance framework within which revenue authorities operate, specifically accountability and anti-corruption; see DFID (2001b) and Barbone et al. (1999) on the World Bank experience. How is this governance framework to be created? The populace has traditionally borne a heavy tax burden – through trade taxation and the indirect taxation of agriculture – without compensating services, and is rightly skeptical about government promises of better services in return for compliance with new forms of taxation. Public resistance to the introduction of VAT in Ghana is one example (Addison and Osei, 2001). DFID's evaluation of its support to revenue mobilization concludes that:

Revenue collection is justified by the expenditure it permits ... Under present conditions it is difficult to justify revenue raising efforts on the basis of their contribution to incremental pro-poor service provision, though this is becoming possible in countries closest to best practice (e.g. Uganda). (DFID, 2001b:18)

Table 3.3 Trends and structure of government revenues in Ghana, 1970–99

	Total revenue[a] (% of GDP)	Grants (% of GDP)	Tax revenue (% of GDP)	Direct tax (% of total)[b]	Indirect tax (% of total)	Goods and services tax (% of total)	Trade tax (% of total)	Petroleum taxes (% of total)[c]
1970–83	10.9	0.05[d]	6.5	20.7	–	27.3	40.4	–
1984–91	12.7	2.30	11.3	21.5	66.9	29.5	37.4	12.02
1992	11.9	3.30	10.8	18.6	71.8	49.2	22.6	19.20
1993–5	18.0	3.80	14.7	18.0	64.1	40.1	24.0	20.10
1996	17.6	2.60	15.1	21.7	63.9	36.7	27.3	17.00
1997	17.3	1.90	14.7	24.8	59.8	34.1	25.8	15.20
1998	18.7	2.70	16.2	22.9	63.6	35.3	28.4	14.10
1999	–	–	–	–	–	–	–	13.30

Source: Addison and Osei (2001) using World Bank data.
Notes:
[a] Total government revenue excluding grants.
[b] Percentage of total revenue excluding grants.
[c] Percentage of total tax revenue. Data obtained from various issues of recent budget statements.
[d] The average does not span the entire period.

Informal businesses are also resistant to the extension of taxation to them, believing, often rightly, that well-connected formal companies will be granted tax exemptions (either de jure or de facto). Formal companies without such connections have deregistered in Zambia to evade taxation. In Ghana and Uganda, informal companies resisted VAT, fearing that they would be driven out of business while bigger operators circumvented the system. Again, partial reform equilibrium exacerbates the problem; the perceived unfairness in the concentration of the benefits of first-generation reforms encourages businesses to evade tax laws. And again there are parallels with the creation of the underground economy in the FSU and the associated difficulties in mobilizing tax revenues (Roland and Verdier, 1999). Success in public expenditure reform will therefore help to convince a skeptical populace and business sector of the merits of tax reform. Accordingly, donor assistance to revenue institutions is unlikely to be fully effective until governments also resolve the partial reform equilibrium in public expenditures.

4 Conclusions

African governments and the region's donors have expended much sweat (and not a little money) on reforming the state. Reform 'ownership' has been the rallying cry for at least a decade or more. But 'ownership' has become a devalued coin. And many state actors – and not a few personnel in the aid agencies themselves – regard it with cynicism. Still, the concept of ownership does reflect a genuine desire to create a specifically African vision of the developmental state. Our difficulty is to move beyond platitudes and to articulate a vision of change that is realistic and appropriate to the region's talents and resources.

This chapter has reviewed some (but far from all) of the key issues. We have seen that the start of economic recession in the 1980s undermined the post-independence social contract, one in which governments promised more public employment and rising living standards in return for acquiescence to one-party rule. Since then we have seen reforms in the areas of civil service management, revenue collection and public regulation. Some have worked, some have failed. What can we conclude from all this? In many countries the new and more desirable social contract is, at best, in the early stages of construction. In the worst cases it is not moving forward at all. For the region as a whole, democratization has advanced – far faster than anyone would have dared to predict a decade ago – but democratic institutions are not yet sufficiently strong vis-à-vis leaderships to achieve a satisfactory resources-for-institutions exchange.

For their part, many leaderships – often long-standing incumbents who have adapted remarkably well to multiparty politics – are yet to be convinced that the *initiation* or *completion* of reform offers them a bundle of resources that improves on the status quo. This is either because they still benefit from the non-reform situation (largely the case in Angola and the DRC) or because they positioned themselves via straddling to do well out of the first reforms and now wish to preserve the distortions that protect their initial gains (Kenya and Zambia).

The mineral resource abundance of many of the non-reformers provides their rulers enough finance to evade donor pressure for change and to defend themselves against usurpers; Angola, Equatorial Guinea and the DRC are in this category. In these countries, we can at best expect slow progress, if pressure from below can be successfully articulated through civil society's democratic forces. Donors can be more influential with the partial reform group, but generally only when internal political dynamics succeed in changing national leaderships. Thus, the change in government in Ghana offers a chance to move ahead, after the Rawlings government stalled with its reform program in the 1990s. It is to be hoped that similar opportunities will arise in Kenya and Zambia in the near future.

We do not possess all the answers to institutional reform in SSA. Still, African societies and their donor partners should not despair. It is all too easy to become overwhelmed. We should remember instead the Ugandan proverb: 'linda kigweyo afumita mukira' (a hunter who waits for the full body of the animal to reveal itself is bound to get only the tail).[13]

Notes

I thank Steve Kayizzi-Mugerwa, Jeremy Clark, Sandra Pepera and participants at the 5–6 May 2001 UNU/WIDER project meeting on Institutional Capabilities, Reform Ownership and Development in Sub-Saharan Africa for helpful discussions. Errors and omissions remain my own.

1. Rosenthal (1998).
2. Source: Turner (2001:8).
3. The term 'prerogative' income is taken from Rosenthal (1998).
4. Over 1980–95, roughly three-quarters of SSA privatizations were in manufacturing (52.0 percent of SOEs sold), agriculture (10.7 percent), hotels and tourism (6.4 percent) and trade (5.3 percent) (Bennell 1997:1790).
5. For example, in World Bank Country Assistance Strategies (see, for instance, World Bank, 2000a, for Mozambique) and project lending (e.g. the Bank's Utilities Sector Reform project in Lesotho). In offering technical assistance in these areas, bilaterals can sometimes draw on considerable national expertise, reflecting either early privatization and thus longstanding experimentation in post-privatization regulation in the donor country itself (the UK's DFID and Crown Agents) and/or particular sector expertise (NORAD utilizes Norway's national expertise in oil and gas sector management – see Norwegian Ministry of Foreign Affairs, 2000).

6. 'Africa's New Leaders' as they were called back in 1997.
7. Donors and the government of Uganda spent US$31 million on civil service reform over 1989–95 (Brown et al., 1996).
8. See, for instance, discussion of Ghana's approach to the CDF in Mackay and Gariba (2000).
9. In fact, the actual figure for military spending in SSA may be double the US$6.6 billion figure because Angola is not included in the aggregate and some estimates put Angola's military spending at US$5–6 billion since the resumption of war in 1998 (Omitoogun, 2000:291). About 40 percent of the Angolan government's expenditure is off budget (IMF, 1999).
10. See also World Bank (1999) on assessing military spending.
11. See the archive of *The New Vision* (www.newvision.co.ug).
12. Revenue instability is nearly three times higher in SSA than in developed market economies, and twice as high in SSA as in Asia (Bleaney et al., 1995:887).
13. I thank Steve Kayizzi-Mugerwa for this apt quotation.

REFERENCES

Addison, T. (ed.) (2001a) 'From Conflict to Reconstruction in Africa,' WIDER Discussion Paper 2001/16, Helsinki.
—— (2001b) 'Reconstruction from War in Africa: Communities, Entrepreneurs, and States,' WIDER Discussion Paper 2001/18, Helsinki.
Addison, T. and L. Laakso (2000) 'Conflict in Zimbabwe: The Political and Economic Determinants,' paper prepared for the UNU/WIDER project on 'Why Some Countries Avoid Conflict While Others Fail,' Helsinki.
Addison, T. and R. Osei (2001) 'Taxation and Fiscal Reform in Ghana,' WIDER Discussion Paper 2001/97, Helsinki.
Addison, T., Alemayehu Geda, P. Le Billon and S. M. Murshed (2001) 'Financial Reconstruction in Conflict and "Post-Conflict" Economies,' WIDER Discussion Paper 2001/90, Helsinki.
Africa Confidential (2001) 'Winners and Losers in Angolagate,' *Africa Confidential* 42(3):1–2.
Albouy, Y. (1999) 'Regulation for Infrastructure Sectors: How to Adapt It to Country Institutions,' *Proceedings of the Annual Meeting of the African Development Bank*, World Bank: Washington, DC (www.worldbank.org/html/fpd/energy/emr/electrictity.reg.htm).
Barbone, L., A. Das-Gupta, Luc De Wulf and A. Hansson (1999) 'Reforming Tax Systems: The World Bank Record in the 1990s,' Policy Research Working Paper 2227, World Bank, Washington, DC.
Batley, R. (2000) 'The Role of Government in Adjusting Economies: An Overview of Findings,' University of Birmingham, International Development Department for DFID (www.bham.ac.uk/IDD/activities/rog/paper41.htm).
Bayliss, K. and B. Fine (1998) 'Beyond Bureaucrats in Business: A Critical Review of the World Bank Approach to Privatization and Public Sector Reform,' *Journal of International Development* 10(7):841–55.
Bennell, P. (1997) 'Privatization in Sub-Saharan Africa: Progress and Prospects during the 1990s,' *World Development* 25(11):1785–803.

Bigsten, A. and K. Ove Moene (1996) 'Growth and Rent Dissipation: The Case of Kenya,' *Journal of African Economies* 5(2):177–8.

Bleaney, M., N. Gemmell and D. Greenaway (1995) 'Tax Revenue Instability, with Particular Reference to Sub-Saharan Africa,' *Journal of Development Studies* 31(6):883–902.

Brown, K. et al. (1996) 'Special Program for Africa: Uganda Civil Service Reform Case Study Final Report,' Overseas Development Administration, London, and DANIDA, Copenhagen.

Chen, D., J. Matovu and R. Reinikka (2001) 'A Quest for Revenue and Tax Incidence in Uganda,' IMF Institute Working Paper 01/24, Washington, DC.

Crawford, G. (2001) *Foreign Aid and Political Reform: A Comparative Analysis of Democracy Assistance and Political Conditionality*, Palgrave: London.

Crown Agents (2000) 'Mozambique Customs Reform Project Extended,' Press Release (www.crownagents.com/default1.htm).

Delay, S., N. Devad and M. Hubbard (1999) 'Reforming Revenue Administration,' School of Public Policy, International Development Department, Birmingham.

DFID (Department for International Development) (2000a) *Making Government Work for the People*, DFID: London.

——— (2000b) *Making Markets Work for the Poor*, DFID: London.

——— (2000c) *Security Sector Reform and the Management of Military Expenditure: High Risks for Donors, High Returns for Development*, report on an international symposium sponsored by the UK Department for International Development, London, 15–17 February.

——— (2001a) *The Causes of Conflict in Africa*, consultation document, DFID: London.

——— (2001b) 'Evaluation of Revenue Projects: Synthesis Report,' DFID, London.

Durevall, D. (2001) 'The Malawian Public Sector: Governance, Accountability, and Reform,' paper prepared for the UNU/WIDER project meeting on Institutional Capabilities, Reform Ownership and Development in Sub-Saharan Africa, Helsinki.

Fozzard, A. and M. Foster (2001) 'Changing Approaches to Public Expenditure Management in Low-Income Aid Dependent Countries,' WIDER Discussion Paper 2001/107, Helsinki.

Haggard, S. (2000) *The Political Economy of the Asian Financial Crisis*, Institute for International Economics: Washington, DC.

Haque, N. U. and J. Aziz (1998) 'The Quality of Governance: "Second Generation" Civil Service Reform in Africa,' IMF Working Paper 98/164, Washington, DC.

Hellman, J. S. (1998) 'Winner Takes All – The Politics of Partial Reform in Post Communist Transitions,' *World Politics*, 50:203–34.

Herbst, J. (2000) 'Understanding Ambiguity during Democratization in Africa,' in J. F. Hollifield and C. Jillson (eds.) *Pathways to Democracy: The Political Economy of Democratic Transitions*, Routledge: New York.

IMF (International Monetary Fund) (1999) 'Angola: Statistical Annex,' IMF Staff Country Report 99/25, Washington, DC.

Kayizzi-Mugerwa, S. (2000) 'Institutional Capabilities, Reform Ownership, and Development in Sub-Saharan Africa,' project discussion note, UNU/WIDER, Helsinki.

———— (2001) 'Privatization in Sub-Saharan Africa: On Factors Affecting Implementation,' Göteborg University, School of Economics and Commercial Law, Department of Economics.

Larbi, G. (2000) 'Government Capacity to Perform New Roles in Adjusting Economies,' University of Birmingham, International Development Department for DFID (www.bham.ac.uk/IDD/activities/rog/paper41.htm).

Lienert, I. (1998) 'Civil Service Reform in Africa: Mixed Results after 10 Years,' *Finance and Development* 35(2).

Lienert, I. and J. Modi (1997) 'A Decade of Civil Service Reform in Sub-Saharan Africa,' Working Paper 97/179, International Monetary Fund, Washington, DC.

Mackay, K. and S. Gariba (eds.) (2000) *The Role of Civil Society in Assessing Public Sector Performance in Ghana*, World Bank, Operations Evaluation Department: Washington, DC.

Mahon, J. E. (2000) 'Globalization and the Exchange of Institutions for Resources,' processed, Department of Political Science, Williams College; paper presented at the 18th World Congress of the International Political Science Association, Quebec, 1–16 August (www.williams.edu/PoliSci/mahon/index. www.html).

Norwegian Ministry of Foreign Affairs (2000) 'Strategy for Norwegian Support of Private Sector Development in Developing Countries,' Government of Norway: Oslo (www.odin.dep.no/ud/engelsk/publ).

Nunberg, B. and J. Nellis (1995) 'Civil Service Reform and the World Bank,' Discussion Paper 161, World Bank, Washington, DC.

Omitoogun, W. (2000) 'Military Expenditure in Africa,' in SIPRI (ed.) *SIPRI Yearbook 2000: Armaments, Disarmament and International Security*, Oxford University Press for the Stockholm International Peace Research Institute: Oxford.

Ottaway, M. (1999) 'Africa,' *Foreign Policy* 114:13–25.

Przeworski, A. and F. Limongi (1997) 'Modernization: Theories and Facts,' *World Politics* 49(2):155–83.

Reinikka, R. (1999) 'Using Surveys for Public Sector Reform,' PREMnote 23, World Bank, Washington, DC.

Roland, G. and T. Verdier (1999) 'Law Enforcement and Transition,' Discussion Paper 1999–22, Centre for Economic Research and Graduate Education, Charles University, Prague (www2.cerge.cuni.cz/dp/DP22_1999.pdf).

Rosenthal, J.-L. (1998) 'The Political Economy of Absolutism Reconsidered,' in R. H. Bates, A. Greif, M. Levi, J.-L. Rosenthal and B. R. Weingast (eds.) *Analytical Narratives*, Princeton University Press: Princeton, NJ.

Salmen, L. (1987) *Listen to the People: Participant-Observer Evaluation of Development Projects*, Oxford University Press for the World Bank: Oxford.

Schiavo-Campo, S. (1995) 'Reforming the Civil Service,' *Finance and Development* 33(3):10–13.

Sköns, E., E. Loose-Weintraub, W. Omitoogun and P. Stålenheim (2000) 'Military Expenditure,' in SIPRI (ed.) *SIPRI Yearbook 2000: Armaments, Disarmament and International Security*, Oxford University Press for the Stockholm International Peace Research Institute: Oxford.

Sulemane, J. A. and S. Kayizzi-Mugerwa (2001) 'The Mozambican Civil Service: Incentives, Reforms and Performance,' WIDER Discussion Paper 2001/85, Helsinki.

Thomson, A. (2000) *An Introduction to African Politics*, Routledge: London.

Tsikata, Y. M. (2001) 'Owning Economic Reforms: A Comparative Study of Ghana and Tanzania,' WIDER Discussion Paper 2001/53, Helsinki.

Turner, M. (2001) 'Kenya Reform Derailed before Leakey Left,' *Financial Times*, 4 April.

Ugaz, C. (2001) 'Privatization of Utilities and the Universal Right to Basic Services,' mimeo, UNU/WIDER, Helsinki.

World Bank (1999) *Security, Poverty Reduction, and Sustainable Development: Challenges for the New Millennium*, World Bank: Washington, DC.

——— (2000a) 'Memorandum of the President of the International Development Association and the International Finance Corporation to the Executive Directors on a Country Assistance Strategy of the World Bank Group for the Republic of Mozambique,' Africa Region Report No. 20521-Moz, Washington, DC.

——— (2000b) 'Africa Database 2000,' CD-ROM, World Bank, Washington, DC.

Wuyts, M. (2000) 'The Agrarian Question in Mozambique's Transition and Reconstruction,' WIDER Discussion Paper 2001/14, Helsinki.

4

Zambian policy making and the donor community in the 1990s

Hendrik van der Heijden

1 Introduction

During the 1980s, and no less so in the 1990s, Zambia's economy spiraled down, virtually without uninterruption, toward extreme poverty and very high levels of human deprivation, aid dependence and debt distress. In stark contrast with the high expectations held in 1991 when a new government, led by the Movement for Multiparty Democracy (MMD), with a large majority in parliament and a strong mandate to reinvigorate the economy through policy reform, was elected. Despite much policy reform in the 1990s, the heavy injection of what became palliative external assistance and modest external debt relief, the MMD government failed to reverse the country's economic decline. Painfully, the economy deteriorated further. Per capita GNP had already fallen from US$650 in 1980 to US$449 in 1990; it then fell by another 28 percent to US$322 in 1999. The Zambian economy has contracted in absolute terms over the past two decades – a period in which the country's population rose by 80 percent to over 10 million people, while per capita income was halved. Zambia became the only developing country for which the United Nations Development Programme's Human Development Index showed a negative trend in the 1990s (UNDP, 1999).

At independence in 1964, Zambia was the second-richest country in Africa; today it ranks amongst the continent's poorest nations. Since 1996 the incidence of extreme poverty has risen from 53 percent to 58 percent.

77

Infant mortality increased from 90 per 1,000 live births in 1980 to 113 today. Zambia is one of the few countries in the world where the under-five mortality rate increased in the 1970–97 period, and one of only two countries in the world where infant mortality rose in that period.[1] Contrary to the widely held view that this phenomenon is almost exclusively the result of the effects of the spreading HIV/AIDS virus,[2] increased poverty was a major cause as well: the incidence of child malnutrition went up from 6 percent in 1980 to 29 percent in 1995. All major indicators of nutrition adequacy – the percentage of underweight children, infants of low birthweight, daily supply of calories, protein or fats – are now below the sub-Saharan African average, which they were not before. In short, during the past two decades, virtually all social and economic indicators that should have gone up, went down in Zambia. And those that should have gone down, went up. Summing up development in Zambia, the World Bank noted that, with a decline in per capita GNP in excess of 30 percent in the 1980s, the country held 'one of the worst records of economic decline of any country not engaged in internal or external warfare' (1993:13).

In the 1990s, development performance was virtually as bad, despite the adoption by the MMD government of an ambitious economic reform program, which led to relative financial stability and brought economic liberalization to the country through far-reaching reforms of the trade and exchange regime, privatization and deregulation.[3] Zambia's persistent and virtually uninterrupted long-term decline was not an act of god, however. Other factors were at work, centering on the incompleteness of the economic reform program and its inadequate implementation. They were the result of the government's half-hearted commitment to the pursuit of broad-based economic development, a weakness that the donor community unsuccessfully tried to assuage through persuasion and by the exercise of financial leverage.

Zambia's development record is the result of its post-independence governments – be it the United National Independence Party (UNIP) or MMD – putting the achievement of non-economic objectives well ahead of those of raising the income and well-being of Zambians. There was pursuit of party or personal interests, as opposed to those of the nation. Clearly, both the UNIP and the MMD governments put far too little political effort and energy into the pursuit of sustainable and widespread economic and human development in the country.

Overhauling the economy of Zambia involved more than a radical change in Zambia's long-established command approaches to economic management. It also required a significant adaptation of hardened attitudes of key personalities in Zambia. Many Zambians had benefited from the command economy of the 1980s, and were still doing so in 1991. They could be counted on to resist radical reform, and they did. They could be found in the universities, within the MMD itself, in the management of parastatal holdings, in trade unions and among managers and miners in the Copperbelt. Overcoming their strong resistance to reform was to be the crucial task of political management in the 1990s. After almost ten years of opportunity to change attitudes, Zambia's political leadership did not succeed in convincing the Zambian nation to embrace fundamental policy reform in full, so that – despite the MMD government's overwhelming support in parliament and its strong mandate to reverse economic decline in Zambia – only a partial and fragile consensus on policy reform appeared to have emerged. The fragility of this consensus continues to hold back further reform: reform is still strongly resisted by the civil service, by managers of large parastatal enterprises and by several groups in both the MMD and opposition parties. Only very recently was resistance to reform overcome to privatize Zambia Consolidated Copper Mines (ZCCM).

The effect of the resistance to reform within ZCCM and by its supporters in the cabinet, as well as by the civil service and parastatal managers, which lasted through much of the 1990s, was to deny to the people of Zambia many, if not all, of the benefits of policy reform, donor aid and debt relief provided to Zambia in that period.[4] If the recently renewed resistance to economic reform is not overcome as a matter of urgency, it will continue to further negate the benefits of external assistance and debt relief in the current decade. Thus, a significant agenda of further reform is still under threat. It includes measures to implement the remainder of the privatization program, vigorous implementation of the public service reform program, measures to raise public savings, improving the development relevance of government expenditures and much more energetic efforts to develop Zambia's non-copper economy, including the agricultural and tourism sectors. It may also include the rolling back of the recently introduced administrative controls on foreign exchange earnings and payments.

2   Increased dependence on donors and creditors

2.1   Failure to reverse the decline of the copper sector and to diversify the economy

A tragic fact of policy making in Zambia has been government failure to maintain, let alone strengthen, the country's engine of economic growth – the copper mines, which in earlier decades, when still in private hands, had brought prosperity to Zambia. This neglect was a serious strategic

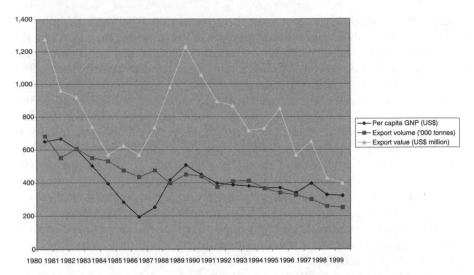

Figure 4.1 Zambian copper exports and GNP per capita, 1980–99
Source: Compiled by the author.

error. It led to a virtually uninterrupted decline in copper production, from 825,000 tonnes in 1969 to 252,000 tonnes today. It was this fall in copper production, and not the often mentioned decline in international copper prices, that led to the dramatic decline in copper export earnings and to the evaporation of the economic and social advances achieved in the post-independence decade (Figure 4.1).[5] Rather than adopting a proactive response to declining earnings from copper, namely investing in the rationalization and expansion of more efficient copper production, the government withdrew resources from the copper sector and converted ZCCM into a milk cow[6] in order to finance what for the government were programs of higher political priority. This approach of looking to the copper sector not as part of the solution to reverse economic decline but, rather, as a problem[7] must be seen as a strategic error of Zambia's postindependence governments. The two MMD governments repeated this error throughout the 1990s until, finally, ZCCM's privatization was reluctantly completed in 2000 (Table 4.1). Thus, despite the MMD's undertaking, included in its 1991 manifesto, that it would 'ensure the development of a self-sustaining mineral-based industry,' the decline of Zambia's copper sector accelerated in the 1990s. Admittedly, copper prices fell in the second half of the 1990s, but the negative effects of that fall could have been mitigated, if not overcome, if the government and ZCCM had addressed the company's increasingly serious production and efficiency problems with vigor.[8] Not one of several emergency programs,

Table 4.1 Zambia: Indicators of government revenue performance, 1980–9

Indicator of revenue performance	1980	1990	1995	1999
Copper exports (1,000 tonnes)	682	440	341	252
Government revenue (% of GDP)	25.5	20.3	19.9	17.5
Public savings (% of GDP)	–	5.5	3.6	0.4
Gross domestic savings (% of GDP)	19.3	16.5	7.3	4.7
Consumption (% of GDP)	80.7	83.5	82.7	94.6
Gross domestic investment (% of GDP)	23.3	17.3	13.1	13.8

Source: Ministry of Finance and Economic Development (various publications).

meant to address the mounting problems at ZCCM, was implemented effectively. This led to the escalation of production costs and, thus, to large and growing company losses.

In addition to the negative income effects of the deteriorating copper sector, governments failed to halt the dramatic erosion of the country's savings, investment and tax efforts. A consumption boom resulted, but it benefited mostly the richest 20 percent of the population, with an average per capita income of US$2,800. The poorest 20 percent of the country's population, whose average per capita income barely exceeds US$200, benefited little, if at all, from the consumption boom.

The second strategic error of the MMD government was its failure to implement a growth-oriented diversification strategy. This would have required the carrying out of a determined program for raising internal savings to finance higher investment in the non-copper sector of the economy, in economic infrastructure and in human development programs. Instead, savings declined – public savings virtually disappeared – and investment fell below its replacement level. This nullified the benefits from the substantial progress that was made in the 1990s with structural reform of the parastatal sector, with far-reaching adjustments to external trade policy and in market liberalization, and explains why Zambia's development performance in the 1990s was in stark contrast to the expectations held in 1991 by the people of Zambia and the donor coalition, which began to support Zambia generously.

2.2   Increased vulnerability and dependence

The two strategic errors described above implied that Zambia's economic reform program would remain incomplete. This led, in turn, to the postponement of the country's access to significant external debt relief in the 1990s, to high levels of external debt distress and to an extraordinarily high dependence on the resources and goodwill of external creditors.

Table 4.2 Zambia: Indicators of debt distress, 1990–9

Indicator of debt distress	1990	1999
External debt as % of exports of goods and services	506	691
Scheduled debt service as % of exports of goods and services	47	63
Net debt service as % of exports of goods and services	6	20
Net debt service as % of GDP	2	5

Source: Ministry of Finance and Economic Development (various publications).

Zambia's dependence on the goodwill of international creditors was already high in the early 1980s. In these circumstances, Zambia's government might have been expected to seek to design and implement policies that conformed to the wishes of the donor and creditor communities in order to ensure adequate debt relief. This was not the case. Largely at the behest of the International Monetary Fund (IMF) and the World Bank, and in return for pledges of external assistance and debt relief, the government adopted several economic reform programs in the late 1980s.[9] However, none was implemented fully and consistently, and external debt relief was thus postponed. This happened again in the 1990s, when, once again, the government failed to meet its commitments.[10] Thus, by 1999, the ratio of Zambia's external debt to GDP had reached 691 percent, one of the highest debt distress ratios in the world (Table 4.2). Scheduled debt service rose to 63 percent of total export earnings, while net debt service absorbed 5 percent of GDP, which is equal to the whole of Zambia's savings in 1999.

With government policies geared to maintaining unsustainable levels of consumption in a period of declining production, Zambia's own savings fell spectacularly in the 1980–99 period (Table 4.3). Thus, after an initial slow decline from 19.3 percent of GDP in 1980 to 16.5 percent in 1990, savings declined precipitously in the 1990s, to less than 5 percent of GDP in 1999.[11] Despite the doubling of external financing in that period, reaching 9.1 percent of GDP in 1999, the large decline in Zambia's own savings caused gross domestic investment (GDI) to fall almost 10 percentage points, down to 14 percent of GDP, a level that was insufficient to maintain Zambia's capital stock. In this sense, over the 1980–99 period, the national contribution to investment fell from four-fifths of the total in 1980 to barely a third in 1999. Public savings, a variable directly under government control, virtually disappeared in the 1990–9 period (Table 4.3). It accounted for only 9 percent of domestic savings in 1999 as opposed to 33 percent in 1990.[12]

Zambia's dependence on external assistance also increased markedly in the 1990–2000 period. From 1990 the contribution of external assistance to Zambia's economy rose by 30 percent, to 13 percent of GDP in

Table 4.3 Zambia: Financing of investment

	1980	1990	1991	1993	1995	1996	1997	1998	1999
Gross domestic investment (GDI) (% of GDP)	23.3	17.3	11.0	15.0	13.1	14.8	13.6	14.4	13.8
Resource gap	4.0	0.7	2.6	3.8	5.8	6.2	5.5	9.2	9.1
Domestic savings (% of GDP)	19.3	16.5	8.4	11.2	7.3	8.5	8.1	5.2	4.7
Public savings	–	5.5	2.5	2.9	3.6	2.6	3.2	2.4	0.4
Private savings	–	11.0	5.9	8.3	3.7	5.9	4.9	2.8	4.2
Public savings as % of domestic savings	–	33	30	26	49	31	40	46	9
Domestic savings as % of GDI	83	95	76	75	56	57	60	38	34
Resource gap as % of GDI	17	5	24	25	44	42	40	62	66

Source: Ministry of Finance and Economic Development (various publications).

Table 4.4 Zambia: Dependence on external assistance

	1990	1999	2000
External assistance as % of GDP	10	13	–
External assistance as % of foreign exchange resources	22	37	–
Net external assistance as % of gross domestic investment	35	62	–
Fiscal dependence (donor financing as % of expenditures)			
All expenditures	32	34	34
Economic sectors	–	–	62
Social sectors	–	–	49
Administration and non-supply	–	–	16
Percent of capital expenditures financed by external grants	69	90	90
Percent of public investment financed by public savings	81	5	–

Source: Ministry of Finance and Economic Development (various publications).

1999. By then, net external assistance financed over 60 percent of all investment, as opposed to only half that in 1990. Donor aid itself accounted for 37 percent of foreign exchange earnings in 1999, up from 22 percent in 1990. By the end of the 1990s, the donor community was financing no less than 34 percent of all government expenditures (current and capital). Donor financing also accounted for 62 percent of all expenditures in the economic sectors and for 49 percent in the social sectors. In FY 2000, no less than 90 percent of public capital expenditures were being financed by donors (see Table 4.4).

Zambia's donor coalition, which normally met annually in Paris as the Consultative Group for Zambia under the chairmanship of the World Bank, had been led to believe by the MMD leadership that, under its stewardship of the economy, external aid would only supplement and not substitute for the country's own development efforts, as had happened in the 1980s.[13] However, in the wake of receding domestic resource mobilization, this did not happen in the 1990s, so that external assistance did no more than substitute for Zambia's own declining development performance. As a result, donor aid and debt reduction did not relieve the savings constraint to investment and economic growth in the country. Similarly, in the wake of falling copper production, aid did not supplement Zambia's own foreign exchange earnings but substituted for these earnings, and thus did not relieve the foreign exchange constraint to investment and growth either. This was not the result of the government finding it difficult to obtain political support for its programs in parliament, where it commanded a four-fifths majority. Rather, the commitment of government itself to economic and political reform weakened progressively in the 1990s as it became increasingly clear that the MMD

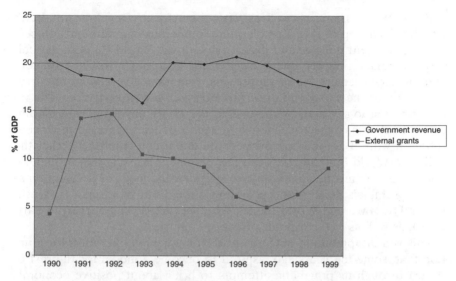

Figure 4.2 Zambia: Government revenue and external grants, 1990–9
Source: Compiled by the author.

was not a homogeneous formation in support of broad-based economic reform but, rather, an alliance of forces that had come together principally for the purpose of ousting President Kaunda in 1991. Zambia's fading self-help efforts, which were largely compensated for by rising external assistance (illustrated in Figure 4.2), inevitably led to a heavy and growing donor involvement in the design and management of Zambia's public sector programs, including those directed at sector investment.

2.3 Loss of policy autonomy or failure of development cooperation?

With the increase in financial dependence on donors, as exemplified by the extraordinarily high cost-sharing ratios mentioned earlier, the concept of national ownership of Zambia's development program was quickly becoming illusory. It should not have come as a surprise then that, as Zambia's external partners began to finance a progressively larger portion of the costs of its development, the government found it difficult to maintain its policy autonomy or full ownership of the design and implementation of its programs. It could not do so, and it did not do so.[14]

Thus, by the second half of the 1990s Zambia's policy autonomy had become seriously circumscribed by the numerous commitments on macroeconomic policy which the government had entered into with the IMF and the World Bank, as well as with the African Development Bank (ADB).[15] On top of this, Zambia made numerous commitments on sector development policies and programs with the World Bank in agriculture, manufacturing, the energy sector, road transport, the environment and the social sectors, water supply and sanitation. There were also programs for public service reform, privatization and governance. It is no exaggeration to say that, by the end of the 1990s, any significant modification to Zambia's macroeconomic or sector policies required prior consultation with, if not the approval of, the donor community, whether the IMF, the World Bank, the African Development Bank or major bilateral donors. The immediate consequence was that the locus of decision making on Zambia's policies and programs shifted out of Lusaka to Washington DC (IMF and World Bank), Abidjan (ADB) and Paris (the Paris Club), as well as to the capitals of donor countries.

This is a disappointing outcome of development cooperation for a nation that, some ten years ago, aspired to become a model for the rest of Africa through its pragmatic attempts to bring about positive economic growth and reduced poverty within a democratic framework. It is also a disappointment from the point of view of the donor community. Donors had hoped that development cooperation with Zambia would show that a combination of economic reforms, democratic governance and generous donor and creditor support could provide the basis required for broad-based and self-sustaining economic and human development in sub-Saharan Africa. The experience of the past two decades in Zambia shows that donors did, indeed, attempt to induce changes in or to respond to the 'performance' of the Zambian government, by adjusting the volume and composition of their aid to fluctuations in its policies. However, the effectiveness of these responses as inducements to strengthen Zambia's development performance was limited, first, because successive governments in Zambia were relatively insensitive to aid adjustments, and, second, because the process by which inducements were applied was not conducive to achieving better policy implementation.

Feeling that Zambia's reform efforts were inadequate, the Bretton Woods institutions had in the 1980s reduced and eventually suspended their aid to Zambia. Yet, bilateral donors continued to maintain a high level of financial support, and even increased it in some cases. In the 1990s these positions were reversed: for several years the Bretton Woods institutions expanded and subsequently largely maintained their aid, whereas bilateral donors curtailed their assistance and phased out their balance of payments support because of what they perceived to be inadequate concern for governance issues (Figure 4.3). The final result was that the efforts of the divided donor coalition to induce the government to strengthen its economic and political governance were not successful,

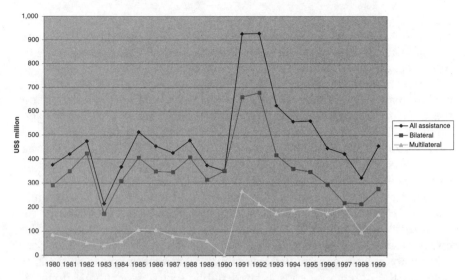

Figure 4.3 Zambia: Bilateral and multilateral assistance, 1980–99
Source: Compiled by the author.

with respect either to the economic area in the 1980s or to political governance in the 1990s. Clearly, the lack of harmonization of donor postures contributed to the low effectiveness of the exercise of leverage in Zambia. The Zambian experience (and, quite likely, the overall experience in sub-Saharan Africa) shows that no amount of aid-supported government policies to promote poverty reduction can be successful if the country's own development efforts are receding.

3 Policy dialogue and conditionality

3.1 Reaching agreement with donors

In reaction to Zambia's declining development performance in the 1990s, which donors highlighted time and again in their dialogue with the government, but which they failed to stem, the donor community cut back its aid to the country significantly. On several occasions creditors also reduced and postponed the provision of debt relief. By 1998, aid disbursements to Zambia had dropped to US$322 million, the lowest annual aid inflow in twenty years (with the exception of 1993), and a far cry from the donor euphoria that greeted the government's burst of policy reforms in the early 1990s. Disbursements of balance of payments support – the most eloquent indicator of donor fatigue – would fall to zero by 1998, leaving Zambia on its own to confront its debt service. Still, these cutbacks and postponements failed to induce improvements in economic and political governance, with most development indicators continuing to reflect negative trends.

Thus, for over ten years, donors collectively engaged the government of Zambia in an interactive process toward reaching a consensus on the focus of economic reform, including its objectives, instruments and timetable for implementation. The World Bank, in its capacity as the chairperson of the Consultative Group for Zambia (CGZ), became the spokesperson for the entire donor coalition on development strategy issues vis-à-vis the government. In this capacity it also undertook policy dialogue with the government on the basis of 'collaborative' economic analysis. However, although the World Bank's own economic work on Zambia, as well as that of the other donors, greatly contributed to the understanding of the economy and the constraints to poverty reduction, there were serious gaps in the coverage.[16] One such gap was the lack of focus on the urgency of consolidated public sector accounts. If done on time, they would have revealed that throughout the 1990s the financial performance of the public sector had deteriorated dramatically, with a highly negative impact on internal savings and investment. In addition, a more in-depth analysis of national accounts data could have shown much earlier that the policies being pursued were increasing consumption at the expense of savings and investment and, thus, were undermining the sustainability of the country's development efforts. This was leading the country towards increased financial dependence on the donor community.

The task of convincing both donors and creditors of the appropriateness of the government's program and of the support that the government was requesting was arduous, however. Indeed, several CGZ meetings in the 1990s ended without donors pledging sufficient support to implement the government's program. Once this task was completed, however, the government would be expected to implement the program as endorsed by the CGZ meeting, and donors would undertake to cover the external financing requirements of the program and would agree to the timely delivery of their financing pledges to make the implementation of the program possible. It was understood that, if the government did not implement its program along the lines it had indicated, donors would not implement their side of the bargain either. Thus, the provision of aid was made conditional on the government's implementation of the agreed upon program. The government expected donors not to move the goalposts during the implementation period of the program – which meant that it expected donors not to deviate from the conditionalities that had been approved, and to deliver their financing in magnitude, composition and timing as had been agreed. Simultaneously, the donors expected the government not to move the goalposts either.

It should be recalled, however, that not one of Zambia's successive adjustment programs, implemented in the 1990s, was carried out in full accordance with its design and intention.[17] Frequently, policy commitments reflected excessive optimism about the timing of the policy reform. There was also excessive optimism about the magnitude of policy change, for example with respect to the number of civil servants to be retrenched. This excessive optimism was most damaging to the reform effort, both with respect to the copper sector and in the macroeconomic areas of public and private savings, public and private investment, and economic growth more generally.[18] Donors, for their part, did not implement their programs in a timely manner either, which often reflected their internal administrative bottlenecks. Nor did they fully deliver their pledged financial support. Sometimes, as when economic governance and political conditionalities would leapfrog, it looked as if donors were moving the goalposts.

To deal with the problem of insufficient trust, and in order to induce the government to implement its program in accordance with its design, donors made certain that there would be a direct link between program implementation and the provision of financial support. To realize this, donors applied several inducement techniques. Sometimes, they would formulate quantitative, qualitative, or structural but timetabled benchmarks for the government action. The meeting of these benchmarks would demonstrate to donors that program implementation was on track, and that the release of financial support was justified. An example is the inclusion in policy framework papers of timetabled policy reform commitments. This technique was also employed by the IMF under its programs and the World Bank in its policy-based operations. It made for very explicit conditionalities. Sometimes conditionalities would be formulated in more general and qualitative terms such as 'making progress with strengthening governance,' which left much room for interpretation. And sometimes there would be no conditionality at all, because the government had already taken all policy measures. But the general principle was that donors would make certain that they could adjust the implementation of their aid programs to changes in program implementation by the government. Sometimes also, and this happened in 1990–1, the government had to adapt its pace of program implementation in response to delayed aid delivery by donors.

The abandonment in the 1980s of nationally prepared development plans and programs, and their replacement by tripartite policy framework papers (PFPs), had two unfortunate effects. First, there would be less national ownership of the country's development strategy and programs. Although the substituting PFPs were formally agreed upon between the government, the IMF and the World Bank, they were mostly drafted by IMF and World Bank staff, in consultation with the finance ministry and the Bank of Zambia; they would not usually involve the very active participation of many other institutions of the government, which, therefore, would not always feel committed to implement the policy undertakings included in the PFPs. In 1998, the draft PFP for 1998–2001, which in late 1997 had been discussed and agreed with the then finance minister, Ronald Penza, was described by his successor, Edith Nawakwi, as having been 'drafted in Washington' and was thus disowned by her. Second, compared with national development plans, PFPs' content was less comprehensive and their coverage largely concentrated on financial issues,[19] with comparatively less attention being given to overall macroeconomic and sectoral development issues and to national investment plans. Although there was a strong movement in the 1990s toward sector investment programs, this did not make up for the loss of the public investment program, which faded away in the 1990s.

3.2   A question of reform ownership

Zambia's ownership of reforms has shifted markedly over time. At the beginning of the 1990s, the government stressed repeatedly that there was genuine Zambian ownership of reforms, and that the policies and programs adopted and articulated had been designed by the government itself. Thus the MMD's new economic recovery program of 1992–4 required much less negotiation with the IMF and the World Bank. The MMD wished to implement reform faster than had been possible under the previous government. At that time, there was also strong national ownership of the program, not just government ownership.[20] Thereafter, there would be little, if any, consultation with non-governmental stakeholders. But the degree of government ownership remained high during the first MMD government in the first half of the 1990s. However, Zambian ownership diminished rapidly after the mid-1990s. The government became increasingly unwilling to undertake far-reaching policy packages, even when fully agreed upon between the IMF, the World Bank, the finance ministry and the Bank of Zambia, in particular those that related to privatization and public service reform.

   A similar development occurred with respect to the letters of development policy (LDPs) that the government submitted to the World Bank (and occasionally to the ADB), and which constituted the basis for the bank's policy-based operations, but for a different reason. In fact, several LDPs of the first half of the 1990s were initially drafted by staff in the finance ministry (see Ministry of Finance and Economic Development,

1997), but, as the ministry's macroeconomic analysis capacity diminished over time, LDPs would thereafter typically be drafted in Washington DC. World Bank staff would also then suggest the areas of policy action that needed to be stressed in the policy reform programs, with staff of the finance ministry providing only comments. At times this would cause problems. For instance, in early 1998, agreement had been reached within the government that the focus of the 1998 policy-based operation from the World Bank should be on measures to stimulate investment, exports and economic growth, and specific proposals had been developed for this purpose. However, at the behest of World Bank staff the focus was redirected towards public service reform, social sector development and, to a very limited extent, export development. In the event, the government yielded to World Bank pressure, but later in the year it became abundantly clear that the core conditionalities regarding public service reform were premature and, thus, did not constitute a suitable basis for this policy-based balance of payments support operation. The result was that this operation shifted into 1999 and balance of payments support from the World Bank was painfully postponed in that year.

With regard to governance, the program for strengthening it was largely foreign owned, even though at the end of 1993 the government had distributed an action program for strengthening governance in Zambia to donors. A very weak aspect of the policy dialogue with the government was that there was no lead agency for the dialogue on governance issues. That also meant that the analysis of these issues was not always adequate and the bilateral donor community as whole could not endorse the conclusions. This led to uncoordinated and ad hoc interventions by the donor community.[21] If there had been such a lead agency, and this function could possibly have been exercised by the European Commission, the bilateral aid community could have approached the challenge of strengthening political governance in Zambia along the lines of a sector investment operation, linking disbursements to the execution of an agreed governance sector program. This may still be possible on the basis of the government's own national program for building capacity in governance, distributed to donors at the CGZ meeting in July 2000.

3.3   Exercising donor leverage in the 1990s

What was the experience in the 1990s with the use and impact of conditionalities in Zambia? As noted earlier, there were several instances when the government failed to implement key portions of the agreed program, to which the donor community then reacted by curtailing or postponing a portion of its committed financial assistance.[22] Such curtailment had at times little or no inducement effect on the government to get back on track with the implementation of its program. For example, the Kaunda government accepted aid curtailment in September 1991 as a logical, albeit regrettable, consequence of its disagreement with donors on reform implementation. It was apparently willing to bear the costs of aid curtailment, which at that time took the form of a suspension of balance of payments support. In addition, because the latter led to defaults by Zambia on its external debt payments, this also provoked a suspension by the World Bank of disbursements on its projects portfolio.

Similarly, on several occasions the MMD government failed to adhere to the timetable for implementing the policy reforms that had been agreed upon with the IMF, knowing full well that this could lead to costly sanctions.[23] These implementation delays – as well as those that occurred under the Enhanced Structural Adjustment Facility (ESAF) program itself – were incurred in the full knowledge that they would lead to delays in Zambian access to funds under the Heavily Indebted Poor Countries (HIPC) program and, therefore, to the avoidable prolongation of the excessive burden of indebtedness on the economy and people of Zambia.

Yet another example of the aid embargo was in 1996 when bilateral donors withdrew balance of payments support in efforts to force the government to rescind the exclusion of Kenneth Kaunda from standing in the elections. This aid embargo had serious consequences for stabilization and growth. However, the government argued that the donors had introduced a new conditionality that had not earlier explicitly been agreed upon – thus the goalposts had been moved. This led to serious conflict between the government and part of the bilateral donor community. But it failed to stop the constitutional amendment.

Thus, in all three cases, rather than take action to implement the agreements reached with the donor coalition and to maintain access to the financing that donors had committed, the government had accepted the negative implications of the postponement on economic growth, poverty alleviation and debt reduction. What is telling, however, is that on these occasions the government failed to take compensatory domestic action to offset the costs of aid cutback, which would have at least demonstrated the government's commitment to reform.

However, there were also cases where the inducement effect of actual or potential aid curtailment stimulated the government into taking corrective policy action. Examples include the UNIP government's corrective, albeit insufficient, policy action to get back on track with the economic recovery program prior to a special meeting with donors in Paris in July 1991, just after the government had decided not to move ahead with the agreed reduction in consumer subsidies on mealie meal, the country's staple, in order to prevent the imminent curtailment of donor support. Another example is the MMD government's corrective policy action in the middle of 1995 to ensure completion of the rights accumulation program by the end of 1995, as well as the special fiscal and monetary policy action in the middle of 1996 to correct significant slippages in the implementation of the 1995–8 ESAF program.[24]

What does the Zambian experience reveal about the effectiveness of donors' application of leverage for the purpose of inducing governments to improve policy performance? First, the magnitude of the immediate cost to the country of not receiving external assistance has a strong effect on the government's response.[25] In the 1990s, that immediate cost was not always high in Zambia. The responses of the donor community were measured and, on the whole, took the form of curtailment of balance of payments support only, which constituted a small and progressively less important portion of the financial assistance received. For example, when in 1996 bilateral donors cut their balance of payments support in response to what they perceived to be inadequacies in the governance area, aid curtailment, at about US$100 million, was only one-eighth of the total volume of external financing to the country. The main components of external financing – project financing, balance of payments support from the World Bank and external debt relief – continued to flow.

The leverage effect of IMF programs was not that strong in the case of Zambia, for several reasons. First, a key objective of Zambia's new economic recovery program of the late 1980s and early 1990s was the normalization of the country's debt servicing to the IMF and the World Bank (Ministry of Finance and Economic Development, 1989). This was important to keep Zambia eligible for further multilateral funding. This objective continued to command high priority during the remainder of the 1990s, superseding the need to use aid curtailment to induce further reforms or to force the government to make up for shortfalls in policy implementation. Although this reflected a form of residual pragmatism, it also had the effect of diluting the IMF's leverage.[26]

A second factor reducing the IMF's leverage was that virtually all the US$1.3 billion from ESAF was released up-front to refinance Zambia's indebtedness to the IMF. Only a small amount was available for government operations, to be drawn on in quarterly installments over a three-year period. Thus the IMF's direct leverage in the 1995–8 period was weak, and remained weak because in 1996 bilateral donors suspended all balance of payments support on governance grounds, and the World Bank did not consistently support the IMF in the matter of disbursing its funds when performance shortfalls arose under ESAF. Hence, during the entire implementation period of the ESAF program, virtually no other balance of payments donor supported the IMF in exercising its leverage. Thus, the government's performance lapses in 1996 and 1997, mostly on its macroeconomic component, the slow rationalization and privatiza-

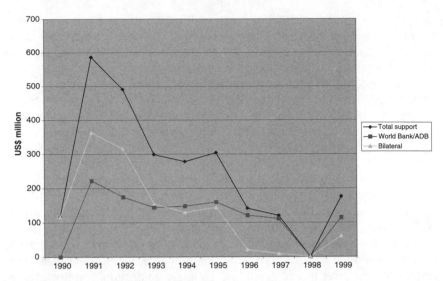

Figure 4.4 Zambia: Evolution in balance of payments support, 1990–9
Source: Compiled by the author.

tion of ZCCM, as well as of other parastatals, and the failure to force-fully pursue public service reform, did not translate immediately into an urgent external financing problem for the government. The World Bank continued to provide Zambia with significant balance of payments support, mainly to preserve economic reforms undertaken up to that time and to allow for improvement in the policy dialogue. It was only in 1998 that the World Bank postponed its balance of payments support on economic performance grounds (see Figure 4.4).

The overall result of this fragmented donor stance in the 1990s was that, through self-imposed limitations on the exercise of leverage, donor efforts to ensure that mutually agreed economic and governance reform objectives were met became ineffective. The reduction in the inducement effect of the threat to cut off aid led to a less than diligent government pursuit of key objectives of the reform program, namely the achievement of economic growth, the early privatization of ZCCM and public service reform. This serious inadequacy in donor coordination helped delay the benefits of economic reform and reduced the development effectiveness of foreign aid. Figure 4.5 illustrates the changing composition of external assistance provided to Zambia in the 1990s.

Even though donors and external creditors reduced their financial support to Zambia, the government did not react by taking compensatory measures that would increase its own development efforts. Instead, it focused on measures that aimed at maintaining consumption, thereby

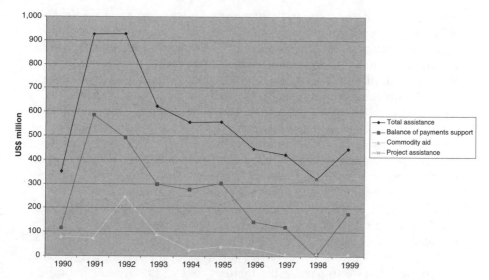

Figure 4.5 The changing composition of external assistance to Zambia, 1990–9
Source: Compiled by the author.

reducing internal savings and compromising the basis for the longer-term development of the economy.[27] Other serious longer-term implications for Zambia, namely the failure by the government to establish a credible record of adjustment under ESAF, in turn led to the postponement beyond 1998 of Zambia's access to debt reduction under the HIPC initiative.

4   Policy discussion and implications for reforms in Africa

Zambia's experience illustrates, first, that for the development dialogue between host government and donors to succeed, so that economic reform can be embraced rather than being imposed from the outside, it should focus on the central issues standing in the way of economic advancement and human development. That was not always the case in Zambia, and the economic analysis was not always focused on these key issues. Second, a government that is not genuinely committed to economic and governance reform is not going to yield to donor pressures if it can avoid doing so.

When the MMD government assumed office in November 1991, it announced that it would maintain and strengthen economic reforms in the country and transparency in government, uphold the rule of law and respect human rights. At that time, the government recognized the importance that the bilateral aid community attached to good governance. After adopting an ambitious economic reform program, the MMD government announced that, unlike Zambia's previous government, it would punctually implement the agreements it had reached with the Bretton Woods institutions. This announcement met with a positive response from donors and creditors alike. Clearly, at that time Zambia had a unique chance, in partnership with the international community, decisively to reduce the country's heavy external debt burden, the key impediment to growth, and to mobilize high levels of external assistance that the government felt were needed to help the country reverse economic decline and reduce poverty. However, this positive policy stance was quickly abandoned and domestic resource mobilization fell. This led to substantially reduced self-reliance and increased Zambia's dependence on the charity of aid donors and external creditors. The final result was reduced national ownership of Zambia's economic reform program.[28]

Dependence on foreign support has had several effects. First, it led to government failure to pay for the maintenance of donor-financed capital stock. Much of Zambia's social and economic infrastructure that had been built up or rehabilitated with the help of foreign aid resources was not maintained properly and deteriorated considerably, therefore requiring further large outlays on rehabilitation. Second, it increased donor involvement in the design and management of public sector programs, including several sector investment programs, so that the composition of expenditure increasingly began to reflect development priorities as donors saw them for Zambia, rather than as Zambia saw them for itself. Third, greater financial dependence led to a reduction in the engagement and commitment of government officials in the design, implementation and evaluation of aid activities. Paradoxically, as aid dependence increased in the 1990s, the quality of aid management declined. Fourth, growth of financial dependence led to a reduction in Zambia's policy autonomy. In the 1990s, ownership in Zambia's development program evolved towards the donor community,[29] resulting in a partnership relationship. However, because of the government's high and increasing dependence on the resources and policy advice provided by the donor community, the government became a junior partner in the development cooperation relationship.

The Zambian experience in the 1990s thus demonstrates that there is an inverse relationship between financial dependence and national ownership. It is important to note, however, that it was increased financial dependence on donors, and not the application by donors of excessive levels of conditionality, that led to a reduction in Zambia's policy autonomy. The reduction in national ownership that occurred in the 1990s reflected the government's weakening commitment to broad-based

Table 4.5 Savings and investment in the developing world, 1980–98

Region	Domestic savings (% of GDP)		Foreign aid (% of GDP), 1998	Foreign aid per capita (US$), 1999	Aid as % of investment, 1998
	1980	1999			
East Asia and Pacific	35	37	0.5	4	1.5
South Asia	19	19	0.9	4	4.1
Sub-Saharan Africa	16	14	4.1	21	24.1

Source: World Bank (2000b).

economic development. This was the trend that the donor community sought to reverse via the imposition of increasingly comprehensive conditionalities in the areas of political and economic governance (in the latter area through conditionalities at the macro or sectoral level). The Zambian experience also indicates that, although it is to some extent possible to substitute domestic savings by donor resources, admittedly with some loss in efficiency on account of the multiple and at times conflicting donor requirements, it is virtually impossible fully and effectively to substitute a waning government's commitment to broad-based development by ex ante conditionalities or policy advice from donors.

Zambia is, however, far from unique and its experience is in large measure applicable to much of sub-Saharan Africa. Overall, the economies of sub-Saharan Africa have been characterized by declining internal savings, high levels of dependence on the charity of aid donors and low levels of self-reliance (see Table 4.5).[30] The high level of dependence on donor financing in sub-Saharan Africa as a whole also appears to have reduced indigenous ownership of development programs. It is therefore not surprising that the World Bank concluded that the development agenda in Africa was 'increasingly being perceived as being shaped by donors' (2000a:18). Neither is it surprising that in the same publication the World Bank signals that 'it remains to be seen how well partnerships can resolve the tensions between the objectives of recipients and individual donors, and how far the behavior of donors will change to facilitate African ownership of its development agenda' (2000a:20).

What is surprising is that the World Bank puts the principal burden of behavior adjustment on the donors' side, rather than on the governments of sub-Saharan African countries. There is ample scope for African governments to take more responsibility for stepping up economic policy reform, internal resource mobilization and investment so that dependence on foreign aid can be reduced and development efforts can be expanded. As Table 4.6 illustrates, there is great need to bring economic and human

Table 4.6 Income per capita and social indicators in the developing world, 1999

Region	Income per capita (US$)	Investment (% of GDP)	Infant mortality (per 1,000 live births)	Life expectancy (years)	Under-5 mortality (per 1,000)
East Asia	1000	33	35	71	43
South Asia	440	22	75	63	89
Africa	500	17	92	52	151

Source: Compiled by the author.

development in sub-Saharan Africa up to more acceptable levels (and to those prevailing in even poorer South Asia). If sub-Saharan Africa genuinely assumed ownership of ambitious and broad-based development efforts, foreign donors would surely support them and refrain from imposing intrusive conditionalities – as they did in Asia, where the issue of ownership hardly ever arose, nor did it need to.

5   Conclusions

Several conclusions can be drawn from the Zambian experience. First, when the national commitment to development wanes, aid cannot fully substitute for it. And, second, if the national commitment to development is genuinely there, conditionalities are not needed. Good policy reform performance, which is reflective of basic trust, can be rewarded by unconditional aid.

Although Zambia's copper mines have finally been privatized, at the beginning of 2001 many of Zambia's key development problems remained unresolved. However, the government shows increasingly strong signs of adjustment fatigue. An unreformed public service continues successfully to resist efforts to make it cheaper, smaller and more effective, thus making it unlikely that poverty reduction programs can be effectively implemented. A poverty-stricken population, also affected by HIV/AIDS, continues to grow at a rate that is far in excess of what the economy can bear. Zambia has an almost unsustainable external debt service burden, and its recent policy reform record is threatening access to the HIPC arrangement by delaying attainment of the completion point. Furthermore, there are strong signs of aid fatigue in the international donor community. Thus, more economic, social and human distress may well be the prospect for the people of Zambia.

A number of lessons need to be learnt, if for no other reason than to prevent a similarly unwelcome result in the current decade. Clearly, there must be a radical change in the government's approach to political and economic governance, which should become much more energetic, results oriented and ambitious, as well as more self-help based. These are the very attributes of national ownership. Only when the national leadership begins to display demonstrable commitment to, and ownership of, its policies and programs can the long-overdue reversal of the country's economic and social decline be initiated.

To meet the challenges of the current decade, a fundamentally different approach is demanded, namely one that does not attempt to achieve economic development by maximizing access to external assistance and debt relief but, rather, aims at maximizing internal development efforts in order to achieve growth.[31] Only by doing more than just helping the country marginally to slow the pace of its persistent economic and social decline can external assistance and debt relief become more effective and make a bigger impact on the country. Thus, there is need to link Zambia's progress toward more self-financed and faster economic growth, via genuine ownership of its economic development programs and policies, with the provision of external support.

Notes

1. Iraq is the other country.
2. The incidence of HIV/AIDS among the adult population has been estimated at close to 30 percent.
3. Zambia succeeded in bringing inflation down from over 100 percent in 1991–2 to 25 percent in 1998. However, inflation rose again in 1999 and stubbornly remained at double-digit levels, reaching close to 30 percent in 2000, reflecting weaknesses in macroeconomic management and fiscal adjustment. Zambia's current account deficit increased from 1.8 percent of GDP in 1991–6 to 6.0 percent in 1996–9.
4. This was bound to happen again in 2001 if the government persisted in its intention not to privatize Zambia's major public utilities (ZESCO, ZAMTEL and ZNOC) and the Zambia National Commercial Bank.
5. Copper prices rose over the 1980–99 period.
6. In 1999, ZCCM's losses were equivalent to 6.0 percent of GNP.
7. Zambia's ills were often wrongly described as arising from an 'excessive dependency on copper' and on several occasions solutions were proposed to diversify 'away from copper' rather than to strengthen the copper sector through cost cutting, productivity increases and early privatization.
8. The obvious approach would have been to privatize ZCCM at the earliest possible opportunity.
9. See, for instance, Ministry of Finance and Economic Development (1989).
10. In fact, Zambia could have qualified for HIPC benefits in 1998 if the Enhanced Structural Adjustment Facility program had been implemented.
11. Zambia's very low savings rate of 4.7 percent of GDP compares with an average of 14 percent for the countries of sub-Saharan Africa, and an average of 19 percent for all low-income countries.

12. These numbers suggest that the government was attempting to pursue economic 'growth from donor resources' rather than primarily from Zambia's own.
13. President Chiluba made this a key point in his first address to donors in December 1991 (Chiluba, 1991).
14. In this connection, the following African proverb is worth mentioning: 'If you have your hand in another man's pocket, you must move when he moves.' See also van der Heijden (1987).
15. This was in the context of the IMF's Rights Accumulation Programme, the Enhanced Structural Adjustment Facilities, as well as the more recent Poverty Reduction and Growth Facility. There were also commitments with the World Bank and the African Development Bank in the context of their annual structural adjustment operations (see IMF, 1994, 1999, 2000; World Bank, 1996).
16. The results of the economic work featured prominently in the discussions of the Consultative Group for Zambia and also helped in the design by government of its adjustment strategy.
17. In a SIDA evaluation report, White states that, 'Whilst there has undoubtedly been reform in Zambia, there have been sufficient departures from the donor's agenda for many in the donor community to feel that that the government is not seriously committed to reform' (1999:9).
18. This is not a new phenomenon in Zambia nor was it limited to the 1990s. In 1991, when reviewing the history of economic reform in Zambia in the 1980s, Phillips and Burrell (economic advisers provided by the Canadian International Development Agency (CIDA) to former President Kenneth Kaunda) made the following point: 'the whole process by which these programmes are negotiated tends to encourage all parties to go beyond what is probably realistically possible, and then express surprise when it cannot be pulled off' (CIDA, 1991:3).
19. This came out starkly in the matrices for policy action attached to PFPs; see, for example, IMF (1999).
20. Finance minister Kasonde mentioned in his budget speech of 1992 that the first MMD programme 1992–4 had benefited from consultation with the private sector.
21. A point made by finance minister Ronald Penza in his budget speech of 1998.
22. Typically applied only to disbursements of balance of payments support and provision of debt relief.
23. This occurred in 1991, 1992, 1994 and 1998, which could have been the year for Zambia accessing the benefits of HIPC, as Uganda and Mozambique did in the 1990s.
24. Inter alia, the introduction of a temporary 5 percent import declaration fee as part of a package to compensate for the government's unsuccessful bail-out of the Meridien Bank.
25. It would probably be more accurate to describe this as the political cost to the government of Zambia.
26. The IMF found itself in a similarly difficult position by end-2000 when it had to consider granting Zambia HIPC status so as to enable Zambia to meet its large annual debt repayments to the IMF.
27. Thus, the MMD government's reaction to the external aid reduction shock was similar to the reaction of the UNIP government to the external copper earnings reduction shock.
28. Nicolas van de Walle defines ownership as 'the engagement and commitment of government officials in the design, implementation and evaluation of aid activities' (1999:340).
29. Even though donors exercised relatively little of their ownership, as evidenced by their reluctance to enforce the agreed upon conditionalities.

30. In fact, in *Can Africa Claim the 21st Century?* the World Bank (2000a:8) wrote, 'Africa is the world's most aid dependent and indebted region.'
31. However, Zambia entered this millennium by not applying this principle: for the third time in a row, in January 2000 (as with the budgets for 1998 and 1999) the government included in its year 2000 budget revenue measures that provide for a net reduction in taxation, thereby extending Zambia's receding internal resource mobilization effort by yet one more year.

REFERENCES

CIDA (Canadian International Development Agency) (1991) *Review of Zambian Economic Advisory Services 1966–91*, CIDA: Ottawa.

Chiluba, F. J. T. (1991) *Presidential Address to Donor Community*, Lusaka.

Heijden, H. van der (1987) 'The Reconciliation of NGO Autonomy, Program Integrity and Operational Effectiveness with Accountability to Donors,' *World Development* 15:103–12.

IMF (International Monetary Fund) (1994) *Staff Report for the 1994 Article IV Consultation and Midterm Review of Rights Accumulation Program*, IMF: Washington, DC.

—— (1999) *Zambia: Enhanced Structural Adjustment Facility Policy Framework Paper 1999–2001*, IMF: Washington, DC.

—— (2000) *Poverty Reduction and Growth Facility*, IMF: Washington, DC.

Ministry of Finance and Economic Development (1989) *New Economic Recovery Programme: Economic and Financial Policy Framework 1989–93*, Lusaka.

—— (1992) *New Economic Recovery Program: Economic and Financial Framework 1992–4*, Lusaka.

—— (1997) *Gearing for High Export-Led Growth*, Lusaka.

—— (various years) *Budget Speech*, Lusaka.

MMD (Movement for Multiparty Democracy) (1991) *Manifesto*, MMD Secretariat: Lusaka.

UNDP (United Nations Development Programme) (1999) *Human Development Report 1999*, UNDP: New York.

Walle, N. van de (1999) 'Aid's Crisis of Legitimacy: Current Proposals and Future Prospects,' *African Affairs* 98:337–552.

White, H. (1999) 'Zambia a Black Sheep among Reformers,' *Evaluation Report*, SIDA: Stockholm.

World Bank (1993) *Zambia: Prospects for Sustainable and Equitable Growth*, World Bank: Washington, DC.

—— (1996) *Zambia: Country Assistance Review*, World Bank: Washington, DC.

—— (2000a) *Can Africa Claim the 21st Century?* World Bank: Washington, DC.

—— (2000b) *World Development Report 2000/2001: Attacking Poverty*, World Bank: Washington, DC.

Part II

Incentive structures and performance in the public service

5

Economic and institutional reforms in French-speaking West Africa: Impact on efficiency and growth

Anders Danielson

1 Introduction

In a multitude of policy assessments, African governments are said to be illegitimate, unable to implement policies and bound to operate with considerable discretion. It is ironic, therefore, that whereas Africa's poor economic performance is often blamed on thc poor bureaucratic culture, the same governments are entrusted by multilateral agencies with the implementation of complex reforms. There is little doubt that governance issues are inextricably linked to the outcomes from the reforms. For example, a government lacking political authority and which is rife with corruption and patronage may find it impossible to stimulate the collective action necessary to bring the fruits of growth directly to the poor. Failure by governments to implement and maintain property rights hurts the poor, as do discriminatory practices in labor, land and credit markets.

This chapter deals with the experience with economic reforms of countries belonging to the West African Economic and Monetary Union (WAEMU) during the 1990s. The potential for reform among these countries differs somewhat from that in other parts of Africa; notably, the institutional nature of the union, which includes a central bank, limits the extent to which individual countries can exercise monetary policy. The region has thus experienced relatively low levels of inflation. The chapter is organized as follows: section 2 outlines the broad characteristics of reforms; section 3 discusses civil service reform; section 4 looks at the social sectors and attempts to assess changes in the efficiency of service delivery; section 5 uses recent data to discuss issues of governance; lastly, section 6 concludes the chapter.

2   Reforms in the West African Economic and Monetary Union

WAEMU was formed in January 1994 in conjunction with the devaluation of the CFA franc (CFAF). The original members were Benin, Burkina Faso, Côte d'Ivoire, Mali, Niger, Senegal and Togo; Guinea-Bissau became a member in 1997. The main purpose for its creation was to strengthen economic collaboration between members by, for instance, adopting a common external tariff to harmonize economic policies, to speed up domestic reforms through peer pressure and to pave the way for integration into the Economic Community of West African States (ECOWAS).

As Table 5.1 shows, the countries display wide differences in economic performance. However, some generalizations are possible. In all countries, except Guinea-Bissau and Togo, recent per capita growth is higher than that for the period 1965–98. This is in contrast to the sub-Saharan average, which shows roughly the same (negative) growth rate in the late 1990s as in the period from 1965. In some cases, the improvement is spectacular: Senegal, with a 1965–98 average of −0.4 percent per annum, had in the late 1990s achieved a per capita growth rate of almost 4.0 percent per annum. Similarly, Côte d'Ivoire increased its rate of per capita growth from −0.8 percent per annum to 3.9 percent over the period. In addition, although per capita incomes are somewhat higher in the WAEMU than in the rest of sub-Saharan Africa, the region masks wide disparities – from Guinea-Bissau's US$160 in 1998 to Côte d'Ivoire's US$700.

Although all countries, except Guinea-Bissau, have been members of the monetary union for a long time, inflation was significant for several members during the 1990s. Recent data suggest, however, a degree of price stability, with five of the eight economies showing falling consumer prices in the late 1990s. Moreover, even though the existence of a monetary union has not harmonized price movements, the fact that average inflation is below that of sub-Saharan Africa reflects the fact that monetizing the fiscal deficit was not a policy option in WAEMU. However, this has not ensured fiscal stability. Leaving the special case of Guinea-Bissau aside, several countries recorded fiscal deficits (before grants) of over 7 percent of GDP, and deficits after grants of around 3 percent of GDP in the 1990s. There are no differences between WAEMU and the rest of

Table 5.1 WAEMU: Basic economic indicators

Country	Per capita growth[a]		Per capita income, MRE[b]	Inflation (%)		Revenue (% of GDP), MRE[c]	Fiscal balance (% of GDP), MRE[c]	External balance (% of GDP) MRE
	1965–98	MRE		1993–8	MRE			
Benin	0.1	1.9	380	9.7	0.32	15.5	2.0	–4.9
Burkina Faso	0.9	3.8	240	6.5	–1.07	13.1	–2.9	–9.8
Côte d'Ivoire	–0.8	3.9	700	7.8	0.79	22.2	–1.8	–5.0
Guinea-Bissau	–0.1	–28.9	160	30.6	–0.70	5.5	–16.2	–15.9
Mali	–0.1	1.3	250	6.5	–1.20	16.1	–2.3	–7.9
Niger	–2.5	4.8	200	8.0	–2.30	9.0	–1.9	–10.0
Senegal	–0.4	3.8	520	6.6	0.82	16.1	0.0	–6.9
Togo	–0.6	–3.5	330	9.8	–0.07	14.3	–5.1	–5.9
SSA average	–0.3	–0.4	340	52.9	11.5	20.0	–3.8	–10.5

Sources: World Bank (2000a,b); IMF (2000).
Notes: MRE = most recent estimate.
[a] Annual average growth of real GDP per capita.
[b] Most recent estimate of GDP per capita in current US$; South Africa is excluded from the SSA average.
[c] Including grants.

sub-Saharan Africa in this respect. Revenue collection is low in the union – lower, in fact, than in the rest of sub-Saharan Africa. Notwithstanding the fact that several WAEMU members are among countries that receive most foreign aid per capita in the world, poor public finances are likely to reduce social service delivery.[1] In all countries, however, reforms were initiated prior to the creation of WAEMU. One issue, which has a strong bearing on the governments' legitimacy and commitment to reform, is the degree to which the reforms were homegrown or imposed from outside by donors. The history of reforms in low-income countries suggests that those arising from a domestic process of consultation have a better chance of success than those imposed by donors or multilateral agencies (Devarajan et al., 2000; White, 2000; World Bank, 1998).

Reforms in the WAEMU countries are characterized by two common themes. In most cases, a rapidly deteriorating economic situation, political turmoil or growing social unrest forced the governments radically to change economic policy. For example, national protests against perceived corruption, followed by social unrest, forced the government of Benin to resign and the successors to dismantle large parts of the bureaucracy. In Côte d'Ivoire, a mounting debt crisis forced the government to accede to reforms. In Mali, a deteriorating economic situation created a political crisis and the transition government widened and deepened the earlier reforms to correct the structural imbalances of the mid-1980s.

In most countries in the region, agreements with the International Monetary Fund (IMF) were typically seen as a last resort. In Burkina Faso, for instance, where the policy of *rectification* has been going on since 1987, the 1991 IMF agreement broadly endorsed that policy.[2] In contrast, Senegal's performance under the homegrown reform program was weak and the 1985 IMF agreement introduced new components, including the amendment of the labor code, dismantling of public monopolies and reorganization of the system of revenue collection. Because reforms were invariably triggered by a rapidly deteriorating situation at home, the financial and technical assistance offered by the multilateral agencies came late and was unable to provide immediate relief. The region as a whole tends to associate reforms with a harsh economic environment (see also Botchwey et al., 1998). In several cases, relations with the IMF have been uneasy, with programs subject to reversal.

Table 5.2 indicates how World Bank staff ranked certain reforms in WAEMU countries in 1980 and 1990/91, that is, before and after reforms had begun. Although the number of non-tariff barriers had diminished markedly in most countries (save for Côte d'Ivoire), progress on deregulation in most of the economies was slow: in six out of eight countries governments did little to remove price barriers, with some countries maintaining price controls as late as 1992. In addition, the indicator of

Table 5.2 WAEMU: Indicators of reform progress

Country	Non-tariff barriers[a]		Export controls[b]		Producer pricing[c]		Change in policy stance[d]
	Before reform	Late 1992	Before reform	Late 1992	Before reform	Late 1992	1981–91
Benin	All	0	1	1	1	2	−0.2
Burkina Faso	Hundreds	19	1	1	1	1	1.0
Côte d'Ivoire	37%	Little change	3	3	1	3	−1.3
Guinea-Bissau	n.a.	n.a.	1	3	1	4	n.a.
Mali	58	0	1	1	1	2	0.5
Niger	Hundreds	9	1	3	1	4	0.3
Senegal	Hundreds	About 15	1	1	1	1	0.5
Togo	20	2	1	1	1	1	−0.2

Source: Compiled from World Bank (1993).

Notes:

[a] Number of commodities subjected to non-tariff barriers.

[b] Indicator of price control on export sales: 1 = public sector monopoly; 2 = parastatals and private sector in competition; 3 = exporters licensed by government or parastatal; 4 = private sector competition. Figure in table is unweighted average for the commodities for which information is available.

[c] Indicator of price controls on producer pricing: 1 = price set at government's discretion; 2 = price set but linked to world market price; 3 = indicative producer price recommended; 4 = no prices set. Figure in table is unweighted average for the commodities for which information is available.

[d] Change in index of policy stance, including fiscal, monetary and exchange rate policies. An increase >1.0 is a large improvement; an increase <1.0 is a small improvement; a decrease is a deterioration. See World Bank (1993:261) for details.

changes in the macroeconomic policy stance reinforces the impression that reforms were slow and reluctantly implemented. Only one country, Burkina Faso, recorded large improvements (partly explained by the fact that the country was moving from a position characterized by pervasive controls), while the macroeconomic situation in two countries deteriorated, despite financial and technical assistance and nominal commitment to reform.

The later part of the 1990s saw progress on the macroeconomic front in most countries (Guinea-Bissau excepted, owing to the 1998–9 conflict), but three weaknesses in the reform programs are apparent. First, the economies display structural fragility: revenue collection is low, the fiscal situation is unstable and exports are concentrated in a few commodities. Second, reforms are being implemented slowly: for instance, privatization is invariably behind schedule; financial liberalization remains superficial, focusing more on expanding numbers of existing banks than on increasing credit availability; and policy integration within WAEMU remains slow. Third, although growth has resumed in most countries, the impact on poverty levels is small. This is to blame partly on the continued fiscal restraint caused by governments' inability significantly to raise revenue levels, and partly on the emerging patterns of growth, which did not emphasize agriculture.

3   Civil service reform

Several countries in WAEMU have taken important steps towards reforming the civil service. Staffing levels have been reduced and the wage bill has been cut. However, the pay structure is still compressed (and even more so following the 1994 CFAF devaluation). In some countries promotion policies are outdated, and there is need to improve the system of remuneration. As in much of Africa, WAEMU members have used the civil service as a tool for employment creation, especially for educated labor. Changing the system is likely to require strong political will.[3]

With regard to remuneration, at least three issues need to be considered. First, to retain competent staff in public administration, the public sector must be able to offer competitive remuneration. To do this without increasing the total wage bill requires a rationalization of staffing. Second, the salary structure within the public sector itself needs to be altered. The 1980s and 1990s saw a serious compression of the salary structure in the public sector. For many high-ranking officials, real wages fell sharply. To compensate for this, alternative systems of remuneration were created, including allowances, fringe benefits and non-monetary compensation. With the current demand for increased budget trans-

Table 5.3 WAEMU: Wage bill and employment in civil service, 1985–98

Country	1985	1990	1994	1995	1996	1998
A. Wage bill as % of recurrent expenditure						
Benin	n.a.	49.6	41.4	38.3	39.3	43.4
Burkina Faso	64.8	53.7	44.3	46.0	48.0	45.6
Côte d'Ivoire	29.2	37.4	34.3	33.2	36.0	37.7
Guinea-Bissau	55.6	25.6	18.3	18.2	20.1	24.9
Mali	63.0	57.4	33.7	35.6	36.8	36.2
Niger	35.5	40.7	43.8	48.7	38.8	36.5
Senegal	48.6	45.3	45.9	48.2	50.7	48.9
Togo	33.7	38.5	39.6	42.2	39.2	38.9
B. Public sector employment as % of total population						
Benin	1.1	0.9	0.6	0.6	0.6	n.a.
Burkina Faso	0.4	0.4	0.4	0.4	0.4	n.a.
Côte d'Ivoire	n.a.	1.0	0.8	0.7	0.7	n.a.
Guinea-Bissau	1.8	1.7	1.8	1.8	1.7	n.a.
Mali	0.5	0.5	0.3	0.3	0.3	n.a.
Niger	0.5	0.5	0.4	0.4	0.4	n.a.
Senegal	1.0	0.9	0.8	0.8	0.8	n.a.
Togo	0.6	0.6	0.6	0.5	0.5	n.a.
C. Public sector employment ('000)						
Benin	46.3	41.3	32.7	32.3	32.0	n.a.
Burkina Faso	28.7	33.5	37.1	39.8	40.0	n.a.
Côte d'Ivoire	n.a.	118.0	108.3	105.2	102.6	n.a.
Guinea-Bissau	16.6	15.9	18.6	19.3	18.5	n.a.
Mali	35.0	39.4	29.1	29.1	29.1	n.a.
Niger	32.7	35.6	39.8	n.a.	40.0	n.a.
Senegal	68.1	65.6	66.7	67.0	67.0	n.a.
Togo	20.1	20.5	21.7	21.8	21.8	n.a.

Sources: World Bank (2000b); Lienert and Modi (1997).

parency, these benefits need to be monetized. Third, there is a need to create performance-based systems of promotion. To date, years of service, rather than performance, determine promotion prospects. To increase efficiency in the bureaucracy and to create incentives for good performance, a benefits system based on clear, transparent and objective criteria is needed.

The state of civil service reforms between WAEMU countries differs substantially. Some countries, for example Senegal, were able to introduce a system of promotions based on merit and seniority and to link this to indicators of service delivery, but other countries, for example Niger, failed to come to terms with their expanding but relatively inefficient bureaucracies (Lienert and Modi, 1997). Table 5.3 (panel A) shows the share of the wage bill in total recurrent expenditure for selected years. Whereas countries such as Burkina Faso and Mali have succeeded in

containing labor costs in the civil service, other countries have not performed as well. In fact, in some countries the share of the wage bill in
recurrent expenditure increased (Côte d'Ivoire, Togo) or remained virtually unchanged (Senegal). Changes in public employment indicate similar patterns (Table 5.3, panel B). In Benin, Côte d'Ivoire and Mali,
public sector employment declined significantly, whereas in other countries (Burkina Faso, Guinea-Bissau, Togo) it remained unchanged. It
should also be noted that high population growth in West Africa partly
explains the high rate of growth of the number of employees in the civil
service (Table 5.3, Panel C).

To reduce public employment, countries have used a number of approaches, including the removal of employment guarantees to new graduates (Benin, Côte d'Ivoire, Niger) and compulsory retirement (Burkina
Faso, Senegal) or a reduction in the statutory retirement age (Togo).[4]
These measures were preceded by censuses that helped weed out 'ghost'
employees. In addition, some countries have tried to use one-to-one recruitment policies (Côte d'Ivoire, Senegal); others (Benin) have used a
three-out/one-in mechanism as the basis of limiting employment in the
civil service.

One argument in favor of retrenchment is that the savings can be used
to raise wages and decompress the salary structure. Ideally, retrenchment
should be targeted at unproductive employees. However, there is no objective mechanism for identifying these. Instead, retrenchment is often
centered on labor in the lower echelons – drivers, messengers and casual
laborers. Thus monetary savings from retrenchment are often insufficient
for the undertaking of substantial salary reforms. Moreover, the fiscal
argument for retrenchment in WAEMU countries was weakened by the
devaluation of the CFA franc in 1994, which led to a decline in real
wages and to salary compression. There is more need now for salary restructuring than earlier (Table 5.4).

A second reason is that in the 1990s donors became more favorably
disposed to financing severance packages. The World Bank's decision to
provide soft loans in this regard as well as the IMF's acceptance of the
practice paved the way for broader public sector reforms. To undertake
retrenchment, governments indeed needed foreign support. Haltiwanger
and Singh (1999) calculated that the retrenchment cost (including severance pay) per worker in Benin amounted to almost US$6,500 and in
Senegal to over US$13,000. The latter is the equivalent of twenty times
Senegal's per capita income. There is also the problem of the revolving door syndrome: owing to poor records and outright corruption, retrenched workers are often rehired, thus defeating the reform effort. The
probability of rehiring was higher in retrenchment programs without a
social safety net component. The inference, of course, is that the pressure

Table 5.4 Real wage per civil servant: index, 1990 = 100

Country	1986	1988	1993	1994	1996
Benin	n.a.	100[c]	120	108	120
Burkina Faso	76	97	85	73	66
Guinea-Bissau	91[a]	104	81	70	65
Mali	121[b]	121	140	133	126
Niger	68	87	116	97	59
Senegal	81	96	105	89	87
Togo	80	97	94	82	79
Non-CFA, average[d]	n.a.	n.a.	93	88	85

Source: Lienert and Modi (1997:Table 8).
Notes: Data for Côte d'Ivoire unavailable.
[a] 1987.
[b] 1988.
[c] 1989.
[d] Unweighted average for Burundi, Ethiopia, the Gambia, Ghana, Kenya, Lesotho, Madagascar, Malawi, Mauretania, Rwanda, Sierra Leone, Tanzania, Uganda, Zambia and Zimbabwe.

to rehire is greater if the retrenchment strategy offers no assistance to workers in transition to the private sector.

4   Education and health sectors

Another focus in WAEMU countries in recent years has been poverty reduction. Sustainable poverty reduction requires economic growth. However, the road from increased growth to reduced poverty is usually long and difficult. Poor people can benefit from increased growth only when it raises the demand for their factors of production. Because the implied time-lag is often measured in years (Thomas et al., 2000), to reduce poverty substantially requires increased social sector spending. Consultations with the poor indicate that improved access to education and health care are among the items the poor put highest on their priority list.[5] Tables 5.5 and 5.6 provide some indications on the progress made with respect to education and health.

Gross enrollment in primary school rose in six out of eight countries. The experience of these countries goes against the flow in the rest of sub-Saharan Africa, where gross enrollment has declined slightly since 1980. Moreover, in some countries the increase is significant. Thus the gross enrollment ratio doubled in Burkina Faso, from less than 20 percent in 1980 to almost 40 percent in 1998. In Senegal it increased by 20 points to almost 70 percent. Adult illiteracy fell in all WAEMU countries,

Table 5.5 WAEMU: Indicators of progress in primary education

Country	Per student expenditure (% of per capita GNP)		Gross enrollment ratio		Illiteracy 15+		Pupil/teacher ratio	
	1980	MRE	1980	MRE	1980	MRE	1980	MRE
Benin	20.2[a]	11.8	66.9	77.6	82.1	66.1	47.5	52.0
Burkina Faso	23.0	16.9	17.5	39.6	89.2	79.3	54.4	50.1
Côte d'Ivoire	22.7	20.7	75.0	71.3	76.9	57.4	38.7	41.0
Guinea-Bissau	32.1	24.4	67.9	61.8	81.2	66.5	22.9	24.1
Mali	31.7	15.5	26.3	45.1	86.4	64.6	42.4	69.7
Niger	26.2[b]	18.1	25.3	29.4	92.0	85.7	41.5	40.8
Senegal	24.6	10.5	46.3	68.2	78.8	65.4	45.8	57.6
Togo	8.2	7.8	118.4	119.6	67.4	46.8	55.1	50.8
SSA average	n.a.	n.a.	80.7	78.0	61.7	40.5	43.5	40.9

Sources: World Bank (2000a,b); IMF/national sources, policy framework papers (various); poverty reduction strategy papers (various); HIPC decision point documents (various).
Notes: MRE = most recent estimate.
[a] 1975.
[b] 1981.

Table 5.6 WAEMU: Indicators of health status

Country	Adult mortality rate (per 1,000)[a]		Under-5 mortality rate (per 1,000)		Public expenditure on public health per capita (US$)	
	1980	1998	1980	MRE	1990	MRE
Benin	418	402	214	140	1.8	4.9
Burkina Faso	426	426	242[b]	210	3.7	11.0
Côte d'Ivoire	431	426	170	143	14.3	10.3
Guinea-Bissau	450	422	290	205	2.7	2.5
Mali	444	420	315[c]	218	4.5	3.9
Niger	464	433	317	250	4.3	3.3
Senegal	477	444	195[c]	121	21.8	6.7
Togo	471	454	188	144	6.2	5.1
SSA average	479	453	188	151	n.a.	n.a.

Sources: World Bank (2000a,b); national sources, poverty reduction strategy papers (various).
Notes:
[a] Simple average of mortality rates for males and females.
[b] 1982.
[c] 1979.

although less rapidly compared with the decline in illiteracy in the rest of sub-Saharan Africa. Pupil–teacher ratios vary a lot as well among WAEMU members.

Although enrollment has increased in some countries, as pointed out above, expenditure per primary pupil as a percentage of per capita GNP has fallen in all countries. This, by itself, does not necessary imply shrinking allocations to primary education, since an expanding economy could have the same effect. However, the WAEMU countries have seen little growth in recent decades so that the decline is in absolute terms. Only three countries experienced positive per capita income growth, and in only one – Burkina Faso – did that growth exceed 1 percent per annum.

Table 5.6 also presents mixed results for health indicators. The adult mortality rate has declined since 1980 in all countries (except Burkina Faso, where it has not changed), and under-five mortality has also declined, but the pattern with respect to monetary allocations to the health sector displays considerable variation. Whereas Senegal allocated almost US$22 per capita to the health sector in 1980, the most recent estimate (from 1997) is less than US$7. Similarly, per capita allocations to health fell in Côte d'Ivoire from US$14 to US$10 during the same period. In

Table 5.7 WAEMU: Primary education spending (CFAF per student, 1995 prices)

Country	1980–3	1984–7	1988–91	1992–4	MRE (year)
Burkina Faso	22,747	17,856	22,754	25,353	n.a.
Côte d'Ivoire	146,258	127,392	115,119	87,494	65,772 (1996)
Mali	n.a.	n.a.	n.a.	20,443	19,611 (1995)
Niger	35,472	n.a	36,273	n.a.	n.a.
Senegal	58,751	49,249	54,692	n.a.	29,830 (1996)
Togo	15,739	18,086	18,396	n.a.	12,425 (1995)

Source: Calculated from data in World Bank (2000a).
Notes: For each column, data are for the most recent year available. Sufficient data for Benin and Guinea-Bissau were not found.

spite of this, health indicators, notably mortality rates, have improved. One explanation for the improvement is the increase in private sector provision. In Senegal the government allocates about 2.6 percent of GDP to the health sector and the private sector about 2.2 percent of GDP. In Côte d'Ivoire, private expenditures on heath are almost twice as large as public expenditures (2.6 versus 1.4 percent of GDP). In Burkina Faso, the public contributes 1.2 percent and the private sector 2.7 percent of GDP. However, Burkina Faso was the only country in WAEMU where adult mortality did not decline.

Table 5.7 presents data on actual spending in education. All four countries with data spent less per student (in real terms) in the second half of the 1990s than previously in the period ranging from the 1980s. In Senegal, per student allocations fell by almost 50 percent between 1991 and 1996, and Côte d'Ivoire registered similar trends. It is difficult to reconcile these figures with the objectives of governments (as reflected in policy framework papers and, more recently, in poverty reduction strategy papers) and donors (as reflected in the general thrust for increased emphasis on social sectors among Development Assistance Committee donors; see DAC, 1996) to increase social spending and reduce poverty. Given a common central bank which controls monetary policy, WAEMU countries face hard budget constraints. It is not obvious how they could increase social spending without recourse to borrowing from abroad.

The reduction in the funds going to primary education had negative impacts, as reflected in the dismal performance of the school system in some countries. In Burkina Faso and Niger, the share of pupils reaching Grade 5 did not increase between 1980 and 1996; in Côte d'Ivoire that share declined by 8 percentage points. In Benin and Côte d'Ivoire, the share of cohorts that repeated grades increased between 1980 and 1997,

Table 5.8 Educational efficiency in WAEMU countries

Country	% reaching Grade 5		Repeaters, primary school (% of enrollment)	
	1980	1996	1980	1997
Benin	60	61	19.6	25.1
Burkina Faso	75	75	17.1	16.0
Côte d'Ivoire	82	74	19.6	24.2
Guinea-Bissau	n.a.	n.a.	28.9	n.a.
Mali	45	81	29.6	16.2
Niger	73	73	14.3	13.0
Senegal	85	87	15.6	13.3
Togo	52	69	35.5	24.2

Source: World Bank (2000a).

and in some countries, such as Benin, Côte d'Ivoire and Togo, one out of every four students failed to graduate to the next grade (Table 5.8).

However, a major obstacle in assessing performance in the education sector is that we usually can observe only a rough measure of inputs (i.e. funds), usually aggregated over sectors and use, and a rough indicator of output (e.g. survival rates, changes in illiteracy), again at an aggregated level. The problems are compounded when we seek, as in this chapter, to compare several countries over a relatively long period. The issues arising are twofold. First, a host of other factors, apart from the volume of funds, affect educational achievement. Moreover, even if funds were available to address constraints such as a lack of qualified teachers, there is usually a substantial time-lag between spending and impact. Second, the standard output indicators are highly aggregated and may not adequately reflect, particularly not in a comparative framework, changes in the way the education system uses resources. Again, the time-lag involved may be substantial and make it difficult to trace changes in output from changes in inputs.

To assess the extent to which economic reforms have been successful in addressing the problems of the education sector, the available data have been compiled for four different aspects of performance of the primary education system:
• apparent intake (that is, gross enrollment in the first grade), which reflects, inter alia, the ability of the education system to absorb new entrants,
• gross enrollment, averaged for all grades in primary school, which reflects ability to absorb entrants at the primary level as a whole,
• net enrollment, averaged for all grades in primary school, which in-

Table 5.9 Impact of reforms in WAEMU countries on primary education

Country	Intake[a]		Gross enroll-ment ratio		Net enroll-ment ratio		Efficiency[b]	
	Before	After	Before	After	Before	After	Before	After
Benin	70.3	75.3*	63.6	67.6	53.2	56.0	47.7	51.0
Burkina Faso	25.7	39.1*	24.1	37.1*	20.1	29.5*	64.7	63.0
Côte d'Ivoire	61.4	61.8	70.3	68.8	55.1	50.5*	66.1	61.2*
Guinea-Bissau	81.6	64.9*	62.0	57.0	52.4	52.0	21.4	21.8
Mali	24.7	33.0*	25.3	32.8*	18.1	23.8*	42.5	54.7*
Niger	23.0	28.5	22.0	27.9*	21.1	24.1	69.6	67.7
Senegal	48.1	62.7*	47.3	61.0*	40.6	51.9*	74.3	75.0
Togo	88.3	98.8	101.1	106.0	67.7	73.5*	38.7	45.6

Source: Calculated from World Bank data.
Notes: Averages were calculated for 'before' and 'after' the reform. The reform years are: Benin 1989; Burkina Faso 1991; Côte d'Ivoire 1984; Guinea-Bissau 1987; Mali 1985; Niger 1984; Senegal 1985; and Togo 1984. The reform year has been excluded from all calculations. In most cases data run from 1970 to 1997; for Côte d'Ivoire and Guinea-Bissau, data series commence in 1975, and for Burkina Faso, Guinea-Bissau, Niger and Togo, data series end in 1996.
[a] Total number of new entrants in the first grade of primary education, regardless of age, expressed as a percentage of the official primary school entrance age.
[b] The ideal number of pupil-years required to produce one primary school graduate as a percentage of the actual number of pupil-years required to produce one primary school graduate.
* Difference between 'before' and 'after' significant at the 95 percent test level.

dicates the ability of the system to provide proper training (i.e. the availability of textbooks, school houses, or properly trained and motivated teachers),
• the coefficient of efficiency, which measures the difference between the ideal number of pupil-years (in the absence of repetition and dropouts) and the actual number required.

The year in which multilateral reforms were embarked on was identified and the data series were averaged before and after that cut-off year in order to see whether indicators were significantly different, that is, whether reforms made a difference.[6] Results are presented in Table 5.9. This table indicates that in half of the cases the difference between pre- and post-reform indicators is not significant. Moreover, in three cases – intake in Guinea-Bissau, net enrollment and efficiency in Côte d'Ivoire – the post-reform indicator is worse than the pre-reform one. There is also enormous variation in performance between countries. In Togo, the apparent intake is virtually 100 percent in the post-reform period; in Burkina Faso, Mali and Niger it is less than 40 percent. Net enrollment varies from almost three-quarters in Togo to less than one-quarter in Mali and Niger. In twenty-four out of thirty-two comparisons, indicators improve after reform, while in two out of the eight 'bad' cases, gross enrollment decreases, which is not necessarily a bad thing as it may be an indication that repetition rates have declined. Reforms have thus been associated with improvements in education indicators, although often modest. However, given the inadequate data, it is difficult to ascertain whether these are due to improvements in funding, efficiency in use of funds or improving institutional quality.

5 Governance and the quality of institutions

The assumption behind most reform programs is that the quality of policies matters. However, data for some of the governance indicators have only recently begun to be systematically collected, and most econometric studies are cross-sectional, typically with one observation per country. In addition, since institutional quality is likely to change only slowly, it is not obvious that – even if the data did exist – variations in institutional quality over time would add much to our understanding of the degree to which it affects growth over time.

Why does institutional quality differ so much between countries? One possible explanation is the historical legacy, including colonial heritage, or ethnic diversity (Barro, 1996a,b). Chong and Zanforlin (2000) suggest that a country's legal tradition has a strong effect on the quality of its institutions. In particular, they find controversially that countries that have inherited a French civil code have less efficient bureaucracies, more corruption and lower credibility of government policies than do countries with a common law tradition. This also suggests by analogy that countries with a French civil code tradition would grow much more slowly than other countries. Another link through which institutional quality may affect growth is suggested by Knack (2000). Here, the quality of institutions is positively associated with economic growth, but higher levels of aid tend to erode institutional quality as measured by indices of bureaucratic quality, corruption and the rule of law. A possible explanation for this surprisingly robust finding[7] is that aid siphons off talent from the bureaucracy, alleviates pressure for reform and encourages rent seeking. Again, the countries in the WAEMU have generally high levels of aid dependence,[8] and thus may be expected to grow more slowly than other countries.

Six indicators are used in Kaufman et al. (1999b) to examine the relationship between institutional quality (or governance) on the one hand and growth on the other.[9] They use a parsimonious specification à la Hall and Jones (1999), writing (the log of) per capita income as a function of the governance indicators. The results

indicate that a one standard deviation improvement in governance leads to between a 2.5-fold (in the case of voice and accountability) and a 4-fold (in the case of political instability and violence) increase in per capita income. These results clearly indicate that there is a large payoff in terms of per capita income to improvements in governance. In other words, governance does matter. (Kaufman et al., 1999b:15–16)

However, a dummy for sub-Saharan Africa (SSA) indicates that the quality of governance does not capture the entire growth difference between SSA countries and other countries – the dummy is significant. A dummy for WAEMU countries, however, is not.[10] Table 5.10 presents the governance indicators for WAEMU countries and the average for SSA and low-income countries. Relative to the rest of sub-Saharan Africa, however, WAEMU countries on the whole score highest on the government effectiveness and corruption and graft indices, but lowest on the political stability/lack of violence index (only three WAEMU countries score above the SSA average).

Looking at the individual countries in Table 5.10 also reveals large differences. Thus, for instance, whereas Burkina Faso and Mali score higher than the SSA average on all six indicators, and Côte d'Ivoire scores higher than the SSA average on five indicators (the exception being voice and accountability), Niger has a lower score on all indicators, and Togo has a lower score on four indicators. Can country dummies explain the governance indices? To investigate that, I identified three groups of countries – WAEMU, sub-Saharan Africa and countries not in the Organisation for Economic Co-operation and Development – and regressed the dummies against the governance indices.[11] The first set of regressions included WAEMU in the SSA group and SSA in the non-OECD group; the second did not. This means that the (WAEMU, SSA, non-OECD) dummy-triple for Benin in the first set of regressions, Model 1, was (1,1,1), and in the second, Model 2, (1,0,0). For Zimbabwe, the triples were (0,1,1) and (0,1,0), respectively. This means that the WAEMU coefficient in Model 1 can be interpreted as the marginal effect of being part of WAEMU as opposed to being an African economy that is not a member of WAEMU. In Model 2, on the other hand, the WAEMU coefficient captures the entire difference between WAEMU members and members of the reference group, in this case OECD members.

Estimated coefficients are in Table 5.11. In Model 1, the dummies for SSA and non-OECD are significant for all indicators of governance, and

Table 5.10 Governance indicators

Country	VOICE	POLSTAB	GOVEFF	REGFRAM	RULELAW	GRAFT
Benin	0.695	-0.937	-0.066	-0.082	-0.422	-0.781
Burkina Faso	-0.213	-0.517	-0.059	-0.038	-0.350	-0.368
Côte d'Ivoire	-0.569	-0.138	-0.180	0.148	-0.335	-0.079
Guinea-Bissau	-0.454	-1.203	-0.334	-1.350	-1.615	-0.176
Mali	0.415	-0.287	-0.052	0.290	-0.465	-0.476
Niger	-0.744	-0.763	-1.387	-0.523	-1.144	-1.567
Senegal	-0.292	-0.871	0.047	-0.338	-0.097	-0.235
Togo	-1.051	-0.906	-0.374	-0.853	-0.799	-0.242
SSA[a]	-0.508	-0.732	-0.566	-0.419	-0.634	-0.526
LDC[b]	-0.298	-0.471	-0.461	-0.242	-0.477	-0.501

Source: Compiled from database described in Kaufman et al. (1999b) and available at http://www.worldbank.org/wbi/governance/datasets.htm#dataset.

Notes: Indices are constructed so that estimates of governance (in the global database) have a mean of 0, a standard deviation of 1 and a range from approximately −2.5 to 2.5. A higher number signifies a better score. VOICE = voice and accountability; POLSTAB = political stability/lack of violence; GOVEFF = government effectiveness; REGFRAM = regulatory framework; RULELAW = rule of law; GRAFT = corruption and graft.

[a] Simple average for all sub-Saharan African countries, including WAEMU.
[b] Simple average for all countries with a 1998 per capita income of less than US$8,500 in purchasing power parity terms.

Table 5.11 Quality of governance by region: Regression coefficients

Indicator[a]	Model 1				Model 2				
	WAEMU	SSA	Non-OECD	$\bar{R}^2$	WAEMU	SSA	Non-OECD	$\bar{R}^2$	n
VOICE	0.21	-0.37*	-1.48**	.36	-0.89*	-1.64**	-1.35**	.31	173
POLSTAB	-0.03	-0.62*	-1.08**	.31	-1.06*	-1.48**	-0.96*	.27	155
GOVEFF	0.29	-0.43*	-1.48**	.45	-0.87*	-1.71**	-1.37**	.41	156
REGFRAM	0.07	-0.37*	-0.90**	.21	-0.69*	-1.10**	-0.79*	.18	166
RULELAW	-0.10	-0.47*	-1.38**	.39	-1.21*	-1.63**	-1.25**	.34	166
GRAFT	-0.01	-0.28*	-1.63**	.49	-1.18*	-1.73**	-1.53**	.46	155
ALL	0.05	-0.39*	-1.33**	.42	-0.98*	-1.55**	-1.22**	.37	174

Source: Data from Kaufman et al. (1999b). Dummies as described in text.
Notes:
[a] Indices are abbreviated as explained in the note to Table 5.10. ALL is the simple average of the six variables.
* significant at the 5 percent test level; ** significant at the 1 percent test level.

have negative signs, suggesting that countries in SSA and non-OECD on average score lower on these indicators than do OECD countries. The WAEMU dummy, on the other hand, is not significant in all instances. Thus we conclude that governance in WAEMU countries is not significantly different from that in other SSA countries. In Model 1, however, there is a significant difference between African and non-African economies, good governance being lower in the latter. Non-OECD countries show an average score of −1.33 for variable ALL (the simple average of the six indicators), and SSA countries an average score of −1.72 for the same variable; the difference between OECD countries and the rest is quite large, much larger than the difference between SSA and other non-OECD countries.[12] This is a pattern common for all estimations in Model 1: the OECD coefficient is between 0.9 and 1.4, and the difference between OECD and other countries is larger than that between non-OECD and SSA.

Turning to Model 2, the WAEMU coefficient now is negative and significantly different from zero for all regressions. Thus, although WAEMU countries may not be different from other SSA countries, they are different from OECD countries. Note, however, that in Model 2 the absolute value of the WAEMU coefficient is smaller than the SSA coefficient for all regressions, suggesting that governance indices are slightly better in WAEMU than in the rest of SSA.[13] A tentative conclusion from this analysis is that there are no significant differences between WAEMU and other African countries. The union has not raised institutional quality above the African average.

6   Concluding remarks

The principal conclusion of this chapter is that reform results have been mixed in WAEMU. Growth has resumed in several countries, but this is far from a general feature. As in other African countries, reforms were triggered by economic and political crises. The reforms have, however, so far been unable to tackle rising poverty and social retrenchment.

Similarly, outcomes from civil service reforms have been limited. Although many countries have managed to reduce the size of the public sector, incentive and pay structures remain inadequate. For example, the 1994 devaluation of the CFA franc helped reduce the cost of the civil service, but it also compressed the salary structure, lowering morale. Signs of serious understaffing are emerging across the region. However, information on social sector outcomes is limited. Conventional indicators on the quality of education and health outcomes have deteriorated in several countries, but it seems that the majority of WAEMU countries have performed better than the SSA average. In particular, enrollment in primary education is significantly higher after reforms, although the impact on education efficiency is less clear-cut.

There are no indications that the quality of institutions in WAEMU is higher than in the rest of sub-Saharan Africa. The quality of institutions also varies between individual WAEMU countries, with scores for Burkina Faso and Mali being far ahead of those for Niger and Togo, for example.

Notes

1. Note, however, that the correlation between aid per capita and income per capita is less than perfect; the poorest members of the union do not receive more aid per capita than the relatively richer members.
2. This policy refers to the gradual dismantling of state controls built up from the late 1960s.
3. The fact that the public sector has often acted as a sponge in anglophone countries as well does not diminish the problem in francophone countries.
4. Note that, although reduction in the statutory retirement age may have an impact on the size of the civil service workforce, it does not necessarily improve government finances, because of both higher pensions and smaller employee contributions.
5. These were made as background to the *World Development Report 2000/01*. Reports from African countries include Rahmato and Kidanu (1999), Kunfaa (1999), Khalila et al. (1999), Ayoola et al. (1999) and World Bank (1999a,b). See also the participatory poverty assessment in Tanzania (Naraya, 1997).
6. In the case of insignificant differences, experiments were made by moving the cut-off year forward in time to allow for the time-lag discussed above. In no case did this make the difference significant.
7. Knack uses instruments for foreign aid to correct for reverse causality, and conducts several sensitivity tests in the form of sample changes and estimation forms. The negative association between levels of aid and institutional quality is not fundamentally affected.
8. Measured as aid per capita, aid as share of GDP, or aid as share of gross domestic investment.
9. Kaufman et al. (1999a) aggregate the indicators under six headings: voice and accountability, political stability/lack of violence, government effectiveness, regulatory framework, rule of law, and corruption and graft. The data set covers up to 173 countries, with one entry per country. Data are generally from 1997 or 1998.
10. And a dummy for CFA zone countries also does not turn out significantly different from zero.
11. However, since WAEMU is a subgroup within SSA and SSA is a subgroup of non-OECD, one can either treat WAEMU as being included in or excluded from the SSA group and similarly for the relation between SSA and non-OECD. I did both.
12. The coefficient for OECD countries for variable ALL in Model 1 is 1.22 with a *t*-value of 9.6.
13. However, the results from Model 1 show that this difference is not significantly different from zero at conventional test levels.

REFERENCES

Ayoola, G. B. et al. (1999) *Consultations with the Poor. Country Synthesis Report Nigeria*, World Bank: Washington, DC.

Barro, R. (1996a) 'Democracy and Growth,' *Journal of Economic Growth* 1.

——— (1996b) 'Institutions and Growth: An Introductory Essay,' *Journal of Economic Growth* 1.

Botchwey, K., P. Collier, J. W. Gunning and K. Hamada (1998) *Report of the Group of Independent Persons Appointed to Conduct an Evaluation of Certain Aspects of the Enhanced Structural Adjustment Facility*, International Monetary Fund: Washington, DC.

Chong, A. and L. Zanforlin (2000) 'Law Tradition and Institutional Quality: Some Empirical Evidence,' *Journal of International Development* 12.

DAC (Development Assistance Committee) (1996) *Shaping the 21st Century: The Contribution of Development Co-operation*, OECD/DAC: Paris.

Devarajan, S., D. Dollar and T. Holmgren (2000) *Aid and Reform in Africa: Lessons from Ten Case Studies*, World Bank: Washington, DC.

Hall, R. and C. Jones (1999) 'Why Do Some Countries Produce So Much More Output Per Worker Than Others?' *Quarterly Journal of Economics* 114.

Haltiwanger, J. and M. Singh (1999) 'Cross-Country Evidence on Public Sector Retrenchment,' *World Bank Economic Review* 13:23–66.

IMF (International Monetary Fund) (2000) *International Financial Statistics*, IMF: Washington, DC, December.

Kaufman, D., A. Kraay and P. Zoido-Lobatón (1999a) 'Aggregating Governance Indicators,' Policy Research Working Paper No. 2195, World Bank, Washington, DC.

——— (1999b) 'Governance Matters,' Policy Research Working Paper No. 2196, World Bank, Washington, DC.

Khalila, S. W., P. M. Mwula and J. M. Kadzandira (1999) *Consultations with the Poor. Country Synthesis Report Malawi*, World Bank: Washington, DC.

Knack, S. (2000) 'Aid Dependence and the Quality of Governance: A Cross-Country Empirical Analysis,' mimeo, World Bank, Institute Center for Governance and Anti-Corruption, Washington, DC.

Kunfaa, E. Y. (1999) *Consultations with the Poor. Ghana Country Synthesis Report*, World Bank: Washington, DC.

Lienert, I. and J. Modi (1997) 'A Decade of Civil Service Reform in sub-Saharan Africa,' IMF Working Paper No. 97/179, Washington, DC.

Naraya, D. (1997) *Voices of the Poor. Poverty and Social Capital in Tanzania*, World Bank: Washington, DC.

Rahmato, D. and A. Kidanu (1999) *Consultations with the Poor: National Report, Ethiopia*, World Bank: Washington, DC.

Thomas, V., M. Dailami, A. Dhareshwar, D. Kaufman, N. Kishor, R. López and Y. Wang (2000) *The Quality of Growth*, Oxford University Press for the World Bank: Oxford.

White, H. (2000) 'Dollars, Dialogue and Development. An Evaluation of Swedish Program Aid,' Sida Evaluation Report No. 99/17, Stockholm.

World Bank (1993) *Adjustment in Africa. Reforms, Results and the Road Ahead*, World Bank: Washington, DC.
——— (1998) *Assessing Aid*, World Bank: Washington, DC.
——— (1999a) *Consultations with the Poor. National Synthesis Report Somaliland*, World Bank: Washington, DC.
——— (1999b) *Consultations with the Poor. National Synthesis Report Zambia*, World Bank: Washington, DC.
——— (2000a) *World Development Indicators*, World Bank: Washington, DC.
——— (2000b) *African Development Indicators,* World Bank: Washington, DC.

6

Reform of the Malawian public sector: Incentives, governance and accountability

Dick Durevall

1 Introduction

Since independence, Malawi's public sector has gone through three distinct phases related closely to the performance of the economy. Between the achievement of independence in the early 1960s and the end of the 1970s, the generally high commodity export prices had led to above-average GDP growth, close to 3 percent per annum and capita. Combined with macroeconomic stability, this period of unbroken growth provided a basis for public sector expansion. Before the end of the period, public investment accounted for two-thirds of total investment. However, the government failed to translate these investment outlays into social welfare improvements. Health and education expenditure remained below 6 percent of GDP in the late 1960s, falling to about 5 percent already by the mid-1970s (Prior, 1990:173).

The second period, 1980–94, saw the economy and the public sector enter a period of serious imbalance. There were severe shocks, including increases in oil prices and transport costs related to external trade, as routes through Mozambique were disrupted by civil war. The war in the neighboring country forced up to 750,000 refugees into Malawi, at a time when it was experiencing severe drought. Investments dropped sharply and foreign reserves dwindled. Growth for the period 1980–94 was only 1.6 percent. The budget deficit, rising to 15 percent in 1980 alone, averaged above 10 percent during 1981–7, and again hit 15 percent in 1994.

In the early 1990s donors withdrew their balance of payments support to Malawi to demonstrate increasing concern with both the poor fiscal discipline of the government and its human rights violations. The donor community also hoped that aid retrenchment would force the government to hold multiparty elections.

The most recent period, from the mid-1990s up to the end of the millennium, saw the election of a democratic government in 1994 and the introduction of a new structural adjustment program in 1995 with broad-based support from the donor community. Aside from policies for macro-economic stabilization, the government also introduced structural reforms with implications for the public sector. They included privatization, deregulation, regulatory reform, liberalization of agricultural markets, including the phasing out of the price control and subsidization regimes, and the reform of the civil service. Towards the end of the 1990s, the reform efforts were starting to bear fruit. The economy, which had earlier stagnated, grew by 5.5 percent per annum during the latter half of the decade. This resumption of growth improved voter sentiment and probably explains the ruling party's re-election in 1999.

In Malawi, the case for a well-functioning public service sector is a stark one. Per capita GDP was only US$163 in 1999, close to 70 percent of the population was living below the poverty line and life expectancy at birth was about 43 years. Given a narrow tax base, recurrent government expenditure is very low, estimated at less than US$30 per capita in the 1998/99 budget year. The government is thus not in a position to meet the huge expenditures on education and training required to reverse the serious shortage of human capital or the investments in infrastructure and maintenance necessary to alleviate the transport constraints of landlocked Malawi. The marginal benefit of improved living standards is hence clearly very large in Malawi. However, the growth-enhancing and poverty-reducing economic policies needed to ensure this require the creation of an efficient and accountable public sector. This is a more crucial precondition for development in poor countries than in much richer countries, where there are fewer growth constraints (Goldsmith, 2000). At least since the dawn of independence, the government has tried to raise public sector efficiency by designing and adopting reform programs (Msosa, 1998). Progress was intermittent, however, making it necessary, with the coming to power of a new government in 1994, to undertake a thorough review of the public sector.

The purpose of this chapter is to study the nature of public sector reforms in Malawi and to analyze their impact on governance and accountability. Section 2 provides a theoretical background to good governance and public sector reform. Section 3 then looks at the evolution of Malawi's public sector reforms. Section 4 looks at changes in employment and wages in the public sector. Section 5 discusses the issue of accountability in government and the steps being taken to ensure that it takes root. Section 6 concludes the chapter.

2 Public sector reform and good governance: The issues

Although public sector reforms are difficult and complex, making a good record of performance hard to establish, they are important for the promotion of good governance in sub-Saharan Africa (see Collier and Gunning, 1999). In our context, governance can be defined as the exercise of political, economic and administrative authority in the management of a nation's affairs. Good governance is when this authority is used to stimulate and promote sustainable development (Mugore, 1997; Schacter 2000). It is thus closely related to the functioning of the state in a democratic society – with separation of powers between the legislature, the judiciary and the executive. The legislature sets policy goals, objectives and rules. The judiciary determines whether the aforementioned are adhered to and sanctions errant practices. The executive, that is, the political leadership as well as the civil service, implements the policies agreed upon. Obviously, for good governance to be realized, the three branches of a democratic society have to work in tandem.[1]

Schacter (2000) has argued, however, that it is almost impossible to find an African government that is more efficient in policy implementation in the new millennium than it was in the 1980s. There are a number of reasons for the poor outcomes. First, there has generally not been a holistic approach to public sector reform in most African countries. In recent years donors have tended to influence the nature and speed of economic reforms more than domestic policymakers have. Structural adjustment reforms are illustrative. The public sector components of the reforms focused on areas emphasized by multilateral and bilateral agencies, such as raising efficiency in the civil service and state divestiture. In the area of legal and judicial reforms, again issues close to the donor constituency, such as human rights protection, were emphasized. Invariably there was less emphasis on issues of coordination of the various reforms to meet domestic needs and enhance local capacities. The recent emphasis on the inclusion of civil society in policy making can also be seen in similar light. It switched the focus once again to issues of access to policymakers and services, via decentralization and empowerment of the citizenry, championed by donors. However, these shifts in emphasis precluded a more systematic and long-term approach to public sector reform in many countries in Africa (Mugore, 1997).

Second, the domestic coordination of public sector reforms has generally been poor. Ministries have conducted their own internal reforms with little attempt at synchronizing with other agencies. Notably, local government reforms have been poorly coordinated with those in the line ministries of finance, health and education. The situation is thus often aggravated by the fact that donors tend to favor portions of the reform project, which they fund accordingly, neglecting the other components that do not appeal to them. This could leave important facets of the reform programs poorly funded, thus making a mockery of the whole.

Third, and rather ironically, although public sector reform seeks to enhance accountability in government, its implementation has in many countries been a study in poor accountability and transparency, with little information reaching the public and with much of the program shrouded in secrecy and poorly explained to the electorate. This has meant that few of the public sector reforms are 'owned' by the populations, and they continue to be seen as impositions from outside.

In spite of the problems of implementation, good governance continues to be highlighted by both donor and recipient governments as crucial for reform success. It is argued in the literature that, by favoring controls and rent-seeking behavior, bad governance crowds out the private sector, generates uncertainty and thus reduces investment. With controls driven to the extreme, governments become seriously inefficient, patrimonial and predatory (Lienert and Modi, 1997; Mutahaba et al., 1993). Corruption is an oft-cited example of the outcomes of bad governance. Although, in the 1980s, corruption was sometimes seen as important for 'unclogging' the rampant system of controls, increasing public sector efficiency by supplying public services at market-determined prices, there is widespread agreement that its effects are negative (Bardhan, 1997). Empirical results relate it to lower investment and thus lower growth. It also lowers expenditure on basic services and generally reduces the productivity of public investment as well as that of the public sector (Tanzi, 2000).

Theory and empirical evidence suggest four determinants of corruption in the public sector: opportunities for corruption; the level of remuneration of the civil service; the extent of controls; and the effectiveness of penalties (Bardhan, 1997; Van Rijckeghem and Weder, 1997). Opportunities for corrupt behavior are directly related to the control regime supported by the government. The proliferation of permits and licenses in a regime rife with shortages creates enormous rents, which accrue directly to those administering the system, and poor remuneration is also often blamed for causing corruption (Van Rijckeghem and Weder, 1997). Still, it is not clear what the optimal wage level in the public sector should be. If civil servants exhibit maximizing behavior, increasing their wages might, on its own, fail to resolve the incentive problem. However, if their behavior is 'satisficing,' they might abstain from corruption when they perceive their wages to be fair. In the latter case, small wage increases will have a large productivity effect (Van Rijckeghem and Weder, 1997). Still, even if wages were to increase, penalties will be effective in reducing corruption only if they are relatively high and their enforcement rigorous.

Among economists, a stable macroeconomic environment, an absence of government-induced market distortions and the efficient provision of social and infrastructure services comprise good policy. However, although broad adoption of adjustment programs in Africa is seen as indicating a willingness to embrace good policies, in practice few sub-Saharan governments have implemented them fully. As a result of factors ranging from poor incentive structures, weak monitoring and supervision, lack of transparency to inadequate legislation, public administration in Africa remains extremely inefficient. This is depicted by poor value for money in service delivery, wastage of resources, low morale among employees and outright corruption.

In the economics literature, the principal–agent model has been used to analyze the impact of poor incentives.[2] The principal–agent problem arises because contracts between agents, for example employees and employers, are incomplete, with compliance requiring monitoring. In trying to reach an incentive-compatible contract the principal is constrained by the need to overcome the agent's participation constraint. The contract offered must at least satisfy the agent's reservation utility. Moreover, to discourage shirking and other costly behavior on the part of the agent, the wage or incentive offered must be such that the threat of dismissal is credible, that is, it is sufficient to instill discipline. However, the principal–agent framework, although insightful, tends to project too simplified a view. Typically, there are hierarchies of principals and agents in the public sector. In a democracy, citizens are the principals of the parliament, which in turn is the principal of the cabinet. The cabinet is itself the principal of the civil service, and so on. There are also principal–agent relations between the president and his ministers, ministers and their permanent secretaries, and the latter and the staff of the ministries. When institutions are weak, such a formal framework tends to be displaced by informal lines of authority based on patronage, ethnic affiliation and corruption (Kaluwa and Musila, 2000; Wescott, 1996).

The monitoring problems in the principal–agent model discussed above arise from lack of transparency. If, for example, the budgetary process of the government is opaque, it is difficult for the parliament to scrutinize the government's intentions as demanded by the electorate. It simply does not have enough information to do so. Similarly, if public sector job descriptions are poorly specified, imposing disciplinary measures or devising an adequate level of remuneration will be next to impossible. The importance of transparency was powerfully demonstrated in Uganda when the government published the amounts of money it was disbursing to the districts in the local newspapers, making recipients aware of what to expect. With regard to primary schools, financial flows from the central government that reached their targets at the district level rose considerably as a result of the increased level of transparency in the disbursement process (Reinikka, 2001).

Evaluation, or after-the-fact monitoring, is another means of ensuring compliance. There is, however, little point in evaluation when poor performance cannot be punished. In practice, especially where job descriptions are imprecise, it can be difficult to prove that employees are guilty of misconduct. Moreover, given the correlation between punishment, the risk of getting caught and the wage level, creating an effective system of deterrents is difficult. If, for example, the penalty is generally considered too hash and thus viewed as unfair by onlookers, enforcers will be reluctant to apply it. Similarly, when wages are low, society takes a more lenient view of corruption in the public service. Since softer deterrents do not work either, the answer seems to lie in fundamental reform of the incentive structure of the public service (Tanzi, 1998).

3   The evolution of Malawi's public sector reforms

3.1   Introduction

Although recent developments have been dramatic, with pressures from all sides, the very first efforts at public sector reform in Malawi were embarked on immediately after the attainment of independence in the early 1960s. A major concern at the time was how to manage the transition from an expatriate-based civil service to one dominated by Africans. With the goal of limiting the cost of running the postcolonial public service, the Skinner Commission, established in 1964, recommended lower salaries and job reclassification for African employees taking over the civil service. These recommendations were adopted and the salary scales were compressed accordingly. However, very little effort was allotted to the more important task of creating incentives in the public sector in order to ensure the efficient provision of basic services in, for example, education, agriculture, healthcare and communications.

With the goal of incorporating these concerns, the Economic Commission for Africa commissioned a study in 1966, which recommended measures aimed at increasing public sector efficiency and improving administrative capacities in state institutions. Still, precisely because implementation capacities were missing in government, few of its recommendations were adopted (Msosa, 1998). Equally ineffective was the Herbecq Review Commission of 1985, whose recommendations on staff structure, career development and job grading, which were meant to improve the quality of the service while putting a cap on employment, were not fully implemented. The number of civil servants continued to grow rapidly during the 1980s.

During the 1990s a number of policy reviews and programs directed at reforming the public sector were attempted, often simultaneously. Among them were a public sector management review, civil service pay and employment study, civil service action plan, poverty alleviation program, functional reviews of the ministries, decentralization and formation of local government policy reform, medium-term expenditure framework, and sector investment programs. Since the earlier problems of paucity of human resources and managerial capacities persisted, the implementation of this new crop of programs was slow and unsatisfactory. However, in comparison to the early 1990s, public sector performance has improved in the past few years (Msosa, 1998; Malawi Government and World Bank, 2000). In the rest of this section I shall look more closely at the civil service action plan on which the government based its hopes for a reformed and efficient civil service.

3.2   The civil service action plan

In 1996, the government launched a civil service action plan (CSAP). It is one of the most comprehensive reform plans ever attempted in Malawi, with a detailed description of the actions and activities to be undertaken, including timetables and deadlines, as well as identification of the ministries or agencies responsible for implementing the various segments of the program. The aim of CSAP was to improve the efficiency and effectiveness of the civil service by restructuring the establishment and retrenching staff. The government also sought to improve financial and human resources management, and generally to manage the process of changing the public sector better (Lungu and Mugore, 1999).

Four years after the introduction of the CSAP, the government had completed a census of the civil service, done strategic and functional reviews of its ministries, laid down plans for contracting out some services (such as cleaning and security provision) to the private sector, and retrenched about 20,000 temporary employees. Nearing completion was a job evaluation and personnel audit for the civil service. However, the above comprises a small part of the total number of actions envisioned when the CSAP was launched in 1996, and much work remains to be done (Malawi Government, 2000).

The slow implementation is partly to be blamed on the low level of political consultation during the initiation of the CSAP. The plan was designed by a small number of civil servants, working under pressure from domestic politicians and donors. There was insufficient interaction with the cabinet, civil servants and other stakeholders. One consequence of this was that neither the members of the cabinet committee on public and civil service reform, which was formed to oversee the reform exercise, nor employees in the ministries felt a high degree of ownership of the program. Moreover, poor consultation aside, the fact that the reform was focused on retrenchment, privatization and contracting out, with little effort expended on capacity and institution building, further alienated civil servants who feared loss of employment. Equally important, absence of the involvement of civil society meant that a potential source of pressure for rapid implementation of the new reforms had been expurgated (Lungu and Mugore, 1999).

The design of the CSAP also had serious flaws. It was, for example, far from clear who was ultimately responsible for the program implementation, monitoring and evaluation. In the case of evaluation, progress was gauged on the basis of very simple indicators. The lack of a clearly defined implementing authority also led to poor sequencing of interventions. Without a plan of implementation, the CSAP became a mere list of initiatives. Line ministries acted autonomously in requesting support from donors for projects and the process became uncoordinated.

The functional reviews of the ministries were an important aspect of the civil service reform. The goals of the reviews included defining mission statements for the ministries, streamlining organizational structures and clarifying issues of accountability and responsibility at all levels of government. Furthermore, the reviews looked at staffing levels with a view to eliminating the duplication of functions by ministries.

The functional review program was managed by a public sector change management agency, which commissioned the reviews and suggested the required interventions to the cabinet. In the beginning the reviews were done more or less according to plan. With time, the speed of execution decreased however. Thus, instead of the work being completed at the beginning of 1998, as planned, it was not completed until the beginning of 2001. Initially, the functional reviews had important policy impacts. For example, the number of ministries was reduced by seven to nineteen, and a number of functions for contracting out were identified. Still, the reduction in the number of ministries does not seem to have reduced the number of civil servants. Individuals and functions were simply transferred to other ministries. Efforts at contracting out activities also encountered serious problems. The contracting-out unit was not ready in time, and the capacity in the private sector for service provision on behalf of the public sector was limited. The government also had a poor record of payment for services rendered, and many private companies were reluctant to tender for the new functions being contracted out. Moreover, for similar reasons, banks were not willing to finance firms, even after being awarded contracts by the government. This cautious response on the part of the private sector meant that the envisaged massive reduction in civil servants owing to contracting out was not realized (see Msosa, 1998).

A typical aspect of the lack of coordination in the CSAP is the omission of the functional reviews regarding decentralization. For example, although the functional review of the Ministry of Education was completed promptly, it was largely irrelevant because it failed to take into consideration the fact that responsibility for the schools was to be transferred to the local governments.

Another key part of the CSAP was the implementation of a medium-term expenditure framework (MTEF). Two pressing issues necessitated its introduction. First, it was necessary to abandon the hitherto incremental basis for recurrent budget preparation for more emphasis on outcomes. Second, budgets were typically prepared for a single year, with a demarcation between development and recurrent expenditures. However, since development budgets generate recurrent expenditures of their own, often not budgeted for, it was important to prepare budgets that anticipate medium-term outcomes. Under the MTEF, the recurrent and development budgets will be integrated. The budget process will change from being an inventory of inputs, adjusted on a discretionary basis, to an outcomes-oriented framework that focuses on outputs, the costing of priority activities and medium-term projections of available resources (Ministry of Finance and Economic Planning, 2000).

The reform of the budget process has turned out to be much more difficult to implement than anticipated. In application, the MTEF entailed more drastic changes in organizational structure and operation of the ministries as well as behavior of civil servants than the government could muster. A recent evaluation has concluded that, after five years of budgetary reform, the budget process remained incomplete (Ministry of Finance and Economic Planning, 2000). Thus, although budgetary allocations to priority sectors, such as health and education, have increased in the recent past, this was more the result of cabinet-level interventions than of improved cost and benefit analyses of expenditure.

4   Employment and wages in the public sector

As in other African countries, the post-independence years in Malawi have seen a rapid expansion in civil service employment, at the same time as wages in the sector experienced a dramatic decline in real terms accompanied by sharp wage compression. At the beginning of the 1960s, the civil service (defined as the public sector less police, parastatal and local government employees) totaled only about 10,700 employees. Partly to cater for the increased demand for services and to create employment, the number of civil servants increased by 13 percent per year during the first twenty years of independence. During the 1990s, the expansion continued, reaching a total of 127,000 civil servants by 1998 (Malawi Government, 1998). However, as part of the civil service reform, the government attempted to stop the expansion of its labor force. Since 1995, about 20,000 temporary employees have been retrenched and ghost workers eliminated (Malawi Government, 2000). Still, by the beginning of the new millennium, the number of civil servants had increased to 130,000.[3]

The focus on numbers seems to suggest that there are still too many civil servants in Malawi, but the opposite might indeed be the case. Looked at as a provider of services for a population of up to 10.5 million people, the size of the civil service is not excessive. Civil servants comprise only about 1.2 percent of the total population. This figure, although comparable to those for other African countries, is very low compared with developed countries in general and with the welfare states of Europe in particular (Lienert and Modi, 1997). Moreover, taking into account that almost half of the civil servants are currently employed as teachers in the education ministry, only about 65,000 are left to run state administration and public hospitals. Thus, on the face of it, there is no compelling reason for reducing the size of the Malawian civil service per se, especially given the serious shortages of personnel in some of the most vital sectors, such as education and health (Malawi Government and World Bank, 2000).

Ultimately, however, the size of the civil service depends on the level that the government can afford, on its own or with the assistance of the donor community. Thus, looked at from the point of view of economic efficiency and affordability, employment in Malawi's civil service is large. The service employs about 20 percent of the formal sector labor force, excluding agriculture and estates. In the 1990s, close to half of the country's professionals and more than two-thirds of its subprofessionals were working for the government (World Bank, 1994). A large civil service that is not adequately remunerated will not only become a burden on state finances but also distorts relative wages in the rest of the economy. What then goes on in the civil service plays an unduly large role in the determination of employment and wages in the rest of the economy. Moreover, the hoarding of professionals and technicians in low-

Table 6.1 Public sector wage costs as a share of GDP and government expenditure in Malawi and sub-Saharan Africa, 1980–98 (%)

	1980–4	1985–9	1990–4	1995–8
Wages/GDP				
Malawi	5.3	5.3	6.5	6.5
Sub-Saharan Africa	3.7	3.3	7.2	7.7
Wages/expenditure				
Malawi	16.4	16.3	18.5	21.1
Sub-Saharan Africa	14.7	12.2	24.6	27.3

Source: World Bank (2000).
Note: Government expenditure is measured as total expenditure and lending minus repayments.

productivity government employment retards the development of the private sector. In the rest of this section, I look at the evolution of wages and wage-related costs in the Malawian civil service, and compare them with those in the private sector. Three questions are asked:

• How have wage costs as well as real wages evolved in recent decades?
• What factors have determined the sharp wage compression in Malawi?
• How do civil service sector wages compare with those in the private sector?

In the 1980s, after close to two decades of relatively good economic performance, the public sector wage bill, at 5.3 percent of GDP and 16.4 percent of public expenditure, was higher in Malawi than in the rest of sub-Saharan Africa (see Table 6.1). For the period from 1990, the pattern was reversed, with wages growing much more slowly in Malawi than in the rest of sub-Saharan Africa. However, in light of the decline in public service provision in the 1990s, it is doubtful whether raising the public sector wage bill, without steps at restructuring the sector, is prudent. As illustrated by Figure 6.1, which depicts developments for selected wage categories (see also Table 6A.1 in the appendix), salaries and wages have declined by more than 60 percent in Malawi since the beginning of the 1980s. Between 1982 and 2000, for example, the top scale in the civil service (S1), that of chief justice, declined by 63 percent, while that of government senior administrative officer (S8) declined by 82 percent. Mid-level grades, for example clerical officers with diplomas (EO/TO), have seen similar declines – an average of 56 percent. For some in the lower grades, declines have been less, below 30 percent, although some categories saw declines of over 50 percent. It is noteworthy that the increasing militancy of the otherwise traditionally docile civil service

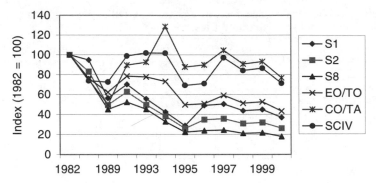

Figure 6.1 The evolution of real salaries and wages for selected civil service grades, 1982–2000 (1982 = 100)
Sources: See Table 6A.1.
Notes: Salary grades are as follows: S1 = chief justice, S2 = attorney general, S8 = senior administrative officer, EO/TO = clerical officer with diploma, CO/TA = technical assistant, SCIV = messenger. Salaries were first converted to constant 1995 Malawi kwachas (MK) using the consumer price index; then all were normalized to 100 in 1982.

workforce, resorting to strikes when need be, has not reversed this downward trend in real wages (Adamolekun and Mvula, 1999).

Another interesting feature of wage developments in Malawi relates to the severe compression that resulted from decades of parsimonious adjustments, via wage reviews and recommendations from commissions, but failed to improve incentives in the system as a whole. Over the period 1982–2000, there were periodic adjustments to wages across the board (Table 6.2). There are two striking features of these changes. First, although the nominal increases were sometimes evenly distributed, most often they were not. For instance, the revisions that took place in 1986 were clearly biased in favor of higher salary grades; this was reversed in 1989 when wages for lower grades rose by well over 40 percent. In 1992, adjustments favored the mid-level grades, then, in the next year, lower grades saw their wages increasing strongly once again. Since 1997, wage increases have been equally distributed across the various grades.

The abrupt and uneven adjustments in the salary scales depicted in Table 6.2 illustrate a lack of continuity in public sector pay policies. The authorities have essentially been crisis managers in recent decades, with little strategic planning. Adjustments were invariably responses to mounting discontent from civil servants rather than the result of well thought out strategies that were consistent with the country's fiscal standing. In the midst of labor unrest, there would be a one-off increase in wages, followed by policy inactivity until the next crisis. Large and

Table 6.2 Malawi: Nominal salary adjustments for selected civil service grades, 1982–2000 (%)

Salary grade	1982–6	1986–9	1989–92	1992–3	1993–4	1994–5	1995–6	1996–7	1997–2000
Super scale									
S1	63	12	80	0	21	44	88	10	83
S2C	–	–	–	–	–	44	47	10	83
S2B	64	12	80	0	18	44	47	10	83
S2A	53	12	81	0	20	44	47	10	83
S2	43	12	83	0	22	44	48	10	83
S3	44	12	83	9	13	44	34	10	83
S4	43	12	83	9	13	44	35	10	83
S5	42	12	81	9	14	44	35	10	83
S6	39	13	78	9	14	44	15	10	83
S7	35	13	73	9	15	44	16	10	83
S8	30	12	68	9	15	44	18	10	83
Administrative & professional									
AO/PO	–	–	–	15	42	44	24	17	83
Executive & technical									
CEO/CTO	30	20	68	15	16	44	24	17	83
SEO/STO	31	30	68	15	24	44	19	25	83
EO/TO	31	54	82	25	50	44	13	25	83
Junior technical/clerical									
SCO/STA	28	20	106	25	50	44	15	25	83
CO/TA	29	25	160	30	122	44	13	25	83
Subordinate staff									
SCI	26	20	80	30	113	44	13	25	83
SCII	25	20	80	30	109	44	13	25	83
SCIII	27	43	92	30	77	44	13	35	83
SCIV	27	85	97	30	59	44	13	47	83

Source: See Table 6A.1.

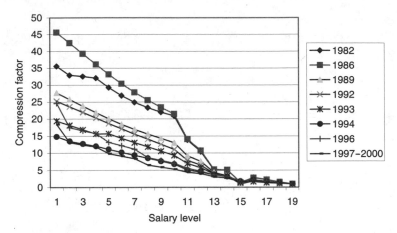

Figure 6.2 Compression factors by year: Major salary grades as ratios of lowest grade (SCIV), 1982–2000
Sources: See Table 6A.1.
Notes: Salary levels range from 1 for chief justice to 19 for messenger. Compression factors were calculated as ratios between each grade and the lowest one (SCIV).

unplanned salary adjustments led to distortions of the economy-wide pay structure, thus affecting overall work effort negatively, especially since they bred discontent in other sectors of the economy and led to inflationary pressure.

The wage compression that resulted from the Africanization of the civil service after independence has remained at the core of the incentive problems in Malawi's civil service. Although the reduction in salary levels had affected those in the top grades most, and the narrowing of wage differentials was probably initially defendable on efficiency grounds, the persistence of wage compression has distorted the incentive structure in the civil service. The government has had to resort to non-wage complements of various types to keep its labor force motivated. Figure 6.2 illustrates the compression factors for major salary grades over the period 1982–2000. They range from the top category (S1), that of chief justice, to the lowest level (SCIV) of subordinate staff (see also Table 6.2). The compression factors are ratios of each grade's salary level to that of subordinate staff. A ratio of unity implies that compression is complete, with all grades enjoying the same salary complement.

Although the compression of salaries has been a common phenomenon in African public services, it has been driven to extremes in poor countries such as Malawi (see Liernert and Modi, 1997; World Bank, 1994).

Thus, whereas at the beginning of the 1980s top government employees were earning up to forty-five times more than the lowest-paid messenger, the gaps had been reduced to only twelve to eighteen times in the decade that followed. The compression has been severer for the mid-range grades, with some ratios falling from above twenty to only about five. The government attempted to reverse the effects of wage compression by inventing a variety of employment benefits, notably housing and transport allowances. Top civil servants travel abroad at frequent intervals, which enables them to generate extra income via per diem and related allowances. Training workshops and conferences, where allowances are paid for attendance, are also common, in many cases sponsored by donors (Government of Malawi and World Bank, 2000). More often than not, however, employees attempt to supplement their incomes by 'privatizing' public property, such as official stamps, demanding a fee for them. Medicines are stolen from hospitals, and government vehicles are used for private businesses. Shirking is common, and some individuals simply abscond from duty while continuing to draw salaries from the government.

How do public sector salaries and wages compare with those of the private sector? Comparing wage levels in the two sectors is difficult. First, within the private sector the pay levels vary across employers, with some paying much less than the minimum salaries in the civil service, whereas others pay up to 30 percent more for staff with similar levels of training (World Bank, 1994). Second, comparisons should ideally be made between jobs held by individuals with similar training and experience. Last, in addition to salaries, one also needs to look at monetary and non-monetary benefits, although the latter can be difficult to quantify.

A study of pay by sector done by the International Labour Organization (ILO, 1989) found that basic salaries among professionals in the private sector were about 150 percent higher than in government, with subprofessional categories in the private sector enjoying 45 percent higher wages. Only among the low-skilled occupations did civil servants earn a little more, 4 percent, than those in the private sector. On the basis of an extensive survey, the World Bank (1994) was able to put a value on the various non-monetary benefits attached to these jobs. When these were added to salaries and wages, the pay gap between professionals in the private sector and in the civil service was reduced to 60 per cent. For the middle and junior grades in the civil service, with subsidized housing, the total remuneration package was in fact better than in the private sector. However, during the period 1993–9, private sector salaries grew much faster than salaries in the public sector. In real terms, salaries for high-ranking civil servants decreased by about 50 percent over the period, while they increased by six times for top jobs in the private sector (Malawi Government and World Bank, 2000). Lower grades similarly lagged behind their equivalents in the private sector. At the end of 1999, a civil service extension worker earned US$41 per month after tax and including benefits, whereas extension workers employed by non-governmental organizations earned three times as much (Moll, 2000).

The health ministry provides an example of the consequences of low salaries and wages. Although the share of public expenditure going to personal emoluments increased from 24 percent to 39 percent over the period 1990–7 as part of a deliberate effort to maintain reasonable salary levels, there were large-scale resignations from the ministry. By 1999, up to 50 percent of the employees had left, mostly doctors, nurses and other clinical staff, and most vacancies remained unfilled (Malawi Government and World Bank, 2000).

In modern economics, a central component of the incentive structure is an ability to relate inputs and outcomes to wage compensation (Lazear, 1995). This approach is, however, rarely practiced in Malawi. The information required for its operation is simply not available. Another reason is that, for most jobs in the civil service, it is difficult to establish a clear link between human resource inputs and the quantity and quality of the service provided. But even when the latter is possible, incentives based on outputs could go wrong. If, for example, health clinics are compensated for the number of vaccinations carried out, they might neglect other aspects of primary care and treatment.

Nevertheless, a job restructuring exercise is under way in Malawi and new employment contracts have been introduced. Some institutions, such as the Anti-Corruption Bureau[4] and the Malawi Revenue Authority, now use employment contracts that relate pay to either individual performance or outcomes. During 2000, senior civil servants from deputy secretary and above were given the option to switch to performance-based contracts of a three-year duration, with pay levels that were about 500 percent above current ones. Still, initially only those close to retirement accepted performance-based contracts, since they had little to lose, while others hesitated for fear of unfair performance appraisals and anxiety regarding the sustainability of the system itself. More recently, however, more individuals have opted for the new scheme.

As already noted, the success of a system based on salary enhancement rests on the ability to design a credible system of performance evaluation. It is not self-evident how to measure the output of a principal secretary, for example. Ultimately, the procedure used must combine objective measurement with a degree of subjectivity. This implies, in turn, that other considerations, such as politics and ethnic bias, might distort the evaluation.

5 Accountability in the public sector

A key goal of the reform of the civil service has been to raise account-ability in the public sector. Lack of accountability has serious impli-cations for the use of resources in ministries and departments. Without accountability, many important initiatives by the government will have little effect. For example, the introduction of a cash budget in Malawi in 1994 was meant to instill a high level of accountability in the budgetary process and also to reduce discretionary expenditures in the ministries. Still, poor accountability led to the build-up of arrears. Private sector firms have been willing to supply goods and services on credit to govern-ment departments on the strength of promises of future payment. This has helped senior officers to maintain their activities. In other cases, cash-strapped departments continue to consume public utilities, including water, electricity and telecommunications, while refusing to pay for the accumulated bills.

To increase accountability in government demands not only reforms of the nature described in the sections above, but also concerted actions directed against corruption in public life. In 1994, a new constitution was written which expressed a commitment to political pluralism and good governance. As a result, the latter part of the 1990s saw the establishment of institutions such as the Ombudsman, the Electoral Commission, the Compensation Tribunal and the Anti-Corruption Bureau (ACB).

Corruption is a big problem in Malawi, as indeed in other parts of sub-Saharan Africa. The new government thus sought support from the World Bank to put in place policies to address it. Already in 1995, par-liament passed the Corrupt Practice Act. The leadership of the ACB was appointed in 1997, with operations commencing a year later. The bu-reau's mandate is to investigate and prosecute offences of corruption, to empower civil society via education and information to fight corruption, and to deter corruption in all its various forms.

The ACB has gained a reputation for efficiency. Its corruption-fighting activities have led to the dismissal of at least four ministers and several senior civil servants. In 2001 a further two ministers were on trial for corruption along with a large number of civil servants. The causes of the ACB's relatively high efficiency are illustrative. First, it enjoys the politi-cal support of the president. This implies that lower levels are not able to interfere. Second, the staff of the institution were hand-picked, with em-phasis put on relevant qualifications and experience. Further, the bureau hired experienced expatriates who brought with them the know-how that gave the institution confidence.

Employees at the ACB work on the basis of three-year contracts. Their remuneration is several times that of civil servants in other departments.

The salary of a senior investigator is, for example, about MK30,000 a month. This is supplemented by a housing allowance (MK15,500), a duty allowance (MK4,500) and a 25 percent taxfree gratuity at the end of the contract. This amounts to approximately MK53,000 (currently US$660). In addition, the investigator gets MK980 per day to cover personal expenses when traveling within Malawi and US$250 when traveling abroad. Moreover, the medical expenses of the employee's family are covered by the ACB.

Monitoring and evaluation of ACB's performance are done every year. Employees prepare a report on their own activities during the year under review and present it to an evaluation team made up of six people, including peers, supervisors and an external human resource officer. The team members then assess aspects of each employee's performance. The average score is used to determine whether the salary should be increased and by how much. These pay increases are purely on merit, but ACB staff also enjoy the salary increases that accrue to the rest of the civil service. So far this system has worked well, and, because discrepancies in assessment by the evaluation team members are small, the system has achieved credibility.

6   Concluding remarks

Since 1994 the Malawian authorities have implemented public sector reforms with the goal of increasing efficiency in the delivery of social services. However, although some institutions, such as the new ACB, appear to perform well above average, the progress made so far has been slow and intermittent. Still, the reform of the public sector is considered a long-term process and it has been important to learn from past mistakes.

Lack of accountability remains a serious impediment to raising efficiency in the public sector in Malawi. A number of issues need to be addressed in this regard, including the incentive structure, transparency, monitoring, evaluation and the disciplinary regime. There seem to be problems with all these factors in Malawi. Basic salaries are low, in real terms and relative to the private sector, and there has been a serious compression of the salary structure since the 1980s. On the other hand, the level of transparency, as well as compliance with rules and regulations, remains low. But a perhaps more serious cause for concern is the lack of a system that sanctions those who break the rules. Before democracy was reintroduced in Malawi (with the elections of 1994), accountability in government was upheld by a strict code of civil service conduct. Then, a mere suspicion of wrongdoing was enough to send civil servants to jail. Since this rigorous system has not been replaced with an effective system of deterrence under the new regime, democracy is sometimes blamed for increasing corruption and lethargy in the civil service.

The low level of accountability has also affected the government's budgeting process. Five years after the medium-term expenditure framework was introduced, there were still large discrepancies between policy goals, implementation and results. Evaluation of the outcomes is made difficult by the poor feedback from end-users, for example those receiving primary health care in the countryside. Lacking this information, it is difficult to assess the impact of the reforms and how to adjust future budgets in order to improve the public sector's capacity to target vulnerable groups.

An important lesson to learn from the Malawian experience is the necessity of public reforms to have champions right across the political hierarchy. At each level of administration, somebody has to take on the responsibility of pushing the reform forward. This also relates to the question of ownership. In many cases, the implementation of a program has depended on the exertion of pressure by multilateral and bilateral donors, often alienating civil servants in the process. Programs so implemented are prone to fail. Many donors now realize that, although they will need to continue providing the requisite financing and technical assistance, Malawian authorities must run the process if it is to have any chance of success. It is also necessary to encourage agencies outside government, such as civil society, business associations and academics, to take an active part in the development debate. This would broaden support for the reforms pursued and check government excesses.

Finally, in spite of the problems in the Malawian public sector listed above and the substantial amount of work still to be done, the government has taken important reform measures in the past few years. The reforms have been of a three-pronged nature. First has been a focus on the creation of incentives for improved performance in the civil service; second is the emphasis on inclusion and a participatory approach; third is the attempt to boost the institutions of the public sector, raising their efficiency and reducing corruption. The enhancement of the terms of service in government in recent years and the creation of an Ombudsman office and the Anti-Corruption Bureau to act as checks on government excesses are examples of the recent policy thrust. So far, progress in public sector reforms has been made thanks to political support from the president. However, for public sector reform to be sustained in Malawi, it will be necessary to incorporate broader sections of the population into the process.

Appendix

Table 6A.1 Malawi: Salaries and wages for selected civil service grades, December 2000

Salary grade	Representative/generic job titles	Annual salaries MK	Annual salaries US$
Super scale, administrative roles			
S1	SPC, chief justice	239,483	2,994
S2C	Deputy SPC	178,397	2,230
S2A	Attorney general	160,785	2,010
S2	Principal secretary	153,034	1,913
S3	Senior DPSS, ambassador	128,010	1,600
S4	DPS	118,467	1,481
S5	Chief, under secretaries	108,325	1,354
S6	Senior assistant secretary	84,018	1,050
S7	Principal administrative officer	76,029	950
S8	Senior administrative officer	68,159	852
Super scale, professional			
P1	Chief specialist	239,483	2,994
P2	Controller, commissioner	153,034	1,913
P3	Principal specialist	128,010	1,600
P4	Senior specialist	118,467	1,481
P5	Chief officer	108,325	1,354
P6	Assistant chief officer	84,018	1,050
P7	Principal officer (medical doctor)	76,029	950
P8	Senior officer (senior accountant)	68,159	852
Administrative and professional			
AO/PO	Professional/administrative officer (1st degree holder)	49,969	625
CEO/CTO	Chief executive/technical officer (accountant)	56,962	712
SEO/STO	Senior executive/technical officer	51,921	649
EO/TO	Clerical officer (diploma holder)	39,907	499
SCO/STA	Clerical officer	35,464	443
CO/TA	Clerical/technical assistant (O-level)	20,023	250
Subordinate staff			
SCI	Messenger	24,387	305
SCII	Messenger	19,366	242
SCIII	Messenger	15,541	194
SCIV	Messenger	12,970	162

Sources: World Bank (1994) and Department of Human Resource Management and Development, Government of Malawi.
Notes: The salaries are minimum salaries within each grade as of December 2000. The exchange rate used was MK80 per US$.

Notes

1. There are countries that have achieved rapid growth and rising living standards without fulfilling these requirements for good governance (e.g. South Korea). However, it seems unlikely that this can be repeated in sub-Saharan Africa given the experience of the last thirty-five years.
2. See Lazear (1995) for reviews of the literature on incentives in organizations.
3. *The Nation*, 1 March 2001.
4. The experience of the ACB is discussed in some detail in section 5.

REFERENCES

Adamolekun, L. and A. Mvula (1999) 'Malawi,' in L. Adamolekun (ed.) *Public Administration in Africa: Main Issues and Selected Country Studies*, Westview Press: New York.

Bardhan, P. (1997) 'Corruption and Development: A Review of the Issues,' *Journal of Economic Literature* 35:1330–46.

Collier, P. and J. Gunning (1999) 'Explaining African Economic Performance,' *Journal of Economic Literature* 37(1).

Goldsmith, A. A. (2000) 'Sizing up the African State,' *Journal of Modern African Studies* 38(1):1–20.

ILO (International Labour Organization) (1989) *Malawi Comprehensive Human Resources Study*, ILO: Geneva.

Kaluwa, B. and J. Musila (2000) 'Pro-Poor Budgeting in the Social Sectors, Efficiency or Uninformed Patronage: Some Answers from Malawi,' unpublished, Department of Economics, Chancellor College, Zomba, Malawi.

Lazear, E. P. (1995) *Personnel Economics*, MIT Press: Boston.

Lienert, I. and J. Modi (1997) 'A Decade of Civil Service Reform in Africa,' IMF Working Paper 97/179, Washington, DC.

Lungu, P. R. and J. L. Mugore (1999) *Review of the Action Plan for Civil Service Reform Part 1*, Malawi Government, Office of the President and Cabinet: Zomba.

Malawi Government (1998) 'Economic Report 1998,' *Budget Document* No. 4, Ministry of Finance and Economic Planning: Zomba.

——— (2000) *Malawi Interim Poverty Reduction and Growth Strategy Paper*, Ministry of Finance and Economic Planning: Zomba.

Malawi Government and World Bank (2000) *Malawi: Public Expenditure Review (Draft Report)*, Malawi Government: Zomba; World Bank: Washington, DC.

Ministry of Finance and Economic Planning (2000) *MTEF Phase Two: Consolidation and Revitalization: Overview of Plan of Action*, Ministry of Finance and Economic Planning: Zomba.

Moll, P. (2000) 'Agriculture Sector Review,' in *Malawi: Public Expenditure Review (Draft Report)*, Malawi Government: Zomba; World Bank: Washington, DC.

Msosa, C. P. (1998) 'Public Sector Reform,' memo, Department of Human Resource Management and Development, Government of Malawi, Zomba.

Mugore, J. (1997) 'Public Sector Reform in Malawi,' unpublished report for UNDP, Lilongwe.

Mutahaba, G., R. Baguma and M. Halfani (1993) *Vitalizing African Public Administration for Recovery and Development*, Kumarian Press: Connecticut.

Prior, F. L. (1990) *The Political Economy of Poverty, Equity and Growth*, Oxford University Press: Oxford.

Reinikka, R. (2001) 'Recovery in Service Delivery: Evidence from Schools and Health Centers,' in R. Reinikka and P. Collier (eds.) *Uganda's Recovery: The Role of Farms, Firms and Government*, World Bank: Washington, DC.

Schacter, M. (2000) 'Sub-Saharan Africa: Lessons from Experience in Supporting Sound Government,' ECD Working Paper Series No. 7, World Bank, Washington, DC.

Tanzi, V. (1998) 'Corruption around the World: Causes, Consequences, Scope and Cures,' *IMF Staff Papers* 45(4).

——— (2000) 'The Role of the State and the Quality of the Public Sector,' IMF Working Paper 00/36, Washington, DC.

Van Rijckeghem, C. and B. Weder (1997) 'Corruption and the Rate of Temptation: Do Low Wages in the Civil Service Cause Corruption?' IMF Working Paper 97/93, Washington, DC.

Wescott, C. (1996) 'Civil Service Reform: Lessons from Africa,' in *Civil Service Reform in Sub-Saharan Africa, Analysis and Policy Document*, UNDP: New York.

World Bank (1994) 'Malawi Civil Service Pay and Employment Study,' Report No. 13071-MAI, Washington, DC.

——— (2000) *African Economic Indicators*, World Bank: Washington, DC.

7

Incentive structure and efficiency in the Kenyan civil service

Damiano Kulundu Manda

1 Introduction

At independence in 1963, the civil service in Kenya was, as in other African countries, dominated by non-African expatriates. Although the policy of Kenyanization saw the lower ranks of the service gradually occupied by African Kenyans, the top levels were retained by Europeans. However, the need to attract high-caliber employees into the service necessitated a high degree of wage differentiation, which became the distinguishing feature of the Kenyan civil service for many years. The Kenyans who eventually took over from the expatriates in the first decade of independence came to enjoy high emoluments, since public wage structures remained largely unchanged (Rempel, 1981). In subsequent years, and in response to the slow job creation in the rest of the modern sector, there was a dramatic expansion in the size of the civil service. An acute lack of space and facilities in government offices followed, and duties were often duplicated.

By the late 1980s it had become clear that the government could no longer sustain such high levels of civil service employment. This was also the view voiced by the donor community as well as the multilateral institutions. Civil service reform, they argued, would help reduce the number of public employees to manageable levels, increase wages and other conditions of service for those remaining in the system, and generally raise morale. Further, the government needed to put in place management and incentive systems that would alter the attitudes and behavior of civil servants, the goal being to create a more results-oriented public sector (see Langseth et al., 1995). Still, as in many other African countries that have been attempting civil service reform in the past decade, economic efficiency arguments have sometimes been superseded by political considerations, notably the need to preserve jobs and the capacity to provide rural services.

The Kenyan civil service is amongst the largest in sub-Saharan Africa, having experienced dramatic growth after independence. In the days of rapid economic growth in the 1960s and 1970s, it was also reckoned to be among the most efficient in the region. This chapter looks at the factors affecting the efficiency of the Kenyan civil service, with regard to service delivery and in meeting the objective of poverty reduction, with emphasis on incentive structures (ranging from wage emoluments, promotion procedures and sanctions against poor performance). On the basis of this analysis, a policy discussion is undertaken that focuses on ways in which policymakers can enhance civil service performance.

The chapter is structured as follows. First, I take a quick look at the development of the Kenyan civil service since independence. Section 3 reviews civil service reforms undertaken since the early 1980s, and their impact on employment and earnings, as well as on social services provision. After a brief presentation of theories of motivation, I look at the incentive structure in the Kenyan civil service, especially following the recent reforms. Section 5 consists of a summary and conclusion.

2   Overview of the public sector in Kenya

2.1   Structure and development

The main features of the public service in Kenya were laid out quite early in the colonial period, with provincial administrations consisting of sub-commissioners, district police and a hierarchy of chiefs, subchiefs and headmen. In the 1950s, twelve fully fledged ministries for public service provision were formed. There was also a parallel expansion in the apparatus of provincial administration aimed at bringing administrative services closer to the people. District officers were posted to every administrative division in the country, accompanied by professional and technical staff. Other important developments included the setting up of a public service commission as well as a police service commission. The two were meant to facilitate the recruitment of personnel and the preservation of regulations and standards in two of the most important sectors of the public service.

The public service commission was first established in 1954. It now consists of a chairman and five members, all appointed by the president. It is not independent from the appointing authority and political pressure has been brought to bear from time to time. The public service commission has not only the power to appoint, promote and transfer but also the power to retire any public service employee who has reached retirement age, or on grounds of ill health or poor discipline. In the latter case it can interdict or suspend the individual concerned from work or withdraw their salary. Lastly, the commission can also punish errant officers through various measures, such as outright dismissal, reduced rank or recovery of any loss caused by default or negligence.

The legal framework relating to the labor market in Kenya has not changed much during the course of structural adjustment. It continues to be guided by the government's desire to keep the labor movement under its control, with a view to ensuring that wages remain at levels that encourage the utilization of labor-intensive technologies. Government legislation has, in this regard, covered such issues as social security, healthcare provision, minimum wage laws and fringe benefits, including paid vacations, severance pay, housing allowances and statutory holidays. However, these laws and regulations are often enforceable only in the formal sector of the economy.

During the past few years, the government's wage guidelines to the private sector have undergone important changes. Upward revisions of minimum wages have, for example, been made at frequent intervals to compensate the lowest cadres for increases in the cost of living (Republic of Kenya, 1995a). It has also been necessary, in an increasingly sophisticated labor market, to accord more weight to labor productivity in collective wage bargaining. Also significant was the change in the legal system allowing employers to appeal against too high wage awards by the Kenyan Industrial Court.

In the 1960s and 1970s, civil service employees were relatively well paid, in some cases better than in the private sector. The government was able then both to attract qualified staff and to motivate them (Republic of Kenya, 1966). In addition, following recommendations from a Commission of Inquiry during 1970–1, civil servants were permitted to own and run private businesses so long as they were publicly declared. This controversial measure has been the subject of debate and criticism ever since. Conflicts of interest have been cited, even after the government adopted a code of ethics for civil servants in 1979 in a bid to address them. Still, sources of income outside the civil service have helped civil servants to supplement their rapidly declining real wages. O'Brien and Ryan (2000) have shown that real wages in the public sector fell by 65 percent between 1970 and 1994.

Given the budgetary constraints mentioned above, the falling real wages were a direct market response to the rapid growth of public sector employment. Throughout the 1970s and 1980s public employment grew much faster than both the economy and the budget itself. For instance, civil service employment grew by 7.4 percent per year, rising from 160,000 in 1979 to 277,600 in 1989 (O'Brien and Ryan, 2000), although the economy itself grew by 4.4 percent per year during the period. The government's blank guarantee of employment to graduates from its tertiary institutions, including universities, was a major contributing factor to the rapid growth of public employment. However, the guarantee was discontinued in the late 1980s owing to its unsustainability following the government's decision to implement a fivefold expansion in enrollment in public universities.

The civil service then simultaneously experienced excess demand for employment at the entry level while more responsible positions, at higher levels, remained vacant for failure to make the remuneration attractive. Although the latter problem was less serious than in neighboring countries, it certainly hampered the implementation of key aspects of the government's program. In the second half of the 1980s, the government received large amounts of budgetary and balance of payments support from the International Monetary Fund and the World Bank. This loosened the budgetary constraints, enabling the government to defer personnel retrenchment and the taking of other difficult expenditure-reducing decisions (O'Brien and Ryan, 2000). However, by 1993, action on fiscal reform was not only imperative, but had also become a key demand of the donor community. A civil service reform program was thus launched in 1993, supported by the World Bank, the United Nations Development Programme and several bilateral donors. On the whole, as will be shown below, the reform has had limited success.

2.2   Employment in the civil service

At least up to the late 1980s, the government had behaved like a residual employer in the modern sector of the economy. The share of the public sector in total wage employment rose from approximately 30 percent at the time of independence in 1964 to 47 percent by 1981 (see Table 7.1). It increased further to 50 percent by 1989, but then declined sharply in the following decade, reaching 41 percent in 1999. The share of the civil service in total public sector employment ranged between 40 and 44 percent in 1981–9, declining thereafter to 31 percent in 1999. Table 7.1 indicates that civil service employment was declining from the late 1980s to the end of the 1990s. The decline was due partly to the declining economy, and partly to the freezing of recruitment and the introduction – very

Table 7.1 Kenya: Wage employment in the formal sector and in the civil service, 1981–99

Year	Total formal employment ('000)	Public sector employment as % of total formal employment	Share of civil service workers in public sector employment (%)	Growth in civil service employment (%)
1981	1,024.3	47.2	44.3	0.2
1982	1,046.0	48.3	42.9	1.0
1983	1,093.3	48.3	42.9	4.5
1984	1,119.7	48.4	42.7	2.1
1985	1,174.4	48.9	43.9	9.0
1986	1,220.5	49.1	43.3	3.1
1987	1,264.5	49.4	43.9	5.7
1988	1,311.0	50.4	40.9	−1.4
1989	1,335.6	50.3	41.1	3.5
1990	1,409.3	49.7	39.1	−2.3
1991	1,441.8	49.6	38.3	0.0
1992	1,462.0	47.4	38.8	−1.7
1993	1,474.9	46.5	39.0	−0.4
1994	1,504.4	45.7	37.3	−4.1
1995	1,557.0	44.3	35.0	−6.0
1996	1,618.8	43.3	32.5	−5.6
1997	1,647.4	42.5	31.3	−3.9
1998	1,664.9	41.9	30.7	−2.3
1999	1,673.6	40.8	30.5	−2.6

Source: Republic of Kenya, *Economic Surveys* (various issues).

much under the influence of the donor community – of civil service retrenchment programs.

In addition to its role of employer, the government undertook measures that had direct effects on the rest of the labor market. During the periods 1964–5 and 1970–1, tripartite agreements were reached between the government, employers and trade union representatives with a view to wage moderation in exchange for employment expansion in both the private and public sectors. It was hoped that up to a 10 percent increase in employment would be realized thereby.

Ironically, although there was excess demand for employment in Kenya, there was also a serious shortage of skills. However, as in other African countries, the skill requirements vary considerably from sector to sector. The main source of skill formation has been the formal school system.[1] The formal education system has seen a rapid expansion since independence, with the growth of school enrollment, at all levels, exceeding the rate of growth of the labor force. Since high wages were ini-

Table 7.2 Employment in the public sectors of East African countries

Country	Government wage bill as % of		Public service workers as % of population
	GDP	Current expenditure	
Kenya	9.4	37.3	2.0
Tanzania	5.2	32.9	0.9
Uganda	3.0	29.7	1.0

Source: IMF (1997).

tially used as a means of inducing an adequate supply response, the returns to education proved to be quite significant, leading in turn to a further demand for education. The government's subsidization of education in general served to magnify its returns. In the early 1970s, the Kenyan education system was acknowledged as the only means to well-paying and prestigious jobs. This was further to enhance the process of certification in Kenya (Republic of Kenya, 1973). However, the rapid expansion of the education system, as well as the high demand for formal schooling, in the face of a stagnating economy led to excess labor supply as the markets began to assert themselves.

The impact of this educational expansion is clear. The level of schooling of those currently in the labor force in both private and public sectors has risen considerably, while the share of those with no education has fallen steadily in the past few years. New entrants to waged employment are more likely to have secondary education than the ones already there. Still, although the expansion in education has been associated with a general reduction in returns to education over time (see Kulundu Manda, 1997; Appleton et al., 1999), returns to university graduates remain high compared with lower levels of education, probably reflecting scarcity of skilled labor.

In terms of skill composition, only a small proportion (10.8 percent) of civil service employees occupy professional and higher technical cadre jobs, and managers account for about 1 percent of the total. The disproportionately small share of professionals and managers in civil service employment explains to some extent the poor performance of the public sector. The government has introduced inspectorates in an attempt to raise productivity. With respect to gender, women constitute about 20 percent of total civil service employees, and only about 9 percent of senior management.

Kenya's public service employment is about 2 percent of total population, which is double the share in its neighbors in East Africa, Uganda and Tanzania (see Table 7.2). In addition, the government spends 9.4 percent of GDP on public services, compared with 5.2 percent for Tanzania and 3.0 percent for Uganda. In terms of the proportion of public expenditure that finances government wages, the Kenyan level is higher regionally, at about 37.3 percent, with Tanzania and Uganda at 32.9 and 29.7 percent, respectively. Whereas in Tanzania and Uganda aid inflows have helped assuage the burden on the budget, in Kenya the government resorted to increased domestic borrowing to finance its wage bill (Wamuyu and Shaw, 1998).

The rapid growth of the public sector has had a number of negative implications. First, the expansion of the civil service has led to rapidly increasing government expenditure. Over 70 percent of the government's recurrent expenditure is spent on wages, leaving only about 30 percent for operational expenses, including vehicles, equipment and other supplies. Relatively low expenditure on operational expenses has meant that existing facilities, including personnel, are underutilized or poorly maintained. Second, it is difficult to increase wages for civil servants without decreasing their numbers substantially, since even marginal increases in personnel emoluments have in the past led to disproportionately large increases in the total budget. Third, for the lower cadres, the rapid expansion of the civil service has led to poor supervision, because the professional categories have grown relatively slowly. Understaffing in the middle- to upper-level positions in the civil service is, as already noted, partly a result of unattractive pay in the civil service compared with the private sector.

3   Civil service reform

3.1   Initiating reform

With the onset of economic crisis in the 1980s, it became clear that the size of the Kenyan civil service was not sustainable. However, although the government first stated its intention to reduce public sector employment in 1986, it was not until the 1990s, when the public works ministry laid off a large number of its casual workers, that the process began in earnest.[2] The government also rescinded its employment guarantees to graduates from higher institutions of learning, notably the universities. From the 1990/91 financial year, the government sought to constrain the growth of central government employment to only 2 percent per annum, and that of employees under the Teachers Service Commission to 5 percent (Ikiara, 1992; Ikiara and Ndung'u, 1987). Other measures included staff redeployment, with emphasis on essential services, and the abolition of the hiring of temporary staff. Earlier, in the mid-1980s, the mandatory retirement age was reduced from 60 to 55 years and voluntary retirement with full retirement benefits to 50 years.

The civil service reform instituted in April 1992 had the objectives of improving the quality of public services, reducing government expenditure, raising the productivity of the civil service and rationalizing staffing levels. It was to be implemented in three phases. The first focused on the reduction of the number of civil servants, in a bid to cut costs. The second phase was meant to bring about a marked improvement in policy analysis and performance. The third stage was to focus on the improvement of finance and general management (Republic of Kenya, 1995a). Marking a departure from earlier attempts, the reform program sought to reduce the size of the civil service, at 272,000 in the early 1990s, at a rate of 6 percent per year for five years. This amounted to 16,000 individuals per year, with up to 6,000 layoffs achieved via normal attrition, and the rest laid off through a voluntary retirement scheme (Republic of Kenya, 1994). Those retrenched were expected to seek employment in the private sector and in self-employment opportunities in either agriculture, small-scale manufacturing or commercial and trading enterprises. 'Golden handshakes' and other severance pay packages and some retraining were offered to the retrenched to facilitate their entry into self-employment in the informal sector or small-scale agriculture.

Although retrenchment has caused much apprehension among civil servants, they have not been able to articulate their grievances collectively. Indeed, collective action on the part of public sector workers has been almost impossible since the banning of the civil servants' union in the 1970s. Attempts have been made to revive the union in recent years, but the government has continued to oppose it, and the threat of losing employment has made civil servants quite docile. The retrenchment program has added pressure to the country's volatile socioeconomic situation, and the political fallout has been considerable as well. For example, attempts to retrench up to 6,000 administrators (including chiefs and their assistants) from around the country were dropped for fear of the political implications.

Still, reform efforts have continued, especially following the introduction of the Civil Service Reform: Medium Term Strategy, 1998–2001. The program aims to retrench 48,000 public service workers, and 25,000 had already been laid off by the end of 2000. The improved state finances will enable the government to enhance public sector terms and conditions of service. But, reflecting the high level of political opposition to civil service reforms, a bill declaring retrenchment to be unconstitutional was recently passed by the Kenyan parliament.

Although it is generally agreed that poor civil service remuneration lies at the center of the incentive problems facing the government, it is still only one of the many causes of poor performance. In the budget speech for 1998/99, the finance minister noted that the recruitment and promotion procedures within the service must also improve. To restore professionalism in the civil service, better remuneration had to go hand-in-hand with career advancement based on merit.

Training has been identified as a key feature in efforts at raising the efficiency and productivity of the civil service. In 1995, the government embarked on a training program to uplift the skills of the civil servants. To ensure that training becomes part and parcel of the civil service reforms, the government has restructured the Kenya Institute of Administration, which now undertakes training, research and consultancy services on a commercial basis. However, in spite of the above reforms, the remuneration of public employees relative to their counterparts in the private sector is still low. Given the number of employees still retained in the civil service, the wage bill is small and further retrenchment might be needed if the government's ambition of offering a competitive wage is to be realized.

3.2 The impact of retrenchment

The retrenchment program has adversely affected the lower job categories in the civil service more than the more skilled levels. First, the lower cadres constitute about 88 percent of the entire civil service, and some 50,000 of them were retired between 1993 and 1998. Second, the opportunities for retraining have been geared towards more skilled workers. Third, prospective job openings, for example the parallel increase in teacher recruitment to improve education services, benefited more skilled categories.

The voluntary early retirement scheme (VERS), targeted mainly at skilled categories, reduced the size of the civil service by 24,080 employees between May 1994 and October 1995. Even with high one-off VERS implementation costs totaling KSh 4.4 billion, the government was still able to save about KSh 1.2 billion in salaries and allowances per year. Some of the resultant savings from the scheme have been ploughed back into the public sector, especially to increase operations and maintenance expenditure, improve the delivery of services and increase the level of job satisfaction among those remaining in the civil service (Republic of Kenya, 1995b).

However, voluntary retirements have not been applied evenly across ministries and districts. There are indications that some job cadres have been affected more than others, with adverse implications for efficiency in some line ministries and for the deployment of personnel and other resources in the more marginalized regions of the country (Republic of Kenya, 1995b).

4   The incentive structure in the Kenyan civil service

4.1   Theoretical aspects

Before looking at incentive structures in the Kenyan civil service, let us briefly present some theoretical aspects related to incentives in the public sector. They can be divided into two broad categories: content theories, which analyze individual employees with the aim of identifying their needs and their variance; and process theories, which try to explain how the reward structure affects employee behavior.

Among the best-known content theories is Maslow's hierarchy of needs (Maslow, 1954), which posits that human needs can be arranged hierarchically. Individuals seek first to satisfy their primary needs, such as food and shelter, but quickly look beyond these motivations as their situation improves. A related theory is that of acquired needs, ascribed to McClelland (1962). It posits that individuals develop the need for achievement, power and affiliation over a period of time and are in turn motivated by these needs. Herzberg's motivation-maintenance theory argues that factors that cause job satisfaction have a stimulating effect on performance and morale, whereas those that cause job dissatisfaction have a negative impact. Positive factors are intrinsic to the job; negative factors are extrinsic. That is, people are happy with their work when they are doing a good job, which enhances their experience and expertise. On the other hand, job dissatisfaction is a result of shortcomings in the workplace, for example when workers are being paid low wages, working conditions are unsafe or workers fear for loss of their jobs (Megginson et al., 1983).

Turning to process theories, expectancy theory predicts that workers' motivation will be low if they feel that the performance level required for promotion is unattainable, they are not confident that high performance will result in career enhancement, or they attach little value or significance to promotion. It is important, therefore, to understand the needs of individual employees and adjust their reward profile accordingly. The second process theory is the equity hypothesis (see Adams, 1963). Here feelings of equity and group solidarity in the workplace play an important role in the behavior of individual employees. Workers feel inequitably treated when their rewards are lower than those for similar employment in their organization or elsewhere. Individuals who feel that they have been overpaid, or who perceive positive inequity, increase the quantity or quality of their work, whereas those who feel underpaid reduce their work effort. Rewards perceived to be equitably distributed increase job satisfaction and thus lead to a higher level of effort and performance. The goal-setting motivation theory, due to Locke and Latham (1984), postulates that well-set organizational goals are important sources of motivation. Employees are made aware of the direction that needs to be taken and can gauge the effort required to achieve the goals of the organization. Lastly, the reinforcement theory, instead of attempting to explain what people do to meet their basic needs or to achieve personal goals, focuses on the external environment and the consequences it holds for individuals within and outside the organizational setting. Positive reinforcement increases or strengthens the frequency of desired behavior by making a pleasant consequence contingent on the occurrence of certain behavior. Negative reinforcement, on the other hand, strengthens desirable behavior via punishment. The above theories throw considerable light on the experience of the Kenyan civil service, particularly the apparent lack of motivation.

4.2   The existing incentive structure

In a study of six African countries, Negandhi (1985) finds that workers in the African civil services, much like in other parts of the world, desire quality employment. They demand job security, opportunities for advancement, good working conditions and an impartial mechanism for promotion and reward (see also Jaeger and Kanungo, 1991). Good governance and a more democratic approach to management in the public sector are also key ingredients in current efforts at reforming the civil service. In a study of Cameroon, Ndongko (1999) notes that, in spite of hierarchical impediments, civil service managers perceived to be democratic in their treatment of staff were also able to explain the rationale behind the reform being attempted and to elicit higher levels of performance from those under them.

In Kenya, the terms and conditions of service are key ingredients in the incentive structure. However, as indicated above, salaries and other benefits in the civil service are reviewed only about every six years, whereas those in the private sector are reviewed every two years, in accordance with the government's wage guidelines. When the period between salary reviews is this long, a cumulative erosion of the purchasing power of civil servants is bound to take place. This affects their morale as well as productivity.

Two important entitlements for civil servants are housing allowances and medical care. The housing allowance has been a key feature in the benefits package since colonial days. In the 1960s, and partly as a deliberate attempt to create an elitist civil service, houses were provided to government workers at very low nominal rents. However, the government's own stock of houses was quickly outstripped by the number of employees in the public sector, necessitating complex non-price rationing procedures, based on seniority and longevity of service. Subsequently, a housing allowance in lieu of a house allocation has become the standard procedure in most urban areas. However, in spite of frequent upward adjustment of housing allowances, they still cover only a fraction of the actual cost of housing. For instance, in 1997 the house allowance was about 15 percent of the monthly wage for a majority of workers in the service. This is lower than the 30 percent recommended by the government. Those lucky enough to be allocated a government house thus enjoy a substantial subsidy. Lower cadres of civil servants now live in seriously crowded neighborhoods, with poor access to social services such as water and sewerage outlets.

With respect to medical care, most civil servants are members of the National Hospital Insurance Fund. However, with the generally rising costs for medical care, the fund can now cover only a small portion of the total costs for treatment. Sickly households, often the poorest, soon find themselves shut out of the system as the amounts for which they are insured are exceeded. There are also a number of other allowances and benefits, including annual leave allowance, subsidized loans and, for senior officers, loans for the purchase of vehicles.

Thus bureaucratic practices in the Kenyan civil service are rules driven. However, the capacity to monitor and implement the rules and regulations remains inadequate. Those in management and supervisory positions share a partiality for exercising power for its own sake. Ultimately, civil service employees tend to see their jobs as a means of meeting their personal needs, as opposed to the broader goal of the efficient provision of social services. The style is quite rigid and subject to coercion (Jaeger and Kanungo, 1991) and few government goals are achieved. The alienation of workers increases when they cannot relate to the goals of the government (Kippis, 1976). This leads, in turn, to a cold and impersonal climate that does not enhance productivity. Government stores, plants and equipment, including vehicles, are often mismanaged. Since maintenance budgets are low or misused, repairs are rare or put off until the equipment breaks down.

How then is performance in the civil service evaluated? In Kenya, the systems for doing this are still very rudimentary, with the majority of civil servants lacking targets against which their performance can be measured. A confidential annual report, done for every employee by the supervisor, is meant to provide the basis for career advancement and other rewards. In practice, however, the document has become highly subjective, since there are no formal criteria for performance evaluation. There are also many cases of 'stagnation' for certain groups, indicating that, in dealing with promotions, the terms and conditions of services are not always adhered to. Since staff morale depends to a large extent on prospects for promotion, a serious lack of fair play and transparency in staff evaluation, as when the process is influenced by politics, affects overall morale negatively. Thus, although performance evaluation is an important tool for making decisions on issues of promotion, rewards, training and staff development, lack of objectivity has reduced its usefulness for policy and planning. The effective delegation of duties is crucial for bureaucratic efficiency. It ensures the proper utilization of employees, the sharing of responsibility and the satisfaction that comes with the achievement of shared goals. Above all, the delegation of duty is crucial for the training of junior officers. However, in a politicized civil service, this ceases to be a management tool and becomes a means for the exercise of patronage. The resulting environment is again not conducive to innovation and personal growth.

In conclusion, a poor incentive structure is the main cause of the failure of the Kenyan civil service to deliver high-quality services. Poorly paid and poorly motivated workers tend to pursue their own utility function, including opportunities for rent seeking, completely neglecting the goals of the government. For example, to make ends meet, civil servants are forced to engage in other income-generating activities, often using government offices as their base. Corruption in the procurement and delivery of goods and services has become a serious problem. All these factors imply that the effort dedicated to government work diminishes markedly.

In Kenya, improving the functions of the civil service has been a central concern of policymakers. The goverment's recent hiring of people from the private sector and the international civil service to rejuvenate the public sector and inject purposefulness in the running of the economy has raised hopes that a turnaround might be achieved. Still, reaching political consensus on the central reforms remains difficult. Moreover, the fact that the government is now ready to rely on a temporary team of private sector technocrats to revamp the civil service reveals the low state to which the public sector had declined, as well as the amount of work that will be required before it is restructured. However, the hiring of these technocrats, who draw market-based wages, introduces a dilemma with respect to future wage policy and manning issues. In the short term, the government might find it difficult to motivate civil servants to pursue the goal of poverty reduction, when, apart from the well-remunerated technocrats, government employees see little improvement in their lot. Many civil servants consider themselves among the poorest groups in the country and demand that their poverty be alleviated first.

4.3   Earnings in the Kenyan civil service

The government affects wage setting in the rest of the economy via its direct influence on wage setting in the public sector and through its minimum wage legislation. In earlier decades, this made the public sector a wage leader. Between 1963 and 1965, real earnings rose by 48 percent in the public sector but by only 6 percent for the private sector. Jobseekers were thus attracted to the civil service. By 1966, however, private sector salaries had started to catch up with those of the public sector (Collier and Lal, 1980). Indeed, as a study by Rempel and House (1978) suggests, the government had ceased to be a wage leader for unskilled labor by the early 1970s. Instead, a subset of firms, operating under imperfectly competitive conditions in the product market, had assumed wage leadership at the lower end of the wage distribution. Although the public sector remained a wage leader among skilled categories for much of the 1970s and 1980s, the private sector's influence on skilled wages increased in the 1990s. In recent years, the government's influence on wage setting in the country is less direct because it is no longer a strong competitor for skilled labor.

The setting of emoluments and terms of service in the civil service has evolved via the formation, from time to time, of civil service review commissions. In 1963, for example, the Pratt Commission submitted recommendations that led to rapid increases in salaries. The Millar-Craig Commission of 1967, for its part, considered a range of criteria for setting public sector salaries, including standard of living levels, comparisons with market-based wages and income equality. Noting that the earnings of civil servants had improved considerably in comparison with the incomes of smallholders, the commission recommended increases for low-wage earners only (Republic of Kenya, 1967). A similar concern for the low paid was expressed by the Ndegwa Commission, 1971, which also suggested increases in wages for the lowest paid in the public sector (Republic of Kenya, 1971). The Ndegwa Commission also established the principle that, as long as a 'code of ethics is observed,' public sector employees could be engaged in private economic activities. The implied conflict of interest, though seemingly mild at the time, became critical with the deterioration in public sector wages.

The 1980 Waruhiu Commission (Republic of Kenya, 1980) considered the extent to which the recommendations for the public service structure and remuneration suggested by the 1971 Ndegwa Commission had been implemented in order to suggest further action. The Waruhiu Commission noted that the state of the civil service, morale, productivity and efficiency had deteriorated in the 1970s and that an environment conducive to efficiency was lacking. It recommended that all public service officers declare their business interests and that implementation of changes in any aspect of their terms of service be conditional on this declaration. Although the recommendations of the Waruhiu Commission on salaries and other terms of service were promptly implemented, the radical restructuring of the civil service that it recommended was never attempted. Similarly, the Ramtu Commission of 1985 reviewed the structure of salaries and emoluments in the civil service and also considered the incentives required to attract and retain competent and qualified personnel (Republic of Kenya, 1985). The commission recommended salary increases for all workers, with proportionately more for those in the lower job cadres, noting that management was crucial for the improved performance and productivity of the civil service.

The Munene Commission of 1997 is the most recent effort at examining the structure of salaries and other terms and conditions of service in the public sector (Republic of Kenya, 1997). Compared with earlier commissions, it had the broader agenda of harmonizing the salaries and other terms and conditions of service of all the branches of the public service, including the education service. Like those before it, the commission noted that the salaries and allowances paid to civil servants were low and inadequate. Lags between salary reviews and phased implementation of compensation were to blame for the poor motivation and low productivity. Moreover, by not making efforts to close the gap between private and public sector pay, the government was risking loss of personnel to the private sector. The most significant recommendations of the Munene Commission were the need to establish a permanent public service pay review board, which would review pay and benefits matters on a recurrent basis and also ensure their harmonization across the public sector. The commission also recommended the development of schemes of service for every job cadre and the monetization of all payments, thus doing away with the current system of allowances and honoraria.

The above review of efforts to improve civil service performance based on the recommendations of government-appointed commissions shows that solutions have not been lacking – what is lacking is the government's willingness to implement them. Commissions became political pressure valves, which provided policymakers with excuses for not taking serious action. Indeed new commissions were appointed before the recommendations of the earlier ones were considered. Thus, in spite of the focus on wage improvements by the commissions, wages in Kenya fell sharply until the mid-1990s, when civil service reforms were embarked on (see Table 7.3). In the period 1991–4, when implementation of structural adjustment programs was disrupted by political problems as well as the aid embargo, which led to inflation, the decline in real earnings was large – over 20 percent in 1993 alone. However, since 1995 there have been

Table 7.3   Kenya: Changes in real earnings in the formal sector, 1981–99 (%)

Period	Private	Public
1981–5	−1.6	−2.3
1986–90	−0.9	−1.4
1991	−7.9	−9.9
1992	−9.2	−12.3
1993	−20.2	−24.2
1994	−8.5	−8.1
1995	22.5	16.1
1996	12.3	10.0
1997	8.8	7.6
1998	12.2	15.4
1999	13.0	9.0

Source: Republic of Kenya, *Economic Surveys* (various issues).

increases in real wages in both the private and public sectors. This recovery was partly a result of the reduction of inflationary pressure, as
weather patterns improved and the government returned to the negotiating table with its donors and the multilateral institutions, thus ensuring
resource inflows. Both the government and the private sector were able
to increase wages in real terms.

The decline and increase in real wages depicted in Table 7.3 indicate,
as already noted above, that wages have been responsive to labor market
conditions. Other African countries experienced similar changes in real
wages. In Côte d'Ivoire (Hoddinott, 1996), and in Africa more generally
(Jamal and Weeks, 1993), labor markets reacted to excess labor supply
with sharp declines in real wages. The same evidence indicates that African public sectors – unlike during the 1960s when Harris and Todaro
(1970) studied African labor markets – are no longer wage leaders. As
such, the centrally determined minimum wage or related legislation
cannot prevent wage erosion in the rest of the economy.

To conclude the wage comparison and to analyze the determinants of
earnings, we estimate, following Mincer (1974), separate semilogarithmic
earnings equations for the public and private sectors using data from a
Welfare Monitoring Survey conducted in Kenya in 1994. We restrict our
analysis to ordinary least squares regressions, with data drawn from the
urban portion of the sample, since it had more complete data. The results
of the regressions are presented in Table 7.4.

As indicated by the R^2, the earnings regression in the equation for
private sector workers in the sample is better explained by the independent variables than is the equation for public sector employees. This reflects the fact that in the public sector the wage-setting process is driven

Table 7.4 Estimated earnings equations for public and private sectors in Kenya

Variable	Private sector		Public sector	
Constant	6.3683*	(0.151)	7.2998*	(0.219)
Experience	0.0590*	(0.010)	0.0158	(0.013)
Experience squared	−0.0010	(0.002)	−0.00001	(0.001)
Skilled workers dummy	0.8381*	(0.075)	0.5787*	(0.073)
Primary dummy	0.0354	(0.132)	0.1017	(0.184)
Secondary dummy	0.4141*	(0.132)	0.2887	(0.181)
University dummy	1.7464*	(0.273)	0.9534*	(0.212)
Male dummy	0.5667*	(0.074)	0.1976*	(0.066)
Coast province urban areas dummy	−0.6905*	(0.102)	−0.1879	(0.117)
Rift Valley province urban areas dummy	−0.6729*	(0.104)	−0.3299*	(0.106)
Western province urban areas dummy	−0.7016*	(0.197)	−0.7749*	(0.134)
Eastern province urban areas dummy	−0.4482*	(0.119)	−0.2558*	(0.111)
Northeastern province urban areas dummy	−1.7608*	(0.274)	−0.5067*	(0.194)
Nyanza province urban areas dummy	−0.3475*	(0.130)	−0.1410	(0.114)
Central province urban areas dummy	−0.2345	(0.123)	−0.0556	(0.126)
R^2	.406		.222	
Number of observations	1,107		693	

Source: Regression estimates based on Welfare Monitoring Survey data of 1994 collected by the Central Bureau of Statistics, Kenya.
Notes: Dependent variable is the logarithm of monthly earnings; standard errors are in parentheses.
* Significant at the 90 percent level and above.

by government-appointed commissions whereas that in the private sector is more market determined. Importantly, experience is significant as a determinant of wage levels only in the private sector. Skill is important in both sectors. However, the premium attached to university education is much greater in the private than in the public sector. Thus, although the public sector is the single largest employer of university graduates, many see it as a place to acquire some experience to give them future access to better-paying jobs in the private sector. Primary education is no longer a determinant of wage levels in the formal labor market in Kenya.

With Nairobi as the area of comparison, the results show that regional effects on earnings are important for employees in both private and public sectors, but are more marked in the private sector. In the private sector, remoteness is a key factor in wage determination. Thus, location in the northeastern province has a large negative impact on private wages, whereas the effect of being located in the central province is much smaller. Table 7.4 shows that location effects on wages are generally milder in government than in private employment, in part a reflection of the relative homogeneity of the civil service labor market.

To summarize the discussion in this section, I have noted that, with the deterioration of the economy, real earnings in Kenya have contracted over time. However, the erosion of earnings has been more marked in the public than in the private sector. Although the government has relied on wage commissions to ensure timely adjustments, in fact commissions have had little positive impact on wages, with commission recommendations implemented in a patchy fashion, if at all. Skilled workers continue to be better rewarded in the private than in the public sector, explaining why it is difficult for the government to find sufficient numbers of qualified people for its management jobs. Clearly, the incentive structure of the civil service must be improved if the manning levels are to stabilize. Although it might be difficult to bring public sector earnings into line with those of the private sector in the medium run, public sector earnings must rise relative to those of the private sector if morale in the civil service is to be improved.

5   Motivating employees in the Kenyan civil service: Summary and conclusions

This chapter has looked at factors affecting efficiency in the Kenyan civil service. The country's civil service expanded rapidly after independence, becoming by far the largest in East Africa. However, by the late 1980s, and in the face of economic decline, it became clear that the government was no longer able to sustain a large public sector. Further, to raise efficiency, extensive civil service reforms were needed. The incentive structure of the civil service also needed changing in order to reflect the government's new priorities. Salaries and allowances for the civil service, especially for skilled workers, are lower than those in the private sector, and lack of equipment and space, poor compensation, the absence of a career development structure and poor delegation lower incentives for civil servants.

In summary, five aspects of incentive realignment in the civil service are worth reiteration. First, salaries and other emoluments of the civil service, once they reach a level deemed conducive to increasing morale and productivity, should be preserved in real terms via periodic reviews and in line with macroeconomic developments. The current huge gaps between government and private sector wages for highly skilled workers should be narrowed if the government is to retain its staff. In recent years, retrenchments have been used to reduce the size of the civil service and to improve productivity. However, the government has been slow in improving its working conditions, notably wages, and the positive impacts of a smaller and more flexible civil service are thus yet to be realized.

Second, the civil service needs to adopt more modern management techniques. This will enable it to respond rapidly to the challenges of development in Kenya, such as poverty reduction, decentralization and fiscal accountability. Better management will also ensure that a higher degree of efficiency in service delivery, especially in the countryside, is achieved. Some of the management practices that could be given more emphasis are management by objectives, performance evaluation, career planning, utilization and effective delegation. Management by objectives, though frequently mentioned in policy statements, has not been practiced to any large extent in the Kenyan civil service. To reach predetermined management objectives demands effective delegation. A general lack of an effective system of delegation in the Kenyan civil service has led to idleness and low morale. It is thus important to make the delegation of responsibilities part and parcel of the management culture in the civil service, as a means of introducing responsibility and mutual trust, and as a basis for leadership training.

Third, job descriptions and evaluations of job performance should become part of the professional culture of the civil service. This entails the introduction and development of clear job descriptions and schedules of work and the setting of targets on the basis of which civil servants are assessed. This would make it possible for the government to appraise individual performance, on which future promotions and other rewards depend, without bias. In relation to this, simple and transparent criteria for promotion should be put in place to eliminate political interference and corruption.

Fourth, civil servants cannot perform their duties effectively without adequate space, supplies and equipment. The bulk of government expenditure currently goes to wage compensation, and very little money is spent on equipment and general maintenance. Lack of space is quite serious in the countryside, and offices at district or provincial headquarters are often overcrowded. Very little improvement will be seen in the public sector's capacity to deliver services until the government increases the share of its budget going towards operational expenses.

Lastly, this study has demonstrated that a well-run civil service is a prerequisite for social economic progress in Kenya, but that a lot remains to be done before the sector acquires the resources needed to raise efficiency in government operations. However, the decline of working conditions in the civil service is not isolated and is closely linked to the poor performance of the rest of the economy. In a stagnant economy, the government was forced to turn the public sector into an employer of last resort for the increasingly large number of people graduating from state institutions. Thus, much as the improvement of the civil service is important for Kenya's economic performance, its reform also crucially depends on the revival of the economy – a mutual interdependence that must be recognized by policymakers.

Notes

1. The other major source of skill formation is on-the-job training.
2. In 1992, Nyayo Tea Zones, a government company, laid off a large number of workers as well.

BIBLIOGRAPHY

Adams, J. S. (1963) 'Towards an Understanding of Inequality,' *Journal of Abnormal and Social Psychology* 67.

Appleton, S., A. Bigsten and D. K. Manda (1999) 'Educational Expansion and Economic Decline: Returns to Education in Kenya 1978–1995,' Center for the Study of African Economies, Oxford University.

Collier, P. and D. Lal (1980) *Labour and Poverty in Kenya 1900–1980*, Clarendon Press: Oxford.

Harris, J. R. and M. P. Todaro (1970) 'Migration, Unemployment and Development: A Two Sector Analysis,' *American Economic Review* 60.

Hoddinott, J. (1996) 'Wages and Unemployment in an Urban African Labour Market,' *Economic Journal* 106.

Ikiara, G. K. (1992) 'Public Sector Retrenchment and Redeployment: The Case of Kenya,' ILO/JASPA Working Paper, Addis Ababa.

Ikiara, G. K. and N. S. Ndung'u (1987) *Employment and Labor Market during Adjustment; The Case of Kenya*, Employment and Training Department, International Labour Organization: Geneva.

IMF (International Monetary Fund) (1997) 'A Decade of Civil Service Reform in sub-Saharan Africa,' IMF Working Paper No. 179, Washington, DC.

Jaeger, A. M. and R. M. Kanungo (eds.) (1991) *Management in Developing Countries*, Routledge: London.

Jamal, V. and J. Weeks (1993) *Africa Misunderstood: Or Whatever Happened to the Rural Urban Gap?*, Clarendon Macmillan: London.

Kippis, D. (1976) *The Power Holders*, University of Chicago Press: Chicago.

Kulundu Manda, D. (1997) 'Labor Supply, Returns to Education, and the Effect of Firm Size on Wages: The Case of Kenya,' Ph.D. thesis, Gothenburg University.

Langseth, P., S. Nogxina, D. Prinsloo and R. Sullivan (eds.) (1995) *Civil Service Reforms in Anglophone Africa*, Economic Development Institute: Pretoria.

Locke, E. A. and G. P. Latham (1984) *Goal Setting: A Motivational Technique That Works*, Prentice-Hall: Englewood Cliffs, NJ.

McClelland, D. C. (1962) 'Business Drive and National Achievement,' *Harvard Business Review* 54.

Maslow, A. H. (1954) *Motivation and Personality*, Harper & Row: New York.

Megginson, L. C. et al. (1983) *Management: Concepts and Appreciation*, Harper & Row: New York.

Mincer, J. (1974) 'Schooling, Experience and Earnings,' NBER: New York.

Ndongko, T. (1999) 'Motivating the Workforce in Africa' in J. M. Waiguchu, E. Tiagha, and M. Mwaura (eds.) (1990) *Management of Organization in Africa: A Hand Book and Reference*, Quorum Books: London.

Negandhi, A. R. (1985) *Organizational Theory in an Open System: A Study of Transferring Advanced Management Practices in Developing Nations*, Dunellen: New York.

O'Brien, S. and T. Ryan (2000) 'Aid and Reform in Africa: Kenya Case Study,' mimeo, Nairobi.

Rempel, H. (1981) 'The Labor Market,' in *Papers on the Kenyan Economy: Performance Problems and Policies*, Heinemann: Nairobi.

Rempel, H. and W. J. House (1978) *The Kenya Employment Problem: An Analysis of Modern Sector Labor Market*, Oxford University Press: Nairobi.

Republic of Kenya (1966) *The Kenya Civil Service: Its Efficiency, Morale and Organization*, Government Printer: Nairobi.

—————— (1967) *Report of the Salaries Review Commission*, Government Printer: Nairobi.

—————— (1971) *Report of Commission of Inquiry: Public Service Structure and Remuneration Commission*, Government Printer: Nairobi.

—————— (1973) *Sessional Paper on Employment*, No. 10, Government Printer: Nairobi.

—————— (1980) *Report of the Civil Services Review Committee 1979–80*, Government Printer: Nairobi.

—————— (1985) *Report of the Civil Service Salaries Review Committee*, Government Printer: Nairobi.

—————— (1991) *Report of the Civil Services Salaries Review Committee 1990–1991*, Government Printer: Nairobi.

—————— (1994) *Economic Survey*, Government Printer: Nairobi.

—————— (1995a), *Economic Survey*, Government Printer: Nairobi.

—————— (1995b) *Report on the Impact Assessment of the Staff Reduction in the Civil Service*, Directorate of Personnel Management Civil Service Reform Secretariat, Office of the President: Nairobi.

—————— (1997) *New Conditions of Services for Kenyan Civil Service*, Directorate of Personnel Management Civil Service Reform Secretariat, Office of the President: Nairobi.

—————— (various issues) *Economic Surveys,* Government Printer: Nairobi.

Wamuyu, G. and R. Shaw (eds.) (1998) *Our Problems, Our Solutions: An Economic and Policy Agenda for Kenya*, Institute of Economic Affairs: Nairobi.

8

Incentive structure, civil service efficiency and the hidden economy in Nigeria

Mohammed Salisu

1 Introduction

It is not my father's work. Work or no work, I must collect my salary. (Sefiya T. Ajayi, former Nigerian Civil Service Commissioner)

As a major instrument for implementing government policies, the civil service in Nigeria is expected to be professionally competent, loyal and efficient. Nonetheless, it is now denounced, as are civil services elsewhere in Africa, for being corrupt, poorly trained and poorly attuned to the needs of the poor. Ironically, the civil service is expected to play the key role in managing and implementing reform programs in the country. This has led to a number of complex agency problems yet to be resolved. However, it is broadly acknowledged, and Nigerian experience attests to this, that, when the incentive structures in the civil service remain poor, its efficiency as well as its ability to effect policy, such as that directed toward reducing poverty, will remain very low.

   The main objective of this chapter is to analyze the incentive structures and efficiency of the Nigerian civil service. Section 2 of the chapter describes the evolving structure of the Nigerian civil service, dwelling on major legislation, wage-enhancing measures, civil service commissions and reform measures since the early 1980s. Section 3 analyzes the nature of incentive structures in the civil service and discusses their impact on work morale, efficiency and corruption. It also provides an empirical analysis of the extent of the hidden economy in Nigeria and its impact on production in the rest of the economy. Section 4 discusses how to approach the incentive problem in the Nigerian civil service, including issues of measurement and analysis. Section 5 concludes the chapter.

2   Evolving structure of the Nigerian civil service

2.1   Structure and functions of the Nigerian civil service

The origins of the Nigerian civil service date back to the beginning of the twentieth century with the introduction of British rule in Nigeria. The colonial masters introduced a dual system of administration: direct rule in the south and indirect rule in the north. A more formal civil service emerged in 1914, when the northern and southern protectorates were amalgamated to form the present geographical space called Nigeria. This, however, did not lead to a unified civil service until 1945, when significant changes were introduced based on the recommendations of the Walayn Committee. These changes included the admission of Africans into higher grades of the civil service and the creation of a central public service board. In 1954, a federal Public Service Commission was established and granted full powers to appoint, promote, dismiss and discipline junior civil servants. At independence on 1 October 1960, the powers of the renamed Federal Civil Service Commission were extended to cover all civil service grades.

The main function of the Nigerian civil service is to implement government policies. However, its ability to do this has depended crucially on the form of government of the day. As will be discussed in more detail later, the traditional role of the civil service in Nigeria has been severely diluted by the politicization of the civil service in recent years, undermining its credibility and integrity. Presidents or state governors have tended to listen more to their close political supporters and advisers than to professional civil servants. As a result, sharp friction arises between the advisers (usually political appointees) and the civil servants (career administrators), with the advisers always getting the upper hand. This has weakened the civil service, with workers lacking motivation because professional prospects are bound to diminish in a politicized civil service.

In a recent summary of the factors affecting the efficiency of the Nigerian civil service, Ajayi (1998) has noted, first, that overstaffing and the closely related poor remuneration of employees in public service are key factors. Secondly, there is poor assessment of labor needs and the use of wrong criteria to appraise staff performance. These two issues have led to poor recruitment procedures, inadequate training and ineffective

Table 8.1 Civil service reforms in Nigeria, 1934–94

	Year
Hunts Commission	1934
Harragin Commission	1945
Foot Commission	1948
Pillipson-Adebo Commission	1954
Gorsuch Commission	1954
Mbanefo Commission	1959
Morgan Commission	1963
Eldwood Commission	1966
Adebo Commission	1971
Udoji Commission	1972
Dotun Phillips	1985
Decree No. 43	1988
Ayida Review Panel	1994

Sources: Ikejiani-Clark (1997); Williams (1997).

supervision. There tends to be a lack of qualified technical support staff, in contrast to the abundance of general staff. The failure to carry out periodic assessment of staffing needs of the various departments leads not only to uneconomic systems of compensation but also to inadequate job description and poor physical working conditions. There has also been considerable political interference in the process of personnel administration, leading to improper delegation of power, ineffective supervision and corruption. The resulting apathy has in turn led to unauthorized and unreasonable absenteeism, lateness, idleness and, notably, poor workmanship.

For the above problems – relating to what is now generally referred to in the country as the 'Nigerian factor' – to be addressed, it is imperative that appropriate incentive structures to raise worker morale be put in place. Although successive Nigerian governments have attempted to address the above problems, it was ultimately not in their interest to tackle the 'Nigerian factor.' It was their means for survival.[1]

2.2   Civil service reforms in Nigeria

The Nigerian civil service has undergone a number of reforms with the aim of enhancing its efficiency and effectiveness. In fact, there have been no fewer than ten major commissioned reports on the problem (Table 8.1). However, the bulk of these reports focused on salaries, wages and conditions of service rather than on the more fundamental structural and attitudinal challenges of the civil service. Two commissions on the civil service, those led by Adebo (1971) and Udoji (1972), deserve special mention here because they attempted to take a broader look at impediments to the performance of the civil service. Whereas the Adebo Commission recommended the setting up of a public service review commission to examine fundamental structural issues,[2] the Udoji Commission focused primarily on the issues of increasing efficiency and effectiveness in the public service. The Udoji Commission recommended, among others, the introduction of an open reporting system for performance evaluation, as well as unified grading and salary structures covering all established posts in the civil services. To enhance policy coherence, the commission also suggested the creation of a senior management group, comprising administrative and professional cadres.

The recommendations of the Udoji Commission found easy passage, thanks to the oil bonanza of the 1970s, which raised government income substantially, but the post-boom period proved more difficult. High public sector borrowing requirements coupled with a growing external debt had forced the government to embark on structural adjustment programs, even as the civil service experienced an unprecedented rise in indiscipline and the rest of society witnessed a general increase in corruption and other crimes (see, for example, Williams, 1997).

As in many African countries, the civil service became unnecessarily hierarchical, less results oriented, conflict ridden, sectarian, and concentrated in urban areas, even following the rapid creation of new states in Nigeria. The environment was clearly not one to encourage high productivity nor was it appropriate for retraining and developing managerial capacities among civil servants. These shortcomings made another restructuring of the civil service inevitable. This came in the form of the Civil Service Reorganization Decree No. 43 of 1988 (see Williams, 1997). Its objectives were to promote a better execution of laws and policy; ensure an efficient and expeditious administration of government business; optimize expenditure and improve the economy; and increase efficiency in the implementation of government policies and programs through encouragement of personnel specialization. The reforms were also aimed at:

- increasing professionalism
- better alignment of the civil service within the presidential system of government
- decentralization and deregulation
- combination of authority with responsibility
- enhanced accountability
- increased checks and balances
- general modernization
- enhanced effectiveness, efficiency and speed of operation.

However, the decree also introduced a number of rigidities into the system that would harm the reform process. First, the posts of head of the civil service and permanent secretary were abolished. The replacement for the latter became a political appointee. Moreover, ministers now became the accounting officers instead of permanent secretaries as in the previous arrangement. The intention had been that a combination of the tasks of chief executive with those of accounting officers would improve ministers' oversight of their ministries and departments, thereby enhancing overall efficiency. This was not achieved.

These and other limitations and constraints meant that Civil Service Reorganization Decree No. 43 of 1988 would not have a lasting impact – Williams (1997) has discussed why this was the case. First, knowledge about its provisions among civil servants and government functionaries was fairly limited. Moreover, fearing that their power would be eroded, some ranking officers slowed down important aspects of its implementation. Above all, the government had had a poor strategy for its implementation. Funds for the introduction and entrenchment of its provisions were lacking, and the deployment of officers, a central feature of the reform, had not been thought through. Thus, ultimately, implementation was piecemeal and lacking, for example, sanctions for infringing the reform's provisions. To address these issues, the government set up the Ayida Review Panel (1994). It led to the repealing of Decree No. 43 and to a comprehensive overhaul of the civil service. The Ayida Review also depoliticized the civil service. The permanent secretary post was revived, as was that of civil service head. The former is now the chief accounting officer in the ministry, while the secretary to the government acts as the head of the civil service.

2.3   The public sector labor market

Any analysis of the Nigerian labor market is likely to be fraught with difficulties, owing to lack of comprehensive statistics on the labor force. Existing labor market survey data are limited and highly aggregative in nature, and the quality of official statistics is questionable because there are wide discrepancies between the information reported by various government agencies. The segmented nature of the labor market – with three distinct categories of urban formal, urban informal and rural – complicates matters further. The public sector is the main employer in the formal sector. However, the formal sector accounts for only about 10 percent of total employment in the country (Collier, 1986; Ikpeze, 1996). The number of civil servants employed by the federal government is very small, and with a male bias (Table 8.2). Informal estimates from the state-level bureaucracies also indicate that proportionately more men

Table 8.2 Employment by gender in the federal civil service of Nigeria, 1988–93

Year	Total (number)	Male (%)	Female (%)
1988	255,579	87.2	12.8
1989	270,020	86.9	13.1
1990	287,278	84.5	15.5
1991	182,254	75.4	24.6
1992	191,329	76.0	24.0
1993	197,202	75.9	24.1

Source: Federal Office of Statistics (1997).

than women are employed by the public sectors. Besides access to education, where men have traditionally been favored, religious factors have played a significant role in this differentiation.

Available statistics indicate a low turnover in the federal civil service, but the bulk of the labor turnover in recent years was on account of retirement rather than outright dismissal or resignation. For example, around 85 percent of the 373 persons discharged from the federal civil service in 1993 had reached retirement age. This figure contrasts sharply with a mere 13 percent of only 109 civil servants discharged in 1990 (Federal Office of Statistics, 1995, 1997). Nearly 30 percent of discharged civil servants had their employment terminated in 1991 and 22 percent were dismissed in 1989. The civil service reforms referred to above have had much influence on the timing and pattern of resignations, terminations and dismissal of civil servants in Nigeria.

Government-owned tertiary institutions have been important in providing training and staff development programs for the public sector. These have been complemented by courses provided by the Administrative Staff College of Nigeria (ASCON), specifically designed for various cadres of civil servants. However, since enhanced skills do not command a premium in an environment that is not supportive of a professional civil service, civil servants have not been too enthusiastic about retraining. In 1995, more than 35 percent offered admission to ASCON failed to take up the offer. This figure is even higher in the case of courses that would normally lead to increased managerial responsibilities, such as personnel management, industrial relations, public administration and project management. There are two possible reasons some civil servants see no direct benefits in retraining in programs of over six months. First, there is fear of displacement. Second, for many civil servants the opportunity cost of training (that is, the lost income from bribery, corruption and other rent-seeking activities associated with their jobs) is very high. Still, there are some civil servants in the country who, although genuinely interested in acquiring vocational training, are unable to do so for lack of political

Table 8.3 Trends in real wages in the Nigerian civil service and inflation rates, 1970–97 (%)

	1970–9	1980–92	1970–92	1992–7
Real wages (annual change)	5.25	−14.12	−34.17	n.a.
Inflation (period average)	14.36	19.79	17.29	36.22
Maximum	29.17	44.00	43.15	72.81
Minimum	3.40	5.56	3.40	7.36

Sources: National Salaries, Incomes and Wages Commission of Nigeria, *Revised and Harmonized Public Service Salary Structure and Allowances for the Federal Public Service* (various); Federal Office of Statistics of Nigeria (various publications).
Note: The trend in real wages was estimated by regressing the logarithm of real wages against a time trend over the different subperiods.

support at the local level. In many cases, it is a case of superiors seeking to eliminate the competition that would arise if more of their staff were trained and hence liable to promotion.

2.4   Wage erosion and political patronage

As stated earlier, the successive civil service reforms in Nigeria had one common objective: to enhance the effectiveness and efficiency of the civil service. This was particularly necessary from the mid-1980s when the civil service was expected to play an important role in the implementation of structural adjustment and other reforms introduced by the government. The reforms tried to address economic growth, wage and employment issues, as well as training and human capital development.

Civil service wages and salaries in Nigeria not only are low, but also have declined in real terms in the past two decades. With the exception of the oil boom period of the 1970s, real wages declined on average by some 34 percent during the 1970–92 period and by about 14 percent during the 1980s (Table 8.3). Much of this decline was on account of the high inflation rates that the economy was experiencing. Although successive wage and salary reviews have tried to reverse these trends, it has been on the whole difficult to protect wages from serious erosion.

A number of other African countries also suffer from declining wage trends and wage compression. For example, Haque and Sahay (1996) have found that, in all but one of thirteen African countries, high-skill wages declined more than low-skill wages during the period 1975–85. Similarly, Nunberg and Nellis (1995) have found that, by the mid-1980s, the salary of top civil servants was less than ten times the lowest-paid rank in many African countries. Although recent attempts have been

Table 8.4 Monthly wages and salaries for semi-skilled workers in selected manufacturing industries in Nigeria, 1990

Industry	Monthly wage (naira)
Dairy products	13,000
Grain mill products	8,000
Soft drinks	22,000
Malt liquor and malt	13,000
Drugs and medicine	9,000
Glass and glass products	18,000
Tires and tubes	23,000
Soap, detergent and cosmetics	10,000
Fabricated metal products	10,000
Electrical and household appliances	11,000

Source: Federal Office of Statistics (1997).

made by some African countries (e.g. Ghana) to decompress salaries, such reforms fall short of the targeted goal of thirteen to one (Rose-Ackerman, 1999).

Civil servants are the lowest-paid group of workers in Nigeria. In 1990, the minimum wage payable to civil servants was about 500 naira per month, and a university graduate on Grade Level 8 Step 10 in the civil service earned less than N5,000 per month. Wages in private manufacturing (Table 8.4) are, for example, much higher than those in the public sector. Although there are no comparative data by grade level, anecdotal evidence suggests that public sector wages in Nigeria are lower than private sector wages. Clearly, there is a need to make the salary structure of the civil service more competitive in order to correct the image of the civil service. A demoralized and disgruntled worker whose image has been unduly tarnished cannot be an effective instrument of change.

Recently, there have been two successive attempts to increase the public sector minimum wage in Nigeria. The first was introduced by the military regime of General Abdulsalami Abubakar in 1998 when the minimum wage was increased dramatically from US$1.20 to US$41.77 per month (using a parallel market rate of N83.80 to US$1.00). The second attempt was undertaken in May 2000 by the new democratically elected administration of President Olusegun Obasanjo. The public sector minimum monthly wage was raised to US$53.91 (at the parallel market rate of N102.02 = US$1.00), that is by about 30 percent in nominal terms, but without compensating sufficiently for the wage erosion of the previous decade. Not only did minimum wages continue to be fixed, and thus quickly eroded by inflation, but they were sometimes beyond the budgets of state governments. The latter were thus unable to pay workers at the new minimum wage, which resulted in conflict between labor and state governments. What was meant as an incentive to public sector workers in a bid to enhance productivity thus became an impediment to the performance of state governments.

Political patronage is an important factor in the incentive environment of the public sector in Nigeria. Civil service appointments tend to reflect this in larger measure than the skills and professional qualifications of the individuals appointed. This has turned the Nigerian civil service into a highly politicized institution, and the changes in Nigerian leadership in recent decades have also led to disruptive shifts within the service. Given this erratic nature of the institution over the years, constructing workable incentive structures – based on better training, wages and promotion and increased responsibility – has been next to impossible. The civil service, in spite of its highly trained cadre of officers, has tended to drift along, overwhelmed by the expectations placed on it by the government and the general population.

2.5   Tension between federal and state bureaucracies

Nigeria operates a three-tier system of government: federal, state and local. At present, the country consists of thirty-six 'autonomous' states,[3] each of which has its own civil service. Each state also consists of a number of local administrative units.[4] There is an administrative gap between the states and between the local administrations within each state.

Generally, there are several formal and informal channels of federal–state cooperation, particularly in areas of housing, national economic planning, agriculture and finance sourcing from both domestic and international markets. The need for cooperation was clearly spelt out in the 1979 Constitution, which emphasizes a coordinated approach in the field of economic planning and socioeconomic development, with the federal government playing the leadership role (Okoroji, 1997). Two intergovernmental sets of bodies play a major role in the management of federal–state relations in Nigeria. One set of organs that enjoys constitutional status is the state council and the national economic council, responsible for advising the president of the federation on economic affairs, especially on measures necessary for the coordination of the economic programs of the various local governments of the federation.[5] Another intergovernmental body consists of committees established by convention (formal channels) specifically to deal with matters relating to education, health and agriculture.

In spite of all this, federal–state relations in Nigeria over the years have largely been characterized by issues that were conducive to tension rather than harmony. Some of these areas of tension between federal and state bureaucracies involve revenue allocation, jurisdictional conflict over the powers of the federal and state governments in certain matters such as land, the role of federal bureaucracy in state capitals and state liaison offices in the federal capital, and the principle of federal character in civil service appointments. Of all these issues, revenue allocation is the most contentious. This was demonstrated recently by the proclamation by some state governments that they would take direct control of the resources (particularly crude oil) found within their own territorial boundaries. This prompted the federal government to take all thirty-six state governments to the supreme court of Nigeria over the resource control issue.

3   Corruption and rent seeking in Nigeria: An investigation

3.1   Introduction

Mismanagement and corruption are major problems in Nigeria, and in many other African countries, adversely affecting the effectiveness and efficiency of the civil service.[6] The phenomenon of corruption poses a number of questions, not necessarily confined to the civil service. What are its socioeconomic determinants? Is it a culture-bound phenomenon? Has economics, as a discipline, anything to offer in explaining it?

Corruption in Nigeria can be analyzed in terms of the forces of supply and demand. There is usually a supply of corruption as well as a demand price for it. It is often argued that bureaucratic interference in the market mechanism is one of the principal causes of corruption. What sorts of interventions raise the demand price of corruption by bureaucrats and in what circumstance will citizens increase their supply price of corruption? Are the demand and supply forces much more different in Nigeria and other developing countries than in developed countries? Do dictatorships such as those that, until recently, ruled Nigeria increase the demand price of corruption? Equally interesting questions arise in the context of the impact of corruption. Some corruption, it is said, is necessary for the smooth functioning of governance – it oils the wheels of the administration.

The *Financial Times* has argued that Nigerians see nothing wrong with 'using public funds to disperse favours to a cousin or to build a well for one's village, as it is an informal means of redistributing wealth.'[7] Such acts are considered as a lubricant or a positive sum game of 'give and take' which is widely practiced in employment offers, the award of contracts and import licenses, and even for obtaining admission to higher education institutions. The visible riches of the corrupt and the greedy spur the poor to imitate their lifestyles and modes of wealth acquisition. But does a market-oriented economy necessarily yield more corruption-free outcomes than a dirigiste economy?

3.2   Causes of corruption and rent seeking: An overview

The literature on rent seeking and directly unproductive profit-seeking economic activities provides some insight into the questions raised above. Policy-induced corruption arises when pervasive regulations exist and government officials have discretion in applying them. Private parties may be willing to pay bribes to government officials in order to obtain some of the rents generated by the regulations. As Tanzi (1994) argues, the problem becomes worse when regulations lack simplicity and transparency. The following are some of the government-induced sources of corruption that have been identified in the literature (see Mauro 1995, 1997):

- trade restrictions
- government subsidies
- multiple exchange rate practices and foreign exchange allocation
- low wages in the civil service relative to private sector wages or per capita GDP.

Table 8.5 shows these and other determinants of corruption, many of which fit Nigeria and many other African countries.

Although the bulk of the theoretical literature on rent-seeking behavior has generally concentrated on quantitative restrictions on international trade, such behavior can be extended to cover other forms of government restrictions on economic activity. Rent-seeking competition may sometimes be legal, but in many instances it takes illegal forms such as bribery, corruption, smuggling and other 'hidden' activities. Multiple exchange rate practices and foreign exchange schemes – whose importance may be proxied by parallel exchange market premia, such as those used by Levine and Renelt (1992) – also lead to corruption. In developing countries, in particular, where state-owned commercial banks ration foreign exchange at the discretion of bank managers, the supply price of bribes could be substantial.

Table 8.6 shows the official and parallel exchange rates for the naira from 1987 to 2000. The gap between the official and parallel rates, a proxy for the incentive structure in the economy as a whole, increased considerably, particularly during the later part of the Abacha regime (1996–8) and Abubakar Abdulsalami's one-year tenure in office (1998–9), when the official exchange rate was fixed at around N22 to the dollar. The democratically elected government of President Obasanjo, however, replaced the official rate with the interbank foreign exchange market

Table 8.5 Determinants of corruption

1. *Wage incentives*
- inadequate pay
- fringe benefits and other financial incentives

2. *Inefficient internal control*
- inadequate supervision and control systems
- lack of explicit standard of performance for employees and organizations
- poor recruitment and selection procedures for personnel
- too few or too many (non-transparent) rules and procedures (red tape)

3. *Insufficient external control*
- no law and order tradition, checks and balances
- lack of information made available to the public and freedom of press
- lack of mechanisms for citizens' participation and complaint
- difficulty of proving cases in court
- high social acceptance of corruption

4. *Statutory penalty rates*
- amount of fine, prison sentence
- administrative sanctions
- prohibition on ever being re-employed in the public sector
- penalties for relatives

5. *Extent of distortion*
- pervasive government regulations
- high statutory tax rates, non-transparent tax regulations
- provision of government services short of demand (government monopolies)

6. *Other factors*
- cultural factors
- culture of bureaucratic elitism and education of civil servants
- leadership
- ethnic diversity

Source: Van Rijckeghem and Weder (1997).

rate, which dramatically reduced the parallel market premium from nearly 300 percent to just 4 percent.

Endowments of natural resources, such as crude oil, provide a major source of economic rents because they can be sold at a price that far exceeds their cost of extraction. Sachs and Warner (1995) argue that resource-rich economies are more likely to be subjected to extreme rent-seeking behavior than are resource-poor economies. In Nigeria, for example, oil wealth is said to be one of the main causes of the pervasiveness of rent-seeking activities and corruption. The oil boom of the 1970s was responsible for the 'Dutch disease' syndrome in Nigeria, including contraction of agriculture (the principal non-oil tradable sector), appreciation of the real exchange rate and the loss of competitiveness of agricultural exports. Although the appreciation of the exchange rate was an

Table 8.6 Official and parallel market exchange rates for the naira, 1987–2000

Year	Exchange rate (N/US$)		
	Official	Parallel	Gap (%)
1987	4.016	4.601	15
1988	4.537	6.048	33
1989	7.365	10.530	43
1990	8.038	11.607	44
1991	9.910	13.425	35
1992	17.298	22.802	32
1993	22.065	n.a.	–
1994	21.996	n.a.	–
1995	21.889	n.a.	–
1996	21.889	82.300	276
1997	21.889	83.800	283
1998	21.889	86.000	293
1999	94.830	98.150	4
2000	98.050	102.020	4

Sources: World Bank (2000); Federal Office of Statistics (various publications).

inevitable response to the oil boom and to a new equilibrium situation, the use of oil boom resources to finance large-scale public expenditure programs introduced large-scale political corruption in Nigeria. The perennial fuel crisis in Nigeria (the world's sixth-largest producer of crude oil) can be attributed to corrupt practices, including hoarding, smuggling and willful damage to government-owned refineries.

Sociological and/or cultural factors such as customs, family pressures on government officials and ethnicity constitute potential sources of corruption. In Nigeria and most African countries, although traditional gifts and tributes to leaders often lead to what Brownsberger (1983) describes as 'polite corruption,' the extent of such corruption is relatively small. Much of Nigerian corruption is underlined by the ethics of dependency relations, ethnic loyalties and attitudinal tendencies, such as greed or love of ostentatious living, either in the culture at large or among a visible clique. It is also noteworthy that poverty, political instability and other societal forces increase public servants' susceptibility to corruption, especially when public officials feel that opportunities may vanish following a coup d'état or defeat at the polls or when their kinsmen place large demands on them (Colins, 1965; Nye, 1961). Similarly, where accumulated wealth for the legal support of their activities or families is lacking, there is pressure on public officials and organizations to use public resources for personal or sectarian ends via embezzlement, to take bribes, or to distribute jobs and contracts politically. These sociological and cultural causes of corruption are likely to continue for a long time in Nigeria, unless credible legal enforcement measures are put in place. The forces that deter corruption are often weak because some, if not most, of the law enforcement agencies are themselves corrupt. In addition, where politicians and civil servants are highly corrupt, professional organizations may be incapable of imposing sanctions on their members. Thus there are no agencies of restraint.

3.3 Magnitude of corruption in Nigeria

Anecdotal evidence on the magnitude of corruption in Nigeria can be found in media sources and the proceedings of various tribunals set up to investigate cases of alleged financial impropriety on the part of government officials. These include the cases of the US$4 billion looted by the Abacha regime, in which the UK Financial Services Authority indicted fifteen British banks,[8] and the US$4.5 billion secret Nigerian debt buyback scheme.[9] The UK Financial Services Authority and the Home Office are now launching their own investigations into the actions of London banks and financial institutions named in the reports. There was also the US$2.5 billion Ajaokuta Steel debt buyback scam involving Abacha's ministers.[10] Similarly, the 'missing' US$12.2 billion excess oil windfalls during Ibrahim Babangida's regime are yet to be accounted for.[11] *Newswatch* also reported fraudulent activities involving the transfer of millions of US dollars abroad by officials of the Central Bank of Nigeria, including a US$80 million overpayment to Chase Manhattan Bank; the reversal of entries on Paris Club debts to the tune of US$10 million; payments of US$27 million to SACE of Italy; large-scale pilfering of vital external debt documents, thereby making reconciliation impossible; and the release of US$25 million to COFACE of France.[12] Numerous cases of smuggling of petroleum products have created unnecessary fuel scarcity in the country.[13]

It should be noted here that Nigeria is not the only corrupt country in Africa. Corrupt practices can be found in many African countries. Although the extent and magnitude may vary between African countries, corruption and rent-seeking opportunities are widespread in most African civil services. In Mozambique, for instance, serious cases of corruption were found in customs, business regulations and foreign aid (Stasavage, 1999). Even Botswana, which provides an exemplary model of good governance in Africa, had its reputation dented during the early 1990s by a succession of scandals involving powerful politicians (Theobald and Williams, 1999).

In spite of the widespread corruption in Nigeria and other African countries, it is noteworthy that the documented cases do not tell the whole story as they relate to isolated acts of corruption. It is therefore crucial to utilize methodological approaches to measure the magnitude of corruption. One such approach is based on techniques for estimation of the size of the hidden economy. Bhattacharyya and Ghose (1998) argue that the disaggregated hidden economy estimates are very informative in identifying the growth of corruption. Evidence from India shows, for example, that the high rates of growth of the industrial sector's hidden economy during the 1980s and 1990s coincided with the timings of a large number of corruption cases uncovered by police departments in India.

A number of techniques have been employed to estimate the size of the hidden economy.[14] One is the factor analytic approach based on the statistical theory of unobserved or latent variables. A variant of this approach is MIMIC (multiple indicators/multiple causes) modeling, which is a special case of the LISREL (linear interdependent structural relationship) statistical model of Zellner (1970), Joreskog and van Thillo (1973), and Joreskog and Goldberger (1975).

A MIMIC model is a structural econometric model for estimating an equation in which the dependent variable is unobservable (latent). Frey and Weck-Hanneman (1984) pioneered the use of MIMIC modeling in the context of the hidden economy. Since then, a number of other studies have employed this technique (Aigner et al., 1988; Giles, 1997, 1999; Schneider, 1997). It is a powerful technique for estimating the underground economy, because it allows for simultaneous interaction between multiple explanatory variables and multiple indicators of the hidden economy. The latent variable is linked, on the one hand, to a number of observable indicators (reflecting changes in the size of the unreported economy), and, on the other hand, to a set of observed causal variables that are considered to be important determinants of the unreported economic activity. The MIMIC model equations can be written as:

$$y = \lambda\eta + \varepsilon \tag{8.1}$$

$$\eta = \gamma'x + \zeta, \tag{8.2}$$

where y is a column vector of indicators of the latent variable η and x is a column vector of 'causes' of η. In other words, equation (8.1) is the measurement model for η and equation (8.2) is the structural equation for the latent variable η. ε and ζ are the measurement and structural errors, respectively, and are assumed to be mutually uncorrelated.

Figure 8.1 shows the interrelationships between the (unobservable) hidden economy (η), its determinants (x) and the indicators (y). The theoretical literature on the hidden economy has identified four broad determinants: the burden imposed by the public sector on individuals

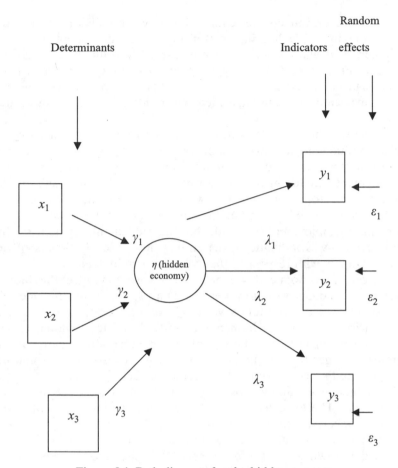

Figure 8.1 Path diagram for the hidden economy

(TB), tax morality (TM), labor market conditions (L) and structural factors (SF). In this context, and for the purposes of estimating the size of the hidden economy (η), equation (8.2) can be rewritten as:

$$\eta = \gamma_1 TB + \gamma_2 TM + \gamma_3 L + \gamma_4 SF + \zeta. \tag{8.2a}$$

The burden on the official economy may consist of the burden of taxation (measured by either the average or the marginal tax rate) and the burden of regulation (measured by the number of regulators or the ratio of the number of public sector employees to total employment). The a priori expectation on the coefficient of the tax burden is negative, implying that an increase in the burden will drive people into the hidden economy. Tax morality, however, reflects the readiness with which individuals leave the official economy. A decline in tax morality will reduce people's trust in government and will consequently increase their willingness to go underground. Frey et al. (1984) suggest that the consequences of tax immorality can be checked by a growing intensity of public controls and a rise in expected punishment, which will reduce the return on hidden activities.

In the case of the labor market, it is hypothesized that the incentive to work in the hidden economy is high for the unemployed, because they can work in the underground economy while at the same time receiving unemployment benefits. It is noteworthy, however, that although the demand for underground activity rises with unemployment, it is also likely that the supply of job opportunities in the hidden economy will fall with rising unemployment. Overall, the effect of unemployment on the shadow economy is ambiguous, depending upon the elasticities of demand and supply with respect to the rate of unemployment.

The level of economic development can also influence the hidden economy. Individuals with low per capita real disposable income will have a strong incentive to hold several jobs and to pay taxes only on the first job (Frey and Weck-Hanneman, 1984). Empirical evidence from Italy, however, suggests that the size of the underground economy in the rich north is larger than in the poor south. This positive relationship between per capita income and hidden economic activity suggests that the supply of hidden economy jobs may increase with an increase in per capita income. The expected sign of the coefficient of the level of development, however, is a priori ambiguous.

The theoretical literature on the hidden economy suggests three indicators: the growth rate of 'official' real GDP, the labor market participation rate and monetary variables. These constitute the elements in the y vector in equation (8.1) above. An increase in the underground economy implies that inputs (particularly labor) move out of the official economy, with a negative effect on the growth of the observed GDP. In the case of monetary aggregates, the literature hypothesizes a positive relationship between hidden economy activity and the cash-demand ratio, because the bulk of transactions are conducted in cash.

In utilizing the MIMIC approach to estimating the size of the hidden economy in Nigeria, I use three types of determinants and two types of indicators of the hidden economy. The causal factors are the tax burden (TAX/GDP), inflation (INFL) and real per capita income (RPERCAP). I have not included unemployment and sectoral variables in the list of determinants owing to a lack of reliable data. The two indicators used in the MIMIC analysis are changes in the male participation rate

Table 8.7 LISREL maximum likelihood estimates of the hidden economy in Nigeria

	RPERCAP	TAX/GDP	INFL
Coefficient	−0.32	0.46	−0.42
Standard error	0.16	0.16	0.13
t-ratio	−2.00	2.88	−3.21

Source: Compiled by the author.
Notes: RPERCAP = real per capita income; TAX/GDP = share of taxes in the gross domestic product; INFL = inflation.

(DMALEF) and changes in the cash-demand deposit ratio (DCPDD). The growth rate of GDP is excluded from the estimation to avoid double counting.

Table 8.7 shows the estimated parameters of the MIMIC model for the Nigerian economy for the period 1960–97. The LISREL coefficients of the tax rate (0.46), inflation (−0.42) and per capita income (−0.32) all possess the expected signs and are statistically significant at the 5 percent level. These estimated coefficients are then normalized to sum to unity for the purposes of determining the size of the hidden economy. Table 8.8 shows the estimates of the hidden economy for the years 1960–97. The size of the hidden economy increased substantially throughout the 1970s then declined in 1984–5, before rising again. The declining trend in the mid-1980s probably reflects General Buhari's measures to curb corruption and indiscipline. Tagged a 'War Against Indiscipline' (WAI), the short-lived Buhari administration succeeded in reducing widespread corruption in both public and private sectors of the economy. But, with the ascendancy of General Babangida to power and the abolition of the decrees that empowered the WAI campaign, the level of corruption rose once again.

Indeed, the Babangida administration was widely seen as the most corrupt military regime in Nigeria, and one that severely marginalized the middle class. Babangida's successor, the late General Sani Abacha, reintroduced General Buhari's WAI policy, renaming it 'War Against Indiscipline and Corruption' (WAIC). This was unable to stem the tide of corruption, although it is now acknowledged that the establishment of the Failed Bank Tribunals in 1995 had reinstilled some financial discipline in the banking system. Still, the hidden economy grew to record levels (over 60 percent of GDP) during the Abacha era (1993–7). The anti-corruption bill signed by President Obasanjo was designed to put in place an appropriate institutional framework for dealing with the menace of corruption in Nigeria.

Table 8.8 Estimates of the hidden economy in Nigeria, 1960–97

Year	Naira million	% of GDP
1960	4,910.2	9.64
1965	7,327.7	11.54
1970	10,076.7	12.83
1973	13,185.4	13.49
1974	24,392.2	22.45
1975	27,217.3	26.43
1980	40,610.9	32.54
1981	37,567.2	34.65
1982	39,555.8	36.57
1983	46,875.5	45.76
1984	30,303.6	31.08
1985	37,972.3	35.50
1986	40,187.8	36.65
1987	40,995.2	37.65
1988	47,578.4	39.76
1989	54,313.8	42.34
1990	56,267.1	40.54
1991	61,690.9	42.43
1992	65,152.2	43.54
1993	83,575.6	54.65
1994	89,138.4	58.65
1995	102,020.7	65.43
1996	107,250.7	64.65
1997	101,304.4	58.76

Source: Compiled by the author.
Note: Estimates are based on the LISREL methodology (see Table 8.7).

3.4   Impact of corruption in Nigeria

To evaluate the effects of corruption on the Nigerian economy, I utilize the estimated size of the hidden economy (a proxy for corruption) in an economic growth framework. The procedure follows a conventional growth model in which corruption is introduced as an input, in addition to labor and capital.[15] Table 8.9 shows estimated equations for labor productivity and the growth rate of GDP in Nigeria during the period 1960–97. In the labor productivity equations, the introduction of the time trend is intended to capture the growth (or lack of it) of total factor productivity. In such a framework, the coefficient on K/L captures the rate of return on capital (the share of capital in output), and the coefficient on L tests for returns to scale. The inclusion of exports in the equation follows the large number of empirical studies that investigate the export-led growth hypothesis (for example, Balassa, 1985; Feder, 1983; Greenaway and Sapsford, 1994; Salvatore and Hatcher, 1991).

Table 8.9 Estimated growth equations for Nigeria, 1960–97

	Dependent variable							
	Labor productivity (log (Q/L))				Change in labor productivity (Δ log (Q/L))		Growth rate of GDP	
	1	2	3	4	5	6	7	8
Intercept	3.55	3.64***	-0.024	-0.034**	-0.034**	-0.03*	1.451	0.982
	(1.07)	(6.68)	(0.72)	(1.99)	(1.99)	(1.99)	(0.22)	(0.11)
Ln (K/L)	0.074*	0.073*	0.083**	0.086**	—	-0.12*	-0.072	0.032
	(1.91)	(2.00)	(2.07)	(2.22)		(1.66)	(0.34)	(0.56)
Ln (HD)	-0.208***	-0.208***	-0.207***	-0.206***	-0.12*	—	-0.058***	-0.173**
	(3.58)	(3.67)	(3.75)	(3.79)	(1.65)		(4.074)	(1.98)
Ln (L)	0.031	—	0.41	—	—	—	0.229	0.178
	(0.03)		(0.34)				(0.91)	(0.67)
Ln (X)	0.230***	0.23***	0.244***	0.242***	0.24***	0.24***	0.274***	0.274***
	(4.82)	(4.90)	(5.09)	(5.16)	(5.16)	(5.16)	(4.38)	(4.25)
Ln $(HD*K/L)$	—	—	—	—	-0.086**	-0.205***	—	-0.024
					(2.22)	(3.79)		(0.74)
Trend	-0.024	-0.023	0.0005	0.0004	0.0005	0.0004	—	—
	(0.77)	(4.64)	(0.66)	(0.62)	(0.62)	(0.62)		
$\bar{R}^2$	.91	.92	.64	.65	.65	.65	.58	.58
Method	AR(1)	AR(1)	OLS	OLS	OLS	OLS	OLS	OLS
LM$_1$	—	—	0.14	0.05	0.05	0.05	2.29	2.29
LM$_2$	—	—	0.30	0.19	0.19	0.19	2.52	2.58
LM$_3$	—	—	1.71	1.78	1.79	1.79	0.09	0.09

Source: Compiled by the author.

Notes: K = estimated capital stock, L = labor force, HD = size of the hidden economy, X = real exports, Q = real GDP, Ln is natural logarithm. For equations 7 and 8, the variables K/L, HD, L and X denote the share of investment in GDP, the ratio of the hidden economy to GDP, the growth rate of the labor force and the growth rate of exports, respectively. Figures in parentheses are absolute t-values. *, **, *** denote an estimated coefficient that is significantly different from zero at the 10, 5 and 1 percent levels, respectively. LM$_1$ denotes the Lagrange multiplier test of residual serial correlation; LM$_2$ denotes Ramsey's RESET test of functional form; LM$_3$ denotes the Jarque–Bera test for residual normality. On the relevant null hypothesis, these test statistics are distributed as χ^2 with 1, 1 and 2 degrees of freedom respectively.

189

All equations were estimated with the ordinary least squares method, except equations 1 and 2, which were estimated using the first-order autoregressive (AR(1)) technique, owing to serially correlated errors. As is widely expected, the estimated coefficient on corruption in all the equations is negative and statistically significant at the 10 percent level or lower. Similarly, the estimated coefficient on domestic investment in equations 1–4 is positive and statistically significant. It is noteworthy, however, that, when an interaction term between the capital–labor ratio and corruption is introduced into the equation, coefficients on both the interaction term and K/L become negative and statistically significant. This result appears to lend support to the widely held view that corruption encourages capital-intensive projects in Nigeria. In other words, the efficiency of investment is severely influenced by corruption. This finding concurs with the conclusions of a number of empirical studies elsewhere (for example, Ades and Di Tella, 1997; Mauro, 1997; Shleifer and Vishny, 1993; Tanzi and Davoodi, 1997) that corruption adversely affects the productivity of public investment and distorts the effects of industrial policy on investment. In the case of the labor force variable, the estimated coefficient is not statistically significant. In equation 2 in particular, the coefficient of the labor force is negative, suggesting decreasing returns to scale in the production function. In contrast, exports, mainly dominated by oil, appear to have an unambiguously positive and statistically significant effect on economic growth in Nigeria.

3.5   Real wages and corruption

As noted earlier, most civil service reform commissions established by successive governments in Nigeria have focused on the review of wages and salaries of civil servants. The aim was to motivate and enhance the efficiency and effectiveness of the civil service with a view to increasing productivity and eliminating or curtailing mismanagement, embezzlement, bribery and corruption. However, the implementation of these schemes has been problematic. What is the relationship between wages and corruption?

To answer this question, a simple wage function is estimated for Nigeria, with corruption introduced into the wage equation as an additional explanatory variable. Table 8.10 contains the estimated wage regression equations for the period 1970–92. The results suggest a negative and statistically significant relationship between real wages and corruption in Nigeria.[16] Although this cannot be used to infer that reduced corruption raises real wages, we can certainly argue that the two are bound to move in different directions. It might well be that in corrupt environments workers augment their wages by privatizing state assets and rent seeking. The non-wage part of their income increases via corrupt practices.

Table 8.10 Estimated wage regression equations for Nigeria, 1970–92

	Equation 1	Equation 2
Intercept	10.48**	11.57***
	(2.55)	(2.88)
Corruption	−0.54***	−0.56***
	(2.93)	(2.99)
Labor force	0.51	–
	(1.15)	
$\bar{R}^2$	.354	.309
LM_1	1.60	1.13
LM_2	0.56	0.38
LM_3	0.52	4.16

Source: Compiled by the author.
Notes: Figures in parentheses are absolute *t*-values. ** and *** denote an estimated coefficient that is significantly different from zero at the 5 and 1 percent
levels, respectively. LM_1 denotes Lagrange multiplier test of residual serial correlation; LM_2 denotes Ramsey's RESET test of functional form; LM_3 denotes the
Jarque–Bera test for residual normality. On the relevant null hypothesis, these
test statistics are distributed as χ^2 with 1, 1 and 2 degrees of freedom, respectively.

3.6   Anti-corruption strategies in Nigeria

The democratically elected government of President Olusegun Obasanjo
has recognized the menace of corruption in the economy. Since coming
to power in May 1999, the government has drafted an anti-corruption
document, which was passed by the national assembly, and has now set
up an Independent Corrupt Practices and Other Related Offences Commission to fight corruption. The main powers and limitations of the commission include: investigating allegations of corruption by public officials
and others and bringing charges against suspects; inspecting the bank accounts, shareholdings and safe deposit boxes of suspects; ordering the
seizure of assets suspected to have been acquired corruptly and their
confiscation if the case is proven. More importantly, the commission has
the power to appoint an independent counsel to investigate allegations
against the president, vice president, chief justice and state governors.
Evidence acquired in such an investigation would then be given to the
national assembly or state assembly. The commission also has a duty to
examine the practices, systems and procedures of public agencies and
parastatals and can direct them to make changes where they are found to
facilitate fraud. In spite of its noble objectives, the anti-corruption commission is unlikely to succeed in curbing corruption in Nigeria unless appropriate institutional and societal reforms are undertaken. The United
States Agency for International Development has identified a number of
anti-corruption measures, including institutional reforms. There are three

aspects to the institutional measure: limiting authority, improving accountability and realigning incentives.

Institutional reforms involving limiting authority consist of genuine privatization measures, competitive procurement, competition in public service and liberalization policies. Nigeria has embarked on privatization of a number of state-owned enterprises, but the process has been severely criticized. On the one hand, proponents of privatization have accused the bureau for public sector enterprises of being sluggish and selective in its privatization program. Much corruption in Nigeria is on account of the Nigerian National Petroleum Corporation, but the government is extremely wary of privatizing the oil sector. In the case of procurement, the World Bank is currently assisting a number of African governments (Uganda, Tanzania, Mali, Malawi, Ethiopia and Benin) to reform their procurement procedures. Competitive procurement allows little or no room for personal discretion and lays down clear procedures and selection criteria.

Institutional reforms involving transparency and accountability have been emphasized by the Obasanjo administration. They include establishing criminal and administrative sanctions, strengthening judicial processes, financial disclosures and an open budget process. All these measures are enshrined in Nigeria's anti-corruption law but, unless there is the political will to implement it, it will remain just so much reference material. President Obasanjo must lead by example: he should declare his assets and be seen to act in a transparent way. And state governors ought to do the same. So far, only one state governor publicly declared his assets upon taking office in May 1999. The rest have not done so or they have done it privately – and Nigeria's anti-corruption agency may simply lack the courage to step on big toes.

Yet another institutional reform measure that may be relevant to Nigeria and other African countries is the realignment of incentives. This relates to the promotion of ethical behavior in civil service. Incentive structures for improving the efficiency and effectiveness of the civil service include, for example, pay incentives and dismissal of dishonest workers. Ghana is a success model of such institutional reform: in the 1980s the government retired or dismissed corrupt tax and customs officials and improved civil servants' pay and conditions of service.

These institutional reforms must be complemented by appropriate societal reforms. Attitudinal laxity on the part of the average Nigerian led to the long presence of military dictators in Nigeria and also allowed politicians to rig elections with impunity. Without dramatic changes in civil society's attitudes toward political processes and the mobilization of the political will for change, governments are unlikely to follow through on anti-corruption reforms once they enter politically complex terrain.

Civic responsibility can be a potent and liberating force in improving the quality of governance at all three levels.

4   Designing incentive structures in the civil service

4.1   Political and economic dimensions

The foregoing analysis suggests that, in spite of all the reforms in Nigeria, the civil service has so far failed to live up to expectations. Corruption remains endemic, as do extremely low levels of efficiency. However, the problems of the civil service are to be blamed more on the distorted incentive structure than on the civil servants themselves. Nigeria's current civilian administration must challenge corruption, using a broad-based approach mandated by its democratic credentials. The anti-corruption bill recently signed by the president marks a step in the right direction. However, since similar legislation was attempted with little success in the past, appropriate incentive structures need to accompany the current legislation if efforts at fighting corruption are to have meaningful results. The approach should have both economic and political dimensions. Politically, the leadership must evolve a culture of honesty based on transparency and credibility. It needs to lead by example, showing zero tolerance for corrupt behavior, even at the highest echelons of government. The legal and institutional framework for dealing with corrupt practices must be independent of political control in order to ensure credibility. On the economic side, the government should scale down regulations on economic activities, as well as other policies, which contribute to the demand for and supply of corrupt activities. On the supply side, this can be done by improving public sector wages towards market-based levels, thereby lowering the premium on errant behavior and making dismissal from the civil service both a painful and a credible threat. At the same time, public sector efficiency would be enhanced. Attractive wages in the public sector demand urgent attention because the perceived high correlation between corruption and inefficiency of public servants may retard economic growth.

4.2   A question of measurement

The extent to which civil service efficiency can be improved will partly depend on the extent to which the sector's inputs and performance can be measured. In this regard, civil service productivity is central; it indicates the efficiency with which resources in the production process are put to use. However, whereas traditional inputs such as labor, capital and land are relatively easy to estimate, the measurement of inputs and outputs in services requires a degree of innovation. In this case, a checklist indicator approach – that is, a set of carefully thought out actions or responsibilities that groups of individual workers must carry out in order to accomplish a particular task or project – is used to estimate productivity. For example, an agriculture extension worker could be set a target of inspecting at least fifteen farming units per day. The cost and quality of such a task will determine the performance of the extension worker during a given period. Target setting can, therefore, play an important role in measuring the efficiency of individual decisionmaking units. In setting effective targets, several requirements must be taken into account (see Ajayi, 1998). First, targets must be challenging but not impossible to accomplish – civil servants should be able to derive satisfaction from their resolution. This implies in turn that the targets must be specific and measurable, as in the case of a social worker who visits a specific number of housebound elderly patients per day. Third, for employees to achieve a sense of participation and motivation to succeed they must be involved in the target-setting process. Fourth, the evaluation of the performance of the employee should be based on results from a trend, hence the need for periodic feedback from all participants.

It is therefore not possible to have a single indicator for measuring the efficiency of the civil service. Rather, different indicators could be used for different ministries, departments or units. Even within these individual units, several indicators may be used. For example, in measuring the efficiency of the health sector, specific targets could be set for, say, the mortality rate, the reduction or elimination of certain kinds of diseases, and the number of patients treated per doctor. In the cases of education and the social services, targets could be set for levels of literacy and for a reduction in the number of people below the poverty line. It is important to note that, in setting targets, due regard should be given to both domestic and international considerations. The targets on mortality rate, literacy rate, school enrollment, life expectancy, and so on may be judged over time and in relation to other comparable countries (see DFID, 1997).

The technique of data envelopment analysis (DEA) can also be used to provide a useful framework for measuring the efficiency of the civil service in Nigeria. This technique has the advantage of incorporating multiple inputs and outputs drawn from within ministries or departments and allows for relative efficiency measures to be determined. In addition to estimating the efficiency of each decisionmaking unit within a particular organization, the DEA method provides information on what it would take, in terms of changes in the production mix, to make the relatively inefficient decisionmaking units efficient. This is done by reference to a weighted combination of the characteristics of the most efficient units. The DEA technique has been widely applied to the evaluation of the efficiency of decisionmaking units in education, banking and manufacturing industry in developed countries.[17] However, the technique is flexible enough to be used with considerable benefit in the ministries or departments of the Nigerian civil service.

5   Conclusions

Successive governments in Nigeria have introduced various reform measures with the main aim of improving the efficiency and effectiveness of the civil service. Unfortunately, the Nigerian civil service has remained weak, inefficient and incapable of reforming itself, let alone the economy. A plausible explanation relates to the endemic nature of corruption and rent-seeking opportunities, inappropriate incentive structures and a lack of the political will to implement 'good' reform measures. There are as yet no operational guidelines for assessing the efficiency of the civil service. The hiring and firing of civil servants are often based on personal acquaintance or vendetta rather than on productivity-related indicators. Specific targets must be set for which the civil service can strive. An efficiency-based incentive scheme that links reward to performance may provide strong motivation. Political interference, which has seriously undermined the credibility and confidence of the civil service in the design and implementation of government policy, should be minimized.

The chapter has also examined the causes of corruption in Nigeria and its impact on productivity and civil service efficiency. The high incidence of corruption and the growth of the hidden economy have combined to render the Nigerian civil service and the rest of the economy inefficient. The phenomenal increase in the hidden or unreported economy, from less than 10 percent of GDP at independence to over 60 percent during the Abacha regime in the late 1990s, reflects the growth of the informal sector, itself fostered by the tax burden, unnecessary regulatory regimes, lack of institutional capacity and weak governance.

A number of reform measures to fight corruption and to curtail the growth of the hidden economy have been highlighted. These include institutional and societal measures aimed at reducing the role of government in economic activities, strengthening transparency, improving incentives in the civil service and encouraging a dramatic change in attitudes toward the political process. In the absence of these reform measures, the anti-corruption bill of President Obasanjo will fall victim to the 'Nigerian factor' syndrome, and the efficiency of the Nigerian civil service will be grossly compromised.

Notes

1. This explains, perhaps, why Ibrahim Babangida once asked the economists in his government to explain why, in spite of the widespread corruption and lack of social capital, the Nigerian economy had not yet collapsed!
2. These included the role of the Public Service Commission, as well as the structure of the civil service and its conditions of service and training arrangements.
3. The number of states has increased dramatically over the years, from 12 in 1967 to 19 (1976), 21 (1987), 36 (since 1990).
4. The total number of local governments in the country is 500, ranging from 11 in Yobe State to 18 in Kano State.
5. This power of the national economic council is explicitly set out in Section 140, Schedule 3, Paragraph 12 of the 1979 Constitution of Nigeria.
6. The simplest definition of corruption is that it is the misapplication of public resources to private ends. In a broader sense, however, corruption can be defined as 'an arrangement that involves an exchange between two parties (the demander and the supplier) which (i) has an influence on the allocation of resources either immediately or in the future; and (ii) involves the use or abuse of public or collective responsibility for private ends' (Macrae, 1982:678).
7. *Financial Times*, 'Survey of Nigeria,' 21 February 1993.
8. *Financial Times*, 20 and 21 October 2000.
9. *Sunday Times*, 2 April 2000.
10. *Today* (Abuja), 1 July 1997.
11. *Newswatch*, 16 January 1995.
12. *Newswatch*, 31 March 1997.
13. Details of some of these large-scale money laundering cases can be found in *Business Age* 8(104), December 2000, or its website (www.businessage.net).
14. For a cogent discussion of these approaches, see Giles (1997).
15. For a detailed discussion on the derivation of the growth regression equation in developing countries, see Balasubramanyam et al. (1996).
16. In fact, the correlation coefficient between real wage rate and corruption is $-.56$, between real wage rate and labor force is $-.65$, and between corruption and labor force is .90.
17. For a detailed account of the DEA technique and its application, see Johnes and Johnes (1993).

REFERENCES

Ades, A. and R. Di Tella (1997) 'National Champions and Corruption: Some Unpleasant Interventionist Arithmetic,' *Economic Journal* 107:1023–42.

Aigner, D. J., F. Schneider and D. Ghosh (1988) 'Me and My Shadow: Estimating the Size of the Hidden Economy from Time Series Data,' in W. A. Barnett (ed.) *Dynamic Econometric Modelling: Proceedings of the Third International Symposium in Economic Theory and Econometrics*, Cambridge: Cambridge University Press.

Ajayi, S. T. (1998) 'Productivity Measurement and Improvement in the Civil Service,' paper delivered at the 32nd Conference of the Civil Service Commissions in the Federation, Kano, Nigeria, 28–29 September.

Balassa, B. (1985) 'Exports, Policy Choices, and Economic Growth in Developing Countries after the 1973 Oil Shock,' *Journal of Development Economics* 18:23–35.

Balasubramanyam, V. N., M. A. Salisu and D. Sapsford (1996) 'Foreign Direct Investment and Growth in Export Promoting and Import Substituting Countries,' *Economic Journal* 106(434):92–105.

Bhattacharyya, D. K. and S. Ghose (1998) 'Corruption in India and the Hidden Economy,' *Economic and Political Weekly of India* 33(44).

Brownsberger, W. N. (1983) 'Development and Governmental Corruption – Materialism and Political Fragmentation in Nigeria,' *Journal of Modern African Studies* 21(2):215–33.

Colins, L. (1965) 'What Is the Problem about Corruption?' *Journal of Modern African Studies* 3:215–44.

Collier, P. (1986) 'An Analysis of the Nigerian Labor Market,' World Bank Discussion Paper, Washington, DC.

DFID (Department for International Development) (1997) *Eliminating World Poverty: A Challenge for the 21st Century*, Stationery Office: London.

Feder, G. (1983) 'On Exports and Economic Growth,' *Journal of Development Economics* 12:59–73.

Federal Office of Statistics (1995) *Annual Abstract of Statistics*, Lagos.

—— (1997) *Annual Abstract of Statistics*, Lagos.

Frey, B. S. and H. Weck-Hanneman (1984) 'The Hidden Economy as an "Unobserved" Variable,' *European Economic Review* 26:33–5.

Frey, B. S., H. Weck-Hanneman and W. W. Pommerehne (1984) 'Has the Shadow Economy Grown in Germany? An Exploratory Study,' *Weltwirtschaftliches Archiv* 118:499–524.

Giles, D. E. A. (1997) 'The Hidden Economy and the Tax-Gap in New Zealand: A Latent Variable Analysis,' Department of Economics Discussion Papers 97-8, University of Victoria, Australia.

—— (1999) 'Measuring the Hidden Economy: Implications for Econometric Modeling,' *Economic Journal Special Supplement* 109:370–80.

Greenaway, D. and D. Sapsford (1994) 'What Does Liberalization Do for Exports and Growth?' *Weltwirtschaftliches Archiv* 130:152–73.

Haque, N. and R. Sahay (1996) 'Do Government Wage Cuts Close Budget Deficits? Costs of Corruption,' *IMF Staff Papers* 13 (December).

Ikejiani-Clark, M. (1997) 'The Civil Service in the Machinery of Government,' paper presented at the National Workshop on the Civil Service and Vision 2010, Abuja, Nigeria, 12–13 August.

Ikpeze, N. I. (1996) 'Role of Nigerian Labor Market in Attainment of Full Employment,' in J. U. Umo (ed.) *Towards Full Employment Strategy in Nigeria*, National Manpower Board: Lagos.

Johnes, G. and J. Johnes (1993) 'Measuring the Performance of UK Economics Department: An Application of Data Envelopment Analysis,' *Oxford Economic Papers* 45:332–47.

Joreskog, K. G. and A. S. Goldberger (1975) 'Estimation of a Model with Multiple Indicators and Multiple Causes of a Single Latent Variable,' *Journal of the American Statistical Association* 70:631–9.

Joreskog, K. G. and M. van Thillo (1973) 'Lisrel: A General Computer Program for Estimating a Linear Structural Equation System Involving Multiple Indicators of Unobserved Variables,' Department of Statistics Research Reports 73-5, University of Uppsala, Sweden.

Levine, R. and D. Renelt (1992) 'A Sensitivity Analysis of Cross-Country Growth Regressions,' *American Economic Review* 82:942–63.

Macrae, J. (1982) 'Underdevelopment and the Economics of Corruption: A Game Theory Approach,' *World Development* 10(8):677–87.

Mauro, P. (1995) 'Corruption and Growth,' *Quarterly Journal of Economics* 110:681–712.

——— (1997) 'Why Worry about Corruption?' IMF Economic Series 6, Washington, DC.

Nunberg, B. and J. Nellis (1995) 'Civil Service Reform and the World Bank,' World Bank Discussion Papers No. 161, Washington, DC.

Nye, J. S. (1961) 'Corruption and Political Development: A Cost–Benefit Analysis,' *American Political Science Review* 56:417–35.

Okoroji, J. (1997) *Federal–State Relations in Nigeria's Second Republic: A Study of Conflict and Cooperation*, VOR Publications: London.

Rose-Ackerman, S. (1999) *Corruption and Government: Causes, Consequences and Reform*, Cambridge University Press: Cambridge.

Sachs, J. and A. Warner (1995) 'Natural Resource Abundance and Economic Growth,' NBER Working Papers 5398, National Bureau of Economic Research, Cambridge, MA.

Salvatore, D. and T. Hatcher (1991) 'Inward Oriented and Outward Oriented Trade Strategies,' *Journal of Development Studies* 27:7–25.

Schneider, F. (1997) 'Empirical Results for the Size of the Shadow Economy of Western European Countries over Time,' Institut für Volkswirtschaftslehre Working Papers 9710, Linz University, Germany.

Shleifer, A. and R. W. Vishny (1993) 'Corruption,' *Quarterly Journal of Economics* 108:599–617.

Stasavage, D. (1999) 'Causes and Consequences of Corruption: Mozambique in Transition,' *Commonwealth and Comparative Politics* 37(3):65–97.

Tanzi, V. (1994) 'Corruption, Governmental Activities and Markets,' IMF Working Papers 94/99, Washington, DC.

Tanzi, V. and H. Davoodi (1997) 'Corruption, Public Investment and Growth,' IMF Working Papers 97/139, Washington, DC.

Theobald, R. and R. Williams (1999) 'Combating Corruption in Botswana: Regional Role Model or Deviant Case?' *Commonwealth and Comparative Politics* 37(3):117–34.

Van Rijckeghem, C. and B. Weder (1997) 'Corruption and the Rate of Temptation: Do Low Wages in Civil Service Cause Corruption?' IMF Working Papers 97/73, Washington, DC.

Williams, F. O. (1997) 'The Civil Service in Nigeria Today,' paper delivered at the National Workshop on the Civil Service and Vision 2010, Abuja, Nigeria, 12–13 August.

World Bank (2000) *World Development Indicators CD-ROM 2000*, World Bank: Washington, DC.

Zellner, A. (1970) 'Estimation of Regression Relationships Containing Unobservable Independent Variables,' *International Economic Review* 11:441–54.

9

The Mozambican civil service: Incentives, reforms and performance

José A. Sulemane and Steve Kayizzi-Mugerwa

1 Introduction

Mozambique, like many other sub-Saharan African countries, has undertaken far-reaching political and economic reforms in recent years with the goal of generating rapid but sustainable economic growth and improving the efficiency of public administration, notably in the delivery of social services and in combating poverty. Many African countries have experienced serious difficulties in implementing these reforms, notably owing to poor implementation and inadequate incentives for those employed in the civil service, but Mozambique's experience has been aggravated by a number of extenuating socioeconomic circumstances, with poverty and poor human resource endowments much more severe than in other countries (see also Table 9.1).

As noted in a UN Development Programme document (Massingue et al., 1995), the process of change in the country has involved several transitions: from a situation of war to one of peace, reconstruction and resettlement; from Marxist–Leninism towards political pluralism; from a planned economy to a market-oriented economy; and from centralized economic and political structures to decentralized ones, emphasizing popular participation. The country achieved its independence in 1975 after a long war of independence which, commencing in 1964, had decimated the social and economic infrastructure. The victory of Frelimo, a party of freedom fighters, saw the departure of over 200,000 Portuguese

Table 9.1 Mozambican welfare indicators by region, 1996

	Incidence of poverty (%)	Adult illiteracy rate (%)	Female illiteracy rate (%)	Access to clean water (% of population)	Infant mortality rate (per 1,000 live births)
Rural	71.2	72.2	85.1	1.0	160.2
Urban	62.0	33.3	46.2	31.0	101.2
National	69.4	60.5	74.1	8.5	145.7
Sub-Saharan Africa	–	39.0	72.5	43.0	92.0

Source: Republic of Mozambique (2000a).

settlers, who had comprised the bulk of the civil service as well as the top echelons of the modern sector.

As one of the frontline states against the apartheid regime in South Africa, Mozambique was the target of considerable external aggression. A civil war broke out in the 1980s, in which government forces were pitted against Renamo, a guerrilla force with considerable support from the central regions of the country. The war led to the destruction of physical capital, rising defense expenditures and sharp declines in social outlays (Brück, 2000). Above all it created uncertainty, which affected the resource allocation decisions of households as well as of government. The civil service lacked the resources, both financial and human, to do its work properly, and the provincial administrations were considerably weakened as well. It was not until after protracted negotiations brokered by several groups and supported by the United Nations that the civil war was ended and multiparty elections were declared in October 1994 (see Alden, 2000).

In rapidly changing regional and international conditions, the government has been forced to redefine Mozambique's place in regional and global terms. Foremost was the need to adjust to the sudden decline of the Soviet Union, a major economic partner and supplier of military equipment. It has, however, also been important to respond to the changing political configuration in southern Africa itself, especially following the achievement of majority rule in South Africa and the search for greater economic collaboration (aside from the traditional export of Mozambican labor to South African mines). In political and economic terms, policymakers in Mozambique have had to adopt a more pragmatic approach, including the adoption of multiparty politics and market-based economic reforms, and the unprecedented incorporation of the country into the Commonwealth, otherwise a grouping of former British colonies.

Responding to these challenges has not been altogether easy. The Mozambican civil service, or what was left of it after the exodus of Portuguese settlers in the mid-1970s, was poorly educated with low incentives. The style of management was based on the East European model of central control, but without the human resources and technical expertise to make a success of it. Moreover, the duplication of central functions at the regional level, in a bid to decentralize power, only led to poor coordination and ineffective use of resources. The role of the state in the new economic dispensation is still a matter for strong debate in Mozambique. The country suffers from chronic poverty and a paucity of human capital, and the protracted civil war still seriously affects social and economic conditions in many parts of the country (Bowen, 1992; Kyle, 1991).

The combination of a war-ravaged economy, poor human capacities and rampant poverty has made the country extremely debt laden and aid dependent. Since the adoption of an economic rehabilitation program in 1987, which was changed to an economic and social rehabilitation program in 1990 to emphasize social sectors and human development, Mozambican policymakers have sought to implement a well-coordinated reform program with support from bilateral donors as well as the World Bank and the International Monetary Fund. The program focused on the following:
• the promotion of private investment
• liberalization of prices
• privatization of state-owned enterprises
• improvement of fiscal policy, by reducing tax exemptions, the tax rate and the budget deficit
• reforming the financial sector
• reforming the foreign exchange market by letting the exchange rate be determined freely in the market (see also Republic of Mozambique, 2000b).

The program has had an appreciable impact. For instance, inflation was reduced from 147 percent in 1987 to an estimated 4 percent a decade later. The rate of growth was, on average, above 6 percent in the 1990s. Thus aside from external shocks, such as floods and drought spells, the reforms helped bring the Mozambican economy back onto the road to sustainable growth.

But, even after a decade of reasonable growth, Mozambique remains a very poor country with overwhelming development needs. A substantial portion of its population remains displaced or cannot return home owing to the threat of landmines or other security hazards. The rural sector still lacks basic infrastructure, including amenities such as primary schools, health centers, adequate roads and food storage facilities. In a consultative group meeting in Paris in 1995, the government reiterated its policies as follows: 'to strengthen governance at all levels; normalize life in the countryside; develop human resources; increase economic growth; and reduce macroeconomic imbalances in the context of growth' (see DANIDA, 1996; Tarp and Lau, 1996). By the end of the 1990s, the government had recorded a number of achievements in its reform efforts, including the development of a medium-term expenditure framework, revision of the civil service career and compensation systems, a reduction and rationalization of direct tax rates and the introduction of value added tax (VAT). Further, an ambitious privatization program saw the sale of the bulk of state-owned enterprises, and the trade regime had been simplified, with import and export taxes reduced.

The government's medium-term objectives, as expressed in its 'Letter of Intent' to the International Monetary Fund for the year 2000, are based on sustaining these achievements with the goal of poverty reduction via high and sustainable growth, reduction of regional inequalities and the consolidation of peace and national unity (see, for example, Republic of Mozambique, 2000a). The achievement of these objectives depends on the efficiency of the public sector. The government has thus embarked on plans to review the machinery of government with a view to raising the quality of governance, including public sector accountability. In the medium term, the government will also seek to adhere to the terms of the HIPC (Heavily Indebted Poor Countries) completion point, which include devising specific strategies for combating poverty and in this context the preparation of a poverty reduction strategy paper (IMF and IDA, 2000).

The main purpose of this chapter is to study the process of institutional reform and transformation in Mozambique during a period characterized not only by social and economic crisis and civil war but also more recently by economic liberalization and a return to peace and growth. The focus of our discussion will be the civil service. The presentation is threefold. First, we provide an overview of the state of the Mozambican civil service and how it has changed during and through the crisis and the economic reforms launched in 1987, as well as since the return of peace. Second, we look especially at the incentive structure in the civil service and assess the impact of the various reforms, such as privatization, on wages and employment in the public sector as a whole. Third, we analyze how the changes in the civil service have affected the delivery of social services in general, with particular focus on health and education. Our discussion of access to social services will also touch on the situation at the regional level, where poor incentives and remoteness from the center have affected the quality and quantity of the services available.

2   The Mozambican civil service in transition

At independence in 1975, the Mozambican civil service had very limited capacity for implementing government directives and policies, and this was especially marked at the provincial and district levels. The country's most acute shortcoming was lack of educated people (Nkomo, 1986). For example, owing to the scant attention paid to African education during colonial rule, only about forty Mozambicans had acquired a university degree at the time of independence in 1975. It is estimated that in the mid-1990s over 60 percent of the adult population was illiterate, and among women the figure was 74 percent.

From 1975, the government had sought to pursue economic development along the socialist principles of a planned economy espoused by Frelimo, the ruling party, and by neighboring countries such as Tanzania. However, the government's support of liberalization movements in southern Africa led, as a countermove from the minority-led governments of the region, to the creation of Renamo, a long-lived rebel group supported in the first instance by Rhodesia and then, after the latter's independence in 1980, by South Africa. The civil war came to disrupt all social and economic activities in Mozambique, especially in the central and northern districts. The resources meant for the civil service were seriously circumscribed, as indeed was the government's ability to deliver social services. By the early 1980s, the government had been forced to abandon its control stance and to embark on a long process of economic and political reorientation. This would see it adopt structural adjustment policies funded by donors and the multilateral agencies and embrace a credible multiparty system of government, following the signing of a ceasefire between the Frelimo-led government and Renamo in 1992.

The economic and political crisis in Mozambique meant that the government was not able to formulate policies to make the civil service – both at the center and in the provinces – more efficient. In the public sector, policies were more determined by short-term fiscal concerns than by those of capacity building, the improvement of job incentives and the efficient delivery of social services. The paucity of skilled labor in Mozambique has been compensated for somewhat by the presence of a large expatriate community, mainly financed by international aid programs. It has been estimated that in 1990, as the country proceeded with its reforms but before the end to the civil war, around 5,000 expatriates were employed in Mozambique (World Bank, 1991). Thus the country has become doubly dependent: on the one hand on the financing from donors and on the other on advice given by the donor-funded expatriates. Although aid coordination remains the government's responsibility, a serious lack of human resources has meant that aid policy remains fragmented and subject to the whim of individual donors (Wuyts, 1995).

On the demand side, a number of factors have contributed to the rapid expansion of the market for skilled labor. The liberalization and return of peace have led to the revival of the private sector as investments from abroad, notably neighboring South Africa, have begun to pour in. Some foreign investment projects, such as the aluminum smelter Mozal, have increased the demand for technicians and engineers, with a very positive impact on their wages. The financial sector, long under state control, has also seen considerable expansion. It now comprises more than ten commercial banks as well as insurance companies.

As a result of the skilled labor shortage, the wage gap between the private and public sectors had reached absurdly large levels by the end of the 1990s. For example, drivers in the private sector or in international organizations earned the equivalent of a lecturer's salary at the government-owned Eduardo Mondlane University. Still, this was an improvement from the early 1990s, when pay differentials between the same categories in the private and public sectors were tenfold (World Bank, 1991). At that time, a janitor employed by an international organization earned a salary that was equivalent to that of a director in the public sector. However, in actual fact directors in government departments had a visibly higher standard of living than janitors in the private sector, because the skewed incentive structure had led to moonlighting by senior civil servants, including the 'privatization' of public services, in attempts to maintain standards. The taking of bribes, absenteeism, and outright theft of public property became the means by which public sector workers compensated themselves for low wages.[1] Thus public administration and the government's own projects were seriously affected by a loss of personnel to the private sector, to projects initiated by the donor community and to the many non-governmental organizations (NGOs), and the shortage of managerial and professional competencies in the government itself disrupted public sector activities. Economic programs have been slow in implementation, and the regulatory weaknesses of the central agencies have affected the pace at which the private sector can expand its activities.

As in other African countries that have experienced prolonged civil strife, the size of the civil service in Mozambique is uncertain. According to the 1980 census, employment in public administration corresponded to about 2 percent of the labor force, that is, about 110,000 workers. However, a census of civil servants conducted by the state administration ministry during 1989–90, and reconciled with the payroll census undertaken by the finance ministry, estimated the number of civil servants to be 105,000, indicating a modest reduction in public employment during the decade in which the country saw an escalation in civil strife (World Bank, 1991). By 2000, however, the number of civil servants had increased to 121,562, indicating growth of about 16 percent over the decade (see Table 9.2).

Table 9.2 indicates that, whereas the total number of civil servants was growing at about 1.6 percent per year over the 1990s, some districts enjoyed more rapid growth than others. The province around the capital, Maputo Provincia, as well as the capital itself saw large increases in the number of civil servants employed in their administrations. On the other hand, remoter regions saw much smaller increases in the number of civil servants, certainly, as in the case of Nampula and Zambezia, not matching their huge shares of the total population. In Cabo Delgado, the number of civil servants decreased by 24.0 percent and that in Inhambane by 2.5 percent. Since the number of civil servants proxies the level of service provision, sharp declines reflect retrenchment in service provision as well as reduction in the income effects associated with civil service employment. The remoter regions thus experienced appreciable negative impacts on local welfare.

Health and education services are important for human resource development, and civil service jobs tend to be concentrated there. In Table 9.2, the shares of civil servants in health and education in 2000 are compared with those in 1990. The number of civil servants in the health services decreased markedly in the 1990s, from 24 percent of the total to only about half that in 2000. Although poor data collection could account for part of the sharp disparity, the general retrenchment in health service provision during the period could explain the reduction in civil servants in the sector. As for education, the share of civil servants in the sector has remained relatively unchanged at about 50 percent. Since the success of the reforms being pursued in Mozambique is dependent on the ability of the civil service to implement policies and to deliver services, it has been important to be able to determine the size of the civil service accurately. Only then can the government put in place effective incentive structures. The government first tried to account for the number of its employees by devising a structure of grades and salaries in 1990 in which to allocate them (Republic of Mozambique, 1990, 1991, 1992). On the basis of a cabinet decree, an improved payroll system, with a unified and decompressed salary scale covering the whole of the public sector, was also devised. It defined three career levels: technical, administrative and clerical. Related to this, criteria for the staffing needs of the various departments and institutions were also set up.

In spite of these measures, a clear conceptualization of the size and role of the civil service had not been achieved by 2000. This was largely owing to the serious constraints faced by the new system, especially

Table 9.2 Distribution of Mozambican civil servants by province and in health and education sectors, 1990–2000

| Region | Share of total population (%) | Approximate number of civil servants in 2000 | Regional share (%) | Increase (decrease) since 1990 (%) | Share of civil servants in | | | |
| | | | | | Health (%) | | Education (%) | |
					2000	1990	2000	1990
Niassa	5.0	7,164	5.9	19.0	11.6	23.7	51.7	46.5
Cabo Delgado	8.5	7,598	6.2	–24.0	14.5	16.6	50.2	66.5
Nampula	18.9	15,776	13.0	17.0	13.6	20.7	57.0	64.0
Zambezia	19.2	12,828	10.5	18.0	12.9	23.0	68.0	61.0
Tete	7.6	8,076	6.6	12.6	15.5	27.8	57.2	49.3
Manica	6.6	7,094	5.8	20.3	14.5	24.8	55.5	51.0
Sofala	8.4	10,061	8.3	5.7	19.0	32.0	39.9	41.5
Inhambane	7.3	7,203	5.9	–2.5	13.7	25.0	59.0	56.6
Gaza	7.0	7,853	6.5	13.0	12.8	23.0	55.0	48.8
Maputo Provincia	5.4	8,694	7.2	97.5	10.7	22.8	51.9	52.4
Maputo Cidade	5.9	13,644	11.2	29.5	9.8	30.0	51.7	58.0
Total	100.0	121,562	100.0	15.8	13.7	24.3	48.0	49.0

Sources: World Bank (1991); unpublished material from Ministry of State Administration and the Ministry of Planning and Finance; and authors' estimates.
Note: Population in 2000 numbered 17.2 million.

the failure to introduce the incentives on which the success of the new approach was premised. For example, although a better definition of careers was meant to make the service more professional, there was an inherent partiality for formal levels of education, in a country suffering a serious shortage of educated individuals. The gaps between the various career stages were also too long, and the terms of reference for the various positions were poorly defined or missing altogether. Although the new incentive structure was supposed to increase competitiveness and raise productivity in the civil service, the reverse was often the case, because high levels of salary compression left little room for income differentiation. Furthermore, the government, while undertaking stabilization measures, had little means of raising wages. Over time, civil service salaries lost their purchasing power, forcing civil servants to look for other means of survival outside the public sector or to engage in unlawful activities within the public sector itself.

Other attempts were made between 1997 and 1998 to ameliorate the conditions of the civil servants and to raise morale in the public sector. However, in devising the new staff salary structure of 1999, there was undue concern for the situation of the senior administrators, who would now get enhanced packages and other benefits. Those at technical levels did not see much improvement in their earnings. Thus the new career and salary structure failed to address the fundamental issues at the center of the poor performance of the public sector. The government needed to approach the problem holistically; piecemeal measures directed at only one section of the civil service – whether those at the bottom of the scale, those with formal education or those in more senior positions – were bound to fail.

In 1990, the average level of qualification of civil servants was quite low. Less than 20 percent of higher-level civil servants had a university degree, and up to 16 percent had no formal schooling at all. This lack of human capital was repeated throughout the various departments of the government. For example, only one-quarter of 247 department chiefs at central level had a college degree; similarly, only one-sixth of 133 provincial directors had a college degree, and only 5 of 199 provincial department chiefs were college graduates. At the district level, all 199 district directors lacked a college degree. In the education ministry, only 60 percent of the over 30,000 elementary and junior high teachers had completed elementary school education (World Bank, 1991). In 2000, the level of qualification of Mozambican civil servants had improved, but not by much. A mere 6 percent of civil servants had a university degree, and up to 40 percent had received only between one and six years of education. Employees without formal education amounted to 18 percent. Since records show that the average length of service for an unskilled civil servant is almost twenty years, there is serious concern that a culture of low skill and low productivity will be perpetuated in the civil service. This also suggests that the human resource management system within public administration has been relatively weak, with few measures aimed at upgrading skills.

3   Incentive structure in the Mozambican civil service

Privileges and incentives for workers in the civil service and the rest of the government are incorporated in the General Statute for State Functionaries (Republic of Mozambique, 1987); additional commitments are added via special statutes for particular categories such as teachers (for example, the statute for teachers). The General Statute establishes the occupation structure with common functions, as well as the ladder associated with promotions. It also defines the conditions for entry, the probationary period, performance and promotions, disciplinary rules, vacations and related issues, and retirement procedures. It confers equal treatment on both sexes for similar work and duties in matters of wages, training and holidays. In the case of women, privileges related to childbirth are also specified.

The changes in pay regime in the public sector can be divided into distinct periods. From 1975 to 1985, the government's main objective was to improve the social welfare of workers at the lowest levels. This was consistent with the ruling Frelimo's egalitarian ethos. In 1975 the ratio between the highest and lowest wages in the public sector was 7.6 (World Bank, 1991). To alleviate shortages at the technical staff level, the government increased wages at this level. For the following five years, however, nominal wages remained unchanged, representing in practice a serious reduction in the purchasing power of civil servants, especially in light of the escalation of prices in the rest of the economy (Republic of Mozambique, 1980).

At the start of economic reforms in 1987, the government attempted to reverse the serious wage compression that characterized civil service wages. However, the structural and financial problems that had accumulated during 1975–85 made drastic improvements impossible. Beginning in 1991, the government embarked on the introduction of a system of professional categories, ranging from A to Z, as well as the harmonization of employee incentives (Republic of Mozambique, 1990, 1991, 1992). In support of the new changes, a series of decrees from the Council of Ministers were used to adjust salaries annually until the system came to an end in 1998. On the whole, the reform led to a more rapid contraction of civil service wages than was good for the maintenance of incentives and discipline. Whereas the ratio between the lowest and the highest wages was 17.0 in 1991, it had fallen to only 7.6 by 1995. Though wage compression had receded by 1998, wage fluctuations in the 1990s were marked, making the government's incentive schemes unworkable (World Bank, 1991; and yearly decrees between 1992 and 1998).

In attempting to improve the incentive structure in the civil service, the government devised new guidelines in 1998 and began to apply them in 1999 (Republic of Mozambique, 1998a,b). These included measures for the revision of professional categories, wage decompression and improved recruitment practices to ensure that jobs are done by qualified individuals. To enhance the skills and competencies of those already in the system, training schemes were also devised. Lastly, the government undertook to decrease the number of cadres at the lower level in line with the supervisory capacity of the civil service. To achieve these objectives, the government reclassified the existing 2,000 occupational categories into 150 general and specialized categories for the areas of diplomacy, higher education, medicine, auditing and inspection, and education. The salary scales were indexed for easy reading and revision. The mechanisms for promotion were now to be based on performance and other objective criteria. Further, more emphasis was to be put on the management of human resources within the public sector. As an indicator of the impact of the new reforms, the ratio between the lowest and highest wages in the civil service rose to 20.

Let us now discuss the evolution of wages in Mozambique since 1975, using examples drawn from the earnings of the various professional and skill categorics (see Republic of Mozambique, 1980, 1990, 1991, 1992a,b, 1998a,b, 1999). Figure 9.1 shows changes in real salaries for the administrative and professional cadres in the Mozambican civil service, in this case permanent secretaries, directors in government departments and specialists with doctorates. Evaluated in 1980 prices, these categories were reasonably well remunerated in the mid-1970s. However, the first decade of independence saw a sharp real wage decline, which was complicated further by the onset of civil war in the early 1980s. It was not until the introduction of economic reforms in 1987 that the downward slide in real wages was stopped. The rapid growth of the economy in the 1990s seems to have helped raise wages, although they remained decidedly below the levels of the mid-1970s. In the second half of the 1990s, peace does not seem to have been wage enhancing for the higher echelons in the civil service, in spite of the fact that for some groups, such as specialized medical doctors, nominal wages were topped up by up to 75 percent of the basic salary. For the lower cadres in the civil service, wage fluctuations were not as marked, although their wages were quite low. For example, whereas the base salary for high-level professional staff was

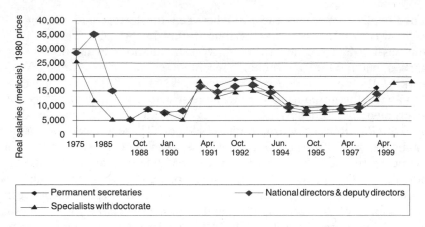

Figure 9.1 Real salaries for administrative and professional cadres in the Mozambican civil service, 1975–99
Sources: See text.

Table 9.3 Ratios of private to public sector wages by category, 1990–2000

Category	1990	2000
Senior administrator	5.6	3.0
Professional staff	3.4	3.8
Clerical staff	10.5	–
Drivers	10.6	–
Unskilled workers	9.5	6.8

Sources: World Bank (1991), and unpublished official data.

about US$240 per month, and the average wage in the public sector about US$120 per month, the lowest cadres received less than US$50 per month.

In comparison with similar professional categories in the private sector, civil service pay was quite low. Whereas private companies are free to set their wages, especially since the liberalization of the 1980s, salaries in the public sector are set administratively, after tripartite meetings between the private sector, the unions and the government. A comparison of salaries in the private sector with those in the civil service shows that, in 1990, salaries for management-level employees in the private sector were up to 5.6 times higher than those in the civil service (see Table 9.3). Those for professional staff, including specialists such as medical doctors, were up to 3.4 times higher. However, the gaps were largest for the medium-skill categories such as clerical staff and drivers, where private sector wages are up to 10.6 times higher. In 2000, the gaps between private and public sector earnings had narrowed somewhat at the management levels, following a series of adjustments in government pay for top employees. Still, private sector wages were 3.0 times higher than public ones at that level. At the professional and specialized levels, the gap remained relatively unchanged. For example, in 2000, a lecturer at the Eduardo Mondlane University earned about US$300 a month, a sum (which included a 60 percent professional bonus) close to the salary earned by drivers in the private sector.

Thus, in both relative and absolute terms, the system of incentives in the Mozambican public sector was far from adequate. It could not ensure that the government retained people with the training and skill necessary to raise productivity in the public sector or to raise the efficiency with which social services are provided. As in other African countries, lack of financial resources was the most immediate impediment to raising remuneration in the public sector. Ad hoc measures have been used in the past to rectify the situation. In 1989 for example, to retain technical staff, the government had devised a monthly subsidy to them in foreign currency, which was deposited in accounts controlled by the finance ministry. However, this scheme proved unworkable in a liberalizing economy. Yet the alternative, of undertaking sharp retrenchment in order to ensure that the remaining officers are paid adequately, is still a difficult choice to make.

In the health sector, regional pay incentives have been created. For example, medical doctors working in the remoter parts of Niassa or Tete provinces could command a 120 percent increase in their basic salaries (Republic of Mozambique, 1999). However, this would still be inadequate if not combined with some other income-generating activity for the professionals or their family. The remote regions of the country do not have such opportunities for extra income generation and thus the government's salary differentiation scheme is unable to attract doctors to these regions in sufficient numbers.

The inability of the government to retain qualified staff has also affected the implementation of donor projects and programs. In individual departments, therefore, there has been a tendency to resolve staffing problems by creating special arrangements. These are based on a variety of allowances, the creation of opportunities for 'consultancies' within projects, which command better pay, or the payment of fees or allowances to employees attending seminars or important meetings. In other instances, such as in the health and agriculture line ministries, specialists and managers have simply been paid directly by donors. More recently, senior managers in government have been given seats on the boards of the partly privatized companies, which has improved their earnings but also demands a considerable amount of their time. Moreover, there is the risk that now they are partly representing the interests of the private sector their allegiance to government policies might be distorted. Serious principal–agent problems are bound to arise.

The various interventions to improve incentives have helped to raise morale among segments of the civil service, but the proliferation of wage enhancement schemes has had a number of negative effects. First, it has encouraged a 'seminar culture,' in which meetings take up a considerable portion of civil servants' worktime that would have otherwise been spent on policy implementation. Since senior managers also attend a considerable number of meetings, decision making tends to be somewhat paralyzed. This problem can be especially cumbersome for policymakers in the remoter regions who are summoned to the capital for meetings. Second, these wage enhancement schemes have led to a lack of wage harmony in the public sector. Relatively junior officers attached to donor-financed projects are able to earn many times more than their departmental superiors. This causes dissatisfaction and even insubordination. Also of concern is the government's very limited capacity to penalize poor performance or to reward success because it has little real influence on the incentive structure.

4   Institutional reforms and governance issues

To move ahead in its political and economic reforms, Mozambique has had to evolve new institutions for governance, at both the national and lower levels. This is in broad terms evidenced by the adoption of multi-party democracy and the introduction of local governments (*autarquias*). The areas so designated have been allowed a measure of self-governance. A major goal behind these changes has been to increase the participation of the population in the decisions that affect their lives. To its credit, the government has recognized that reform of the public sector will be a long-term process. At the end of the 1990s, it put together a program, to be implemented over a period of ten years, that would address many of the institutional problems outlined above. The central objectives of the program include:

- the modernization of the public sector,
- improvement of its ability to formulate and implement policies, including the efficient use of public resources,
- decentralization, including planning for and deployment of resources,
- improving systems for human resource management, including wage structures,
- improvement of governance, that is institutional development at both the central and regional levels.

The program is divided into phases. The first phase started in August

2001 and will run to mid-2004. During this phase, the government hopes to establish the financial management systems as well as remuneration and incentive schemes for the public sector that will be more robust than those attempted in the past. With these in place, the government will then be in a position to improve the implementation of its policies, with the help of a better-motivated civil service. As a first step in implementation, an interministerial commission for reforms in the public sector was created by presidential decree in March 2000 to establish mechanisms to manage the process. The commission incorporates line ministries, including the ministries of planning and finance, education, labor, health and justice, and agriculture and rural development. A unit to deal with the technical aspects of reform was also created to assist the commission in planning, coordinating and monitoring programs and projects within the reform process. As an indication of the priority given to public sector reform, the commission is chaired by the prime minister and reports to the Council of Ministers (Republic of Mozambique, 2000c,d).

The government has also sought consultation with the people at various levels. This could, for example, be via the implementation of sector-wide projects, such as those in agriculture, health and education supported by donors, with consultations between NGOs, the private sector and the beneficiaries thought to be key to project effectiveness. At the district or regional level, new forms of public management revolving around the new *autarquias* have been established. The goal is to increase local participation while bringing services closer to where they are needed. Although this is a promising departure from the relative bureaucratic aloofness of the past, it is not quite clear how these new entities will raise revenue, or what specific activities, as opposed to those of central government, they should focus on. Part of this confusion of roles is because the legislation setting up these new entities is not quite complete. They still rely almost exclusively on transfers from the state budget, and their operational independence is thus substantially limited. Weak auditing systems also imply that the keeping of accounts is irregular. Still, the new administrative forms could well become the basis for the devolution of power to the lower levels, and develop horizontal, as opposed to vertical, planning modes to support the decentralization process.

In Nampula, a pilot decentralization project, which includes almost all the districts within the province, has been undertaken with good results. Based on this experience and a previous rural development project supported by the World Bank – and also taking into account that there is some competition among donors to replicate the Nampula experience in other provinces of Mozambique – a larger project is now being designed within the ministry of planning and finance. These types of actions and experiments are seen as necessary for providing a basis for solutions to some of the country's critical problems.

However, as already noted, serious human capacity problems remain, making many of the reforms difficult to implement. For example, financial accountability, budgeting and monitoring are important for the success of the new structures and to eradicate corruption, but in reality there is very little bookkeeping at the local level, although current stipulations are that books should be audited bi-annually. With a view to strengthening accountability, the government has embarked on the process of drafting a law to govern the use of public finances. Without government implementation, however, accountability will not improve.

The government has also had to consult broadly with respect to broader national policies, including macroeconomic policy, judicial reforms and privatization. In a society that has suffered various forms of cleavage in the past, ranging from external aggression to civil war, this has not been an easy task, however. Parliamentary democracy is a very recent phenomenon, and political opposition is still viewed with suspicion in government circles. In the wake of the peace process many new social and political groupings have emerged, collectively referred to as civil society. They are expanding their influence and demands on the government. Domestic and foreign NGOs, and by extension the donor community, have also had to be incorporated in various ways into the reform process. In this regard, the biggest challenge has been to establish credible, democratic institutions that would bridge the sharp social dichotomies, repair the collapsed economy and stem rising poverty, especially in the remoter regions of the country.

With regard to interaction with donors, aid management has caused much concern. This is for two interrelated reasons, the first of which is the proliferation of aid operations in the country. Owing to its immense needs, but also its strategic importance in southern Africa, Mozambique has attracted a large donor community and multifaceted aid programs. On the host side, up to seven agencies at the national level are involved in aid administration. Although the planning and budget directorate of the planning and finance ministry is the lead agency in this respect, a number of other agencies are also involved: the treasury, the directorate for international cooperation, customs, the central bank, the industry and trade ministry, and a national institute for natural disasters and calamities (which registers aid in kind). The donor agencies, notably the IMF and the World Bank, also register and monitor the volume of aid inflows. The proliferation of contracts, administrative cultures and interventions implied by the 'aid problem' has diverted the government from implementing its programs and delayed the time when the government can claim to be the main force behind domestic policies (Plank, 1993).

Second, as already noted above, the capacity for aid implementation remains weak. Donors use expatriates to manage their projects, thus putting sustainability into question (Harrison, 1998). Of most concern is the fact that only a portion of the aid inflows is registered as budgetary resources. The persistence of 'off-budget' resources is a result partly of the unwillingness of donors to lose control over their pet projects, with which they have sometimes been associated for decades, and partly of a genuine fear that, given management capacity constraints, the projects will fail. However, donors have recently shown a willingness to abandon project aid and instead provide general budget support. To achieve the effectiveness they desire, donors are now focusing on how to help the government improve its human resources and technical competence in budgetary matters in order to ensure a higher degree of accountability in the use of resources. This would, for example, reduce corruption in the civil service, which is acknowledged to be a serious impediment to policy implementation.

With regard to the reform of the judiciary, it is clear that, after thirteen years of economic reforms, many aspects of the legal system, including the judiciary and the courts, are no longer appropriate and must be abandoned. The expansion of the private sector, especially since the government embarked on privatization in the early 1990s, has necessitated improvements in property rights, the creation of mechanisms for settling business disputes and the formulation of a law of bankruptcy (see Brück et al., 2000). Overall, business disputes need to be expeditiously foreclosed in order to lower costs and to speed up investment. Moreover, a commercial code was needed to enable the development of a favorable business environment. Donors have also insisted that the government make important improvements in its judiciary and other legal institutions. As a result, the restructuring of the legal sector has become an important aspect of the overall economic and political reforms in Mozambique.

5   Reforms, social sectors and poverty reduction

An overriding goal of the reform process in Mozambique, as indeed in other African countries, has been poverty eradication. Measurements based on the 1996/7 household survey show that close to 70 percent of the population is classed as poor. Moreover, there are some serious regional disparities, with the remoter areas having a higher poverty incidence than areas closer to the capital (see, for example, De Sousa et al., 1999). Thus in the government's program for the period 2000–4, poverty reduction has become the core goal of economic policy. The first poverty assessment was done in 1998, enabling the government to embark on strategies for the reduction of absolute poverty. An action plan for the reduction of absolute poverty was finalized in December 1999. This document was the basis for an interim poverty reduction strategy paper, which, after IMF and World Bank endorsement, made it possible for the country to accede to the enhanced HIPC initiative in 2000.

To encourage reform ownership and ensure sustainability, the approach used in the production of the action plan was geared towards capacity building, favoring local intellectual input and undertaken almost entirely by the staff of the ministry of planning and finance. The remaining challenges include devising the consultation methods that must go hand in hand with poverty reduction programs. Until very recently, the government was poor at discussing policy issues with the major stakeholders. Thus consultation, given the requirement that it should relate directly to overall planning and budgeting, will also become a learning process for the civil service and the government as a whole. Moreover, consultation helps to keep stakeholder demands and expectations within realizable limits.

A key element in poverty reduction is the adequate supply of social services, notably education and healthcare. In November 1977, following independence in 1975, the Frelimo government introduced a health bill that in effect socialized medical care. However, the civil war had a negative impact on the economy, and there were few resources to cater for the health and education needs of the population. Even after a number of years of relative peace, the quality of health service delivery in public institutions remains questionable, and donor support is still important in ensuring the supply of a modicum of services, especially in the rural areas.

Table 9.4 shows that, on the whole, the health infrastructure in Mozambique remains rudimentary, with, for example, a total of only 14,000 beds for a population of over 17 million. Although the earlier socialist experiment had helped spread health units throughout the country, today many of them lack adequate supplies of medicine and materials. Many hospitals are in a poor physical state. The supply of doctors and specialists is much better in Maputo and surrounding regions than in the remoter northern areas. Although newly graduated doctors have to spend a period of internship upcountry, they soon return to the urban areas where the opportunities for augmenting incomes are much better. In a bid to improve the supply of medical services, the government introduced special clinics, where patients would be treated for a fee. Fully private-run clinics were soon introduced as well. Although the new approach has improved services for the more affluent groups, it has split the loyalties of the medical workers, because they can now earn many times their official

Table 9.4 Mozambican national health infrastructure by province, 1997

Region	Share of total population (%)	Number of health units	Regional share (%)	Approximate number of beds	Regional share (%)	Number of personnel	Share of doctors (%)	Number of vehicles
Niassa	5.0	107	10.0	696	4.9	368	3.0	26
Cabo Delgado	8.5	84	8.0	857	6.0	535	5.2	32
Nampula	18.9	157	14.9	2,124	14.8	1,050	4.3	38
Zambezia	19.2	166	15.7	1,340	9.4	802	3.0	38
Tete	7.6	84	8.0	1,041	7.3	515	5.2	31
Manica	6.6	75	7.0	728	5.1	453	5.3	29
Sofala	8.4	121	11.5	1,641	11.5	847	5.8	68
Inhambane	7.3	76	7.2	1,220	8.5	634	2.0	32
Gaza	7.0	85	8.0	1,312	9.2	581	4.0	23
Maputo Provincia	5.4	61	5.8	921	6.4	362	5.5	25
Maputo Cidade	5.9	38	3.6	2,362	16.5	1,553	13.7	49
Total	100.0	1,054	100.0	14,305	100.0	7,700	6.2	391

Source: Compiled by the authors from official sources (see reference list).
Note: Population in 2000 numbered 17.2 million.

217

wage by working for a few days in the private sector. They do not wish to abandon the public sector all together since they still enjoy the non-salary benefits attached to public employment. The wealthier groups have, increasingly, sought treatment in neighboring South Africa.

To address the shortage of human capital, the government embarked on a strategic plan for the education sector to cover the period 1999–2003. Its goals include universal access to primary education, improvement of the quality of education and ensuring that the system is flexible, decentralized and sustainable. However, like many other reforming countries in Africa, Mozambique has been confronted by the dilemma of attempting to improve the quality of social services, especially in education, with little means of defraying the costs of expanded provision. With the majority of the population characterized as poor, cost-sharing measures have achieved very little in improving services. Thus, any expansion in the numbers accessing school without offsetting increases in expenditure on education has meant declining quality of services. Dropout rates have also been substantial.

Over the period 1980–6, before the civil war had ruined the economy, the education budget comprised 17–19 percent of the general state budget. In 1987, with the civil war reaching a higher intensity, the budget fell to below 10 percent of the state budget, as service expenditure competed with that of the military. In adjusting to this shock, wages in the education sector fell in real terms by about 50 percent, and the supply of materials was also seriously curtailed. The sector was saved from collapse by foreign aid, which in total exceeded what the government was spending on education.

Since embarking on the liberalization of the economy in the late 1980s, Mozambique's modern sector has experienced a sharp increase in the overall competition for skilled labor. The backlog in training that was caused by the civil war and economic crisis led to severe skill scarcities across the board. In 1990, for example, the number of Mozambicans with a university degree was estimated at only 3,000 in a total labor force of almost 6 million. The 1997 census estimated that this number had increased to about 8,000 people, which is still only about 0.1 percent of the adult population. The distribution of those with degrees by residence and occupational category indicates serious regional disparities: degree holders are invariably resident in urban areas, which account for only 30 percent of the total population.

Three institutions provide higher education in Mozambique and are the main source, apart from some training abroad, of professional and managerial cadres in the civil service: Eduardo Mondlane University, the Higher Institute of International Relations and the Pedagogical University; all three offer diplomas, bachelor's degrees as well as *licenciatura*.

Only the Pedagogical University has educational activities based outside the capital, Maputo, with branches in Beira and Nampula. In 1994, the three institutions admitted a total of about 1,200 students, with women accounting for about 26 percent. Since the mid-1990s, and as a general reflection of the liberalization trend in Mozambique, three private colleges have been established: the Catholic University, with campuses in Beira, Nampula and Cuamba in Niassa Province, a polytechnic (ISPU) with campuses in Maputo and Quelimane, and an Institute for Science and Technology in Maputo.

Table 9.5 depicts aspects of the Mozambican dilemma in education. School attendance at the lower levels seems to be evenly spread among the provinces, and the student/teacher ratios are not seriously divergent, but attendance rates for the country as a whole and for the rural provinces in particular fall rapidly after the 5th grade. In 1997, the country had only about 6,000 students in the 11th–12th grades, attendance rates that were much lower than for neighboring countries. It is obvious that the numbers currently filtering through the school system are simply too low to provide the level of human capital consistent with sustainable development and poverty reduction. There is thus a strong case for giving priority to the education sector in subsequent reforms (Shoeman, 1999).

6 Conclusions

Owing to its history of conflict-ridden colonial rule and post-independence civil war, it might be tempting to consider Mozambique and the evolution of its state structures as a special case. However, the challenges related to the reform of its civil service in the 1990s are similar to those in the rest of sub-Saharan Africa. First, it is important for the government to establish credibility not only with the general population but, even more crucially, with employees in the public sector. Civil servants have in the past been expected to behave differently from the rest of the population and to continue to provide services to the population under inadequate conditions of service. Credibility will, however, not be achieved by the adoption of discretionary measures directed at strategic elements of government. Higher wages and terms of service for chosen individuals and groups such as doctors and university teachers can go only so far in enhancing public sector productivity. Sustainable improvements demand that the government undertake comprehensive measures that encapsulate the whole of the public sector.

Second, improving incentives in the public sector should not be conceived of as an isolated exercise, since it is part and parcel of overall economic reform. Very little improvement in employment conditions in

Table 9.5 School attendance by province and level, 1997

Region	Share of total population (%)	Grades 1–5		Grades 6–7		Grades 8–10		Grades 11–12	
		No.	Student/ teacher ratio	No.	Student/ teacher ratio	No.	Student/ teacher ratio	No.	Student/ teacher ratio
Niassa	5.0	79,818	46	5,735	27	1,694	19	334	21
Cabo Delgado	8.5	121,972	55	6,657	32	2,522	28	309	13
Nampula	18.9	269,747	53	15,143	33	4,159	29	583	17
Zambezia	19.2	330,253	65	15,628	40	3,748	49	382	25
Tete	7.6	124,304	49	9,748	27	3,124	36	341	19
Manica	6.6	101,004	59	11,136	48	2,392	30	201	13
Sofala	8.4	111,179	56	12,127	38	3,814	27	574	30
Inhambane	7.3	159,838	68	16,567	47	3,262	27	220	12
Gaza	7.0	173,737	79	14,995	50	3,940	43	284	18
Maputo Provincia	5.4	130,344	83	14,786	41	4,328	28	426	25
Maputo Cidade	5.9	142,853	63	31,960	41	12,228	55	2,689	38
Total	100.0	1,745,049	61	154,482	39	45,211	35	6,343	24

Source: Compiled by authors from official sources (see reference list).
Note: Population in 2000 numbered 17.2 million.

the public service and in the delivery of social services can be achieved when the rest of the economy remains in disarray. This is especially true in light of the current efforts at decentralizing government functions in Mozambique and elsewhere in sub-Saharan Africa. Access to social services demands not only an adequate level of infrastructure (at its most basic, roads), but also stable macroeconomic conditions.

Third, much of the progress made in public sector reform in Mozambique has been largely thanks to the goodwill of the donor community and the multilateral institutions. However, this has also meant that donors have tended to influence the agenda at the expense of domestic initiative. In the medium to long term, however, the question of the ownership of the development agenda will have to be addressed. It is only when policies are internalized, and the reform thrust is from within, that improvement in the public sector can become sustainable.

Lastly, engaging in far-reaching reforms without sufficient domestic resources risks subordinating the government's political agenda to that of the donor community. This is the dilemma facing most African governments. However, given Mozambique's recent history of civil war and weather shocks, financial independence will not be achieved in the near future. Still, efforts at improving capacities in the public sector in general and in the civil service in particular could ensure that future reforms will be driven from within.

Note

1. In the more remote provinces, where the scope for parallel activities was limited, public officials absconded from duty altogether.

REFERENCES

Alden, C. (2000) 'Swords into Ploughshares? The United Nations and Demilitarization in Mozambique,' *Journal of Humanitarian Assistance*, http:/www.jha/articles/a026.htm.

Bowen, M. (1992) 'Beyond Reform: Adjustment and Political Power in Contemporary Mozambique,' *Journal of Modern African Studies* 30(2):255–79.

Brück, T. (2000) 'Macroeconomic Effects of the War in Mozambique,' QEH Working Papers, 11, Queen Elizabeth House, Oxford.

Brück, T., V. FitzGerald and A. Grigsby (2000) 'Enhancing the Private Sector Contribution to Postwar Recovery in Poor Countries,' QEH Working Papers, 45(3), Queen Elizabeth House, Oxford.

DANIDA (Danish International Development Agency) (1996) *The Danish As-*

sistance to the Fisheries Sector Mozambique: Main Report, Ministry of Foreign Affairs: Copenhagen.

De Sousa, M., J. Sulemane and C. Matusse (1999) *Rapid Assessment of Mozambique National Anti-Poverty Program*, UNDP: Maputo.

Harrison, G. (1998) 'Clean-ups, Conditionality and Adjustment: Why Institutions Matter in Mozambique,' *Review of African Political Economy* 26(81):323–33.

IMF (International Monetary Fund) and IDA (International Development Association) (2000) *Republic of Mozambique – Decision Point Document for the Enhanced Heavily Indebted Poor Countries (HIPC) Initiative*, IMF: Washington, DC.

Kyle, S. (1991) 'Economic Reform and Armed Conflict in Mozambique,' *World Development* 19(6):637–49.

Massingue, V., A. Muchanga and R. Labelle (1995) *Mozambique Document, Sustainable Development Networking Program*, UNDP: Maputo.

Ministry for Health (various) *Informacão Estatística Sumaría*, Ministry for Health: Maputo.

Nkomo, M. O. (1986) 'A Comparative Study of Zambia and Mozambique: Africanization, Professionalization and Bureaucracy in the African Postcolonial State,' *Journal of Black Studies* 16(3):319–42.

Plank, D. (1993) 'Aid, Debt, and the End of Sovereignty: Mozambique and Its Donors,' *Journal of Modern African Studies* 31(3):407–30.

Republic of Mozambique (1980) 'Salários para Técnicos Superiores e Médios,' *Decreto* 4/80, Maputo.

——— (1987) 'Estatuto Geral dos Funcionários do Estado,' *Decreto* 14/87, Maputo.

——— (1990, 1991, 1992) 'Tabela Única de Vencimentos na Administração Pública,' *Decreto* 41/90, *Decreto* 41/91, *Decreto* 26/92, Maputo.

——— (1992a) 'Adequação do Sistema Salarial no Aparelho do Estado e nas Instituições Estatais,' *Ministério das Finanças Circular* 12/GAB-VMF/92, 30 September, Maputo.

——— (1992b) 'Sistema Nacional de Gestão de Recursos Humanos,' *Decreto* 40/92, Maputo.

——— (1998a) 'Sistema de Carreiras e Remuneração,' *Decreto* 64/98, Maputo.

——— (1998b) 'Alteração de Algumas Disposições do Estatuto Geral dos Funcionários do Estado e Legislação Complementar,' *Decreto* 65/98, Maputo.

——— (1999) 'Ministérios da Administração Estatal e Ministério do Plano e Finanças, Classificação das Áreas Territoriais para Efeitos de Atribuição do Bónus Especial,' *Diploma Ministerial* 23/99, Maputo.

——— (2000a) *Interim Poverty Reduction Strategy Paper*, Maputo.

——— (2000b) *Memorandum of Economic and Financial Policies of the Government of Mozambique for 2000–01*, Maputo.

——— (2000c) 'Criação da Comissão Interministerial da Reforma do Sector Público – CIRESP,' *Decreto Presidencial* 5/2000, Maputo.

——— (2000d) 'Criação da Unidade Técnica da Reforma do Sector Público – UTRESP,' *Decreto* 6/2000, Maputo.

Shoeman, S. (1999) 'Transforming Education in South Africa: Lessons from the Mozambican Experience,' *Africanus* 29(1):33–44.

Tarp, F. and I. M. Lau (1996) *Mozambique: Macroeconomic Performance and Critical Issues*, Institute of Economics, University of Copenhagen.

World Bank (1991) 'Mozambique: Public Sector Pay and Employment Review,' MOZ Reports 9815, World Bank, Washington, DC.

Wuyts, M. (1995) *Foreign Aid, Structural Adjustment and Public Management: The Mozambican Experience*, Institute of Social Studies: The Hague.

Part III

Developing institutional capabilities

10

Privatization in sub-Saharan Africa: On factors affecting implementation

Steve Kayizzi-Mugerwa

1 Introduction

A characteristic feature of the African economy in the 1990s was the speed with which governments extricated themselves from the direct ownership and management of businesses. Although the process was part of a global trend, it has tended to have larger economic and political connotations in Africa than elsewhere (Bennel, 1997; Drum, 1993). This is because African governments had embraced state ownership of the formal economy much more strongly than had other parts of the world outside the former socialist bloc.[1] This attempt at controlling the 'commanding heights' coincided with severe external shocks, however, and was not sustainable. The structural adjustment programs that were embarked on in the 1980s presented an alternative approach based on less intrusive government, and with privatization and the restructuring of state-owned enterprises (SOEs) seen as important for the success of economic reform.

Privatization implies the transfer of ownership from the public to the private sector, as well as changes in income flows between groups. Hence it has important socioeconomic implications for the various interest groups, not least the bureaucratic elite. Thus, politically and in terms of administrative resources, privatization and public sector reforms have been more demanding than the 'stroke of the pen' measures such as exchange rate and price reforms, which brought about macroeconomic stability. Furthermore, in recent years, donors and multilateral agencies have made privatization a key conditionality. Indeed, more African countries undertook privatization in an effort to assuage donor fears over domestic reform commitment than out of ideological or economic conviction. Privatization thus touches on a complex set of issues, including property rights, nationality, ethnicity, bureaucratic practices, donor conditionality and the nature of markets and politics.

The purpose of this chapter is to analyze the factors affecting the implementation of privatization in sub-Saharan Africa. Anecdotal evidence suggests that there have been wide differences in the way privatization strategies and plans have been introduced, debated and executed in Africa. Whereas some governments quickly overcame opposition to privatization from influential groups, such as labor unions and consumer groups, and were able to sell off the bulk of the parastatals, others failed to go much beyond the initial divesture of small companies or the return of shares acquired during earlier nationalizations. Ironically, it is not always the capitalist-oriented African economies such as Kenya and the Côte d'Ivoire that are the most keen privatizers. Formerly socialist-oriented ones such as Mozambique and Tanzania have been faster in implementing privatization.[2]

Among the questions addressed in this chapter are the following: What strategies have been used to initiate privatization, especially in light of domestic opposition? Which factors have influenced the evolution of the privatization debate in the various countries and what impact has this had on the pace of implementation? Why have some countries kept a steady course in implementing privatization, whereas in others the process has stagnated or failed altogether? Which issues have emerged as privatization evolved from the divesture of small firms to that of large corporations, and how have they been resolved?[3] In other words, is there a 'privatization learning curve'? If so, how have the transition costs, political as well as economic, been addressed?

2   Theoretical overview

Theoretical analyses project two main views on privatization. The normative view is that privatization is necessary to curb waste, raise economic efficiency and develop the activities of the private sector via increased domestic and foreign investment.[4] The main driving force is the eradication of the 'soft budget' constraints that make public firms a major cause of fiscal imbalance, because they encourage waste and obstruct the flow of services (Harsch, 2000; Kornai, 2000). The normative theory also presupposes benevolent governments and politicians. The latter are assumed to be altruistic, their main concern being to maximize aggregate welfare. They are willing to abandon a discretionary system for one where market forces determine performance. Since the welfare benefits of privatization take time to realize, however, the normative view provides a long-term rationale for public sector divestment, since the process is in the context not as important as the outcome.

The point of departure for the positive view is that in sub-Saharan Africa, as in many other developing countries, privatization is a politically charged subject. This relates to the agency and credibility problems that are unleashed by the exercise, as well as its income distribution implications. In managing SOEs, politicians and bureaucrats enjoy rents and are also able to exercise political patronage, for example the creation of jobs for their supporters as well as targeting credit and other benefits to them. In turn they are assured re-election or other means of retaining power. Why then would politicians who are pursuing group interests and, under them, bureaucrats with discretionary powers be willing to commit to a privatization policy that does not favor particular groups or agree to the establishment of an impartial regulatory mechanism after privatization?

The answer from the positive theory is that privatization goes ahead only when politicians see clear-cut economic and political benefits. In their application of the model on sub-Saharan Africa, Laffont and Meleu (1999) conclude that the speed of privatization is directly related to the shares that politicians or their relatives can fetch in the privatized firms to compensate themselves for the loss of the rents previously enjoyed under state ownership. Similarly, interest groups or constituencies, depending on the amount of political influence they wield, can also affect the speed and sequence of privatization (see Table 10.1). Thus governments could end up maximizing group rather than aggregate welfare. For example, since the divestiture of loss-making SOEs implicitly lowers the tax burden, privatization rewards taxpayers, often the middle classes, while reducing the rents and employment opportunities enjoyed by senior bureaucrats and other public sector employees.[5] There is thus a tradeoff between the goals of economic efficiency postulated by the normative approach and the issues of income distribution and voter maximization of the positive approach (Gupta, 1998; Talley, 1998).

However, bureaucratic collusion and political patronage need not be the only spur to privatization. As already noted, privatization was undertaken in many African countries as a direct response to demands from the donor community and the multilateral agencies to get governments out of business. Indeed, in Kenya and Zambia the privatization of key

Table 10.1 Threats and benefits to interest groups in the privatization process

Interest group	Potential threats/benefits
1. Government leaders and their representatives on the boards of the state-owned companies, as well as bureaucrats in the line ministries	Threats include possible loss of political patronage and income. On the other hand, privatization reduces the fiscal burden and sends positive signals to the donor community
2. Parastatal managers and employees	Risk of loss of employment and income during privatization and post-privatization restructuring
3. Participants in the markets for goods and services: consumers, suppliers of inputs, financiers, competitors, etc.	Since many parastatals were moribund pre-privatization, their divesture tends to increase market activities, benefiting participants. However, even non-performing parastatals still received huge subsidies from government; their loss affected some groups seriously
4. Influential domestic groups, including political parties, religious leaders, labor unions, parliamentarians and academics	The unequal distribution of privatization benefits as well as 'foreignization' are seen as threats by a large number of groups ex ante. Still, an expanding private sector soon begets its own support groups, and views change rapidly ex post
5. Donors and multilateral agencies	On the whole, donors and multilateral agencies see no threats in privatization, only benefits. To them, privatization signals commitment on the part of national policymakers to economic reform and to efficiency in government

Source: Compiled by the author.

companies was a precondition for further financial assistance. There is one important reason why donors would have influence in the context. The inflow of aid keeps government bureaucracies operative and sometimes even increases their activities and wages. It can also be argued that for many regimes, for example those that had forcibly nationalized or expropriated properties belonging to multinationals and non-indigenous groups, as in Uganda in the early 1970s, privatization became a means of signaling the end of the old ways and the beginning of legality. That governments were tying their own hands, for the sake of private sector development, also indicates how weak they had become compared with the 1960s, for example (Kumssa, 1996).

3   Learning to privatize

Even after privatization, as a concept, has been internalized by policy-makers, debate often continues around issues such as the divestiture sequence, the size of the firms to be sold and the speed at which privatization is to be undertaken, as well as the method to be used. In many countries in Africa, the divestiture of small firms, almost exclusively sold to 'nationals' or simply liquidated, elicits little controversy, even when the companies end up in the hands of bureaucrats and politicians. It is the privatization of large companies, especially those thought to be 'strategic,' that leads to controversy. First, these companies are often too big for domestic capitalists to afford and thus end up in foreign ownership. Second, the concept of 'sunk costs' is not well appreciated by the general population and the politicians. They expect large SOEs to be worth at least a good fraction of the millions spent on their rehabilitation or on loans to them by the government. The sale of 'national treasures' at 'distress prices' causes much political dissatisfaction. In deference to this, many African governments embarked on privatization with lists of companies that were to remain in state ownership. In the case of Uganda, the list included, among others, the government-owned newspaper *New Vision*, the national airline and the electricity board (an electricity utility monopoly). It is an illustration of how fast the process has evolved since the early 1990s that none of the above firms remains on the priority list, with Uganda Airlines in de facto liquidation.

With the help of Figure 10.1, we portray the evolution of the privati-

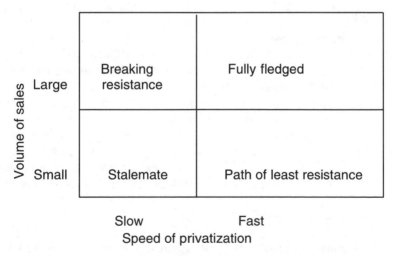

Figure 10.1 Typical phases in privatization in sub-Saharan Africa

zation process for a typical group of sub-Saharan countries. On the vertical axis of Figure 10.1 is the accumulated volume of sales in an appropriate currency, say US dollars. This ranges from the proceeds of 'small' businesses with fewer than five employees to 'large' corporations employing thousands of workers. On the horizontal axis is the speed of privatization, measured as the time it takes to achieve a given volume of sales. It could be 'slow,' which for convenience also includes no activity, or 'fast.'

3.1   Stalemate

Stalemate describes a position of minimal movement, with slow privatization and a small volume of sales. This was the case for many African countries in the late 1980s, before the privatization process achieved momentum. Owing to social strife and political difficulties, some countries have not moved far from here.

3.2   Path of least resistance

The 'path of least resistance' refers to a scenario, quite common in sub-Saharan Africa, in which governments embarked on rapid privatization of small firms but balked when it came to large companies. This was, for example, the experience of Zambia during the first five years of privatization in the 1990s when close to 200 companies were divested and the government was praised by donors and multilateral agencies for undertaking one of the fastest and most transparent privatizations in Africa (Kayizzi-Mugerwa, 2001). The Zambian government claimed at the time that when it came to privatization there were 'no sacred cows.' However, altogether the companies sold thus far were worth only a fraction of the assets of Zambia Consolidated Copper Mines (ZCCM), the mining conglomerate, whose controversial privatization was long drawn out and not completed until the end of the 1990s.[6]

Eventually, the stock of small firms in the 'path of least resistance' phase is exhausted and governments must resort to privatizing larger ones. At about this time, the privatization process begins to generate its own dynamics. This is partly a process of learning from earlier mistakes and strengthening the administrative and financial aspects of the process, including the introduction of new legal codes to remove loopholes.

3.3   Breaking resistance

The third phase of privatization in Figure 10.1 can be referred to as 'breaking resistance.' This characterized the bulk of sub-Saharan countries in the first half of the 1990s. At this stage, privatization has been accepted in principle, and institutional and legislative modalities for its implementation are in place. However, owing to institutional and political constraints – for example, as symbols of national independence, larger firms have considerable sentimental value in Africa – privatization is much slower than before. The political mood is still against the divestiture of large companies. Some governments were able to privatize one or two large companies – for example, Kenya Airways in the mid-1990s and the electricity conglomerate CIE in Côte d'Ivoire in 1990 via the issue of a ten-year lease contract to a French company. The privatization of a big company is often what is needed to help break domestic resistance. The privatization of 'national treasures' is no longer impossible, becoming just a question of time.[7]

3.4   Fully fledged privatization

The last phase, so far reached by only a few African countries, involves a more fully fledged privatization effort, including firms formerly considered strategic in sectors such as telecommunications, electricity, water and other utilities. The phase is reached when political and institutional constraints to privatization have been removed, enabling rapid divestiture, with big companies coming on stream relatively quickly and with sales to foreigners causing little or no controversy. This phase differs from the 'big bang' privatization that was common in the transition economies of Eastern Europe, notably the voucher privatization schemes in Russia, the Czech Republic and, to a lesser extent, Poland. The rationale there was that, for reasons of fairness, every citizen had to be given an equal share of the former property of the state. For the big bang to succeed, however, central bureaucracies, such as those of the postsocialist era in Eastern Europe, must have suffered serious credibility problems, making it difficult for them to defend themselves against the serious onslaught on their incomes and rents implied by the rapid diminution of the public enterprise sector. Voucher privatization has not been attempted in sub-Saharan Africa. In the fully fledged privatization phase, governments have more experience and are able to make the necessary adjustments, notably with respect to strengthening the legal framework. Typically, the debate regarding the rationale for privatization has at this stage been transcended, with the focus now on how the benefits of privatization are allocated.[8]

4   The privatization process in sub-Saharan Africa

In this section, I use the framework discussed above to analyze issues arising during the privatization process. I look specifically at the stages of initiation, consolidation and fully fledged privatization. The factors determining performance during each of these phases, as well as the transition from one to the other, will be illustrated using examples and data from a range of sub-Saharan countries, although the experiences of Côte d'Ivoire, Ghana, Kenya, Mozambique, Tanzania, Uganda and Zambia will form the core of the discussion.

4.1 Factors at initiation

Privatization and public sector reforms mark what have been termed 'second-generation' adjustment policies, an attempt at distinguishing them from the 'first-generation' policies, which focused almost exclusively on economic stabilization. In most sub-Saharan African countries, privatization was embarked on because of pressure from the donor community; rarely was it a country's own policy initiative (Appiah-Kubi, 2001).[9] Still, when privatization began, a number of domestic factors came into play. As a result, some privatization episodes were relatively smooth whereas others were protracted and controversial, in some cases forcing the government to postpone or cancel the process altogether.

SOEs are often an amorphous group of companies covering most sectors of the economy, acquired under a variety of political ambitions and held together by a number of statutes and legal provisions. The bulk of SOEs – not just utility companies supplying electricity, water, transport and telecommunications, but also huge mining companies – were inherited from the colonial governments at independence. However, governments then acquired whole or partial stakes in multinationals and other foreign-owned companies during the socialist revolutions of the 1960s and 1970s – this included areas such as banking, transport, agriculture, mining and manufacturing.

In most countries, nationalization was completed after protracted negotiations with incumbent owners, with governments compensating them for their nationalized assets (in the case of Zambia even borrowing on international markets in order to do so), but there were a number of exceptions. In Mozambique, nationalization was a result of the assumption of power of the socialist guerrilla movement (Frelimo), which saw private ownership as synonymous with Portuguese alienation and something to be eliminated entirely (Pitcher, 1996). The properties left behind by the fleeing Portuguese settlers were nationalized en masse. In Tanzania, following the declaration of socialism in the second half of the 1960s, a similar nationalization of businesses took place, with the government or cooperatives ending up with many more of the smaller businesses than happened in neighboring countries. Uganda provides yet another variation. In the early 1970s the military government expelled citizens of non-

African origin, with Asian business families being the main target, and expropriated all their properties with little or no compensation. However, unlike in Mozambique and Tanzania, the smaller businesses were acquired by indigenous Ugandans close to the political leadership; only the bigger businesses were taken over by the state.[10]

Governments also set up their own companies, seeing this as an important means of providing dynamism to their economies by helping to create employment while enabling governments to ensure regional balance in economic development. SOEs were created in a number of areas, including airlines, banking, insurance and tourism. In francophone Africa in particular, perhaps as a legacy of metropolitan France itself, state ownership became quite entrenched. In Côte d'Ivoire, for example, a country generally considered capitalist in orientation, the government still has extensive business holdings in most areas of the economy. This policy stance resembles that of Kenya. In both countries, state ownership of businesses has not excluded multinational corporations and private individuals from holding large stakes in the economy, although there have been complaints over lopsided competition.

4.2 Evolution of the privatization debate

In most African countries, privatization has been followed by serious debate. The exchange between politicians, bureaucrats and other stakeholders has sometimes been acrimonious, and the conditionality attached to privatization by donors and multilateral agencies has caused sharp disagreement.

African governments had heralded the nationalizations of the 1960s and 1970s as marking the real beginning of independence. Besides political independence, Africans would also control their economies for the first time. Thus, although many of the businesses acquired by governments were very poorly run, with low capacity utilization and serious dependence on state subsidies, SOEs were seen as national possessions worth preserving in the public realm.[11] However, although state ownership of the larger companies could be justified on the grounds of scale economies, employment creation and regional balance, governments had gone well beyond 'strategic' considerations in acquiring businesses. This was because in many of them nationalization was equated with indigenization, with businesses belonging to foreign-born ethnic minorities especially targeted for takeover.

During privatization, the foreign ownership debate has thus returned, with governments trying to ensure that indigenous Africans get a 'fair' share of the assets on sale. However, apart from the small enterprises, governments have not been in a position to tilt the ownership structure in favor of Africans. There was no attempt to adopt the voucher-type privatizations of Eastern Europe, discussed earlier, and the stock exchanges, which would have provided an alternative means of privatization, remain small and fragile.

Privatization seems irreversible in many countries in Africa, but local opinion still refers to it as a loss of 'resources to abroad,' 'foreignization' and 'loss of independence.' In Uganda, which has gone further than most other sub-Saharan African countries in its privatization efforts, President Museveni has made an insightful analysis of the politics of the process (Museveni, 1993). He argues that, simply because his government was returning assets to their former Indian owners and selling off large companies to foreign companies and individuals, this is not reason enough to claim that Uganda was 'being sold to foreigners.' He notes that the 'local middle class' that propagates this view is not in a position to purchase the assets on sale and the government has no money to lend them. He concludes that the tension is not surprising since in his estimation the national interest rarely coincides with the interest of the 'local middle class.'

The second area of contention relates to who should determine the pace, extent and depth of privatization. As already noted, the multilateral agencies and the donor community are very much involved in the implementation of privatization in many African countries. They help set up and finance the institutional structure for privatization and ensure that the process remains on track by attaching it to their overall conditionality. In the earlier phases of privatization, it was generally felt that donors had much more influence on the process than domestic actors. In Uganda, for example, members of parliament argued that, although they considered privatization a fait accompli, they worried about how little influence they and, by analogy, their constituents had had on the process as a whole (UMACIS, 1998). African labor unions had been so weakened by the economic crises of the 1970s and 1980s that they were not able to resist privatization via strikes or other industrial action.

The third source of controversy relates to the valuation of assets and the use to which the proceeds are put. As already noted, although many of the enterprises were non-operational at the time of privatization, the general public still believed that they were worth much more than the buyers were offering. The secrecy surrounding the privatization proceedings often aroused public suspicion, leading to charges of collusion, especially when assets were sold cheaply to 'foreigners.'

4.3 Setting up the institutional structure for privatization

Although domestic opposition to privatization delayed the process in many countries, a more serious impediment was the lack of an institutional structure for privatization. Even after reaching a consensus on the need for privatization, it took much longer than expected for governments to nullify statutes that had sustained state monopolies and to put in place an adequate body of legislation to support privatization, including revisions of laws covering areas such as taxation, bankruptcy, land ownership, competition and regulation.

The existing legislation for the setting up of the institutional framework for privatization and public sector reforms was introduced almost simultaneously by many African countries in the early 1990s, assisted by the donor community. The laws and related documentation share a number of issues; for instance, explaining why it was necessary to privatize, commercialize or bring about changes in the operations of SOEs. The documents and laws also define the structures and powers of the units and institutions set up, within ministries or as independent entities, to supervise the privatization and reform process. However, although the thrust and direction are quite similar, the documents nevertheless reveal some subtle differences in emphasis across countries, reflecting a number of political concerns.

In this section I provide a brief review of some of the laws, proclamations and ordinances introduced by a cross-section of African countries: Ethiopia, Ghana, Guinea, Mozambique, Tanzania, Togo, Uganda and Zambia. The group exemplifies a range of political and economic experiences. Ethiopia, Mozambique and Tanzania had in the past pursued a socialist approach to development, although only Tanzania was spared the ravages of civil war; the rest of the countries in the sample had practiced varying forms of state control and, excepting Zambia, were led at some stage by the military. Uganda, in particular, went through over a decade of political and economic chaos in the 1970s and 1980s. In this section I look at the legislation setting up the privatization structures in the individual countries and the extent to which affirmative issues were taken into account (see Table 10.2).

The objective of the newly created agencies was 'to carry out the process of privatizing public enterprises in an orderly and efficient manner' (Government of Ethiopia, 1994). However, few countries gave the agencies complete autonomy, and the composition of their boards was steered to a large extent by the governments themselves. For example, although the Ethiopian Privatization Agency was to be an autonomous agency with its 'own legal personality,' its five permanent board members were designated by the government and it was accountable to the prime minister in all matters. With respect to interest group representation, the chairperson of the board of the enterprise under privatization as well as the worker representative sitting on its board were allowed to represent the company during the agency's negotiations for its sale.

Table 10.2 Legal and institutional structures for privatization: Board composition of the agency and the affirmative action content of the legislation

Country	Laws and policy declarations	Board composition of the privatization agency	Affirmative action
Ethiopia	Ethiopian Privatization Agency Establishment Proclamation No. 87/94; Establishment of the Board of Trustees of the Privatized Public Enterprises Proclamation No. 17/96	Five permanent members designated by the government. When a company is in the process of privatization the chairperson of its board and the worker representative on the board would participate in the agency's deliberations, as non-voting members	The proclamations establishing the privatization agency as well as the board of trustees for privatized public enterprises make no explicit mention of the need to favor Ethiopian nationals in the privatization process
Ghana	Ghana Divesture of State Interests (Implementation) Law, 1993, establishes a Divestiture Implementation Committee	A chairperson who had to be a member of the then ruling Provisional National Defence Council (PNDC). A representative each from the following: trade union congress, armed forces and Committee for the Defence of the Revolution, plus three other people chosen on the basis of their 'experience or specialized knowledge.' The executive secretary of the committee was automatically a member. All members of the committee were to be elected by the PNDC (i.e. the government)	No explicit affirmative action provisions are made by the divestiture law

Guinea	Loi L93 fixant les règles de la privatisation des entreprises publiques, 1993, sets up a privatization committee	A representative of the Minister for State Assets, two representatives from the ministry to which the company belongs, a representative from the professional bankers' association, and two representatives from the chambers of commerce of agriculture and industry. The mandate of the members would be enforced by decree	Article 8 of the 1993 law states that the privatization should be conducted with national interests in mind. Measures in support of the employees of the privatized companies, including their acquisition of some of the shares, had to be put in place, and labor unions had to be consulted frequently during the process
Kenya	Policy Paper on Public Enterprise Reform, 1992, announces creation of Parastatal Reform Program Committee (PRPC), with the Executive Secretariat and Technical Unit (ESTU) as implementing agency	The board membership of PRPC and ESTU is not specified, although the vice-president was to head PRPC at initiation. The work of the two agencies would be 'insulated from any government or political interference'	With respect to the overall reform of the parastatal sector, the government refers to the need for safety nets to counter the effects of labor retrenchment. The reform measures are also aimed at broadening ownership of assets in the country
Mozambique	Decrees, laws and a ministerial diploma (1989–93) create the Inter-Ministerial Commission for Enterprise Restructuring (CIRE), implementation agency (UTRE), with an Executive Privatization Commission (CEP) for each large company. National and provincial agencies created for smaller firms	CEP membership includes the following: one representative each from the planning and finance ministry, the Bank of Mozambique, the ministry to which the company belongs and the unions. All are nominated by the prime minister	For the purchase of bigger companies, favorable interest rates are offered to nationals. They can also mortgage up to 60 percent of the acquired asset before full payment. Acquisition of smaller firms is faster and tilted in favor of nationals

Table 10.2 (cont.)

Country	Laws and policy declarations	Board composition of the privatization agency	Affirmative action
Tanzania	Amendment of Public Corporations Act, 1992, in 1993 creates Parastatal Sector Reform Commission	The president, upon advice from the finance minister, appoints seven–nine members of the commission, including chairperson	Affirmative action not explicit
Togo	Ordonnance No 94 002/PR Portant Désengagement de l'Etat et d'Autres Personnes Morales de Droit Public des Entreprises, 1994	Nine members, including the chairperson, to be nominated by decree of the Council of Ministers	A hierarchy for privatization specified: firm employees, Togolese persons (physical and legal), similarly for WAEMU countries and ECOWAS. A key goal was 'to protect national interest'
Uganda	The Public Enterprises Reform and Divestiture (PERD) Statute, 1993 (Revised 1998), establishes a Divestiture and Reform Implementation Committee (DRIC), the Privatization Unit (PU) and a Parastatal Monitoring Unit (PMU)	Members of DRIC are: finance minister as chair, attorney general, privatization minister, chairperson of the parliamentary committee on the economy, chairperson of parliamentary committee on parastatals, chairperson of investment authority, three eminent Ugandans who are not ministers. All are government appointees	No explicit affirmative action imbedded in PERD Statute, although among its objectives was 'the promotion of local entrepreneurship'

| Zambia | The Privatization Act, 1992, sets up the Zambian Privatization Agency | Board members are: permanent secretary, Ministry of Commerce, Trade and Industry; permanent secretary, Ministry of Finance; the attorney general; a representative each from the congress of trade unions, the employers' federation, the law association, the Institute of Certified Accountants, the Dean of the School of Business of the Copperbelt University, the churches, the bankers' association, the farmers. The chairperson and the deputy would be elected from among its members. Members would be chosen by a select committee of the national assembly, ratified by the national assembly and appointed by the president | The government may retain a share in any privatized enterprise and could convert it into a golden share. Related to this is the establishment of a privatization trust fund, in which government would hold shares to be purchased later by Zambians. Citizens could also be offered shares (small number) at a discount, and management and employees wishing to buy into the state-owned company would be able to pay for shares in installments |

Sources: World Bank Privatization Transaction Data; and national sources.

A similarly centralized approach to privatization was evident in Ghana in the early 1990s (Republic of Ghana, 1993). The purpose of the Divestiture Implementation Committee was defined as 'to implement and execute all Government policies in respect of divesture programs.' All the committee's recommendations were submitted to the Provisional National Defence Council (PNDC) for approval. The PNDC appointed the members of the committee, whose chairperson and executive secretary were PNDC members. Other members included a representative each from the trade unions, the armed forces and the Committee for the Defence of the Revolution.

In Guinea, the Minister for State Assets assumed authority over the privatization exercise, signing transfer documents on behalf of the government and supervising the work of the privatization committee. A representative from the state assets ministry would chair the committee, which would comprise two representatives from the ministry to which the enterprise on sale 'belonged,' a representative from the bankers' association and two representatives from the chambers of commerce of agriculture and industry. Although there was no explicit representation on the privatization committee for workers, the committee was admonished to keep the labor unions 'informed of the progress of the privatization process.'

The Kenyan and Tanzanian privatization legislation is light compared with other sub-Saharan African examples (Republic of Kenya, 1992; Republic of Tanzania, 1992, 1993). These more modest models contrast sharply with that of Mozambique. To get the privatization process started there required five decrees, three laws and a 'ministerial diploma,' as well as the creation of layers of institutions at the national and provincial levels. The process is also marked by considerable affirmative action to ensure that Mozambicans benefit.

Togolese privatization also favored a centralized approach, with the minister in charge of public enterprises having the main responsibility. The privatization committee, composed mainly of officials chosen by cabinet decree, would consult the minister on each operation, including justifying the choice of object for privatization, as well as on the nature of the negotiations and their conclusion.

In Uganda, the Public Enterprises Reform and Divestiture (PERD) Statute came into force on 8 October 1993, establishing the Divestiture and Reform Implementation Committee (Republic of Uganda, 1993). The committee included the finance minister, as chairperson, the attorney general and the minister responsible for the parastatal on sale. It also included the chairpersons of the parliamentary committees on the economy and the parastatals, the executive director of the investment authority and three 'prominent Ugandans' (not ministers) appointed by the cabinet. The PERD Statute differed from the privatization and reform statutes presented above in that it also laid out the complete portfolio of Ugandan SOEs from the outset, dividing it into four groups: those in which the state would continue to have 100 percent ownership; those in which the state would require majority shareholding in the future; enterprises to be fully divested; and enterprises to be liquidated. The PERD Statute was revised in 1998 to improve the transparency of the privatization process and increase the private sector's representation on the committee. The number of parastatals slated for outright privatization was also increased, and those to remain in government control were reduced drastically.

Unlike many African countries, where the authorities or ruling parties decided to undertake privatization only after pressure from donors and multilateral agencies, Zambia's own privatization effort was part of the ruling Movement for Multiparty Democracy's (MMD) election manifesto. After coming into power in 1991, the MMD embarked on a rapid enactment of laws and institutions to enable the process to go ahead. Parliament passed the privatization bill in July 1992, and the Zambian Privatization Agency was established two months later (Republic of Zambia, 1992). The agency's board comprised twelve members, drawn from as many interest groups as possible, appointed by the president of the country but subject to scrutiny by a select committee of the national assembly and to the assembly's ratification. The breadth of the board, including representatives from churches as well as labor unions, is credited with Zambia's success in the earlier phase of its privatization program.

Turning briefly to the question of affirmative action – that is, to ensure that nationals are favored in the acquisition of the assets on sale – this is not as emphasized as one would have expected, and even then more by implication. The Kenyan document, for example, refers to the need to 'broaden ownership of businesses,' and Uganda's to the 'promotion of local entrepreneurship' as a goal of privatization. Notably, Ethiopia, Ghana and Tanzania, all with long experience of collectivism, have no explicit affirmative provisions in their legislative statements on privatization, which is of course not to say that policymakers did not have any such ambitions in mind.

The privatization laws from francophone Guinea and Togo (République de Guinée, 1993; République Togolaise, 1994) are thus significant in their insistence on enabling citizens to acquire some of the businesses on sale. For example, article 8 of the privatization law of the Republic of Guinea states explicitly that privatization should 'safeguard the national interest' and protect the social wellbeing of the workers in the privatized firms. Moreover, 'labor unions should be involved in discussions related to the treatment of workers in the privatized industries.' Further, the law demands that the privatization committee set aside enterprises for acquisition by Guineans.[12]

In the case of Togo, the privatization committee is charged with setting up a priority list of those who would have the first right of refusal on the assets on sale; notably, employers wishing to take over management of a company, individuals or legal persons of Togolese origin, individuals or legal persons from the West African Economic and Monetary Union (WAEMU), and individuals or legal persons from the Economic Community of West African States (ECOWAS). In a similar law, drafted earlier by the Senegalese government, the need to reserve shares for employees who wished to participate in the process was emphasized; significantly, even employees who had since retired were to be included.[13] Mozambique also has a strong affirmative element, with nationals able to mortgage up to 60 percent of an acquired asset before even paying it off.

With respect to conflicts of interests, which sub-Saharan African experience has shown to lie at the center of the privatization process, legislation has been mild or silent. Here also, the Guinean privatization is significant, taking a tough line on abuse of office by members of the privatization committee. For example, those who accept payment or seek employment or other benefits in the privatized companies would be liable to imprisonment and a large fine.[14] In comparison, the Togolese privatization law, named above, refers only to the need for 'professional secrecy and integrity' in the work of committee members, with no legal consequences indicated for transgression. The Ugandan law (Republic of Uganda, 1993), on the other hand, demands (article 7) that committee members with 'direct personal interest' in the matter being considered should as soon as possible 'disclose the nature' of this interest to the committee and not partake in decisions relating to it. Even here, no sanctions are specified for any transgression of the provision.

What can be concluded from the above examples is that governments were well aware of the political implications and serious conflicts of interest implied by the privatization exercises. The response to these challenges, not only in the drafting of privatization laws but also in applying them, very much depended on the politics of the individual countries, the history of past ownership structures and the extent of donor leverage.

5   Privatization in practice

As already noted, privatization is not a uniform process, not least because of its politicized nature. Comparisons among countries are also made difficult by the differences in methods used to privatize. Among the methods used to privatize companies have been direct sale, usually via tender or direct negotiation, public offer (via the stock exchange), joint venture, lease (for example of hotels in national parks), sale of assets, and liquidation. Moreover, governments have tended to bunch up their sales, for example selling hotels, banks or textile companies at about the same time. The need to prepare sector strategies and legal documents also tends to bring the affected companies on stream at about the same time.

Table 10.3 indicates that direct sale has been the most common method used – 100 percent in the case of Mozambique – although stock exchanges, well developed only in Kenya, Ghana and Nigeria among the sample countries, have been used. In Kenya, the sale of Kenyan Airways was undertaken partly via the stock exchange as well as through a commercial bank. Nigeria undertook 72 percent of its privatization via the stock exchange, although generally its privatization rate has been slow, to be characterized as in the 'breaking resistance' phase.

Although liquidations featured in a number of countries, they have been significant only in Kenya. It can also be argued that, since liquidated companies are written off the books, this might be an easy way for bureaucrats to get hold of the assets cheaply, without arousing political interest. Tanzania has undertaken more joint ventures than other countries in the sample. Besides the fact that its stock exchange is quite new and unable to cater for large transactions, joint ventures reflect the latent resistance to fully fledged privatization by the Tanzanian bureaucrats (Due, 1995; Due et al., 2000). Zambia is the only country recording cases of management buyouts, with many of these involving companies providing services to the Copperbelt mining industry. In both Uganda and Zambia, privatization has also included restitution of companies to their original owners. As argued earlier, privatization enabled these countries to erase their history of private property confiscation in their bid to attract investors.

Tables 10.4 and 10.5 present privatization outcomes for a sample of African countries over a decade. Although Mozambique undertook by far the largest number of privatizations over the 1990s, it is important to note that it also had one of the largest holdings of SOEs in Africa. When Frelimo took power in the mid-1970s, it simply annexed the thousands of small businesses and shops owned by the fleeing Portuguese settlers. During privatization, many of these were sold cheaply to nationals as part of the country's affirmative action. Thus, in spite of the large number of firms for sale, the government has, perhaps intentionally, realized only modest revenues from privatization. It might also be the case that privatization, coming after a long period of civil war, was seen as a part of the postwar reconstruction by policymakers; maximizing returns was thus not necessarily the goal (see also Harris and Lockwood, 1997).

Table 10.3 Privatization in sub-Saharan Africa by method of sale of company, 1990–8 (%)

Country	Stock exchange	Direct sale[a]	Joint venture	Liquidation	Lease	Management buyout	Return of assets and pre-emptive rights
Côte d'Ivoire	24	76	–	–	–	–	–
Ghana	4	89	5	2	–	–	–
Kenya	35	44	–	21	–	–	–
Mozambique	–	100	–	–	–	–	–
Nigeria	72	28	–	–	–	–	–
Tanzania	6	53	21	10	10	–	–
Uganda	2	86	6	2	–	–	4
Zambia	–	87	–	–	–	6	7

Sources: World Bank Privatization Transaction Data; and national sources.
Note:
[a] Direct sale here also includes restricted tender, public tender and negotiated tender, auction and management buyout.

Table 10.4 Privatization outcomes for a sample of sub-Saharan African countries, 1987–97

Country	Sample period	Peak year	Peak sales (no.)	Total sales (no.)	Sales by sector (%)			
					Services	Industry	Finance	Agriculture
Côte d'Ivoire	1990–6	1995	17	45	17	23	2	24
Ghana	1989–96	1994	82	193	12	52	2	9
Kenya	1992–7	1995	65	153	13	61	5	11
Mozambique	1987–96	1994	136	549	21	36	–	6
Nigeria	1989–94	1990	36	60	4	20	30	27
Tanzania	1992–6	1996	34	123	5	45	–	31
Uganda	1991–7	1995	35	85	24	30	4	5
Zambia	1993–7	1996	107	213	22	30	2	19

Sources: World Bank Privatization Transaction Data; and national sources.

Table 10.5 Value of total sales over sample period and share of foreign purchases

Country	Sample period	Total sales (US$m)[a]	Value of foreign sales as % of total sales	Largest foreign sale (US$m)	Largest foreign sale as % of total sales
Côte d'Ivoire	1990–6	477.0	70	193	40
Ghana	1989–96	800.0	71	398	50
Kenya	1992–7	170.0	15	26	15
Mozambique	1987–96	139.7	43	14	10
Nigeria	1989–94	763.4	65	500	65
Tanzania	1992–6	133.9	79	55	41
Uganda	1991–7	151.4	56	21	14
Zambia	1993–7	417.0	93	220	53

Sources: World Bank Privatization Transaction Data; and national sources.
Note:
[a] Total sales data refer to amount agreed to at the time of sale. In many countries, payment has been tardy, with some buyers even asking for renegotiation of contracts.

Taken individually, many countries in the sample reached a peak in terms of the number of companies sold in the mid-1990s, that is, about five years after the launch of the privatization process across the continent. In terms of sales value, however, peaks were not reached until substantial numbers of the larger companies were privatized towards the end of the 1990s. The bulk of the companies sold were in the industrial sector, but with a good number in agriculture and services. Table 10.5 indicates that foreign sales have been important for the returns from privatization. Excepting Kenya and Mozambique, foreign purchases contributed to over 50 percent of total sales – well over in the case of Zambia (93 percent) and Tanzania (79 percent). In a number of cases a single foreign purchase was worth over 40 percent of total sales; this includes Ghana's sale of Ashanti Gold on the London Stock Exchange as well as Zambia's sale of part of ZCCM.

With respect to the country of origin of the buyers, there has been considerable variation. Table 10.6 indicates, for example, that buyers in Ghana included companies originating from Britain, France, Germany, Malaysia and the USA. The London Stock Exchange sale of Ashanti Gold of course implies an even broader participation in Ghana's privatization process. Buyers of Ugandan companies are equally diverse. It is only in Côte d'Ivoire that France is the dominant purchaser, although companies from Britain and Switzerland have also purchased businesses (Plane, 1996). The relatively low diversity of participation is probably because, compared with Ghana and Uganda for example, Côte d'Ivoire

Table 10.6 Major foreign purchases during privatization in a sample of sub-Saharan African countries by country of origin, 1988–98 (US$m)

Buyer's country of origin	Ghana 1989–98	Côte d'Ivoire 1991–8	Kenya 1988–98	Mozambique 1989–98	Nigeria 1989–94	Tanzania 1992–6	Uganda 1991–7	Zambia 1993–7
Belgium	–	45.0	–	–	–	–	–	–
Britain	12.0	5.1	–	0.9	–	10.0	20.0	68.2
China	–	–	–	–	–	–	1.5	20.0
France	24.3	220.0	–	–	500.0	–	5.4	–
India	0.2	–	–	–	–	–	20.5	2.0
Japan	2.8	–	–	–	–	–	–	–
Germany	39.4	–	–	–	–	–	–	–
Malaysia	43.9	–	–	21.0	–	–	11.0	–
Netherlands	–	–	26.0	–	–	–	11.2	–
Norway	4.0	–	–	–	–	–	–	–
Portugal	–	–	–	20.0	–	–	–	–
South Africa	2.0	–	–	18.0	–	45.5	6.8	376.0
Sweden	–	–	–	–	–	1.3	–	–
Switzerland	–	91.0	–	–	–	71.5	–	–
USA	9.8	–	–	–	–	–	–	–
Other[a]	597.2	4.0	0.4	2.5	–	–	17.0	12.0

Sources: World Bank Privatization Transaction Data; and national sources.
Note:
[a] For Ghana, 'other' includes purchases of shares of Ashanti Gold on the London Stock Exchange, involving a number of institutional investors. For other countries, it includes mostly purchases of small companies jointly by local and foreign investors, without specification of the country of origin of the latter.

still retains a huge parastatal sector. The recent political problems in the country have prevented the implementation of plans – quite advanced in the late 1990s – to embark on rapid privatization of the remaining companies using the regional bourse, which has its headquarters in Abidjan.

6   Conclusions

Although privatization in Africa did not become the political battleground that many predicted it would, it nevertheless was opposed by broad groupings in many countries. Policymakers nevertheless went ahead, initially because they really did not have much choice given that the donor community demanded it. In many countries, economic assistance was conditional on the progress made in privatization and public sector reforms. Domestic resistance was also less than expected because many countries were faced with more pressing concerns, which included the transition to multiparty politics, poverty eradication and, in some countries, civil war. Moreover, many parastatals performed poorly, failing to deliver the basic consumer goods and utility services on which their creation was premised. The official or normative justification for privatization is that it increases economic efficiency and productivity and, thus, raises general welfare. However, African experience indicates that political considerations have also been important determinants of the pace at which privatization has been designed and implemented. Politicians went ahead only when they were sure that the benefits to themselves and their supporters exceeded the costs, including loss of rents, of denationalization. The reasons for this are threefold.

First, even where net revenues from privatization were modest, the process generated its own economic and political dynamics. Economically it improved resource flows in the form of new investment and donor aid, which rejuvenated whole sectors. Politically, the expansion of economic activities improved governments' finances and their capacity for patronage.

Second, privatization helped improve the image of many African governments in the eyes of foreign and domestic investors. In earlier decades, governments had forcibly nationalized businesses and properties, of both multinationals and non-indigenous citizens. Privatization can thus be seen as signaling that past behavior has been abandoned and respect for property rights reinstated.

Third, privatization is not the threat to politicians that it is sometimes said to be. Policymakers in many countries, as well as their supporters, have benefited directly or indirectly from privatization, by buying up some of the assets on sale or by ensuring themselves access to the proceeds from privatization. In a number of countries these economic and political factors have converged positively to ensure a well-sequenced privatization process, thereby helping to revive investment as well as overall economic activity. In many more countries, however, the verdict on privatization is still pending. Many newly privatized firms have not been able to 'graduate' and still depend on or expect direct and indirect support from the government to survive. Weak internal markets and vulnerability to foreign competition have turned them into lobbyists for increased protection.

Notes

1. See, for example, the article in *Africa Analysis*, 18 October 1996:4, 'Selling off the Icons of State Socialism.'
2. Two reasons can be given for this. First, state-owned companies in Tanzania and Mozambique were close to bankruptcy and had lost their original purpose of bolstering domestic employment and generating government revenue. The second point, also advanced in the text, regards the need by governments to send signals to domestic and foreign investors that a new page had been turned.
3. This concern is altogether different from that related to how to ensure that privatization contributes to private sector development.
4. For example, on announcing its privatization/divestiture program in 1992, the government of the Republic of Kenya (1992) listed the following objectives for privatization: enhance the role of the private sector in the economy; enhance efficiency and the use of the scarce resources; rationalize the operations of the public enterprise sector; improve the regulatory environment; broaden the base of ownership and enhance capital market development; reduce the fiscal burden on government; raise revenue for the government.
5. Avishur (2000) has argued that privatization might not amount to a Pareto-dominating mode of operation. Note, however, that in Uganda the 'privatization' of coffee marketing greatly improved peasant incomes, thus reducing poverty.
6. The slow process of privatizing ZCCM eventually led to an aid embargo on Zambia by donors and the multilateral agencies. Post-privatization restructuring of the mines has been slow. Ironically, the former chief executive of ZCCM was made the chair of a committee put in place to privatize it, probably partly explaining the twists and turns of the process.
7. The notion of what was strategic has changed radically over the years. Utilities, railways and airlines had been declared strategic in the late 1980s when the privatization process began, and thus to be retained, but few areas, if any, were still designated as such by the late 1990s.
8. The allocation of benefits has proven to be an important issue. Few governments had a good strategy for using the money that privatization generated. In Uganda, some of the privatization proceeds were lent to companies in the private sector to improve their operations. Sales proceeds were also used to 'fatten' other companies before sale or to pay off workers. There was inevitably considerable confusion, which eventually led to direct intervention by parliament.
9. Only Zambia, under the Movement for Multiparty Democracy (MMD), embarked on privatization of its own volition.

10. In Uganda, regime shifts also meant a reallocation of the businesses acquired from the departed Asians. Indeed, the businesses became an important source of patronage. This also meant that security of tenure was tenuous and the businesses attracted little investment (see Bigsten and Kayizzi-Mugerwa, 1999).
11. For example, at the beginning of privatization in Mozambique in the late 1980s, only 42 percent of the companies were operational, and many of these were operating at a very low level of capacity utilization (see *Unidade Técnica para a Reestraturacão de Empresas*, various issues).
12. This right would, however, be valid for a limited period only, after which the companies would revert to the common pool. I have freely translated the legal texts from the French original (see République de Guinée, 1993).
13. See Loi 87-23 du Août 1987 Portant privatisation d'entreprises of the Republic of Senegal (1987).
14. For example, the fine for taking advantage of knowledge gained in the exercise of duties on the privatization committee would lie between CFA 5 million and CFA 10 million (that is, up to US$15,000).

BIBLIOGRAPHY

Appiah-Kubi, K. (2001) 'Privatization in Ghana,' *Journal of Modern African Studies* 39(2):197–229.
Avishur, A. (2000) 'A Positive Theory of Privatization,' *Journal of Applied Economics* 3(1):247–68.
Bennel, P. (1997) 'Privatization in Sub-Saharan Africa: Prospects during the 1990s,' *World Development* 25:1785–803.
Bigsten, A. and S. Kayizzi-Mugerwa (1999) *Crisis, Adjustment and Growth in Uganda. A Study of Adaptation in an African Economy*, Macmillan: London.
Drum, B. (1993) 'Privatization in Africa,' *Columbia Journal of World Business* 28:144–9.
Due, J. M. (1995) 'Comparison of Privatization of Economies of Eastern Africa and Europe,' *African Development Review* 7:50–75.
Due, J. M., A. E. Temu and A. A. Temu (2000) 'Privatization in Tanzania. A Case Study, 1999,' Research Report, Department of Agricultural and Consumer Economics, University of Illinois; Department of Agricultural Economics and Agribusiness, Sokoine University of Agriculture, Morogoro.
Government of Ethiopia (1994) *Ethiopian Privatization Agency Establishment*, Proclamation No. 87/1994, Addis Ababa.
—— (1996) *Establishment of the Board of Trustees of the Privatized Public Enterprises*, Proclamation No. 17/1996, Addis Ababa.
Gupta, G. S. (1998) 'Privatization: Theory, Practices and Issues,' *Indian Economic Journal* 46(2):96–106.
Harris, N. and D. Lockwood (1997) 'The War-Making State and Privatization,' *Journal of Development Studies* 33(5):597–634.
Harsch, E. (2000) 'Privatization Shifts Gears in Africa,' *African Recovery Online* 14(1).
Kayizzi-Mugerwa, S. (2001) 'Explaining Zambia's Elusive Growth: Credibility

Gap, External Shocks or Reluctant Donors?' in M. Lundahl (ed.) *From Crisis to Growth in Africa?* Routledge: London.

Kornai, J. (2000) 'Making the Transition to the Private Ownership,' *Finance and Development* 37(3):12–30.

Kumssa, A. (1996) 'The Political Economy of Privatization in Sub-Saharan Africa,' *International Review of Administrative Sciences* 62:75–87.

Laffont, J.-J. and M. Meleu (1999) 'A Positive Theory of Privatization for Sub-Saharan Africa,' *Journal of African Economies* 8:30–67.

Museveni, Y. K. (1993) 'Why Privatization Is a Correct Strategy,' Statement on privatization given to the National Resistance Council, 18 April.

Pitcher, A. M. (1996) 'Recreating Colonialism or Reconstructing the State? Privatization and Politics in Mozambique,' *Journal of Southern African Studies* 22(1):49–75.

Plane, P. (1996) 'La privatisation des services publics en Afrique subsaharienne: enjeux et incertitudes,' *Revue Economique* 47:1409–21.

Republic of Ghana (1993) *Ghana Divestiture of State Interests (Implementation) Law, 1993*, Accra.

Republic of Kenya (1992) *Policy Paper on Public Enterprise Reform and Privatization*, Nairobi.

Republic of Mozambique, Technical Unit for Enterprise Restructuring (UTRE) (1997) 'Privatization in Mozambique: On the Home Stretch in 1997,' Ministry of Planning and Finance Report No. 30.

Republic of Senegal (1987) *Loi 87-23 du Août 1987 Portant privatisation d'entreprises*, Dakar.

Republic of Tanzania (1992) *Public Corporations Act 1992*, Dar es Salaam.

—— (1993) *Amendment of Public Corporations Act 1992*, Dar es Salaam.

Republic of Uganda (1993) *The Public Enterprises Reform and Divestiture Statute – Uganda, 1993*, Kampala.

Republic of Zambia (1992) *The Privatization Act 1992 – Zambia*, enacted by Parliament of Zambia, 4 July.

République de Guinée (1993) *Loi L93/037 du Août 1993, fixant les règles de la privatisation des entreprises publiques*, Conakry.

République Togolaise (1994) *Ordonnance No 94 002/PR Portant Désengagement de l'Etat et d'Autres Personnes Morales de Droit Public des Entreprises*, Lomé, June.

Talley, W. K. (1998) 'The Indirect Cost-Sharing Hypothesis of Privatization: A Public Transport Labor Earnings Test,' *Journal of Transport Economics and Policy* 32(3):351–64.

UMACIS (Uganda Manufacturers Association Consultancy and Information Services Limited) (1998) 'Privatization and Private Sector Participation in Infrastructure,' Privatization Unit Workshop for Members of Parliament, Entebbe, 2–4 April.

Unidade Técnica para a Reestraturacão de Empresas (various issues), Republic of Mozambique, Maputo.

11

Decentralization, local bureaucracies and service delivery in Uganda

Moses L. Golola

1 Introduction

Uganda is one of only a handful of countries in sub-Saharan Africa that have taken part in the new wave of decentralization. The process differs from the efforts of the 1960s and 1970s in that this time governments seem ready to cede real power to the lower (local government) levels. It is also taking place alongside broad economic and political reforms and with the support of the donor community, which is convinced that aid is most beneficial in countries where recipients are able to participate in the political process that determines its use.

However, as was the case in the 1960s, it is sometimes easy to romanticize about the benefits of decentralization and thus fail to take into account the detailed work required before it benefits people at the local level. In many African countries, an important impediment to decentralization has been lack of financial and human resources. These two deficiencies work interactively. Local governments find it difficult to raise enough revenue and therefore are unable to hire able administrators and other officials to manage programs. To ensure the provision of essential services, local leaders often have no alternative but to fall back on funds from the center. The combination of lack of managerial resources, inadequate finances and poor access to markets implies that the concept of independence at the local level is illusory, with the center dictating the development agenda and local bureaucrats continuing to be beholden to the line ministries.

The purpose of this chapter is to analyze the impact of decentralization on the local governments' capacity to undertake development activities in Uganda and, in particular, to evaluate how the new policies have affected the provision of services at the local level. After a brief theoretical appraisal, the chapter discusses key aspects of the reform of local administration in Uganda implemented by Yoweri Museveni's National Resistance Movement since 1986. I investigate what impact the reforms have had on local bureaucracies, and especially how local populations have been mobilized for development programs and the extent to which they have participated in policy decisions. I then look at some of the problems encountered in the course of implementing decentralization.

2 Issues in rural institutional reform and decentralization

Interest group politics suggest that politicians at the center have little wish to cede their vast powers, notably those over public finances, to the local level. They embark on meaningful rural reforms, including decentralization, only when they detect real benefits to themselves and their political supporters from incorporating the countryside into the mainstream political process – for example, when this gives them a political advantage over their competitors at the center or when, to generate welfare-enhancing growth, create broader markets for urban-based industries or support the agricultural activities of the elite, it becomes necessary to liberalize the economy as well as domestic politics.

In earlier efforts at rural mobilization and social engineering, past African leaders had embarked on measures collectively referred to as 'African socialism.' These were exemplified by Nyerere's 'ujamaa' and, on a milder scale, by Kaunda's 'humanism' and Obote's 'common man's charter.' As detailed in studies by Kasfir (1976) and Hydén (1980), these radical political postures bore little fruit. Kasfir notes that all these efforts at incorporating rural dwellers and the poor into the political process during the first decade of independence in the 1960s paradoxically seemed to serve the opposite purpose of alienating them further. Thus the politics of national unity that had preceded independence had broken down into ethnic groupings, leading to a 'shrinking' political arena. Hydén argues, on his part, that, though seeming to be the direct and indirect objects of the political attention of the post-independence leaders, peasants remained decidedly 'uncaptured.' This was partly because there was precious little attempt to translate the ambitious development agendas of the 1960s and 1970s into practical measures to develop the countryside and raise rural welfare. At one extreme, the controls introduced in a bid to improve resource husbandry had broken down into a crude exploitation of the countryside via commodity marketing boards and import substitution schemes undertaken with the help of foreign exchange controls (Bunker, 1987).

What then has changed in recent years to justify the current optimism regarding the developmental impact of decentralization? Three factors can be noted in this regard. First, decentralization, at least in theory, holds great potential for development.[1] It can be said to possess a dual mandate. Decentralized government provides space for people to participate in the formulation of policies that affect them directly, including the setting of local taxes, provision of social services and ensuring security of life and property. It is also assumed that it is easier to exercise inclusive politics, which enable communities and groups to influence policies that affect their daily lives, at the local than at the national level. Indeed, for many aid agencies local participation has become the focus of their aid programs. In recent years, this has led to the strengthening of 'civil society' as a counterweight to central government powers. The most visible exponent of this trend has been the growth of the non-governmental sector (NGOs) in many African countries, to the extent that worries have been expressed over the negative impact that the bypassing of the state might have on public sector effectiveness. Besides, decentralization is assumed to improve decision making at the local level and to raise the quality of governance. Also, by encouraging local participation, decentralization enhances resource mobilization, including development aid, and ensures a more efficient use of resources. This increases the production of goods and services and thus local welfare (Bossuyt and Gould, 2000).

Second, the process of decentralization in sub-Saharan Africa has coincided with, and perhaps even been dictated by, efforts by the donor community to reorient aid policies. Today, countries that emphasize broader political participation and show a high degree of ownership of domestic reforms, including a focus on poverty reduction, are apt to get more support. Since populations in sub-Saharan Africa will remain predominantly rural for the foreseeable future, rural-based policies, emphasizing decentralization of power as well as local participation, will continue to attract aid resources (MacLure, 1995).

Third, the structural adjustment policies pursued in the various African countries have changed the urban–rural terms of trade, especially in countries with a traditional cash crop sector. In many countries one now finds urban groups that are in many ways worse off compared with rural groups (Jamal and Weeks, 1993; Kiggundu, 1998). The removal of commodity marketing boards and other marketing monopolies has increased the incomes of farmers in some countries and thus raised their bargaining power vis-à-vis the center. This is certainly true for parts of Uganda and Ghana. However, although proximity to political leaders and influencing policy at the local level are thought to be important, it is naive to think that power structures at the local level are radically different from those at the center. Among rural power structures, the relatively well-off still dominate the top, and, as a rule, at most levels men hold the reins of power. Thus, even at the local level, the most disadvantaged members of the community – women, the aged, the handicapped and children – have poor access to policymakers and, thus, exert little real influence on policy (Guwatudde, 1997; Obbo, 1988).

Recent reforms, especially those focusing on poverty eradication, have sought to incorporate all social groups in the development process. In fact, the poverty reduction strategy papers meant to be the basis for poverty reduction in individual countries are partly based on a participatory process of interviews, meetings and other interaction with all segments of society. However, the politics of inclusion have been complicated by the sheer number of interventions undertaken so far, as well as the number of groups engaged in the exercise.

3 Local government in Uganda: A short history

Throughout Uganda's colonial history, the issue of how to govern the various districts of the country was a source of constant debate. During the earlier part of the twentieth century, a policy of governance known as 'indirect rule,' which had been tried with some success in Nigeria, Zambia, Malawi and Tanganyika, was introduced in Uganda in areas that had kings or established chiefs (Golola, 1977). In the rest of the country, a more direct form of local administration was used (Low and Pratt, 1960). It can also be argued, however, that, although indirect rule enabled the UK to conserve its financial and human resources, it meant that the form of local administration that was adopted in Uganda was fairly unimaginative. The Buganda Kingdom, which evolved its own system of local government well before colonization, comprised the administrative center of the colony. Its privileged position at the center, with encouragement from the new rulers, helped it to export its institutions, notably the hierarchical power structures, to the rest of Uganda, in the process enjoying a form of suzerainty over major parts of the country.

On Uganda's attainment of independence in 1962, some powers were devolved to the kingdoms. However, the post-independence constitution was short-lived and was abrogated in April 1966 following the overthrow of the titular head of state. A new (and republican) constitution was promulgated in 1967. Under it, a new Local Administration Act (1967) was enacted with provisions that totally ignored the relevance of local government councils, instead transferring and concentrating most of their earlier powers into central government. For example, not only were local government budgets subject to approval from the local government minister, local bylaws were subordinated to the local government ministry, which also had the power to revoke them. In terms of financing, ultimate accountability was to the local government minister and not directly to the local people. Finally, the local government minister had the power to terminate the mandate of the local councilors and to dissolve local government councils as well.

These features greatly constrained the independence of local governments and reduced their flexibility and ability to innovate. Ultimately, local government councils had very little power over their employees, with local employment creation sometimes used by politicians at the center as an avenue for exercising political patronage. In fact, according to the 1967 Local Administration Act, even the lowest-ranking employees in local government were appointed by the president (Nsibambi, 1998).

The situation was further radicalized when Milton Obote introduced his 'Move to the Left,' which envisioned a socialist future for Uganda, in which the common man had ultimate authority in the running of the country. In his 'Communication from the Chair,' delivered at the beginning of the 1970s, Obote (1970:8) declared that 'from now on there would be one public service embracing all public officers in the government.' Further, the president saw no reason for public officers to receive allowances for working outside their duty stations, since this gave the impression that some parts of the country were more desirable to work in than others. Such allowances were thus abolished.

However, the new reforms were overtaken by Idi Amin's coup d'état of early 1971. The stature of local governments probably reached its lowest point during Amin's tenure in the 1970s. He abandoned his initial attempts at incorporating civilians into his cabinet, bringing in soldiers instead. These had little interest in public affairs. In attempts at removing potential competitors from the barracks, he also established provincial administrations, along with provincial governors, most of them fellow soldiers. However, this fitted poorly into the overall administrative structure of the country. The military governors had few real tasks, and were known to undertake such mundane tasks as personally arresting smugglers at the borders or, in the case of the Kampala governor, arresting banana sellers who had 'inflated' their prices (Bigsten and Kayizzi-Mugerwa, 1999).

When Milton Obote assumed power in Uganda for a second time in 1980 (referred to as Obote II), he was initially very successful in returning the economy to stability, partly thanks to assistance from the World

Bank and the International Monetary Fund. Policy statements at the time even suggest that changes in the country's administration were being planned. However, Museveni's guerrilla insurgence embarked on in the early 1980s reversed this and Obote II increasingly diverted resources to the military. There was very little focus on local government reforms at this time. This was roughly the state of affairs when the National Resistance Movement (NRM) under Museveni captured power at the beginning of 1986. On attaining power, the NRM initiated the process of empowering local government through decentralization. It marked the most far-reaching measures to decentralize administration that had ever been attempted in the country (Langseth and Mugaju, 1996).

4   Innovations of the local council system

Museveni's NRM saw decentralization and the devolution of power as key means of introducing popular democracy and fostering local governance. They would promote capacity building at the local level and ensure that there are local inputs in the decisionmaking process, especially with respect to service delivery. These factors would in turn help foster a local sense of ownership of development programs. The decentralization and local government reforms started with a commission of inquiry headed by a Makerere University academic, Mahmood Mamdani. Following the commission's report, the first step towards reviving the local government powers and functions was the enactment of the 1987 Resistance Council/Committees Statute No. 9, which legalized the resistance councils and gave them powers of jurisdiction at the local level.[2]

The decentralization policy in Uganda is based on a hierarchy of local councils (LCs) and committees at the village (LCI), parish (LCII), sub-county (LCIII), county (LCIV) and district levels (LCV). Each level is headed by a chairperson, and district-level council meetings are chaired by speakers.[3] The local councils have a number of committees, including those on finance, education, works and transport, security and gender. These political structures were legalized by the 1993 Resistance Council Statute, which was in turn enshrined in the Uganda Constitution of 1995, with amendments made by the Local Government Act, 1997 (MISR, 2000:2). The main objectives of decentralization were the following:

- to transfer real power to the districts and thereby reduce the workload on remote and underresourced government officials at the center,
- to bring political and administrative control over services to the point where they are actually delivered,
- to improve financial accountability and responsibility by establishing a clear link between payment of taxes and provision of services,

Table 11.1 Decentralization in Uganda: Goals, policy innovations and outcomes

Goals	Policy innovations	Comments on outcomes
1. Involvement of local people in the management of their own affairs	Identify local problems and find solutions to be implemented by locally elected organs	Raising local people's interest in the management of their affairs is probably the strongest outcome of the decentralization effort in Uganda
2. Democratization of the decisionmaking process	Elect local leaders instead of having them appointed by central government	Local-level democracy is taking longer to take hold, probably for lack of precedent. Many chairpersons are said to be 'dictators' who are difficult to remove
3. Mobilization of local resources	Make budgets and prioritize expenditure according to needs at the local level	Few local governments are financially independent from the center and they continue to be beholden to government
4. Reduction in costs for service delivery	Improve social infrastructure and expand social service provision in the countryside	Scarcity of resources makes the undertaking of extensive infrastructure and social service extensions difficult
5. Improved efficiency and accountability at the local level	Enhance human resources by appointing professional staff to run local services	The quality of staff recruitment at the local level is improving, though lack of resources implies that many positions are not filled

Source: Author's notes.

- to improve the capacity of local councils to plan, finance and manage the delivery of services to their constituents.

What impact have these far-reaching interventions had on local government's ability to deliver services, and to what extent have local populations been involved in the running of their affairs? I have assembled the main goals of the decentralization process in Uganda, along with policy innovations intended to achieve results, in Table 11.1. Five goals have been identified: to involve local populations in the decision and problem-resolving process, thereby empowering them; to democratize the decisionmaking process; to enhance the mobilization of resources at the local level; to reduce costs for service delivery; and to raise efficiency and accountability at the local level. To what extent have these innovations led to the results expected and what have been the actual outcomes? I shall discuss the extent to which these goals have been achieved in turn.

4.1 Empowerment

The empowerment of local populations by involving them in the identification of their problems and the finding of solutions has been the driving feature of decentralization in Uganda. As already noted, local councils are composed of elected local people, who often hold personal stakes in the welfare of the area. Such individuals are expected to have considerable interest in the deliberations of the councils and to defend the interests of their constituencies against, for example, the demands of the central government.

In a study of the evolution of decentralization in Uganda and its impact on rural communities, Brett (1993) notes a number of admirable outcomes. He argues that, in ethnically divided countries such as Uganda, peace and development crucially depend on the presence of effective local authority structures. Because Ugandan authorities have been persistent in their devolution efforts, Brett sees the possibility of getting the diverse groups in the country to start feeling that 'they are getting a fair deal' in terms of access to resources. Furthermore, the new decentralization system, by involving hundreds of thousands of people, hitherto totally ignored, in the political process at the local level, has stimulated a rapid growth in social responsibility and political creativity. The local council system has also increased the involvement of women in local politics. Women are reserved a certain number of seats on the councils, and a gender committee focuses on their special interests. However, analysts feel that impediments to women's development in Uganda, especially in matters related to property ownership, remain formidable (Guwatudde, 1997).

4.2 Democratization of decision making

Through local councils and committees, the powers and responsibilities for making decisions over issues of local concern in the district have been democratized. This represents a fundamental shift from the traditional procedure where policies implemented at the local government level were made by state bureaucrats based in the capital city, and thus far away from the people affected by those decisions. Similarly, it has been argued (Kisakye, 1996; Kullenberg and Porter, 1999:12; Lubanga, 1998:56) that, compared with earlier systems, the local council system has proven superior in helping communities reach consensus on political and development issues. This is because the new system moves away from the unbridled and comprehensive subordination of locality to center of the past to a relationship steeped in consensus building, participation in policy formulation and negotiation. Increased transparency in local government has improved the stakeholders' capacity to expose the practices of malfeasance and corruption, which in the past often went undetected at the central level, and to initiate corrective action (Kwagala, 1998:113).

4.3   Mobilization of local resources

Following the old adage 'no taxation without representation,' policymakers believed that the system of local councils, in which elected representatives took part, would improve the mobilization of local resources, including taxation. Proximity to local policymakers would increase tax compliance, because the population not only would be able to see the direct benefits, in terms of improved services, but also would be able to monitor the use of resources and, via the local councils, hold errant officials accountable for abuse of office. The Local Government Act of 1997 allows district and subdistrict councils to collect and expend revenue from certain sources, such as market dues and graduated tax. However, the tax base in Uganda differs markedly between districts and regions. Thus, although local inputs have made an important contribution to local government activities in some parts of the country, in others there has been a more than disproportionate dependence on central government funding.

4.4   Improvement of service delivery

Resource mobilization is closely related to the local government's capacity to improve service delivery. In the past few years, local councils have assumed a number of functions that were previously performed by line ministries. These include political administration, judicial services involving minor cases, monitoring and supervision of development projects at the local level, and maintenance of community roads. However, not all local governments have the financial or human resources required to provide an adequate level of services. At the lowest levels, much of the work done by councilors is voluntary. Some local council members even complain about 'poor facilitation' and the fact that they have to abandon their income-generating activities to attend to council work without compensation. Such people might be difficult to hold accountable to the local communities.

4.5 Efficiency and accountability

To what extent have accountability and transparency in local government been enhanced by the decentralization measures? Lack of transparency and, indeed, corruption are among the spurs for faster decentralization. However, part of the reason corruption and abuse of office were so rampant at the center was poor managerial capacities. Thus it has been argued by some that care should be taken lest rapid decentralization lead to decentralized corruption. This would be especially true where local administration capacities are weaker than at the center.

According to Lubanga (1998), however, the government has undertaken important changes that might assist in curbing corruption at the local government level. First, central government allocations to local governments (intergovernmental transfers) are governed by objective criteria. These funds are currently divided into 'conditional' and 'unconditional' grants. Conditional grants are disbursed when the local governments fulfill the agreements with the government regarding certain targets, such as recruiting teachers, purchase of drugs or provision of extension services. These grants cover recurrent expenditure, whereas unconditional grants cover local capital expenditures. The government plans eventually to decentralize the development budget to the districts. Second, funds for local government operations are no longer routed through line ministries. Instead, the finance minister remits funds directly to the accounting officer of each district. An innovation is that the amounts disbursed are published in local newspapers. This enables the local populations to know what to expect in terms of service provision and acts as a deterrent to financial abuse. Furthermore, 'ghost' employees at local levels have been spotted and eliminated.

In a paper on the experience of the Rakai district in southern Uganda, Semakula (1999) is categorical that the institution of local government councils and committees with full authority over their areas of jurisdiction has resulted in improved efficiency, accountability and transparency in the execution of local government business. He argues that the fact that all public servants in the district and lower tiers are accountable to the local population, via the local councils, has been a crucial determining factor.

It ought to be remarked that, before decentralization, most local governments began spending money before their budgets were approved. Since their expenditures were thus technically unauthorized, no budget performance evaluation was ever undertaken. However, since the start of financial decentralization, all councils have been required to have their budgets approved by the appropriate committees as a first step toward making the budget management process transparent. This also makes it possible to use the budget as a management tool. Furthermore, local budgets enable the center to 'monitor and evaluate the budgetary and financial management performance of local governments' (Lubanga, 1998:93). In addition, more streamlined budgets have made it possible for authorities to undertake frequent audits of financial statements. This reduces financial abuse and leads to the apprehension of culprits. This is a vast improvement on the earlier system, when it took the public accounts committee of the parliament years to examine the books of accounts of the district administrations, if at all.

Closely related to efficiency and accountability is the skill level of the local bureaucrats. Although the Local Government Act of 1997 provides district councils with powers to recruit their own staff members as they see fit, funds for recruiting and motivating educated personnel have been scarce in most local governments. Thus, whereas the more affluent districts closer to the capital have been able to lay off incompetent or unqualified individuals inherited from the central government and replace them with more competent ones, poorer districts have seen little change. Thus, in general, it has not been easy to improve administrative structures by hiring new individuals, and implementation capacities remain low in many districts. At the district level, service committees have been set up to handle issues related to employment within local governments, with powers to hire, discipline and dismiss employees. This streamlining of the local governments' employment process has helped reduce instances of irregular appointments. On the whole, the recruitment of personnel has been easier in the richer districts, to the south of the country, than in the poorer ones to the north, where lack of opportunities for generating extra incomes has made it difficult to attract competent staff.

However, there is little agreement on what qualifications the districts' political leaders, as opposed to their employees, should have. Remembering the brutalities unleashed by Amin's 'uneducated horde' in the 1970s, there have been demands that leaders at all levels should be highly qualified. Such demands are feasible in urban areas, notably for the parliament, but they become less realistic the further from the capital the district lies.

5   Constraints on local governance

Having reviewed key features of decentralization and the devolution of power in Uganda, I shall now look at some of the constraints faced by local administrations in realizing the promise of administrative autonomy (refer also to comments on outcomes in Table 11.1). The constraints and challenges to decentralization can be presented in three broad categories. The first question is whether the difficulties are caused by a general lack of financial and human resources, which have hindered policy innovation and limited the independence of local governments. The second question is whether the complex center–locality relations, whereby political confrontations at the center, at least their results, have tended to spill over to the districts and below, are altering policy parameters at the local level. The third aspect to take into consideration relates to the political and economic dynamics at the local level itself; instead of enhancing unity in supposedly homogeneous entities, political autonomy has in some districts tended to unleash clashes of personalities and aspirations. Has decentralization led to fractionalization instead of the reverse?

5.1   Lack of resources leads to program failure and reduced independence

Lack of their own resources is probably the single most important impediment to local governance in Uganda. It has severely limited the extent to which local leaders can deliver on their electoral promises, notably improvement of social services, and limits their ability to resist demands and interference from politicians at the center as well as those from line ministries. With their independence thus curtailed and lacking their own funds, local governments run the risk of becoming instruments for the propagation of political schemes or for the exercise of patronage by politicians at the center.

Lack of resources also limits the extent to which local leaders can motivate their staff and retain them in the now stiff competition between the public and private sectors for educated and efficient employees. Traditionally, the wage levels in local government were very low compared with those of the center, especially since local governments very seldom employed university graduates. It has been necessary over the past few years to adjust wage levels upwards, though, given the resource constraints noted above, not many graduates have been absorbed into the local administrations. This might not have been serious if local governments had embarked on retraining programs to upgrade the skills of their labor force. This again has been impossible owing to serious lack of resources. A shortage of skilled staff has thus put a limit on the amount of intervention that local governments can embark on successfully. It also implies that important aspects of accountability, for example keeping the books in order, refining policies or designing new ones, cannot be undertaken easily. It could be argued, however, that this shortage of skilled personnel is only transient, being caused mainly by the low salary levels. Given that Uganda's educated labor force has expanded substantially in the past two decades, the problem of skills shortage might be resolved when local governments design more attractive terms of service, including improved remuneration.

Thirdly, lack of resources causes a serious shortage of supplies, equipment and physical structures, making daily operations difficult and the realization of policy targets all but impossible. Although lack of basic facilities and tools is partly a result of serious under-capitalization in past decades, areas of the country that experienced long periods of political strife in the 1970s and 1980s saw their social infrastructure, including schools and clinics, destroyed, making their situation even more precarious today. In these areas, employees have had to improvise in a multitude of ways to be able to perform their duties. Children are still taught under trees in some areas, and local government offices are often derelict structures, poorly protected from the elements.

5.2   Center–local relations remain complex

As argued above, the central government's wish to control the periphery made a nonsense of many earlier attempts to cede powers to local authorities. Direct coercion, including legislation, was often necessary to restrain the clamor for autonomy at the district level (Roberts, 1982). To what extent, then, has the new approach to decentralization, based on local councils, reduced the tension between the center and the districts in matters of policy coordination, budgeting and accountability?

Critics of the decentralization process in Uganda have claimed that the policy was introduced too hurriedly, with little preparation of stakeholders, notably the local populations. At the technical level, the legislation required to formalize many of the changes came after the fact. This left considerable room for discretion to politicians. Also owing to the speedy implementation of decentralization, between 1986 and 1989 some confusion developed over who determined policies at the local level, whether it was the newly created resistance council (later renamed local council) officials or government-appointed 'chiefs' from earlier years. Although resistance council leaders had taken over the formal duties of the chiefs in the regular local administrations, the traditional organs of the state, such as the police and magistrates, were not giving the resistance council leadership the recognition and support required to establish effective administration (Makara, 1998:35).

This policy opaqueness at the local level made it difficult for the rural population to internalize the new system. Since the new system's credibility depended to a large extent on local people's reaction to its provisions and their ability to penalize poor performance, it was imperative that they understood the issues involved. The Local Government Statute of 1993 was the central government's attempt to remove the confusion of roles at the local level. It presented a decentralized structure of government with sufficient powers for councilors at local levels to make decisions designed to encourage development projects in their localities. The statute was the precursor to the Local Government Act of 1997.

However, advocates of gradualism have also been opposed (Byaru-gaba, 1997; Kayizzi-Mugerwa, 1993). The argument is that decentralization implies a system shift and as such will threaten various interest groups including politicians. Indeed, whenever there are changes in the political system there is bound to be resistance and sometimes apathy. These reactions do not mean that change promises little benefit to the population. Since it introduces new ideas and policies and alters the way things are done, change might be the key contribution of decentralization to development.

But perhaps the most important source of conflict between center and local administration relates to money. Decentralization would have had little content if the central budget had not been similarly decentralized. Thus the goal of financial decentralization was to assign responsibilities and taxes between the center and local governments, as well as to enable the transfer of grants and other resources from the center. First, a block grant was devised whereby the central government allocated funds to the districts based on the number and quality of programs of the line ministries in each district. This was, however, seriously flawed, seeming to favor areas that already had good access to public resources. It was replaced by an allocation system based on a 'needs-based formula,' with a weighting of 10 percent for area of district, 10 percent for the size of the general population, 40 percent for the size of the school-going population and 40 percent for child mortality. Still, because the weighting scheme does not take into account the capacity of regions to collect taxes, a degree of inequality in resource distribution remained.

Beginning in the 1993/4 financial year, there was a phased financial decentralization, which began with thirteen districts; another fourteen districts were decentralized in the 1994/5 financial year. The process was completed in the 1995/6 financial year when the remaining thirty-five districts also entered the process. Besides block grants, there are two other grants. The conditional grant, as the name suggests, was to be based on certain conditions to encourage districts to undertake projects in areas such as poverty reduction that would have been ignored otherwise. However, the conditions have been difficult to define and these types of grants have been given to districts, but without the accompanying conditions, thus becoming a form of block grant. The equalization grant was to be based on assessment of resource endowments, with poorer districts compensated accordingly.

However, for the system of transfers to succeed in achieving the goals envisaged by the center and the local government, there is need for a high degree of accountability. This has been very difficult to establish in most districts. Local councils have failed to deliver monthly accounts of expenditure for purposes of planning and budgeting to the center, as for example requested by the finance ministry. In trying to reconcile the budgetary process at the center, the finance ministry has thus resorted to threats, including withdrawal of funding from districts not complying with its directives and publishing a list of such districts in the local newspapers. On the other hand, the financial decentralization exercise was intended to reduce total expenditure and personnel in the line ministries, but local governments complain that this has not been the case. With decentralization, departments in line ministries were also supposed to reduce their functions to those of policy making and supervision, relegating operations and related expenditures to the district level. This has not happened to the extent expected, and the bulk of government expenditure is still undertaken at the center.

5.3   Center politics often spill over

Decentralization was also meant to insulate local governments from the political whims of the center. However, politics at the center tend to spill over to districts in a variety of ways. Here I shall illustrate with three cases: the sudden abolition of the poll tax during the general elections of 2001; the issue of land reform; and the maintenance of local security.

During the presidential campaigns of 2001, President Museveni announced the abolition of 'graduated tax.' In spite of its name, this tax was in reality a poll tax imposed on all adult males, irrespective of their employment status. It was unpopular not only because it was not means based, but also because its collection, especially at the lower levels, involved considerable coercion, including the deployment of armed guards at times.[4] It also happened to be an important source of income in the districts, because the funds collected were retained at the district headquarters. In some districts, graduated tax accounted for up to 40 percent of local government revenue. The sudden abolition of the tax, seemingly without prior consultation, led to serious loss of revenue in the districts. The lack of consultation with the local authorities, which were very dependent on the tax, illustrates the fragility of their powers in the face of political competition at the center. Subsequently, local governments have petitioned the central government for a 'special stabilization grant' to compensate them for the revenue loss. Since the government has not responded adequately, many local authorities have decided to scale down their operations, especially the delivery of services.

The second illustration relates to land. In Uganda, indeed as in other agrarian economies, land issues are at the center of economic and political debate. Decentralization has brought many of these issues into sharp relief in recent years. As part of its vision for Uganda, the ruling NRM has advocated far-reaching land reform in order to ensure more efficient land use and egalitarian land distribution. In July 1998, a new land act came into force. It vested the powers to handle land disputes in sub-county and district land tribunals. In the country as a whole there were to be 45 district land tribunals and over 700 subcounty tribunals. The system of specialized land tribunals was introduced when land disputes threatened to swamp lower courts and local councils in long-drawn-out disputes, which hampered work in other areas of the local economy. However, the government did not have sufficient funds to put the tribunals into operation. The high court then became the only institution that could handle land disputes in the country. This in effect grounded all land cases. In this light, the judicial service commission recommended that, at least for the time being, the old order, whereby local councils and lower courts adjudicated land cases, should be restored.

The last example relates to security. The NRM's proudest boast is that it returned peace to Uganda. To increase security in communities, the government introduced a system of local defense units (LDU), with one unit in each locality throughout the country. The unit was under the control of the local council. Members of the LDU would be from the communities themselves and selected by community members. The original idea was that the LDUs were to be maintained by the communities themselves, while the government provided equipment and training.[5] However, although first created in 1986, when Museveni took power in Kampala, in early 2001 LDUs were not yet formalized by parliament as an armed force in the country. This illegitimacy has meant that the welfare of LDU officers and men is not given the same serious attention as that of the regular army. Some members of the force have been blamed for engaging in violence, including robbery. Short of resources, the local councils have also had an ambivalent relationship with their LDUs. They have not been able to maintain these forces or to supply them with even very basic equipment.[6] Moreover, the central government has not been willing to cede control over armed groups to local councils. As a sign of the control still exercised by the center, the government recently brought the LDUs back into its fold. In the future they will be seen as a department of the regular armed forces. This was also probably done because the government feels the need to keep a close watch on the activities of the LDUs, especially given the insecurity that currently affects the Great Lakes region.

The conclusion to draw from the above examples is that the new local institutions and their bureaucracies are not yet strong enough to resist political pressure from the center. Graduated tax was retrogressive and was bound to be eradicated eventually. However, it was a major source of revenue at the local level and abolishing it without consultation dealt a serious blow to the planning and budgetary processes at the local level. However, it is clear that the timing of its abolition was meant to garner votes for the presidential incumbent. In the case of land issues, as well as local security, the illustrations above show that the wishes of the center will continue to influence events at the local level.

Most recently, members of parliament have sought to sit in on the meetings of the local councils in their constituencies.[7] They argue that this will enable them to use their vast experience at the national level to assist deliberations at the local level. However, there is a danger that if this is institutionalized local councils will lose their autonomy, with the spillover from national politics being felt much more than before. It is also possible that the local councils might then become arenas in which the proxy battles for political succession at the center will be fought. Thus, given institutional weaknesses in local governments, the rules of the game will continue to be dictated by the center. For some time to come, local authorities will be left to adjust to them as best they can.

5.4   Decentralization and fractionalization

To what extent has decentralization led to fractionalization at the local level? Since the onset of decentralization in the mid-1980s, there has been a tendency in Uganda to split up districts into ever smaller entities in the belief that atomization will create the dynamics of self-governance and ability to influence decisions that are emphasized by the National Resistance Movement.[8] However, given the dearth of human and financial resources, this has also caused considerable confusion. In many instances the newly created districts have had to start from scratch without buildings or other infrastructure. Normally, they have to draw staff, with accompanying equipment, from the headquarters of the older district. This has proven to be quite disruptive and conflict ridden.[9] The 'break-away' district is sometimes embargoed by the part of the older district that retains the old headquarters. There are thus costs to atomization, especially since the splitting up of a district seldom emanates from a clear-cut strategy of maximizing local benefits but is often done in response to the wishes of important pressure groups and political supporters of the central government.

Are atomization and homogeneity good or bad? They are certainly not uniformly good. It can be argued, for example, that conflicts are managed better in urban areas because urban dwellers are more heterogeneous by origin but similar in education and other characteristics, such as consumption and leisure patterns. It is the latter accoutrements rather than commonality of ancestral origin that dictate the speed at which communities absorb new ideas, including the benefits of political collaboration.

6 Assessing the impact on production, service provision and welfare

As argued above, decentralization has meant policy intervention on a vast scale. However, although the benefits of decentralization seem to be fairly obvious in theory, in practice there is no unequivocal method of measuring them with certainty. This is because, lacking counterfactual history in real life, it is often difficult to say whether the observed change is a result of policy or of exogenous events. This can be illustrated by the situation of households in northern Uganda. There the failure of poverty to decline dramatically in recent years, as has happened in the southern parts of the country, is more to blame on continued armed insurgence, which has weakened local capacities, than on the failure of decentralization itself. Still, recent household surveys as well as participatory poverty assessments (Republic of Uganda, 1999) give us some idea of the evolution of production and welfare trends during the era of decentralization in Uganda.

Indicators of the impact of decentralization and local institutional reforms can be divided into effectiveness indicators and response indicators. The former might illustrate the extent to which the goals of reform have been achieved, for example whether proximity to health and education services in the rural areas has improved or whether agricultural extension services have become more effective. Other indicators of effectiveness would be whether the rate of infant mortality has declined or whether rural livestock have better access to water. Response indicators, on the other hand, are governance related, showing the speed at which local officials are responding to local demands and the speed at which they embark on the resolution of disputes and the redressing of complaints. Let us look briefly at the impact of decentralization on the following areas:

- primary health
- education
- agricultural extension and livestock services
- roads and water
- security.

As noted above, local councils operate under a serious financial constraint that restricts their capacity for intervention. Moreover, the councils located in the south of the country, and with a broader tax base, are in a much better position to raise revenue and thus operate more effectively than the councils in the north. Still, Goetz and Jenkins (1998) note considerable innovation in the primary health sector in Uganda. The charges (cost sharing) at the clinics are set by the local authorities and the level of service provision has improved markedly in recent years. Many local councils have introduced local tender boards, which encourage competition between suppliers of materials, medicines and equipment. Although many clinics have been able to keep charges at affordable levels, instances of corruption as well as the need to bribe health workers have persisted. During the recent presidential election campaigns, Yoweri Museveni declared the 'cost sharing' of healthcare fees, that is, the payment of fees at public clinics, abolished.[10] It is difficult to say whether this new policy is fully funded, however. In any case, the abolition reflects the fragility of local institutions as well as their power, since such a decision should have been discussed first within the local levels themselves.

With respect to education, especially primary education, the main thrust has been the central government's introduction of universal primary education. This has been a major reform, probably the defining achievement of the NRM government. However, local authorities have had to do a great deal to make a success of it. There is still a serious shortage of school buildings, and teachers too have been scarce. Local councils that have mobilized populations in the construction of school buildings and that have plans for increasing teacher numbers via better salaries have been able to provide their school-going populations with a much improved service, as is reflected in performance in the centrally administered primary school examinations. Unfortunately, the disparity in performance between districts that are near the capital and those at a remove remains quite large and will probably be difficult to bridge in the medium term.

At the local level the supply of agricultural extension services and services related to transport and water infrastructure is sparse. This is directly related to the lack of capacities mentioned above. Again, the richer districts are ahead of the others, but overall progress here is not as marked as in healthcare provision and education.

Peace is an important ingredient in the Ugandan context, and it is probably here that local councils have made their biggest contribution. In many areas of the country, decades of lawlessness had led to declining respect for property rights, with legal cases taking years to be brought to court and much longer to reach closure, if at all. Local councils have been able to return the rule of law to many areas, and thereby a sense of security, which has enabled households to re-engage in income-generating activities in many districts. In this regard, the political wrangles in the districts also reflect the fact that, given peace, politicians find it worthwhile to compete in the market for political ideas. Lack of dissent and acrimony during a period of rapid social and economic change would have been quite odd.

Finally, on the general issue of governance, there has been a necessary period of learning-by-doing, and performance has varied greatly between regions. It is only recently that firmer mechanisms have been put in place to ensure accountability at the local level. A number of local-level officers have lost their jobs as a result of poor accountability and corruption. Citizens at the local level are also becoming more assertive in their demands for services and higher accountability, in some cases even threatening not to pay taxes. This has been recognized by the government, which now announces all its disbursements to local governments in the newspapers in order to ensure local monitoring of expenditure and to ensure that services are actually delivered (Ablo and Reinikka, 1998).

7 Conclusion

In many African countries, the creation of effective local institutions for decentralization has only just begun. It will thus take a while before the information systems, local-level tender boards, drug procurement procedures, auditing systems, sanctions for poor performance, and the establishment of accountability to the center are in place. There is, however, genuine concern that in the midst of decentralization the center continues to claim the bulk of resources, those generated internally as well as donor and other foreign inflows. Urban concentration of resources leads to a boom in economic activity in areas already relatively well off, while shortage of resources causes lethargy and dependence on the center in the countryside.

It is worth stressing, however, that decentralization is a process whose success hinges on a whole range of factors: political, social and economic. In Uganda the tenets of the process are now in place, including well-defined political structures and how they will relate and be accountable to the communities and the central government. For perhaps the first time since independence in the 1960s, local communities can now directly influence the policies that affect their daily lives. Successful decentralization takes time and is also resource demanding. What is important, however, is to ensure progress in building local institutions. It is the strength of these that will guarantee the success of decentralization.

Notes

1. See, for example, Collins and Green (1994).
2. 'Resistance councils' were carryovers from Museveni's guerrilla war. They were converted to 'local councils' since, after achieving power, there was nothing to resist any longer. Note, however, that the National Resistance Movement has retained its name.
3. At lower levels, the chairperson calls and chairs the meeting; hence the frequent charges of dictatorship at these levels.
4. In some districts, tax collectors raided homes early in the morning before menfolk had left. This sometimes forced defaulters to sleep in the 'bushes' until the tax collection campaigns were over.
5. *The Monitor* newspaper (31 August 1999) estimated the total LDU force in the country at 3,000.
6. A typical LDU funding scheme in the Kampala area could look like this: the Kampala City Council pays about 15 dollars per month to each LDU soldier, and the fees collected from citizens for communal security top this up. But because the volume of fees collected fluctuates considerably, and between districts of the city, the pay is quite uneven – another reflection of the non-regularized nature of the LDU functions.
7. See, for instance, the article 'MPs Want Ex-Officio Status in Districts,' *New Vision*, 8 February 2001. MPs have, for example, claimed that the district leaders have 'hijacked government programs and given credit to themselves.' The wishes of the MPs have more or less been conceded, although there have been worries that MPs would then dictate the agenda, which would be counteracting the decentralization efforts (see also Prud'homme, 1995).
8. The scope of the decentralization effort can be given by the fact that there are 45,000 villages, 5,000 parishes, 900 subcounties and 170 counties (each county being represented by a member of parliament). In elections at the parish level, the process cannot go ahead until 30 percent of the electorate are assembled.
9. There have also been problems with pensions, with new districts not wishing to assume the pension liabilities for retired civil servants now belonging to their local government.
10. This was the second tax 'abolished' during the run-up to the elections of 2001. Even here, the timing suggests that the move was more politically strategic than economic. In the aftermath of the ban, medicines began to 'disappear' from hospitals and clinics once again.

REFERENCES

Ablo, E. and R. Reinikka (1998) 'Do Budgets Really Matter? Evidence from Public Spending on Education and Health in Uganda,' mimeo, World Bank, Washington, DC.

Bigsten, A. and S. Kayizzi-Mugerwa (1999) *Crisis, Adjustment and Growth in Uganda: A Study of Adaptation in an African Economy*, Macmillan: London, and St. Martin's Press: New York.

Bossuyt, J. and J. Gould (2000) 'Decentralization and Poverty Reduction: Elaborating the Linkages,' Policy Management Brief No. 12, ECDPM: Maastricht.

Brett, E. (1993) *Providing for the Rural Poor, Institutional Decay and Transformation in Uganda*, Fountain Publishers: Kampala.

Bunker, S. (1987) *Peasants against the State: The Politics of Market Control in Bugisu, Uganda 1900–1983*, University of Illinois Press: Urbana Campaign.

Byarugaba, F. (1997) 'The Role of Major Stakeholders in the Transition to Democracy in Uganda,' *Makerere Political Science Review* 1(1):43–60.

Collins, C. and A. Green (1994) 'Decentralization and Primary Healthcare: Some Negative Implications in Developing Countries,' *International Journal of Health Sciences* 24(2).

Goetz, A. M. and R. Jenkins (1998) 'Creating a Framework for Reducing Poverty: Institutional and Process Issues in National Poverty Policy – Uganda Country Report,' mimeo, Institute for Development Studies, Brighton, UK.

Golola, M. L. (1977) 'Central Malawi under the British with Particular Reference to Lilongwe District,' Department of History, Makerere University, Kampala.

Guwatudde, C. (1997) 'Engendering National and Local Budgets,' *Gender Bulletin*, Ministry of Gender and Community Development, Kampala.

Hydén, G. (1980) *Beyond Ujamaa in Tanzania: Underdevelopment and an Uncaptured Peasantry*, Heinemann: London.

Jamal, V. and J. Weeks (1993) *Africa Misunderstood*, Macmillan Series of ILO Studies, Macmillan: London.

Kasfir, N. (1976) *The Shrinking Political Arena: Participation and Ethnicity in African Politics, with a Case Study of Uganda*, University of California Press: Berkeley.

Kayizzi-Mugerwa, S. (1993) 'Urban Bustle/Rural Slumber: Dilemmas of Uneven Economic Recovery in Uganda,' in M. Blomström and M. Lundahl (eds.) *Economic Crisis in Africa, Perspectives on Policy Responses*, Routledge: London.

Kiggundu, R. (1998) 'Economic Reforms and Rural Households in Uganda,' in S. Kayizzi-Mugerwa, A. Olukoshi and L. Wohlgemuth (eds.) *Towards a New Partnership with Africa: Challenges and Opportunities*, Nordiska Afrikainstitutet: Uppsala.

Kisakye, J. (1996) 'Political Background to Decentralization,' in S. Villadsen and F. Lubanga (eds.) *Democratic Decentralization in Uganda: A New Approach to Local Governance*, Fountain Publishers: Kampala.

Kullenberg, L. and D. Porter (1999) 'Decentralization and Accountability: Recent Experience from Uganda,' *Agriculture and Development* 6(1).

Kwagala, B. (1998) 'The Role of NGOs in the Delivery of Health and Water Services,' in A. Nsibambi (ed.) *Decentralization and Civil Society in Uganda*, Fountain Publishers: Kampala.

Langseth, P. and J. Mugaju (eds.) (1996) *Post-Conflict Uganda: Towards an Effective Civil Service*, Fountain Publishers: Kampala.

Low, D. A. and R. C. Pratt (eds.) (1960) *Buganda and British Overrule, 1900–1955*, Oxford University Press: Nairobi.

Lubanga, F. X. K. (1998) 'On-going Reforms to Curbing Corruption: The Contribution of Decentralization,' in A. Ruzindana, P. Langseth and A. Gakwandi, *Fighting Corruption in Uganda*, Fountain Publishers: Kampala.

MacLure, R. (1995) 'Primary Health Care and Donor Dependency: A Case Study of Non-Government Assistance in Burkina Faso,' *International Journal of Health Services* 25(3):539–58.

Makara, S. (1998) 'Political and Administrative Relations in Decentralization,' in A. Nsibambi (ed.) (1998) *Decentralization and Civil Society in Uganda*, Fountain Publishers: Kampala.

MISR (Makerere Institute for Social Research) (2000) *Decentralization: Human Resource Demand Assessment from the Perspective of the District*, Makerere University: Kampala.

Nsibambi, A. (ed.) (1998) *Decentralization and Civil Society in Uganda*, Fountain Publishers: Kampala.

Obbo, C. (1988) 'Catalysts of Urbanism in the Countryside – Mukono, Uganda,' *African Studies Review* 31(4):39–47.

Obote, M. (1970) *Communication from the Chair*, Government Printer: Kampala.

Prud'homme, R. (1995) 'The Dangers of Decentralization,' *World Bank Research Observer* 10(2).

Republic of Uganda (1999) *Uganda Poverty Status Report 1999*, Ministry of Finance, Planning and Economic Development: Kampala.

Roberts, A. F. (ed.) (1982) *Uganda's First Republic: Chiefs, Administrators and Politicians 1967–1971*, African Studies Center, University of Cambridge: Cambridge.

Semakula, G. M. (1999) 'Rakai District in Development: Consequences of Decentralization,' in S. Villadsen and F. Lubanga (eds.) *Democratic Decentralization in Uganda: A New Approach to Local Governance*, Fountain Publishers: Kampala.

12

Institutional development in Africa: The case of insolvency law

Clas Wihlborg

1 Introduction

The view that the quality of institutions supporting economic activity is an important determinant of economic growth and welfare has become widespread in the development literature (North, 1990; Olson, 1993). Particular groups that gain power may be able to shape institutions and policies so as to enrich their members and, if these groups represent narrow interests, this may take place at the expense of the majority. Others argue that legal institutions defining, contracting and enforcing property rights are particularly important, although the development of law is not independent of political institutions. These issues have been prominent in the governance and accountability debate raging in many African countries. In a recent study, Beck et al. (2001) find empirical support for the view that legal institutions are particularly important for financial development. Well-functioning financial intermediation and markets would influence economic growth because they enhance the supply of external financing and the quality of corporate governance. Other channels through which legal institutions affect economic growth are technological deepening and the productivity of investments.

Clarke (2001) finds, for example, that the impact of institutional variables such as rule of law and risk of expropriation on expenditures on research and development relative to GDP is robust, even for low- and middle-income countries. Following the above results, we can interpret

the results of Devarajan et al. (2001), who investigate whether low productivity of investment as opposed to slow accumulation of capital explains weak economic growth in Africa, as also pointing to institutional
deficiencies. They find that the productivity of investment has been so
low in Africa that one can talk about overinvestment rather than under-
investment, in spite of the observed low investment rates.

The legal institution emphasized in this chapter is insolvency law. The
procedures for dealing with insolvent firms are particularly important for
the financial sector, and they reflect the prevailing social attitude to contracts and property rights. As Wood (1995) writes,

Insolvency law ... is the most piercing indicator of the doctrines that divide the
world's legal systems in the context of financial law. It is the destructive force of
bankruptcy which has moulded the central tenets of commercial law and it is
bankruptcy which is the ultimate test of a jurisdiction's ability to realize its own
view of fairness, equity and legal civilization.

Insolvency procedures may be determined by formal law or by informal
rules and practices. The scope of informal procedures depends on properties of the law and its enforcement. In formal law it is common to dis-
tinguish between bankruptcy law, referring to rules for the liquidation of
firms, and restructuring law, referring to rules for reorganization, debt
restructuring and rehabilitation of firms without a change in ownership.
Sometimes insolvency and bankruptcy are used synonymously, however.
In this chapter, bankruptcy is used in its narrower definition. The objective of this chapter is to evaluate the economic effects of insolvency procedures in sub-Saharan African countries in particular, and to develop
principles for economically efficient procedures. Since quantitative data
and information about insolvency law and its enforcement in Africa are
limited, the focus is on principles rather than actual procedures and their
specific consequences. The discussion is limited to insolvency procedures
for firms in the manufacturing and services sectors, excepting banks.

In section 2, I look at the role of insolvency procedures in an economic
growth process and in economic crises.[1] A distinction is made between ex
ante and ex post efficiency of law. The latter refers to the time of distress,
whereas the former refers to the time of lending and investment decisions. The variation in formal insolvency law across countries is described
in section 3,[2] where insolvency law is also classified in different ways.
Most often laws are classified as more or less creditor or debtor oriented,
but this classification says little about the law's contribution to economic
restructuring and the fate of different stakeholders in a distressed firm. A
more interesting classification from an economic point of view is the extent to which the law recognizes and enforces contracts voluntarily en-

tered into. The practical implementation of insolvency law and its contribution to restructuring in different countries are discussed in section 4. Enforcement of law is identified as a particular weakness of insolvency regimes in most developing countries. This aspect of insolvency procedures in Africa is discussed in section 5. Indicators of the quality of the legal system in Africa are presented, and it is argued that continued financial repression and recurring financial crises are partly explained by the low quality of insolvency procedures. Important aspects of the design of insolvency law in emerging market economies are discussed in section 6. Concluding comments follow in section 7.

2   The role of insolvency law and procedures

'Bankruptcy is a collective procedure for the recovery of debts by creditors. It also protects individuals who have become overburdened by their debts' (Wood, 1995: Preface). There is a potential benefit to both creditors and debtors in bankruptcy. Creditors wish to recover debts to the extent possible in a speedy manner from a borrower who is unable to pay all creditors fully. From the borrower's point of view, bankruptcy should allow the speedy resolution of debts. Thereafter, the borrower can devote his or her remaining resources to new ventures. Insolvency procedures, including informal, voluntarily agreed upon procedures for settling the debts of an insolvent borrower, play an important role in the restructuring process of an economy. Without agreed-upon procedures in contracts or in laws specifying, for example, priority among creditors, conflicts of interest between debtor and creditors and among creditors could hinder any resolution of claims. Expecting such a situation, debtors could try to recover loans as soon as they suspect a borrower to be heading for distress. Thus, positive value projects may be prematurely abandoned if one or more creditors are able to recover a loan. An important efficiency aspect of insolvency procedures is, accordingly, that they provide a timely resolution of claims, as emphasized by Posner (1992). In the following subsections I discuss the role of insolvency procedures for firms in economic and financial distress, and the contribution of insolvency procedures to growth and crises. Finally in this section, a distinction is made between ex ante and ex post efficiency of procedures.

2.1   Economic and financial distress

In Table 12.1, a distinction is made between 'economic' distress and 'financial' distress. In economic distress, the net present value of a firm's assets is negative and, from a financial valuation point of view, the firm

Table 12.1 Types of distress and efficient action at the time of distress (ex post efficiency)

	Definition	Action
Economic distress	The net present value of assets is negative under any management team	Piecemeal liquidation of assets
	The net present value of assets is positive under a different management team	Sale of assets as a going concern to enable a change of management
Financial distress	The present value of cash flows is positive but is lower than the value of claims by non-shareholders	Debt reduction in combination with restructuring and/or ownership change, if value of assets can thereby be enhanced
	Liquidity problem	Debt-rescheduling Liquidity-enhancement

Source: Compiled by the author.

should be shut down in its present form. It is possible, however, that under different management the physical assets would produce a positive net present value. If so, it would be efficient to auction or sell the firm as a 'going concern' to new owners who would be able to improve management. Under 'financial distress,' the net present value of the assets is positive but the value of debts exceeds the present value of cash flows generated by assets. Thus, a firm in financial distress is insolvent but its assets produce a positive value from a social point of view. In this case, debt reduction and rehabilitation, possibly in combination with more fundamental restructuring, such as a change in control, would be efficient. A firm may also find itself in financial distress because of liquidity constraints, even if the present value of cash flows from assets exceeds the debts. This situation presumes that the financial system for one reason or another is failing in its role of providing liquidity to solvent firms. The obvious remedy is rescheduling of debt or liquidity infusion.

2.2   Insolvency procedures in growth and crisis

Insolvency procedures provide only one way to restructure an economy in which assets need to be reallocated continuously in response to changes in preferences, technology and human skill. Insolvencies are inevitable, however. Procedures that are ill suited to deal with them can be the cause of recessions and economic crisis, they can deepen a crisis, and they may extend or shorten the duration of a crisis by influencing the speed of recovery.

The procedures can be the cause of a crisis if disincentives to bankruptcy, in combination with a politically influenced banking system and state support of banks and firms, contribute to an accumulation of surviving, economically distressed firms. This has been a point of concern in many African economies.

An existing crisis may be deepened and prolonged if financially distressed firms are not rehabilitated but are forced to shut down. Similarly, a crisis is deepened if liquidity problems cause the shutdown of operations in a credit crunch. Widespread financial distress in a country may be caused by severe macroeconomic shock, large exchange rate changes or increases in interest rates. We certainly observed this type of deepening of a crisis in the hard-hit Asian economies of Indonesia, Korea, Malaysia and Thailand (Hussain and Wihlborg, 1999).

There exists strong evidence that the lack of effective insolvency procedures can contribute to a banking crisis and to the ability of banks to recover from a crisis. In a study by Caprio and Klingebiel (1996), severe banking crises in sixty-nine countries between 1980 and 1995 are recorded. Crises in twenty-six countries are studied in more detail with respect to their causes and their resolution. In a large share of the latter countries, politically influenced lending practices by banks were seen as a contributing cause of the crisis. An inefficient legal framework hindered the resolution of crises in many countries.[3] I return to evidence with respect to Africa in section 6.

2.3 Ex ante versus ex post efficiency

One reason an incumbent owner may value a firm more highly than others is that he or she may have 'invested' in or acquired firm-specific human capital (knowledge). However, it is not only a distressed firm's owner who risks loss if the firm were discontinued as a going concern. Employees, suppliers, customers, the surrounding community and the state may have made firm-specific investments as well. If so, they have a strong interest in the distressed firm's survival and may actually be willing to reduce their claims and contribute to a reorganization. Procedures for handling negotiations and overcoming conflicts of interest must exist or be developed for a solution to be found. These considerations lead to the argument that there could be a social good in having a distressed firm continue under the old ownership without risking possible shutdown if it is declared bankrupt and liquidated. Employment considerations in particular have led many countries to favor rehabilitation and restructuring over bankruptcy. Wood (1995) observes that legislation favoring rehabilitation has generally been implemented after severe economic downturns, when the consequences of bankruptcies have been felt.

Insolvency procedures affect economic incentives not only at the time of distress but also at the time various stakeholders enter into contracts with a still healthy firm. Procedures that increase the likelihood of firm survival increase the incentives of stakeholders to invest in firm-specific capital. The same procedures would reduce the expected return on financing the firm, if survival is accomplished at the expense of the lenders. As a result, the costs of financing a healthy firm would increase. Uncertainty about procedures increases these costs further. An economic efficiency analysis of these considerations is sensitive to, for example, assumptions about the relation between asset specificity and return on projects, the substitutability between general and specific assets, and the supply of debt financing. Bebchuk and Picker (1993) argue that allowing managers/shareholders to retain a stake in the assets in case of bankruptcy (deviation from absolute priority) may enhance ex ante efficiency under limited liability. Gangopadhyay and Wihlborg (2001) show that the existence of credit rationing offsets or reverses these results, and they conclude that an absolute priority rule minimizes the cost of capital. Cornelli and Felli (1996) link the incentives to monitor to the position of senior and junior creditors in bankruptcy. They find that neither absolute priority nor a more debtor-friendly rule is efficient with respect to monitoring the incentives of all creditors. The issue of the ex ante efficient priority rule in bankruptcy remains unresolved even when a rather narrow range of specific assets is considered. What can be said is that ex ante efficiency is enhanced if:

(a) insolvency procedures are flexible enough to allow different types of resolutions for firms with different types of stakeholders,
(b) recontracting is possible at the time of distress for services provided with specific assets,
(c) insolvency procedures are well defined ex ante – in other words, the rules for dealing with insolvency should not be subject to uncertainty,
(d) insolvency procedures allow speedy resolution of distress.

Viewing priority rules as one aspect of a firm's ex ante contracts with different stakeholders, points (a)–(c) above indicate that, from an economic efficiency point of view, rules should allow the different stakeholders to obtain the types of contract they find suitable. I return to the implications of this view below.

3   Orientations of insolvency procedures across countries

It is common to denote insolvency procedures as either creditor oriented or debtor oriented. These terms indicate whether the procedures tend to

Table 12.2 Creditor/debtor orientation of corporate insolvency law

Orientation[a]	Country[b]
1	**Former British colonies (except South Africa and Zimbabwe)**
2	England, Australia, Ireland
3	Germany, Netherlands, Indonesia, Sweden, Switzerland, Poland
4	Scotland, Japan, Korea, New Zealand, Norway
5	United States, Canada (except Quebec)
6	**South Africa, Botswana, Zimbabwe** (all Dutch based); Austria, Denmark, Czech and Slovak Republics
7	Italy
8	Greece, Portugal, Spain, most Latin American countries (except Paraguay, which protects security interests strongly)
9	**Former French colonies, Egypt, Zaire** (Belgium)
10	France
No insolvency law	**Liberia (and many Arab countries)**
Not classified	Russia, Belarus, Ukraine, Khazakstan

Source: Adapted from Wood (1995).
Notes:
[a] The orientation refers to explicit law, disregarding the practical implementation through the court system. Scale: 1 = extremely pro-creditor, 10 = extremely pro-debtor.
[b] African countries are in bold type.

favor creditors or debtors in terms of claims on the distressed firm's assets and in terms of control over these assets in and after legal proceedings for bankruptcy or restructuring. Table 12.2, with African countries highlighted, is based on Wood's (1995) assessment of the degree of creditor or debtor orientation of formal procedures in different countries. Wood defines a creditor-oriented law as one that recognizes the claims of creditors to the greatest extent in insolvency. A debtor-oriented law allows debtors to retain a stake and/or control in insolvency although there is no equity left in the firm. This classification of creditor orientation amounts to recognition of ex ante contractual relations after filing for bankruptcy or restructuring.

Important determinants of orientation are the scope and efficiency of security and the existence of a rehabilitation statute or restructuring law. The existence of an easily accessible restructuring law generally favors debtors, since such a law – if it is mandatory – implies a constraint on the range of contractual solutions in distress situations. If incumbent owners are permitted to retain a stake and/or control after insolvency, then informal workouts with a lesser stake to be retained by the incumbent owners are hindered. More debtor-friendly restructuring law has been implemented in recent decades in a number of countries: the French law of 1967 changed the orientation strongly; Chapter 11 of the US bankruptcy code was enacted in 1978; British 'administration proceedings' have been possible since 1986; Australia allowed formal restructuring in 1992; and Germany and Sweden enacted restructuring laws in 1994 and 1996 – the latter two laws are not much different from already existing highly inaccessible composition laws.

Table 12.2 rates traditional British law as the most creditor oriented and current French law as the most debtor oriented. The implementation of formal procedures for restructuring (administration) in 1985 and 1986 made British law less creditor oriented, but it is still rated as marginally more creditor oriented than German, Dutch and Swedish law. Japanese and US laws are rated in the middle as more creditor oriented than Italian, Spanish and French law. Most developing countries base their insolvency laws on the law of the former colonial power, while the former members of the communist bloc seem to have adopted an insolvency law akin to one of the West European laws.

4   The practical application of insolvency law

In this section I look at the empirical evidence that may have a bearing on the efficiency of different insolvency law regimes. Both industrialized and emerging market countries are discussed.

Thorburn (2000) analyzes the results of 300 liquidation cases in Sweden between 1987 and 1991. She finds that in 75 percent of cases the bankrupt firms survived as 'going concerns.' Sweden has a strongly creditor-oriented law and allows floating charges, like the UK. Restructuring law was and remains inaccessible. On the other hand, the incidence of bankruptcy is very high in an international comparison. The procedure employed by the courts in bankruptcy is a 'cash auction' of the firm, meaning that the courts take over the insolvent firm and try to sell the whole entity to the highest bidder. Stromberg (2000) argues that the Swedish cash auction system tends to lead to a sale of assets back to the original owner in cases where the bank benefits from this solution. The probability of such a sale-back increases with the specificity of a firm's assets. Thus, it seems that the auction system under creditor-oriented law to a large extent accomplishes what restructuring laws are designed to accomplish.

Franks and Sussman (2000) present complementary evidence for Britain. In a study of three banks' handling of distressed firms, they show that the banks implemented elaborate informal rescue processes. The majority of distressed firms remain outside formal procedures, and the rate of liquidation does not seem particularly high when banks remain in control of the insolvency procedure.

Wood (1995) notes that the greatest disincentive to informal workouts of distress situations is the existence of relatively debtor-friendly re-structuring law. The evidence for Sweden and the UK seems to confirm this observation.

The conclusion that may be drawn from the evidence presented is that the absence of restructuring law has not hindered the survival of viable firms in financial distress during normal times, and has probably speeded up the shutdown of economically distressed firms. However, the anecdotal evidence from Sweden during a period of severe macroeconomic crisis in 1991–3, including a banking crisis, indicates that the Swedish informal system for restructuring did not function as well as during normal times. The willingness of banks to supply credit for survival was reduced, and there were few potential buyers with the means to buy distressed firms as going concerns. It is possible that the only effective remedy is to resolve a threatening banking crisis quickly.[4]

I turn now to emerging market economies where explicit insolvency law plays a lesser role. InsolvencyAsia (1999) reports that, prior to the Asian crisis in 1997, bankruptcies were almost non-existent in Indonesia, Korea, Thailand, Taiwan and the Philippines. Only Malaysia, Singapore and Japan among the East Asian economies had and have insolvency law that is actually applied with any frequency. There are three possible reasons the actual insolvency procedures in a country can look very different from the system described in formal law. First, the credit allocation process of banks may be influenced by political factors and specific groups with strong relations to a bank. Second, the legal process for dealing with insolvency according to the law may be ineffective, time consuming and/or corrupt. Third, creditors and debtors may prefer informal procedures, perhaps because their value system differs from the one expressed in law.

Among the East Asian countries, Korea, Thailand, Indonesia and the Philippines had banking systems before the crisis that did not impose hard budget constraints on firms, and political influences on credit allocation were strong, as shown in Hussain and Wihlborg (1999). In these four countries, as well as in Taiwan, the judicial procedures were ineffective or unpredictable in terms of judicial handling. Insolvency procedures thereby became de facto relatively debtor oriented. In Hong Kong, informal procedures seem to have been preferred in spite of the existence of an effective legal system. Taiwan too seems to have had effective informal procedures, although the legal system was unpredictable. Malaysia is the anomaly in Asia. The country was hit hard by the crisis in spite of effective formal procedures for dealing with firms in economic distress and a reasonably sound credit allocation process. However, the effective formal procedures seem to have contributed to a relatively fast recovery from the crisis in Malaysia.

Indian insolvency procedures are discussed in Wihlborg and Gangopadhyay (2001). In spite of its British-inspired creditor-oriented law, India's debt recovery and restructuring systems are extremely ineffective. Large firms in distress enter administrative restructuring proceedings that in effect protect debtors for years. Small firms, on the other hand, are subject to legal proceedings, but these are very time consuming. There is also a draconian law threatening debtors with imprisonment for certain arrears of payment. Such draconian consequences of distress do not contribute to the process of rehabilitation of a firm, however. The incidence of bank-led informal workouts of viable firms seems to be low in India.

Insolvency procedures in Latin America are discussed in Rowat and Astigarraga (1999). They describe insolvency procedures as 'woefully inadequate' in most countries of the region. The procedures are rigid and formalistic, they give judges too much arbitrary power to serve what they consider the 'general interest,' there is widespread cynicism about political influences overriding judgments, there is a powerful bias in favor of labor claimants, and corruption is rampant. Although the procedures are seemingly debtor oriented, they do not provide debtors with effective means to preserve going concern value.

Turning to the former socialist countries in Eastern Europe, many have implemented modern insolvency law but few have managed to enforce the laws successfully. Poland and Estonia are the countries that have progressed the most in terms of developing a functioning insolvency system based on law.[5] However, lack of capacity in the legal system is a problem in all the countries. Uncertain and ill-defined property rights have naturally been a hindrance to secured lending in Eastern Europe.

Insolvency procedures in Russia are discussed in, for example, Gaddy and Ickes (1999a,b) and Freinkman and Starodubrovskaya (1995). There is a modern insolvency law but the procedures seem to be used for asset diversion of enormous magnitudes through the activities of 'arbitration managers' appointed by court to lead the insolvent entity after bankruptcy filing. Large resources of industrial groups are spent on influencing the choice of arbitration manager.[6]

With hard data lacking, the African evidence is impressionistic but consistent. In a Senior Policy Seminar organized by the African Development Bank (ADB, 1997), legal institutions in most of Africa are described as inappropriate and lacking qualified personnel. The credit allocation process is strongly influenced by political factors and 'relations.' As a result, there is a large overhang of non-performing loans in most countries and there is no effective legal system for recovery of loans and security. In spite of a heritage of formal laws from the previous colonial powers in sub-Saharan Africa, these laws seem to have little effect on in-solvency procedures in practice. In the next section I review some evidence on the enforcement of insolvency law and indicators of the quality of legal institutions in Africa.

5   Enforcement and the quality of legal institutions and the financial sector in sub-Saharan Africa

The evidence presented in the previous section shows that, in large parts of the world, lack of enforcement renders the letter of insolvency law nearly meaningless. Creditor-oriented law in many countries becomes de facto debtor oriented in practice. Without court enforcement of in-solvency law, the actual rights of creditors at the time of a borrower's insolvency are uncertain and the stakeholders that are able to influence court proceedings or banks' credit allocation stand to gain the most. In this section, enforcement of insolvency law in Africa is studied. First, evidence with respect to the financial sector is considered. Then indicators of the quality of the legal systems are presented.

5.1   Financial crises and financial repression

Financial sector reform has been on the development agenda in Africa since the 1970s when McKinnon and Shaw coined the term 'financial repression' to characterize a financial system lacking the ability to supply credit to a great number of viable projects, and misallocating the scarce existing resources. By lifting interest rate ceilings for the banking system, financial resources were expected to be mobilized and channeled by banks. By privatizing or, at least, commercializing the banking system, the credit allocation mechanism would be improved. Financial sector reform initiated in a large number of countries during the 1980s followed these principles. The results have been disappointing. In a summary of the research results of the Second Senior Policy Seminar organized by the African Economic Research Consortium in November 1996, it was stated that 'it is now broadly confirmed that the response of investment to the variety of reform measures being widely pursued in the region has been quite poor, ... the banking sector has retained its character of providing short-term finance and capital markets remain either weak or absent in the majority of cases' (ABD, 1997).

The accumulation of bad loans in commercial banks has led to banking crises in many African countries when the burden on the public sector of supporting banks with large credit losses became overwhelming. Table 12.3 lists twenty-two African countries where banking crises reached sys-

Table 12.3 Banking crises in Africa, 1980–95

Country with episode in 1980–95	Causes include politically motivated lending	Regulatory shortcomings	Debt recovery hampered by legal environment	Recurrent problems
Benin	Yes	Yes	Yes	No
Cameroon	No	n/a	No	Yes
Congo	No	n/a	No	Yes
Central African Republic	No	n/a	No	Yes
Chad	No	n/a	No	Yes
Côte d'Ivoire	Yes	Yes	Yes	No
Eritrea	No	n/a	No	No
Ghana	Yes	Yes	n/a	Yes
Guinea	n/a	n/a	Yes	Yes
Mauritania	No	n/a	No	Yes
Kenya	Yes	Yes	n/a	Yes
Madagascar	Yes	n/a	Yes	Yes
Mozambique	No	n/a	No	Yes
Nigeria	Yes	Yes	n/a	Yes
Senegal	Yes	Yes	Yes	No
South Africa	No	n/a	No	n/a
Tanzania	No	n/a	No	Yes
Togo	No	n/a	n/a	Yes
Uganda	No	n/a	No	Yes
Zaire	No	n/a	No	n/a
Egypt	No	n/a	No	Yes
Morocco	No	n/a	No	Yes

Source: Caprio and Klingebiel (1996).

temic proportions between 1980 and 1995. In a majority of countries, politically motivated lending and regulatory shortcomings were considered major causes of the crises. With few exceptions, the crises were not resolved but considered to be 'recurrent problems.'

One reason the crises tend to be recurring is that the legal environments in the sub-Saharan countries do not seem to support debt recovery, as noted in Table 12.3. Efficient procedures for closing or rehabilitating have been lacking and the recovery of assets pledged as security for loans has been time consuming and uncertain. Popiel (1994) states that the recovery of non-performing assets has been 'disappointing' in all countries except Ghana, and that banking crises must be resolved jointly with the restructuring of the borrowing firms. Ghana, along with Uganda, has established 'non-performing assets trusts' separating the bad loans from the healthy parts of the banks. These trusts focus entirely on debt recovery, which includes contributing to the restructuring of distressed firms.[7]

Another perspective on the financial sector in Africa is offered by surveys conducted in the mid-1990s within the framework of a World Bank project – the Regional Program on Enterprise Development (RPED). The RPED surveys focused on enterprise finance, technical efficiency, the structure of wages and the impact of regulation. Three rounds of surveys were conducted with more than 200 firms of varying sizes in each of seven countries: Burundi, Cameroon, Ghana, Kenya, Tanzania, Zambia and Zimbabwe. Biggs and Srivastava (1996) report that, in all countries, lack of credit was considered the most severe obstacle to firm expansion among twenty possible obstacles including lack of demand, lack of infrastructure and labor regulation. It is, of course, to be expected that an interviewed manager would say that lack of credit is a problem when the firm has been denied credit, whether the credit was to be used productively or not. Nevertheless, the prominence of 'lack of credit' as a problem in comparison with many alternatives (the manager could select only the three most severe problems) among twenty is an indication that something is amiss in the markets for finance.

Data on sources of financing confirm that credit supply is seriously constrained. Table 12.4 shows the percentage of firms in different size classes receiving a bank loan during the previous five years, and bank loans as a percentage of sales. Among small firms with 10–20 employees, the share of firms having received a bank loan lies between 20 percent (in Tanzania) and 49 percent (in Cameroon). The figures for large firms with more than 100 employees are 47 percent and 85 percent. Even in large firms the ratio of loans to total assets is low. For example, in Kenya the ratio of loans to total assets in large firms in 1993 was around 30 percent according to an RPED country study (Isaksson and Wihlborg, 2002). The pattern for bank overdrafts used primarily as working capital is similar, although the figure for 'share of firms' is slightly larger for overdrafts, and the total amounts are smaller.

The same studies reveal that informal borrowing does not compensate for lack of bank credit. The amounts for informal borrowing are 5–10 percent of the amounts for bank loans, and the country that relies most on bank credit – Cameroon, with formal loans amounting to 22 percent of sales – also has the largest market for informal loans, with an amount of 2 percent of sales. The informal loans are to a large extent from 'business angels,' including family and friends for micro and small firms. Another observation is that the firms obtaining bank loans are mainly the ones also receiving trade credit, although in Zimbabwe and Tanzania the

Table 12.4 Firms with access to bank loans and value of loans relative to sales in African manufacturing

Country	Firm size				Average for all firms
	Micro	Small	Medium	Large	
Cameroon					
% of firms receiving loan	31	49	48	85	
Loan as % of sales	17	27	25	15	22
Kenya					
% of firms receiving loan	16	46	68	66	
Loan as % of sales	14	14	10	18	14
Tanzania					
% of firms receiving loan	12	20	25	47	
Loan as % of sales	4	7	2	19	10
Zimbabwe					
% of firms receiving loan	20	32	53	62	
Loan as % of sales	4	27	18	8	11
Zambia					
% of firms receiving loan	12	27	37	63	
Loan as % of sales	n.a.	n.a.	n.a.	n.a.	n.a.

Source: Biggs and Srivastava (1996).

share of small firms receiving trade credits is substantially higher than those receiving bank loans. Trade credits are most important for large firms, however.

For Kenya, Isaksson and Wihlborg (2002) show that a large share of micro and small firms rely entirely on cash transactions, although around 30 percent of such firms are able to obtain advance payments as a financing source. About half of the small firms owned by ethnic Asians are also able to obtain trade credits. Except for the latter group of firms, the results indicate that different forms of credit are not substitutes for relaxing the financial constraint. However, they may be substitutes for firms that have access to several kinds of credit.

Additional light on the financial constraints firms face is shed by figures for the value of collateral assets relative to the size of loans. Biggs and Srivastava (1996) mention that firms in Zimbabwe must offer collateral to a value of four times the loans, and in Kenya the figure is six. Isaksson and Wihlborg (2002) report similar figures for Kenya, and that the explanation given for the high collateral to loan value is uncertainty about banks' ability to claim the collateral in case of default. One example of uncertainty associated with collateral in Kenya is that so-called land control boards can invalidate the collateral by simply deciding that a bank's claim on a collateral asset must not be enforced, allowing the borrower and owner of the asset to keep it.

Kenya and Zimbabwe are neither special nor extreme in the sub-Saharan region. Biggs and Srivastava (1996) provide similar information for Ghana and Cameroon. Statements from the African Development Bank (ADB, 1997) and Popiel's (1994) observations indicate that political intervention in court proceedings and the overruling of court decisions are common in many African countries. Furthermore, proceedings may take several years to complete. The slow pace of court proceedings adds costs to the process of debt recovery for the creditors, and provides debtors with opportunities to evade debt obligations. These stylized facts support the view that there are important institutional hindrances to an effective financial sector in most African countries. The *African Development Report 1997* calls for a more enabling business environment, including a 'credible legal and judicial framework that supports private economic rights and which is enforced equitably and transparently ... Laws relating to business contracts, property rights, collateral and debt recovery, commercial dispute resolution and arbitration will need to be enacted and effectively enforced' (cited in ADB, 1997:8).

Bankruptcy law and, more broadly, institutions supporting debt recovery are clearly the legal areas singled out for attention as a potential source of continued financial repression.

5.2 Indicators of legal system quality

The causes of a lack of enforcement by the legal system may be low capacity of the legal system, lack of expertise and tradition, uncertain or ill-defined property rights, asset diversion/stripping by borrowers, arbitrary powers of courts and corruption. These factors may also contribute to a soft budget constraint imposed by banks, because if a bank faces little likelihood of being repaid it may extend existing credit lines in the hope of a turnaround or of future state support. Weak property registration, accounting and reporting standards contribute to the ability of debtors to divert assets from an insolvent estate.

Corruption is a widespread problem favoring particular groups. Naturally, the prospect of political intervention breeds corruption, as do the great arbitrary powers of judges reported for Latin American countries above. In Africa, on the other hand, arbitrary powers of judges do not seem to be the main source of corruption. Instead, the ability of politicians and administrative bodies, such as land control boards, to influence or overrule court decisions may breed corruption.

La Porta et al. (1997a,b) analyze the relationship between the supply of external finance and quality indicators of the judicial system based on

Table 12.5 Indicators of legal system quality in Africa

Country	Efficiency of judicial system[a]	Rule of law[b]	Corruption[c]	Risk of expropriation[d]	Risk of contract repudiation[d]
Egypt	6.50	4.17	3.87	6.30	6.05
Kenya	5.75	5.42	4.82	5.98	5.66
South Africa	6.00	4.42	8.92	6.88	7.27
Nigeria	7.25	2.73	3.03	5.33	4.36
Zimbabwe	7.50	3.68	5.42	5.61	5.04

Source: La Porta et al. (1997b).
Notes:
[a] Efficiency of judicial system: efficiency and integrity of the legal environment as it affects business, particularly foreign firms, produced by Business International Corporation; average 1980–93; scale of 0–10, with 10 for high efficiency.
[b] Rule of law: assessment of the law and order tradition in the country, produced by International Country Risk (ICR); average 1982–95; scale of 0–10, with 10 for strong tradition.
[c] Corruption: ICR's assessment of the (lack of) corruption in government (for example, 'bribe connected with import and export licenses, exchange controls, tax assessment, policy protection and loans' indicate corruption); average 1982–95; scale of 0–10, with high score indicating low corruption.
[d] Risk of expropriation and of contract repudiation: assessment by ICR; average 1982–95; scale of 0–10, with high score indicating low risk.

data for a large number of countries worldwide. They show that legal institutional factors are important in the variation across countries in the supply of external financing.[8] Table 12.5 shows scores for the efficiency of the judicial system, rule of law, corruption, risk of expropriation and risk of contract repudiation in four sub-Saharan countries and Egypt. The figures are averages for the period 1980–95. A high score indicates high quality (high efficiency and rule of law, low corruption and risk), with the highest possible score being 10. With the possible exception of risk of expropriation, the different measures of quality of the legal system would seem to capture different aspects of enforcement. South Africa scores relatively well on corruption and risk of contract repudiation, indicating that banks' lending and debt recovery decisions would be relatively free from political influences and that contracts are upheld in court. On efficiency of the judicial system, South Africa's score is mediocre; its rule of law score is very low, which reflects the apartheid past. The other scores reflect that South Africa has at least had a functioning legal system supporting contractual arrangements, including insolvency procedures, based on Dutch law. Nigeria and Zimbabwe score relatively high on efficiency of the judicial system but very low on the other dimensions. This

Table 12.6 Index of Economic Freedom with respect to property rights in sub-Saharan Africa

Country	Index[a]	Country	Index[a]
Botswana	2	Chad	4
Cape Verde	2	Congo, Rep.	4
Mauritius	2	Ethiopia	4
Namibia	2	Guinea	4
Swaziland	2	Ivory Coast	4
Djibouti	3	Mauritania	4
Egypt	3	Mozambique	4
Gabon	3	Niger	4
The Gambia	3	Nigeria	4
Ghana	3	Tanzania	4
Kenya	3	Togo	4
Lesotho	3	Equatorial Guinea	5
Madagascar	3	Guinea-Bissau	5
Malawi	3	Rwanda	5
Mali	3	Zimbabwe	5
Senegal	3	Angola	N/R
South Africa	3	Burundi	N/R
Uganda	3	Congo, Dem. Rep.	N/R
Zambia	3	Sierra Leone	N/R
Benin	4	Somalia	N/R
Burkina Faso	4	Sudan	N/R
Cameroon	4		

Source: Heritage Foundation (2001).
Notes: N/R = not recorded.
[a] Property Right Grading Scale: 1 = very high (private property guaranteed by the government, and efficient court system enforces contracts; expropriation unlikely); 2 = high (private property guaranteed by the government, but enforcement lax; court system is inefficient or subject to delays; expropriation unlikely); 3 = moderate (government recognizes some private property rights, but property can be nationalized; expropriation possible; judiciary subject to influence); 4 = low (property ownership limited, with little legal protection; expropriation likely, and government does not protect private property adequately; judiciary subject to influence, possible corruption within judicial process); 5 = very low (almost all property belongs to the state; expropriation certain, *or* country so corrupt and chaotic that property protection is nonexistent).

could indicate that courts work relatively fast but with unpredictable and arbitrary results relative to original contracts.

Table 12.6 shows the 2001 scores for the scope and the enforcement of property rights for most sub-Saharan countries and Egypt. These scores represent one aspect of the Heritage Foundation's Index of Economic Freedom. The scores are on a scale from 1 to 5, with a low score indicating high quality, i.e. wide scope of property rights that are well enforced. The table's note describes the meaning of the scores, and shows that only the best score (1) is consistent with strict enforcement of insolvency and other laws pertaining to contracts with respect to property. All Western market economies obtain the highest score. A score of 2 means that enforcement is lax, and a 3 indicates uncertain rights, insecure contracts, weak enforcement and possible corruption. As seen in the table, only five countries – of which two are islands – score better than 3 (Botswana, Cape Verde, Mauritius, Namibia and Swaziland). These data constitute a harsh judgment of the legal systems in sub-Saharan Africa. They go a long way in explaining the financial repression and financial crises discussed above, and in explaining a wide difference beween the letter and the implementation of insolvency law.

6   Issues of design of insolvency law as a contract

Insolvency law is a relatively complex body of law. There are many dimensions both to formal law and to enforcement. A number of issues that countries must face when reforming insolvency procedures are discussed in Wihlborg and Gangopadhyay (2001):

(1) Is insolvency law necessary and, if so, must it be mandatory?
(2) Which contractual obligations of a distressed firm should be recognized in insolvency?
(3) What priority shall be given to liabilities to employees and tax authorities and to other social objectives?
(4) Is there a need for a formal process for restructuring? If so, should access be restrictive and incentives to use the process weak or strong?
(5) How will legislation deal with foreign claims on the firm and by the firm?
(6) How can enforcement of the law be assured?
(7) Do market-oriented solutions provide an alternative?

The discussion here is limited to the relatively controversial issues (1), (4) and (6).

6.1   Is insolvency law necessary and, if so, must it be mandatory?

A fundamental principle of a market economy is that contracts voluntarily entered into should be respected. Insolvency law determines how involuntary breach of certain contractual obligations shall be dealt with. Clearly, the procedures for dealing with such a failure can be regulated in ex ante contracts between the firm and various stakeholders. The complexity of financial obligations is so high, however, that transaction costs (negotiation, information and enforcement costs) could be very high if there were no 'standard form contract' provided by the legislature in the form of insolvency law. *Enabling law* is a standard form contract that can be amended and changed as desired in mutual agreement by the contracting parties; or there is no explicit law but only recognition and enforcement of voluntarily entered contracts. The purpose of having a prespecified, enabling standard form contract is that the standard form provides information about what aspects of a contract parties need to think of, and it provides a 'default contract' for those who do not want to enter negotiations on many details. *Mandatory law* not only prespecifies a standard form contract but provides the only legal contract. Macey (1992) and Wihlborg (1998) argue that mandatory law tends be less efficient than enabling law, but that mandatory law is necessary for lawmakers to achieve objectives other than economic efficiency (in a dynamic sense). The political interests of the state and employees, in particular, are often given special weight.

Even if insolvency law is made mandatory with respect to particular social objectives, it can be designed in such a way that it provides strong incentives for and enables efficient workouts outside court, as noted in section 3. If debtors are given a strong position and contracts are cancelled, debtors have an incentive to delay resolution of insolvency. During a delay they will not have to repay debts, assets can be diverted in their favor, or they may hope for a turnaround of fortunes. On the other hand, if creditors are given strong rights, and their claims are largely preserved, they have an incentive to resolve the insolvency in a way that maximizes the value of the estate and their claims. Thus, if they can contribute to a solution whereby the firm continues as a going concern, they would do so. If the current management is the best suited to continue in control, then the creditors would want to contribute to a solution that allows such a resolution. Evidence was presented in section 4 that senior creditors in Sweden and the UK generally help to preserve going concern values, either by contributing to court-led resolutions or through informal reorganizations of distressed firms.

6.2   *Is there a need for a formal process for restructuring? If so, should access be restrictive and incentives to use the process weak or strong?*

As noted, informal restructuring is likely to occur in a creditor-oriented insolvency system recognizing ex ante contracts. Thus, there are great advantages to a creditor-oriented regime with very limited opportunities for court-led restructuring, since the existence of formal restructuring law acts as a disincentive for informal solutions. It was noted in section 3 that the role of restructuring law should be determined in coordination with other rules for financial markets in general, and banks in particular. For example, reliance on effective informal arrangements requires that banks' incentives are consistent with the maximization of the value of assets. It is therefore very important that state guarantees of the banking system are abandoned, and that banking crises are resolved in a speedy manner in order to maintain banks' incentives to maximize assets.

6.3   How can enforcement of the law be assured?

Enforcement is perhaps the most intractable problem in the area of insolvency law. A viable market economy requires that parties to a voluntary transaction feel secure that traded property will change hands securely, with a minimum of transaction costs, and that each party must have some recourse to corrective action, other than threat of violence, in case of non-performance by another party to the transaction. One requirement for this security is that the buyer knows that the seller has the right to sell. Enforcement of financial contracts requires that the property of a delinquent borrower can be identified. Similarly, contractual arrangements with and among firms require that the property of the firm and the individuals signing are identifiable. Thus, firms as legal persons must be registered with the names of individuals acting as their agents. Apart from these registration requirements, security of contractual relations in the absence of detailed law requires that the state enforce voluntary and 'reasonable' contracts, that is, contracts that are not entered into under duress. Some kind of arbitration and dispute settlement mechanism is necessary, although such a mechanism can be agreed upon in contract. Thus, even in this case 'enforcer of last resort' can be required.

In the absence of state-supported enforcement, contract fulfillment must rely on self-enforcement, and the most important mechanism of this kind is reputation. The threat of lost reputation is sufficient for transactions involving established firms with repeated transactions within a well-defined group. Other types of self-enforcement (for example, requirements for advance payments, a bond or the internalization of transactions within a firm) are more costly. However, reputation as an enforcement mechanism is not likely to work well unless repeated transactions are expected. It is a mechanism that cannot be relied upon in insolvency negotiations, except possibly in countries where a strong social stigma would be associated with opportunistic behavior.

Without court enforcement of insolvency law, the actual rights of creditors at the time of a borrower's insolvency become uncertain, and the creditors who are able to apply influence of some kind will be the ones who have the strongest security. If the influence of the debtor in political or physical terms is substantial, then even a strictly creditor-oriented insolvency law becomes de facto debtor oriented. Enforcement touches on the very fundamentals of the political and economic system of each country. Powerful groups must find it necessary for their political survival to create an effective legal system, and old networks of influence must be destroyed.

Some first steps toward enhancement of the efficiency of the legal insolvency procedures are proposed for Latin America in Rowat and Astigarraga (1999). These steps have the objectives of increasing transparency, legal competence and the capacity of the legal system. Enforcement problems in the area of insolvency law have also been recognized in recent initiatives from the World Bank, the Asian Development Bank and the African Development Bank.[9]

7 Concluding remarks

Pistor et al. (2000:330) state: 'The effectiveness of legal institutions has a much stronger impact on external finance than does the law on the books.' This statement is supported by the review of insolvency procedures across the world in this chapter. Emerging market economies, with few exceptions, do not support the letter of the law with effective application and enforcement. Either the banking system allocates credit such that insolvency procedures are made irrelevant, or the legal system is so slow, unpredictable or corruptible that written law and its intent lack force. Most sub-Saharan countries perform very poorly both in terms of the banking system's ability to allocate credit and in terms of the effectiveness of the legal system. The letter of insolvency law is essentially meaningless, although there are examples of countries where there are ongoing efforts to improve enforcement of debt contracts – Ghana and Uganda are such examples.

I have noted that changes in the legal system and its enforcement mechanisms take time. Evidence from Indonesia and Latin America indicates that strong enforcement of existing law lacks support among powerful groups. Effective enforcement requires public support for the intent of the law, as well as respect for legal institutions. This evidence has a bearing on Africa as well, indicating that public attitudes to private property and contracts and the independence of the judicial system from the political and economic powers are both essential ingredients of the practical implementation of formal insolvency law. With respect to the economic role of insolvency procedures in Africa, the relation between the financial system and insolvency procedures is particularly important. A financial system that allocates credit based on relations and political power renders insolvency procedures nearly meaningless, and accumulates bad loans until the government can no longer afford to support the banks. At this stage the lack of effective insolvency procedures hinders the restoration of both the financial system and firms.

Among issues of the design of insolvency law, the design of so-called rehabilitation or restructuring statutes is controversial. There is a tendency to implement more easily accessible restructuring law, but the implementation of such statutes may not increase the survival rate of viable but insolvent firms, or decrease the rate of survival of firms producing negative value.

Notes

1. This section is based on Wihlborg and Gangopadhyay (2001).
2. An expanded version of this section can be found in Wihlborg and Gangopadhyay (2001).
3. Debt recovery was hampered by the legal system in the following heterogeneous group of countries outside Africa with recent banking crises: Indonesia, Thailand, Brazil and Hungary. These observations indicate that a large number of countries with different legal traditions on all continents have insolvency procedures that contribute to or prolong economic crises.
4. The role of capital requirements in supplying liquidity in a macroeconomic crisis is another factor deserving research.
5. See, for example, Coates and Mirsky (1995), Gray (1996, 1997) and Montes-Negret and Papi (1996).
6. See Wihlborg and Gangopadhyay (2001) for an elaboration on this.
7. The share of non-performing loans of Ugandan commercial banks fell from 60 percent in 1994 to 30 percent in 1997 and to 12 percent in 2000 (Nannyonjo, 2002).
8. Demirguc-Kunt and Huizinga (1998) show that interest spreads on corporate debt issued by firms in different countries are influenced by an index of contract enforcement.
9. The main World Bank initiative is called the Global Insolvency Law Database, a database covering insolvency law across the world, developed and made accessible through the World Bank website. 'Best practices' principles for insolvency law are also developed.

REFERENCES

ADB (African Development Bank) (1997) 'Report on the Second Senior Policy Seminar on the Impact of Financial Sector Reform on Domestic Resource Mobilization for Investment in Africa,' *African Development Review* 9(1).

Bebchuk, L. A. and R. C. Picker (1993) 'Bankruptcy Rules, Managerial Entrenchment, and Firm Specific Human Capital,' University of Chicago Law and Economics Working Paper No. 16.

Beck, T., A. Demirguc-Kunt and R. Levine (2001) 'Law, Politics, and Finance,' World Bank Working Paper No. 2585, Washington, DC.

Biggs, T. and P. Srivastava (1996) 'Structural Aspects of Manufacturing in Sub-

Saharan Africa: Summary Evaluation from RPED-Surveys,' World Bank Technical Working Paper No. 346, Washington, DC.

Caprio, G., Jr. and D. Klingebiel (1996) 'Bank Insolvencies: Cross Country Experience,' World Bank Policy Research Working Paper No. 1620, Washington, DC.

Clarke, G. R. G. (2001) 'How the Quality of Institutions Affects Technological Deepening in Developing Countries,' World Bank Working Paper No. 2603, Washington, DC.

Coates, R. D. and A. E. Mirsky (1995) *Restructuring and Bankruptcy in Central and Eastern Europe*, Deloitte Touche Tohmatsa International: New York.

Cornelli, F. and L. Felli (1996) 'Ex Ante Efficiency of Bankruptcy Procedures,' *European Economic Review* 41(3/5):475–85.

Demirguc-Kunt, A. and H. Huizinga (1998) 'Determinants of Commercial Bank Interest Margins and Profitability: Some International Evidence,' World Bank Working Papers No. 1900, Washington, DC.

Devarajan, S., W. R. Easterly and H. Pack (2001) 'Is Investment in Africa Too Low or Too High? Macro and Micro Evidence,' World Bank Working Paper No. 2519, Washington, DC.

Franks, J. and O. Sussman (2000) 'The Cycle of Corporate Distress, Rescue and Resolution: A Study of Small- and Medium-Sized UK Companies,' London Business School Working Paper No. 306, London.

Freinkman, L. M. and I. Starodubrovskaya (1995) 'Restructuring of Enterprises' Social Assets in Russia: Trends, Problems, Possible Solutions,' World Bank Working Paper No. 1635, Washington, DC.

Gaddy, C. G. and B. W. Ickes (1999a) 'Russian Virtual Economy,' *Foreign Affairs* 77(5):53–67.

———— (1999b) 'Stability and Disorder: An Evolutionary Analysis of Russia's Virtual Economy,' World Bank Working Paper No. 276, Washington, DC.

Gangopadhyay, S. and C. Wihlborg (2001) 'The Impact of Alternative Bankruptcy Rules on Risky Project Choice and Skill Formation under Credit Rationing,' Scandinavian Working Papers No. 2001-5, Stockholm.

Gray, C. W. (1996) 'Bank-Led Restructuring in Poland (I): The Bank-Conciliation Process in Action,' *Economics of Transition* 4(2):349–70.

———— (1997) 'Bank-Led Restructuring in Poland (II): Bankruptcy and Its Alternatives', *Economics of Transition* 5(1):25–44.

Heritage Foundation (2001) http://www.heritage.org/index/2001.

Hussain, Q. and C. Wihlborg (1999) 'Corporate Insolvency Procedures and Bank Behavior: A Study of Selected Asian Economies,' IMF Working Paper No. 99/135, Washington, DC.

InsolvencyAsia (1999) 'Insolvency Law Reforms in the Asian and Pacific Region,' Report of the Office of the General Counsel, Asian Development Bank, Manila.

Isaksson, A. and C. Wihlborg (2002) 'Financial Constraints on Kenyan Manufacturing,' in A. Bigsten and P. Kimuyu (eds.) *Structure and Performance of Manufacturing in Kenya*, Palgrave: London.

La Porta, R., F. Lopez-de-Silanes, A. Shleifer and R. W. Vishny (1997a) 'Law and Finance,' *Journal of Political Economy* 104:1113–55.

―――― (1997b) 'Legal Determinants of External Finance,' *Journal of Finance* 52(3).

Macey, J. (1992) *Corporate Law and Governance Once in Sweden: A Law and Economics Perspective*, SNS Publishing: Stockholm.

Montes-Negret, F. and L. Papi (1996) 'The Polish Experience in Bank and Enterprise Restructuring,' World Bank Working Paper No. 1705, Washington, DC.

Nannyonjo, J. (2002) 'Financial Sector Reforms in Uganda (1990–2000): Interest Rate Spreads, Market Structure, Bank Performance and Monetary Policy,' Ph.D. dissertation, Ekonomiska Studier No. 110, Department of Economics, Göteborg University.

North, D. (1990) *Institutions, Institutional Change, and Economic Performance*, Cambridge University Press: Cambridge.

Olson, M. (1993) 'Dictatorship, Democracy, and Development,' *American Political Science Review* 87:567–76.

Pistor, K., M. Raiser and S. Gelfer (2000) 'Law and Finance in Transition Economies,' *Economics of Transition* 8(2):325–68.

Popiel, P. A. (1994) 'Financial Systems in Sub-Saharan Africa,' World Bank Discussion Paper No. 260, Washington, DC.

Posner, R. A. (1992) *Economic Analysis of Law*, 4th ed. Little Brown: Boston.

Rowat, M. and J. Astigarraga (1999) 'Latin American Insolvency Systems. A Comparative Assessment,' World Bank Technical Paper No. 433, Washington, DC.

Stromberg, P. (2000) 'Conflicts of Interest and Market Illiquidity in Bankruptcy Auctions: Theory and Tests,' *Journal of Finance* 55(2):641–91.

Thorburn, K. S. (2000) 'Bankruptcy Auctions: Costs of Debt Recovery and Firm Survival,' *Journal of Financial Economics* 58(3):337–68.

Wihlborg, C. (1998) *The Role of Enabling and Mandatory Company Law for Financial Systems Efficiency: The Limits of Government: Policy Competence and Economic Growth*, City University Publishing: Stockholm.

Wihlborg, C. and S. Gangopadhyay (with Q. Hussain) (2001) 'Infrastructure Requirements in the Area of Bankruptcy,' Brookings-Wharton Papers on Financial Services, Washington, DC.

Wood, P. R. (1995) *Principles of International Insolvency*, Sweet & Maxwell: London.

13

Non-formal institutions, informal economies and the politics of inclusion

Aili Mari Tripp

1 Introduction

African governments and donors have gradually come to accept informal economic institutions as a source of survival for large sections of the population who cannot rely on the formal economy for employment or adequate incomes. Rather than simply seeing the informal sector as a manifestation of casualization to be eliminated as the formal sector strengthens, today donors and governments alike are looking for ways to provide microfinance and other support to this sector. There is growing recognition that the vitality of this sector can be attributed to the fact that it is owned and controlled by the operators to a greater extent than happens in many other sectors of the economy. Nevertheless, government policy has a long way to go in addressing the needs of this sector.

This chapter draws on the theoretical and empirical findings of the growing literature on informal economic institutions, especially as they relate to Africa, to explore economic responses to the failures of state economic policy, poor infrastructure, incomplete information, insecurity and problems of risk. It explores some of the particular characteristics of non-formal market institutions within which the informal economy operates by examining both the underlying norms, economic rationales and motivations of small-scale entrepreneurs as well as the associations within which their economic activity is embedded. I refer to these institutions as 'non-formal' but even this term does not fully capture the complexity of African markets. Thus, the study is an attempt to respond, by looking at the informal economy, to the observations made by Marcel Fafchamps (1997:733) about African markets more generally.

We know little about how markets operate in practice. Perhaps the best measure of this lack of knowledge is our propensity to call 'informal' everything that is not of Western inspiration. The truth is that market activity in Africa is not without form; it is only without economic formalization. It may escape our present understanding, but it does not defy explanation – African market realities are much richer than is often recognized. The problems that indigenous institutions attempt to solve are the usual ones – commitment failure, asymmetric information and transaction costs – but the solutions often are original. African market realities are nothing but a transformed image of those in advanced countries. Studying markets in Africa forces us to rethink the very nature of markets themselves. The poor understanding of African markets was especially evident with the widespread failure of structural adjustment programs throughout much of Africa. Economic reforms were intended to eliminate irrationalities in economic policy and practice. Although their aim was to strengthen the formal sector and eliminate the need for informal markets, in reality the reforms often strengthened the informal sector and its efficiency. In particular, the informal sector expanded employment opportunities and the growth of new firms in response to structural adjustment in Africa (Parker et al., 1995:3).

Whereas formal financial institutions responded poorly to economic reform measures in countries such as Malawi, Nigeria, Tanzania and Ghana, informal financial agents responded dynamically and proved to be more efficient. Default rates for small-scale creditors in Tanzania, for example, were 0.1 percent and 2.5 percent for rotating savings and credit associations, whereas for commercial banks they were 80.0 percent (Aryeetey et al., 1997:198, 205). Moreover, unlike formal lending institutions, which concentrated only on large manufacturing companies, informal institutions expanded their clientele significantly. Poor integration between the formal and informal financial sectors, however, did not permit a spillover effect from informal institutions to formal ones. In many ways, these outcomes challenged expectations. Excessive government control of financial systems had been seen as encouraging fragmented financial markets, resulting in a market that favored certain borrowers while forcing the majority to seek credit in inefficient, expensive informal markets. According to this view, the elimination of restrictive financial policies should have allowed for the expansion of the formal sector, improved access to formal financial institutions, reduced the need for informal lending, improved efficiency, and lowered the differential between borrowing and lending rates (Steel et al., 1997). Instead, the lifting of controls led to an expansion of the informal financial institutions.

In case study after case study, the evidence overwhelmingly points to tremendous vitality in the informal sector in response to economic reform when contrasted with the formal sector. Kenneth King's latest study of the *jua kali* informal sector in Kenya showed how informal sector operators – both rural and urban, large and small scale – had experienced differentiation and greater dynamism, more diversity and sophistication in technologies, when he contrasted his earlier 1970s study with what he found in the 1990s. Because of the potential of the informal sector in contrast to the low wages and insecurity of the formal sector, there has been significant migration from the formal to the informal sector in Kenya (King, 1996:519). My findings in Tanzania are virtually identical (Tripp, 1997).

Section 2 of this chapter uses comparative analysis of African informal economies to examine key distinguishing characteristics of the informal sector in Africa. Section 3 outlines the economic rationales that drive these informal economies to show how their logic derives from social and human considerations that are often at odds with the goals of business expansion. Section 4 then maps out some of the institutional terrain within which the informal sector operates that derives from these rationales. Finally, section 5 analyzes the extent to which government policies in Africa have facilitated and constrained the informal sector: What are continuing impediments to the growth of local and informal markets? What incentives would enhance informal institutions?

2   Dimensions of the informal economy

Informal economic activities are untaxed, unlicensed and unregulated economic activities. Sometimes, though not always, they are characterized by their small scale of operation. However, the lines between informal and formal activities are often blurred. Overlaps between the two sectors are numerous, and so to a large extent we may also be talking about local markets and local economies, and especially small-scale production, microfinance and small-scale trading, commerce and service businesses. One further distinction is necessary. The informal economy can be divided into at least two types of activity: licit and illicit activities. Illicit activities have no legal counterpart in the society in question. Depending on the social and political context, illicit activities might include embezzlement, drug dealing, bribery, extraction of rents, kickbacks and other forms of criminal activity. The informal economy also includes licit or legitimate activities, which do have a legal counterpart in the society in question (Tripp, 1997). For example, making oil lamps without a license is a licit informal activity because one could potentially obtain a license for that activity. There is naturally a fine line between licit and illicit forms of informal economic activity, with many gray areas in between. Most importantly from an empirical standpoint, there are many connections between various kinds of licit and illicit activities. In this chapter I am referring primarily to licit informal activities.

As much as the informal economy blends into the formal economy, it also differs from the formal economy in particular ways in Africa. For example, in most African countries the informal sector contributes more to GDP than the formal manufacturing sector does. It accounts for the majority of the urban labor force and a growing portion of the rural population. Moreover, informal entrepreneurs primarily serve local markets. Small-scale entrepreneurs provide local consumers with affordable products, often tailored to meet the specifications of the individual. Informal international trade is as big as or bigger than that of the formal sector. It is facilitated by foreign exchange and commodity shortages, price differentials and foreign exchange differentials across the borders. The fact that similar ethnic groups and peoples cut across national borders also makes such trade easier (DPCSD, 1996:14). A large proportion of total urban incomes are found in the informal sector. In Tanzania I found that nine-tenths of urban household income was obtained from informal income-generating projects, while the other one-tenth came from formal wages. Thus, the informal economy provides incomes to people that come much closer to meeting their needs than formal wages do. The fastest-growth wages are in the informal economy (Tripp, 1997).

The overwhelming majority of new job creation is in the informal sector. The informal sector has resulted in the expansion of small enterprises in recent years (DPCSD, 1996:10–18). In Uganda, for example, there are 800,000 micro-enterprises employing roughly 1.5 million people, mostly women, 80 percent of whom are based in the rural areas. They have an annual labor force growth rate of about 20 percent. Indeed this is the fastest-growing job growth sector in Africa, accounting for as much as 40 percent of GDP and providing at least 70 percent of all new employment (Charmes, 1997). The informal economy has often provided opportunities for sectors of society, such as urban women, youth and the elderly, who have limited opportunities for formal employment. Much of the expansion is due to the growth in numbers of new enterprises rather than as a result of an increase in vertical growth. In fact, Africa has some of the highest proportions of people who are entrepreneurs, and the numbers of people who are self-employed, heading their own firms, is much higher than one would find in Western economies. Moreover,

African households frequently combine farming with crafts, trade, services or production (Fafchamps, 1997:734).

The informal economy has absorbed a large percentage of the population who otherwise might be considered unemployed. One way in which the informal sector is able to accommodate these income and employment demands is through the creation of similar new enterprises rather than through internal expansion or hiring. Once apprentices or family members who have been working for an enterprise gain enough capital, they break off and form their own business, perhaps hiring (often a distant relative) or in partnership with another individual. This effectively and intentionally keeps many enterprises small in size. Tinker (1987) has referred to this splitting off to form a new enterprise as an 'amoeba-like' activity, in contrast to the alternative expansion route of forming a larger hierarchical enterprise. It is interesting to note that in Tanzania even firms with greater capital tend to keep employees at a minimum, while permitting this amoeba-like expansion to occur (Bagachwa and Ndulu, 1996). Thus, capital and resources do not remain in the hands of a few, but are more widely distributed among a larger segment of the population, whereas large-scale enterprises tend to concentrate capital in the hands of the state or a few capitalists. Because informal activities usually are labor intensive, employment takes place at relatively low capital cost. Small-scale and micro-entrepreneurs rely primarily on local inputs, unlike formal industry, which is heavily dependent on foreign exchange and the importation of inputs.

Small enterprises tend to be more efficient in the resources they use and as such are critical to African potential in employment and productivity (Young, 1994:1). Small-scale producers in Tanzania, to take one country, have proven to be at least five times more productive than their large-scale counterparts in terms of output measured per unit investment (Kim, 1988:96). Although individual accounts may be small in scale, when the many accounts are aggregated they represent substantial amounts of internal investment and saving.

In most African countries, informal savings and financial activities predominate and have limited linkages to formal lending institutions (Adams and Fitchett, 1992; Bouman, 1995a,b). Most funding to start enterprises is self-generated but also with high rates of loans coming from family and friends (Buckley, 1997:1082). The majority of informal sector activities are trade related rather than in the manufacturing and service sectors. The average size of commercial enterprises is about one-quarter or one-fifth of service businesses or production activities (DPCSD, 1996:10).

Women constitute the major labor force within the informal sector in most parts of Africa. Although estimates of informal sector participation tend not to be very reliable, the general pattern of female involvement is clear. For example, Congo has 94 percent female involvement in the retail trade sector, Gambia 89 percent, and Zambia 91 percent (DPCSD, 1996:11; Grey-Johnson, 1992:74–5). Although there is considerable regional differentiation in the extent to which women participate in the informal economy, where they are most active, women are primarily responsible for meeting household needs, including food, clothing, healthcare and education-related expenses, whereas men are more likely to spend their income on themselves. Patterns throughout Africa show that women's surplus income goes first to the care of children, secondarily to the household, and lastly to the expansion of their businesses. This makes women entrepreneurs, in particular, a key leverage point in influencing the welfare of the household overall. Yet they frequently have the hardest time accessing capital to invest in their enterprises that sustain their households (see also Tripp, 2000).

3   Organizing principles of the informal economy

A variety of rationales drive these informal institutions, especially small-scale micro-enterprises. It is difficult to generalize because much depends on the broader cultural and economic context and the size of the enterprise. Also, people vary strategies and are not necessarily consistent. But many of the poorest microbusiness operators, especially women, commonly adopt operating principles that defy conventional neoclassical assumptions that business people simply are self-seeking individualists singlemindedly bent on maximizing their profits. Many will seek to lessen market competition by sharing product and marketing ideas with others; by making profit a secondary consideration when it comes to family crises; by lowering prices for poorer customers; by assisting other business people who sell similar products in the same location; and by combining collective income-generating strategies with individual ones. It is necessary to understand such rationales and values in order to comprehend, for example, why vertical integration is not always a preferred strategy or why profitability and expansion are sometimes limited. Such value preferences help explain why people might not always respond to policy incentives in expected ways. Moreover, these alternate logics of operation mitigate against the expansion of linkages between the formal and informal economies.

To comprehend the vitality of the informal economy is to comprehend the norms of reciprocity, mutuality and fairness that drive it. Although it is linked to and overlaps with the formal economy, there are rationales that drive this more localized, smaller-scale, informal economic activity that are not as evident in highly developed market economies, where economic activity is more disembodied from social life, individuals are more atomized and markets are the driving force in society (Booth, 1994:657–60). Participants in a given community share a common plight in which survival is the driving force. Moreover, they share a common perception that their survival is contingent on that of others in their community. Community, family or kin interests rather than the market define values governing economic activity in what could be considered a 'moral economy.' Many of the operating principles of the informal economy are at cross-purposes with the expansion of businesses, competitiveness and even efficiency. But they are important to consider because they explain in part the high levels of feelings of ownership that participants have of their economic activities. They also reflect considerations that have to do with the strengthening of community, trust, social capital and quality of life.

3.1   Accumulating social capital

In a study I conducted of small businesswomen in Uganda in the early 1990s (see, for example, Tripp, 1994, 1998a,b), I found that they were as likely to cooperate as to compete. Underlying these strategies was the strong conviction that women's individual and household survival is tied to that of their community and to that of others. They believed that, by seeking cooperative strategies, they could enhance their own well-being and that of their household. This idea is summed up in the acronym for one savings club, the West Road Women's Association (WERWA), which translates into 'give of yourself.' As a member of this organization explained, 'it is important that you first give of yourself and think of others and only then you can think of yourself.' When I asked why, under such harsh economic conditions, women do not think first about their self-interest, she answered, 'because you cannot survive if you only rely on yourself, we all need one another.'

You help others because you might be the one in need the next time around. You forgive someone who, on a rare occasion, defaults on a payment in a rotating savings club, because next time you might be the one who needs forgiveness. This is by no means limited to business strategies, but it is a way of life for the urban and rural poor alike. Valdo Pons (in Wallman et al., 1996) describes a Kampala neighborhood as a 'moral community' in which neighborliness and respectability are highly valued, especially by women, who are integral to the cohesion of the community. Women are obligated to look out for the well-being of neighbors and care for them when they are ill (Wallman et al., 1996:88–9). Favors of this kind are ways to build social wealth (Vélez-Ibañez,

1983) or social capital, to borrow a term popularized by Robert Putnam (1993:163–85). In other words, these Ugandan women are building up networks made up of family, friends, acquaintances and business associates that are based on trust and reciprocity as a way of banking on assistance in the future. The larger the network, the greater the accumulation of social capital that can be drawn on in a future time of need.

3.2   Mutual assistance

Cooperative strategies take many different forms. Enid Rwakatunga is a Kabale woman who ran a secretarial service firm and had started a mushroom-growing business. She had begun encouraging and training rural women's groups to get into the mushroom business so that she could provide them with spawn and they would grow the mushrooms. When I asked her why she was doing this, she first talked about how she had grown up in a polygamous rural family and was still haunted by how much her mother and sisters were suffering. She felt it was her duty to educate rural women with what she knew about how to grow mushrooms and other income-generating activities to help them improve monetarily. She said she was also keen to educate them about nutrition because of the low levels of awareness she felt rural women in her area had about how to feed their children properly. I then began to probe to see how important these concerns were to her relative to the profitability of her own business, since these women would be selling her their mushrooms, which she would then market. She admitted that she would give her own business priority, but this was because she would not be in a position to help them if she could not get her own seed-supplying business off the ground. But she insisted that the women would benefit because in Kabale the mushroom business is much more lucrative than selling handicrafts, which is a common income-generating project for women but one where sales are tough because the market is flooded.

I pushed Rwakatunga even further and asked what she would do if a wealthy businessman came to town who had the means to grow large quantities of mushrooms. He was willing to buy her seeds at considerably higher rates than she was asking from the rural women. Would she sell to him? I asked. She responded, 'I would not buy from him even if we were to get better price. Only one person would be benefiting. But by supplying rural women, several homes would be developed.' This was no hypothetical question for her. She had given it considerable thought since her husband, as manager of an American-owned pyrethrum business based in Kabale, had already been forced to choose between working with large numbers of poor rural women or with a few men who had large farms and could supply large quantities of pyrethrum. 'Let me tell you how he struggled to get women in rural areas.' To supply individuals with big farms 'would have only benefited one person. He would not go in for that.' From his example she drew the lesson that to supply one wealthy individual 'I would only be thinking of my own factory, I would not be thinking of rural women. Don't you see?' By now she was imploring me to understand, until I finally relented and admitted that I 'got it.'

The entrepreneurs in my study formed business associations explicitly to share ideas for products and markets, to teach each other how to improve their bookkeeping and accounting and how to manage their businesses and to encourage them to save. Other entrepreneurs established groups to encourage other women to get into business or to save money.

3.3   Avoiding competition

Entrepreneurs would often go to great lengths to minimize competition, sometimes writing provisions into their trade association or cooperative constitution or into market rules to ensure that a collaborative non-competitive ethos prevailed. Thus, in the context of a market, the rules would stipulate that one seller would not try to divert customers who were engaged in a purchase with another vendor. Market vendors selling the same product side by side would not encroach on each other's regular customers, and would even go to great lengths to help each other out in making sales and covering for each other if one had to leave the stall temporarily.

3.4   Profit and economic efficiency as secondary considerations

Some norms suggest that the profit motive is tempered by other considerations. A trader might dip into her business savings to pay for the medical treatment of a child. In Kumasi market in Ghana, most women traders kept their working capital separate from disposable income, but would use it willingly to meet a family emergency, including medical, funeral or schooling expenses. They were, nevertheless, careful not to overextend themselves in this way (Clark, 1994:146). In urban Tanzania (Tripp, 1997) I found extended family members being hired to help an entrepreneur with her business, allowing the relative a source of livelihood but not always out of considerations of business economic efficiency.

The profit motive was minimized in other ways among Ugandan small-scale businesswomen I interviewed. Rules could be bent and prices were negotiable. Often, prices on goods and services were not fixed or even marked. Tailors, market sellers and medicine men/women, for example, all included these considerations in their economic decisions. The means of the customer were often factored into price determinations. Those who appeared to have greater means might have to pay more, whereas those who had less might not be charged as much or, in some cases, at all. Also the customer's relationship with the person selling a service or good might be taken into consideration, not to mention their bargaining ability and style. Valdo Pons (in Wallman et al., 1996) found that moral considerations at times prevented Kampala herbalists and diviners from asking for payment when the patient lacked resources. I found similar patterns among local healers in Tanzania in my study of the informal economy in Dar es Salaam (Tripp, 1997). Healing was their destiny and, because their ability to heal was a gift from God (*upaji*), a patient should not be charged if they did not have the payment means. The purpose was to heal, not to make money. Many healers were suspicious of other healers who use their occupation solely as a means of making money.

3.5   Building trust

The economic activities of the poor often revolve around activities predicated on high degrees of trust. The importance of trust is abundantly evident in the running of rotating savings and credit associations (ROSCAs). In Dar es Salaam, one woman talked about how, when she first joined a savings club (*upato*) of close friends in 1972, the purpose of the club was '*kutunzana*' as she put it in Swahili, which is an endearing way of saying 'in order to care for or to look out for one another.'[1] The one characteristic of these savings societies that women stressed time and again was the fact that they necessitated trust in order to function. As one woman said, 'because we trust ourselves we can save on our own.'[2] She was a seamstress who also made and sold fried maandazi buns. Another woman, who along with eighteen other women put one hundred shillings in a kitty every three days, said much the same thing, '*upato* is like putting money in the bank, but you need trust.'[3]

Trust manifests itself in a variety of ways in business practices. In Kumasi Market in Ghana, women traders sought to establish long-term relationships with buyers, suppliers and relatives. These were relationships they could tap into if they found themselves in need of loans. Strictly commercial loans were made in secret and were regarded as shameful because they suggested a lack of well-established relations with others and were associated with insolvency and unreliability because they were not based on trust (Clark 1987:16). Trust often needs to be earned. In Cameroon, for example, the ROSCAs (*njangi*) allow even the lowest-income groups to gain access to credit without collateral, paying interest or drawing up legal documents. However, individuals can participate only in a certain level of *njangi* based on their creditworthiness and ability to repay. No one moves up to a higher division unless they have proven themselves at a lower division (Bouman and Harteveld, 1976). In Africa more generally, it is the ROSCAs' simplicity of procedures, their flexibility, the smallness of the group, the speed with which loans can be negotiated, the use of collective shame to ensure repayment and their informality that make them more appealing than formal financial institutions. People believe that they save more in these groups than if they were saving as individuals because of the discipline imposed by group pressure (Bouman, 1983; Miracle et al., 1980).

Some have found that fostering reciprocity and trust in the urban setting requires more clearly defined mechanisms to promote accountability because groups are not based on affective familial, clan, ethnic or other close ties as they might have been in the rural areas. The National Organization for Women's Associations of Uganda, for example, reported a significant rise in the 1990s in the number of businesswomen's groups seeking assistance from them in drafting constitutions.[4] Even the most informal savings clubs I found in Uganda drew up constitutions and adhered to strict procedures to strengthen mechanisms of accountability. This was the case regardless of how much the members emphasized the importance of 'trust' and irrespective of the size of the club.

3.6 Flexibility

There is a flexibility in this informal economy that is not evident in more formal economic institutions. When I asked one member of a Kampala savings club why her group was unregistered when they might be able to apply for credit if they registered, she replied:

These organizations will collapse if they become formalized. We work so well informally. We have no office. Everything is nice and simple. The minute we become formal we will collapse. The minute we try to get credit, we will go to shambles. The group is based on trust, mutual confidence, flexibility. You do what you want, the organization is yours. What would we do if we registered? We would have to have a location, an office, and we can't afford that. We would have to get registered and do the proper paperwork. Who would have time to go around and do all that? We are all working women. Then they would want us to be a cooperative and we do not want that. They would want a fee and we can't afford that. We just want things nice and simple.[5]

These attitudes are replicated in diverse contexts throughout Africa. One 62-year-old woman from Bassa, Cameroon, made a similar comment about the ROSCA she belonged to:

If there's an emergency over the weekend, no bank will open to help you. Sometimes you just can't wait for your money. And, in the banks, well you sometimes can't even get your money out. With the *tontine* [ROSCA], you can get credit immediately, without paperwork or waiting. They are your sisters, and they understand when you need help. (Brusky, 1995)

3.7   Combining income generation with service

Another common feature of Ugandan businesswomen's organizations was their public-spirited orientation. Some combined income-generating projects with caring for the disadvantaged, such as orphans, young girls who had been expelled from school for becoming pregnant, the disabled, the old and others. Another typical pattern involved urban groups that would reach out to rural women's groups because they believed they had something to offer them. Others involved educated women who worked with groups of uneducated women for the same reasons. And women came together to find ways to provide the whole community with a service such as a health unit or daycare center or to help find markets for goods produced in the community.

In Kampala, one businesswoman who had been involved in several savings clubs with friends and in a *munno mukabi* (farming group) was able, through her savings and a small grant from a women's organization, to start a 'mother and child center' in Wabigalo, a low-income part of Kampala. It was a daycare center for market women, but it was also a place where various groups of market women could meet to exchange ideas and discuss their trade and marital problems and child-raising issues. Other groups met to learn how to manage their accounts or how to read. The director also raised chickens and sold eggs wholesale to the market women, who then sold them at the market. These patterns suggest just how much business enterprises, especially for women, are woven into the web of daily life; they do not constitute a discrete activity apart from caring for children, for the old, for the sick and for those who are more disadvantaged. The demands of daily life impinge directly on the ability of businesses to expand and to enhance productivity, efficiency and, ultimately, profitability.

4   Institutional terrain of the informal economy

The informal economy exists in the context of an associational life that reveals some of the norms and organizing principles of this economy.

They suggest ways in which social capital is formed to meet the needs of this economy in culturally relevant ways. They also show ways in which people have compensated for state failure by seeking alternate solutions to poor infrastructure, lack of relevant formal financial institutions and problems of state-related corruption. They serve also as responses to collective poverty, insecurity, the difficulty of taking risks and the uncertainty of the overall economy. Many informal market associations, credit associations, trade organizations, cooperatives, farming and marketing groups, ethnically based development associations, and other societies emerged in the 1980s and 1990s to assist the growing informal sector and give it a political voice, especially at the local level.

Rotating savings and credit associations (ROSCAs) are enormously popular throughout Africa as a source of savings and credit. Studies in Liberia, Côte d'Ivoire, Togo, Cameroon and Nigeria have found that participation in ROSCAs ranged from 50 to 95 percent (Bouman, 1995a).[6] A study of microfinance in Kenya, Ghana and Malawi found that ROSCAs are highly efficient. Group solidarity forms the basis for risk management. Defaulters are punished by not being paid in future rounds, but the use of social sanctions can be limited because participants understand each other's life situation and realize that they may be in need of forgiveness at a later date. Money flows from one group member to another such that savings match credits without any need for interest rates or collateral and where transaction costs are kept at a minimum (Buckley, 1997:1085). Some ROSCAs serve as a kind of rotary club, allowing business people to network, exchange relevant information and build good will (Haggblade, 1995). They are generally durable because they meet all the criteria of successful long-standing resource management organizations: they establish clear organizational rules, use graduated sanctions and establish low-cost mechanisms to resolve disputes.

Some organizational strategies have arisen out of a need to avoid excessive state interference and political manipulations. In Benin, for example, the military regime had attempted to control all business and market sellers, according to John Heilbrunn (1997). Merchants selling cloth, liquor and food in urban centers and villages all belonged to one organization. Military commander Major Mathieu Kérékou formed the Union Nationale des Commerçantes Béninoises (UNCOBE) in 1976, hoping to bring all market women under the government's control. But the women purposefully kept their activities locally based and outside of state regulation, channeling much of their business into the informal economy, especially into the trade with Nigeria. Others evaded outside control by forming associations within associations. For instance, market leaders of the association oversaw market vendors who, in turn, presided over ROSCAs embedded inconspicuously within the UNCOBE structure. UNCOBE eventually withdrew its support from the regime after the banks crashed in 1989, and it continued to press demands for freedom of association, political pluralism and a free trade zone (Heilbrunn, 1997).

Hometown development associations are another form of economic association that became increasingly visible in the late 1980s as urban dwellers sought to provide assistance to the rural towns from which they originated. They used these associations to build schools, orphanages, libraries and clinics; to establish projects to conserve the environment; and to raise funds for flood relief and other such causes. They assisted businesses by helping build infrastructure (roads, water pipelines, electricity supply, telephone facilities) but also by disbursing soft loans to women's groups and entrepreneurs engaged in business (Barkan et al., 1991). The strengthening of local development associations and the emergence of new ones since the late 1980s are directly attributable to the weakness of local government, especially in the context of economic decline. In Tanzania, many of these associations are taking over functions of local government; for example, they are taxing local coffee and cotton producers. Similarly, informal sector associations formed around particular trades became increasingly popular in the 1990s. Kenneth King identified about 400 *jua kali* informal sector associations in Kenya in the 1990s, and they had also formed national apex bodies. They were based on locality rather than trade and had become a vital part of civil society in Kenya (King, 1996:419).

Dual-sex organizations in West Africa play an important role in regulating and supporting informal economic activities along with other spheres of activity. In Nigeria, for example, Ibo Women's Councils, which have their origins in precolonial Africa, continue to be important institutions governing the social, political, economic and spiritual affairs of women. Their flexibility and capacity to respond to changing situations account for their durability. The Ibo Women's Councils, for example, intervene in matters that concern the market, ensure moral behavior, penalize men who violate women's rights in the community, govern multiple smaller organizations and lobby for women's interests at the national level (Nzegwu, 1995). In this dual-sex governance system, representatives of each sex govern their own members through a council. These organizations, according to Nzegwu, are autonomous of the state, yet their decisions are binding regardless of social status, education or income level. Moreover, the local councils can represent women living as far away as Lagos, Kano or New York. They are distinct from organizations modeled on Western patterns in that they promote a sense of 'shared communitarian values rather than perceived divisive individualistic values,' as Nzegwu puts it. Their economic functions are simultaneously embedded in a wide range of social, cultural, religious, economic and political issues.

Such associations offer legitimate sources of authority because they embody culturally relevant ways of ensuring accountability. Accountability is maintained by a strict monitoring system where nothing is hidden and the threat of public humiliation and ostracism weighs heavily as a deterrent to violations of council norms. Accountability is tied to community validation, which is an extremely effective constraint on corruption in this context. Once again, the pattern of authority, accountability and legitimacy diverges considerably from formal non-governmental organizations that follow more Western models of organization.

5 Government policy toward the informal economy

Government policies have both facilitated but mainly constrained the informal sector in Africa. Although there is greater recognition of the importance of the informal sector, it is still treated as separate from other sectors of the economy in policy making. There is little recognition of the complementarity and interconnectedness of the informal and formal sectors. Industrial policies still favor large-scale industry, both public and private, through tax exemptions, tariff protection, direct and indirect subsidies, and access to capital and foreign exchange. A self-employed tailor in Burkina Faso pays 50 percent customs duty when importing a sewing machine, whereas a company registered under the investment code is exempt from this tax (DPCSD, 1996:27). The lack of foreign exchange means that informal sector operators have poor access to technology and quality inputs that could make them more competitive. Pricing policies favor production technologies and the capital goods sector. Meanwhile, the constraints on the informal sector remain almost unchanged. Integration between formal and informal financial systems that would improve the flow of financial resources to high-potential enterprises has been poor (Aryeetey et al., 1997). Informal sector operators often pay high rates of interest on loans, sometimes as high as 1,000 percent annually if they are borrowing from moneylenders. Yet they have difficulty accessing formal banking institutions because they do not have the collateral. The lack of integration between the informal sector and formal financial institutions means that small-scale operators do not have access to cheaper loans.

The government contributes in other ways to the broader environment within which the informal economy operates. The weakness or absence of property rights is a major constraint on small-scale enterprises, making it difficult to plan, take business risks, transfer property and ensure secure inheritance arrangements (Tomeko and Aleke-Dondo, 1992). Often uncertainty of business location means that informal sector operators are less likely to invest in improving the workplace and working conditions, leading to greater levels of theft, fire, flood and injury. For women, the lack of or insecurity of property and inheritance rights and the frequent need to access capital, land and resources through husbands or fathers place additional constraints on their capacity to conduct business.

Little attention has been devoted to improving markets and the quality of products or to upgrading trade, literacy, management and accounting skills. Low levels of education make it difficult for informal sector activities to expand. Ministries of education have rarely integrated practical and accounting skills relevant to this sector into primary school curricula or encouraged the expansion of the numbers of vocational, trade and technical schools. Technical schools need to provide skills in business management, bookkeeping, procurement and supply management, staff supervision and marketing. Distance education via the radio and TV needs to be expanded to provide some of these courses. Adult education courses need to address these concerns as well, especially through short courses in the rural areas. School days should be organized to accommodate children who work in the informal sector to minimize high levels of absenteeism and lower levels of enrollment. Technical and vocational schools need to provide opportunities for informal sector workers to take short courses to upgrade their skills. Much of the education of micro-entrepreneurs takes place on the job in the form of apprenticeships. Although apprenticeships are an ideal way to learn a trade, they have limitations that could be addressed in a school setting. Apprenticeships exclude those who do not have access to skilled workers. They do not necessarily expand the menu of skills and variety of enterprises, nor do they provide avenues for improving technical skills.

Labor ministries do almost nothing to monitor labor conditions in this sector. Moreover, finance and planning ministries have virtually ignored questions of how to create a conducive business environment for this large sector, while focusing their energies on policies directed at the minuscule private sector. There has been little consideration of restricting the importation of goods widely produced by the informal sector. Few concerted efforts have been taken to improve the infrastructure, transport and communications, water and power supply specifically in the areas where informal sector workers are concentrated.

Government involvement with this sector frequently ends up being repressive. Harassment by city officials of informal sector operators continues unabated in many cities. Laws restricting this sector are outdated, and there are unnecessarily tedious, lengthy registration procedures to navigate. Paying for a business license, registration, buying land, obtaining a loan, clearing goods through customs or getting a public health certificate for a restaurant frequently necessitate bribing a government official, which undermines the development of an entrepreneurial culture (Buckley, 1997:1090). Excessive government corruption makes legitimate business cumbersome since it does not seem worth the effort to obtain proper documentation when the bribes are excessive. It undermines state legitimacy and creates serious disincentives for informal entrepreneurs to expand their businesses and become more formal.

Youth and women have high levels of involvement in the informal sector, and they frequently end up being the targets of government harassment, especially if they do not have proper licenses or are operating in non-sanctioned locations. In Dar es Salaam, the militia usually extract bribes from them or confiscate their goods. This kind of harassment confounds most people, who cannot see the logic in making the poorest members of society pay for the right to seek a living, especially poor women who are already supporting many family members from their business and are shouldering many expenses including school fees, healthcare and care for the elderly – all basic needs that the government could not even come close to covering.

One woman entrepreneur from Mwanga, a rural village in northern Tanzania, described this alternative logic in a seminar for small-scale businesswomen.[7] I quote her at length because she clearly and eloquently describes the illogical nature of government licensing and harassment of the poorest micro-entrepreneurs, who gain nothing from the government yet provide a social security net for the children, the old, the sick and the poorest members of society (Tripp, 1997:126).

You may see that a mother is selling her cassava, when she sells her cassava, she gets money, at that time you may see that that mother has borrowed some money from someone and bought cassava, carried it, carried firewood and roasted it, you may think that this is just a simple thing and say 'this mother is just roasting cassava'. But this mother is feeding five kids, has her husband, has her mother-in-law, father-in-law, sisters-in-law, children of her sisters-in-law. If that woman gets 200 sh profit, she will buy 1 kg of maize flour, spinach and cook for the family that day and be satisfied.

You may think that being a mother is a simple thing, and that is why problems are happening. Municipal officers, city council officers and village officers do not see that these women are trying to be self-reliant by employing themselves, raising the family.... They do a lot in the family and in the society....

I ask for these important people to know that these poor people have a big task of being self-reliant. They don't ask for your money ... they don't ask you for school fees ... they ask you nothing because they are self-reliant. They should be encouraged, and the important people should recognize their presence.

She then went on to caution City Council officials from harassing the women by trying to extort money from them through bribes.

6   Conclusions

The resilience of the informal economy in the face of failed economic reform initiatives and the difficulties experienced by the formal economy call for serious reflection on what has and has not worked in Africa and why. This chapter begins to point us in some new directions, suggesting that it is necessary to consider more seriously the nature of African markets and their particular characteristics. African institutions, whether we call them 'non-formal,' 'indigenous' or 'informal,' may resemble similar institutions in other parts of the world (for example, ROSCAs). But they do not necessarily resemble Western idealized perceptions of markets. By examining how real African economies function, we will understand better the possibilities for enhancing economic development.

Notes

1. Interview by author, 20 January 1988, Buguruni, Dar es Salaam.
2. Interview by author, 7 November 1987, Manzese, Dar es Salaam.
3. Interview by author, 11 November 1987, Manzese, Dar es Salaam.
4. Interview with Florence Nekyon, 21 May 1993.
5. Interview by author, Kampala, 2 June 1992.
6. They go by many names in different parts of Africa: *tontine* in much of francophone Africa, *njangi* in Cameroon, *susu* in Ghana, *upato* in Tanzania, *chiperegani* in Malawi, *stockfelds* in South Africa, and so on (www.gdrc.org/icm/rosca-names.html; Bouman, 1995a).
7. Comments made at a seminar on Women Entrepreneurs in the Local Economy, hosted by Umoja Wanauchumi Wadogo Wadogo wa Mwanga (Small Entrepreneurs Association of Mwanga), 7–10 March 1994.

REFERENCES

Adams, D. W. and D. A. Fitchett (1992) *Informal Finance in Low-Income Countries*, Westview Press: Boulder, CO.
Aryeetey, E., H. Hettige, M. Nissanke and W. Steel (1997) 'Financial Market

Fragmentation and Reforms in Ghana, Malawi, Nigeria, and Tanzania,' *World Bank Economic Review* 11(2):195–218.

Bagachwa, M. and B. Ndulu (1996) 'Structure and Potential of the Urban Small-Scale Production in Tanzania,' in M.-L. Swantz and A. Tripp (eds.) *What Went Right in Tanzania? People's Responses to Directed Development*, University of Dar es Salaam Press: Dar es Salaam, 69–97.

Barkan, J. D., M. L. McNulty and M. A. O. Ayeni (1991) 'Hometown Voluntary Associations, Local Development, and the Emergence of Civil Society in Western Nigeria,' *Journal of Modern African Studies* 29(3).

Booth, W. J. (1994) 'On the Idea of the Moral Economy,' *American Political Science Review* 88:653–67.

Bouman, F. J. A. (1983) 'Indigenous Savings and Credit Societies in the Developing World,' in J. D. von Pischke, D. W. Adams and G. Donald (eds.) *Rural Financial Markets in Developing Countries*, Johns Hopkins University Press: Baltimore, MD.

—— (1995a) 'ROSCA: On the Origin of the Species,' *Savings and Development* 19(2):117–46.

—— (1995b) 'Rotating and Accumulating Savings and Credit Associations: A Development Perspective,' *World Development* 23(3):371–84.

Bouman, F. J. A. and K. Harteveld (1976) 'The Djanggi, a Traditional Form of Saving and Credit in West Cameroon,' *Sociologica Ruralis* 16(1–2).

Brusky, B. (1995) 'Women and Rotating Credit Associations in Cameroon,' unpublished paper.

Buckley, G. (1997) 'Microfinance in Africa: Is It either the Problem or the Solution?' *World Development* 25(7):1081–93.

Charmes, J. (1997) 'Progress in Measurement of the Informal Sector: Employment and Share of GDP,' *Proceedings of the Expert Meeting in Household Satellite Accounts*, United Nations Statistical Division: New York.

Clark, G. (1987) 'Pools, Clients and Patrons: Relations of Capital and Risk Control between Kumasi Market Women,' unpublished manuscript.

—— (1994) *Onions Are My Husband: Survival and Accumulation by West African Market Women*, University of Chicago Press: Chicago and London.

DPCSD (Development for Policy Coordination and Sustainable Development), UN Office of the Special Coordinator for Africa and the Least Developed Countries (1996) *Informal Sector Development in Africa*, United Nations: New York.

Fafchamps, M. (1997) 'Introduction: Markets in Sub-Saharan Africa,' *World Development* 25(5):733–4.

Grey-Johnson, C. (1992) 'The African Informal Sector at the Crossroads: Emerging Policy Options,' *African Development* 17(1).

Haggblade, S. (1995) 'Africanization from Below: The Evolution of Cameroonian Savings Societies into Western Style Banks,' *Rural Africana* 2:35–55.

Heilbrunn, J. R. (1997) 'Commerce, Politics, and Business Associations in Benin and Togo,' *Comparative Politics* 29(4):473–92.

Kim, K. (1988) 'Issues and Perspectives in Tanzanian Industrial Development with Special Reference to the Role of SADCC,' in M. Hood (ed.) *Tanzania after Nyerere*, Pinter Publishers: London.

King, K. (1996) 'Microenterprise: Macroeconomic Environment: Revisiting Kenya's Informal (Jua Kali) Sector against the Background of the Formal Globalizing Economy,' *International Journal of Educational Development* 16(4):417–26.

Miracle, M., D. Miracle and L. Cohen (1980) 'Informal Savings Mobilization in Africa,' *Kyklos* 43(2):701–24.

Nzegwu, N. (1995) 'Recovering Igbo Traditions: A Case for Indigenous Women's Organizations in Development,' in M. Nussbaum and J. Glover (eds.) *Women, Culture and Development: A Study of Human Capabilities*, Clarendon Press: Oxford.

Parker, R. L., R. Randall and W. F. Steel (1995) 'Small Enterprises Adjusting to Liberalization in Five African Countries,' World Bank Discussion Papers, African Technical Department Series No. 271, Washington, DC.

Putnam, R. D., with R. Leonardi and R. Nonetti (1993) *Making Democracy Work: Civic Traditions in Modern Italy*, Princeton University Press: Princeton, NJ.

Steel, W. F., E. Aryeetey, H. Hettige and M. Nissanke (1997) 'Informal Financial Markets under Liberalization in Four African Countries,' *World Development* 25(5):817–30.

Tinker, I. (1987) 'The Human Economy of Microentrepreneurs,' paper presented at the International Seminar on Women in Micro and Small-Scale Enterprise Development, Ottawa, Canada.

Tomeko, J. and C. Aleke-Dondo (1992) *Improving the Growth Potential of the Small-scale and Informal Sectors*, Kenya Rural Enterprise Programme: Nairobi.

Tripp, A. M. (1994) 'Gender, Political Participation and the Transformation of Associational Life in Uganda and Tanzania,' *African Studies Review* 37(1):107–31.

—— (1997) *Changing the Rules: The Politics of Liberalization and the Urban Informal Economy in Tanzania*, University of California Press: Berkeley and Los Angeles.

—— (1998a) 'Local Women's Associations and Politics in Contemporary Uganda,' in H. B. Hansen and M. Twaddle (eds.) *Developing Uganda*, Ohio University Press: Athens, OH, 120–32.

—— (1998b) 'Gender, Political Participation and the Transformation of Associational Life in Uganda and Tanzania,' in P. Lewis (ed.) *Africa: Dilemmas of Development and Change*, Westview Press: Boulder, CO, 232–57.

—— (2000) *Women and Politics in Uganda: The Challenge of Associational Autonomy*, University of Wisconsin Press: Madison, WI.

Vélez-Ibañez, C. G. (1983) *Bonds of Mutual Trust: The Cultural Systems of Rotating Credit Associations among Urban Mexicans and Chicanos*, Rutgers University Press: New Brunswick, NJ.

Wallman, S. (ed.), in association with G. Bantebya-Kyomuhendo, V. Pons, J. Jitta, F. Kaharuza, J. Ogden, S. Freudenthal (1996) *Women Getting by: Well-*

being in the Time of AIDS, James Currey, Fountain Publishers, Ohio University Press: London, Kampala, and Athens, OH.

Young, R. C. (1994) 'Enterprise Scale, Economic Policy, and Development,' International Center for Economic Growth, Occasional Paper No. 52, San Francisco.

14

The relevance of the Nordic model for African development

Arne Bigsten

1   Introduction

In many ways, the Nordic countries (Denmark, Finland, Iceland, Norway and Sweden)[1] epitomize the technological advances and high living standards achieved by countries of the North, whereas sub-Saharan Africa depicts the extremes of poverty and social disharmony of the South. And yet the Nordic region was a poor agrarian outpost at the European periphery just over a century ago. Poverty was extensive and, compared with the rest of Europe, the industrial revolution arrived late. In spite of these poor starting conditions, Nordic countries are today fully fledged welfare states that have virtually eliminated poverty and created technological niches that have placed them, in spite of their small populations, at the frontier of economic and human resource development. The countries have evolved institutions that have led to peaceful coexistence, political pluralism and social compassion. Today, similarly to the Nordic countries about one hundred years ago, African economies are still well below the global technological frontier. In terms of growth strategy this means that they will have to rely more on catching-up growth than frontier growth. In other words, they will have to borrow and apply technologies from abroad rather than develop new technologies of their own. For the catch-up process to work, however, the countries need to have an effective institutional structure in place. When institutions are supportive of innovative activity and productivity improvements, the resulting growth can be sustained for a long time. However, if the institutional structure is not favorable, it will soon halt the growth effects from innovations and investment activities.

The chapter is structured as follows: section 2 summarizes the main strands of the Nordic model, including a discussion of the institutions, both economic and political, that have sustained it; section 3 asks what lessons African countries can derive from the Nordic experience with respect to the creation of an environment for private enterprise and the definition of an appropriate role for government and judiciary; section 4 concludes the chapter.

2 Outline of the Nordic model

The development of the Nordic countries in the past century and a half demonstrates that economic backwardness and poverty need not be immutable. Around 1870 the Nordic countries were all relatively backward compared with countries in the rest of Western Europe. Since then, however, their position has improved dramatically. The main features of the Nordic model, with emphasis on its Swedish exponent, are outlined in Table 14.1.[2]

An activist stabilization policy has been an essential feature of the Nordic model since World War II. Full employment was a central aim of the Nordic strategy, and during the first decade of the postwar era unemployment was kept below 3 percent. In the case of Sweden under the Social Democrats it was felt that a strong budget stance was necessary to ensure that the government had some scope for action and intervention when there was a risk of increasing unemployment. One significant dimension of the Swedish strategy was the creation of an investment fund system, whereby firms could deposit untaxed profits into an interest-free account at the central bank on which they could draw with government permission when the business cycle was going down. Similar concerns lay behind controls on the credit market. A major aim was to keep interest rates low, making it possible for firms to invest and expand. This was achieved by combining credit market controls with a closed capital account and a fixed exchange rate. Real interest rates were negative part of the time.

The Nordic model is also distinguished by its liberal approach to business, in spite of left-of-center governments. The Nordic governments did not encourage large-scale nationalization, although companies in Sweden faced high taxation on the portion of profits that was distributed to shareholders. However, as noted above, as long as profits were reinvested in the business they were taxed only lightly.

Table 14.1 Main strands of the Nordic/Swedish model

Feature	Main characteristic/target	Comment
Activist stabilization policy	A strong budget stance to provide scope for government to intervene in markets to ensure 'full employment'	Introduced in the 1930s by the Social Democrats to combat mass unemployment in Sweden
Control of the credit market	The maintenance of low interest rates	Real interest rates were negative for part of the time
Liberal attitude towards business	The model did not favor large-scale nationalization and governments were generally supportive of private enterprise	Under a left-leaning government, Sweden was able to encourage the growth of some of the world's largest multinationals
Rehn–Meidner model	Compensatory measures to try to combine low levels of unemployment with low inflation	Selective measures were used to create jobs in regions with unemployment, and high profit taxes were used to lock profits inside firms
Role of union–employer relations	Harmonious and peaceful employer–labor relations became a major characteristic of the Nordic labor markets	This was partly ensured by the 'solidarity-based' wage policy, which discouraged wage drift in profitable branches. However, a state-directed incomes policy was opposed by the parties
Market interventions	The goal in the labor market was to improve mobility; in financial and capital markets it was to 'direct' investment	The Nordic countries were late in opening their financial markets, and interventions in the labor market remain
Liberal trade policy	As small countries, they espoused free trade	Firms have not been able to exploit domestic monopoly positions, thanks to foreign competition
Welfare state and social climate	Extensive provision of tax-financed social services. High and progressive taxation ensured the transfer of resources from the better off to the poorer segments of the population	The good employment climate and safety nets enabled a considerable amount of social engineering

Source: Compiled by the author.

In the 1950s, the fiscal stance supported by the government, as well as the wish to maintain low inflation, called for a policy fine-tuning. In Sweden the solution was the Rehn–Meidner model (Meidner and Rehn, 1951). It recognized that in a market economy there would be some regions or sectors that did well, while others would lag behind. Effective resource use would then require the transfer of resources from the poor sectors to the booming sectors. At the same time, selective measures were needed to create jobs in the regions of unemployment. It was also felt that, if profits were highly taxed, there would be less pressure for inflationary wage settlements in the economy as a whole. The policy was also meant to be growth supporting, since it knocked out the low-productivity firms, while the most productive could make large profits and thus invest and expand. The Rehn–Meidner model clearly had an impact on labor–employer relations as well. However, harmonious labor market relations date back to the 1930s. The degree of unionization was very high then and an increasing centralization of wage negotiations made it possible to achieve peaceful and comprehensive wage settlements. In the 1950s, the Rehn–Meidner model introduced a solidarity-based wage policy, which discouraged wage drift. However, wages have essentially been set in free negotiations between employers and unions. Since the 1980s, wage settlements have become more decentralized, though an informal coordination of settlements in various areas of the labor market persists.

The above policy stances implied extensive market interventions. In the case of the labor market, the strategy was to improve mobility by the creation of labor exchanges and payment of mobility subsidies. In financial and capital markets, controls were extensive. Banks were forced to buy government bonds or to finance housing investment. These amounted to a guided investment policy. As small economies with extensive trade-based activities, the Nordic countries have pursued free trade and resisted protectionism. However, with regard to domestic competition, Sweden has not had any extensive legislation. It has used free trade as a substitute. Firms have been unable to exploit domestic monopoly positions, since foreign goods inflows have provided a check on price increases (Hjalmarsson, 1991).

All these aspects tie in with the overall goal of creating a welfare state, together with a social climate that supports change. The welfare state had two basic components: first, extensive provision of tax-financed public services; and, second, a comprehensive system of social insurance. To support the system, there were high and progressive income taxes, wealth taxes and large payroll taxes, plus, from the 1960s onwards, extensive indirect taxes. With the growth of the middle class relative to the working class in past decades the system has gradually been adjusted to preserve the support of the middle class. There is a fear that, if that support dissipates, the existing comprehensive welfare system will begin to crumble. The implementation of many of the policy features enunciated above demanded a social climate that was supportive of change. During the glory days of the model in Sweden, the system was controlled by Social Democrats in close collaboration with the trade unions. It is notable that, when the model ran into trouble in the late 1970s, the Social Democratic hegemony was broken as well. Since then the liberal–conservative opposition has been in power several times in Sweden and other Nordic countries. Still, consensus across political blocs on welfare issues has been extensive, and one may note that the basic ingredients of the welfare state have remained in place even when right-of-center parties are in power.

3   Relevance to the African experience

3.1   The importance of economic flexibility and market integration

Among the lessons of the Nordic experience has been the importance of structural and policy flexibility for economic development. Although the industrialization drive in the region began in about 1870, between 1840 and 1870 the Swedish government had already undertaken major reforms of the economic system, including removal of domestic restrictions on trade, opening up the economy for international trade, reforms of company law as well as banking legislation.

During the first half of the nineteenth century, Swedish per capita incomes grew at 0.5 percent per year, while the population grew by about 1.0 percent per year. The growth during this period was based mainly on agriculture. New land was planted and land ownership was consolidated. The limits of ownership became better defined and farmers moved out of villages to live on their consolidated farms. It was like the Ujamaa reform in Tanzania in reverse. The process of growth led to a market expansion, which supported some growth of handicraft and small-scale industry. Still, the most important event during this period, in a longer-term perspective, was probably the emergence of new growth-supporting institutions. The government invested heavily in the creation of a transport infrastructure in the form of a national rail network, largely financed by loans from the European capital market. Furthermore, institutional changes, such as free trade, free capital movements and increased mobility of people, made the markets more flexible. Trade increased and technology and immigrant entrepreneurs came in from Western Europe. The export activities, based as they were on raw materials and agricultural commodities, meant that broad segments of the population could benefit from the expansion (trickle down). Since the production technology was simple, a lot of unskilled labor was employed initially. Resources that had previously been virtually worthless, such as marginal land and forest in the north of the country, became valuable. There was to some extent a vent-for-surplus export expansion at work here. At the beginning of the industrialization process, Sweden was rich in natural resources and labor, but poor in capital (much like Africa today). The market integration led to large inflows of capital to Sweden. The capital importers were largely the state, counties, banks and other financial institutions, which then on-lent to investors in industry and agriculture or invested in infrastructure and urban development.

With recourse to international capital and investment, wages increased, as did consumption. During the period 1850–1910, Sweden had a virtually permanent deficit on the current account. At the start of World War I it was probably the most indebted country in the world in per capita terms. Swedish external debt at the time is estimated to have been 75 percent of GDP. If these loans had not been forthcoming, investments would have been lower and growth and structural change slower. The integration of the world also meant that more than 1 million Swedes (in a total population of 5 million) emigrated to America during the half-century preceding World War I. Thus, with capital moving in and labor out, factor prices changed dramatically in Sweden. Between 1870 and 1910 wages increased more rapidly than elsewhere. It was only the other Nordic countries that came close to this. Real wages increased faster than GDP (2.8 percent vs. 1.7 percent), which meant that sectors dependent on traditional comparative .advantages of cheap labor and abundant natural resources came under pressure relative to those sectors that used more advanced techniques and capital. O'Rourke and Williamson (1999) show that much of the Swedish catch-up in terms of wages was owing to labor emigration rather than trade and the standard Stolper–Samuelson effect.[3] The African countries of today are obviously not able to attract very much foreign capital, and labor emigration is also severely restricted. Factor movements have so far not been as effective as in the case of Sweden in helping equalize factor prices. The firms that grew during this period were largely created at the turn of the century and then consolidated in the 1920s and the 1930s, although a few new ones also emerged, such as TetraPak, IKEA and H&M. It was mainly capital-intensive industries that grew during this period, whereas labor-intensive sectors, such as textiles, clothing, food and agriculture, shrank. This structural change did not arouse too much opposition, since those laid off tended get new jobs relatively quickly, not least in the expanding public sector.

The pressure for structural change was increased in Sweden by this process. The transformation meant that industrial workers became a more important group at the expense of those depending on agriculture. Some of the basic ingredients of the Swedish model emerged from the experience of structural changes occurring alongside or causing rapid increases in real incomes. The labor movement and industrial owners shared a positive view of Swedish international dependence; they thus appreciated the need to rationalize industry to make it more competitive and accepted structural change. Access to international markets for goods and capital is also crucial for the development of African countries. Much needs to be done on the side of the governments to ensure that resources begin to flow.

3.2 Defining a credible role for the state

Nordic countries have probably had a higher degree of government intervention than occurred in other developed regions of the world, excepting perhaps Japan. However, governments were careful to ensure that this did not overly distort markets or lower incentives and thereby productivity. In the 1930s, a long period of political hegemony for the Social Democratic Party was established. This party advocated a more active policy stance vis-à-vis the mass unemployment of the early 1930s. Keynesian stabilization policies, as advocated by leading Swedish economists (the Stockholm School with Lindahl, Myrdal, Ohlin and others), were introduced in Sweden as early as around 1930. It was also felt that the government should improve the social security of the population in the new and more turbulent economic situation. The majority of the population were now dependent on wage income. The idea that income needed to be redistributed from the better off to the poorer segments of the population was firmly established. The Social Democratic Party launched a new social contract labeled 'folkhemmet' (the people's home). Nobody was to be left out of this new home.

Sweden managed to get through the Great Depression of the 1930s better than many other countries. This was owing to some extent to an expansionary Keynesian policy, but probably more so to the fact that Sweden left the gold standard in 1931 and had a large devaluation of the currency. This ensured a good competitive position for Swedish exporters throughout the decade. The 1950s and 1960s were decades of record growth in Sweden and elsewhere. The war-torn economies needed rebuilding and new industries grew. The role of the state increased as it invested in infrastructure and public services such as health and education. There were also some modest elements of nationalization of industries, but essentially Sweden has been a private capitalist economy.

The debate on such issues as the nationalization of the banks was very heated in the late 1940s, but the opposition won the debate and since then it has been subdued (except for the period after 1968, when it briefly resurfaced). Internationally the global financial system was formed at Bretton Woods and gradually the economies started to integrate again. International free trade areas emerged, such as the European Economic Community and the European Free Trade Association. There was increasing internationalization at the same time that government interventions increased. Sweden grew fast, but the countries that had suffered during the wars started to catch up.

The Swedish model meant the development of the welfare state and a more interventionist stance with regard to labor and capital markets. The aim was to achieve high and rapid growth, at the same time spreading the benefits reasonably evenly. The welfare state took over some of the obligations that previously had rested with the family, and this eventually paved the way for the broad entry of women into the labor market. Many of these women actually entered the public sector, producing services in education, health, childcare and care for the elderly. The role of the public sector as a provider of services increased rapidly. At the same time, the public sector developed extensive transfer activities in the form of child allowances, pensions, unemployment benefits, sickness benefits, and so on. The transfers were as large in monetary terms as the actual government activities. The level of taxation obviously was increased dramatically. It must be noted that all the Nordic countries have extremely efficient systems for tax collection, whereas African economies are at the other end of the global spectrum in terms of collection efficiency.

For the interventions in production activities the aim was to make it possible to exploit comparative advantages and, thus, grow fast to create resources for the welfare state. Sectors that were competitive were to grow, and those that were not were allowed to shrink. A strong pressure for structural change was created by the so-called solidaristic wage policy, which meant that wages should be equalized across sectors. Those that could not bear the cost would be squeezed out, whereas those that were profitable were actually favored by labor not demanding the maximum the firms could pay. At the same time, capital markets were controlled and investments were favored. Firms' dividends were heavily taxed, but as long as funds were reinvested they were taxed lightly. This meant that existing profitable firms could grow fast, but capital mobility across activities was hampered. This later on would turn out to be a problem, when there was a need to shift profits from mature firms to newly emerging sectors. Labor-intensive industries declined, as did agriculture. In the old controlled setting, large firms had developed internal capital markets as a substitute for an external one, but when really extensive structural changes were required the system could no longer efficiently reallocate capital.

The 1960s were a period of record growth, but at the same time a structure emerged that was vulnerable. Investments were concentrated in heavy industry, which reinvested its profits in its own activities in the form of real capital. This was supported by the existing policy incentives. The Swedish model also favored investment in house building and the public sector. These trends meant that Sweden was locked into a structure that lacked flexibility. It seemed for a while that the Swedish economy could carry an ever-increasing level of taxation, but eventually it ran into incentives and distortions that hampered efficiency. This happened in a situation in which the state apparatus was honest and fairly efficient, which suggests that in the case of Africa this stage of decreasing returns to intervention would come earlier. Given the weakness of the African state, one must thus be very cautious when drawing conclusions from the Nordic experience about state interventions. The high levels of corruption and inefficiency set definite limits to what should be tried in Africa. The appropriate approach there would be to seek to find robust and simple solutions that do not require discretionary and detailed interventions.

3.3   Governance issues and the rule of law

What lessons are there for African countries in the area of governance? One feature of the development in the Nordic countries of interest to African countries is how these countries managed to create institutions that contributed to the creation of an increasingly egalitarian and wealthy society. This is obviously a huge topic that would deserve extensive historical analysis. Still, what can be said against the background of the brief history sketched above?

Between 1890 and 1910 the modern institutions of the Swedish industrial society emerged, such as the Social Democratic Party, the Federation of Employers and the Central Trade Union Organization. However, it was not until the period between the 1930s and the 1950s that economic policies were reformed and the system that came to be known as the 'Swedish model' developed. The period between 1950 and the early 1970s may be regarded as the golden age of the Swedish model, when growth was very rapid and the country finally moved to the top layer of nations in economic terms. In 1970 Sweden was ranked as number four in the world in terms of purchasing power per capita. We may note that, although Nordic countries were involved in extensive international wars until the time of Napoleon, since 1815 Sweden has been at peace. Norway and Denmark were occupied by Germany during World War II, but have otherwise been at peace. Finland has had a more violent history, with wars against the Russians. Still, overall these countries have been among the more peaceful in Europe during the past century and a half. The relatively peaceful environment has been conducive to economic development. Africa, on the other hand, has recently seen an increase in violent conflicts, with detrimental effects on economic development. There are, however, no easily transferable lessons from the Nordic countries on how international conflicts should be avoided, although it seems that African poverty has increased the likelihood of cross-border conflicts.

Democratic institutions emerged gradually in the Nordic countries over a very long time, until the countries became fully democratic around 1920 when women got the vote. There have of course been political conflicts, but these have generally been solved in a consensual and pragmatic fashion. This way of solving conflicts of interest is the end result of a very long historical process, in which it is hard to point out exactly which factors have been the most important. One factor that may have made it a bit easier than in the African context is that the countries, at least until World War II, were ethnically and linguistically very homogeneous.[4] Africa, with its ethnic diversity, has little to learn from the Nordics about how to treat minorities.

One aspect of Nordic society is the extensive network of civil society organizations. They have been there for a very long time in the rural areas, but during the industrialization phase there were very active political parties, trade unions, temperance societies, independent churches, sports clubs, and so on. The Nordic countries might be a good example of a culture in which trust has been built through extensive and peaceful interchange between individuals and groups in a range of organizations. There is also a tradition that agreements are negotiated between the relevant parties. Before the government introduces new laws there are generally committees, with the relevant parties invited to produce a report that is then sent out to all interested parties for comments. These are then taken into account by the government before it presents its bill to parliament. There seems to be an increase in the number and influence of civil society organizations in Africa in recent years, and involving them more in the decisionmaking process would be something that African countries could learn from the Nordics. The mode of political operation is also clearly reflected in the style of leadership. In the Nordic countries, a typical African leader, trying to be all-powerful, would not be well regarded. The Nordic model is much more one of consensus building, with some similarities to the Japanese approach to decision making; the leader is expected to be a consensus builder.

The Nordic countries have decentralized administrative structures –

local councils take a lot of the decisions regarding how to organize schools, health services, and so on. This has meant that local citizens are very much involved in political decision making, and that there is a relatively small distance between voters and at least local politicians. This probably has contributed to confidence building. Assuming that the local politicians are better able to gauge the desires and needs of the local community than central policymakers are, this may also have made decision making more efficient. The local authorities have extensive powers of taxation and thus a good source of income. This ensures them a measure of independence from the central powers. African leaders have been less willing to let so much power be delegated to authorities outside their control. If African governments could achieve a higher degree of legitimacy, they would be less unwilling to share power. That would then also increase participation and maybe the efficiency of policy making. Still, in countries with large regional differences in income levels, there will always be a great need for a system of transfers from the better off to those worse off, although decisions on spending could be taken locally.

One ingredient of the Nordic model has been close links between the government, labor and industry. Some have referred to this as a system of corporatism, in which the lines of demarcation are blurred and it is unclear who is ultimately responsible. In the Nordic countries, such close links have helped in several ways, but in Africa such links have often been harmful. Bigsten and Moene (1996) argue that straddling, that is, individuals in government having a foot in business as well, may have negative effects on the efficiency of the economic system, being one of several channels of corruption. On the other hand, it is useful if policymakers appreciate the needs of business. Still, there need to be checks and balances. Corruption and rent seeking are among the major constraints on African economic development.

3.4   The fundamentals of the welfare state: Social insurance, social inclusion and conflict management

What ingredients of the welfare state can be replicated in Africa? We may first note that in the case of Sweden the churches had for a long time had a responsibility for teaching the population to read and write, but since the 1840s primary education has been compulsory. This has meant that essentially the whole population has been literate, and this has been a major advantage. It seems to me that this is an area where African economies should follow the Nordic example. The ambition to provide extensive education has surely been there, but economic stagnation in African economies has hindered the realization of the ambition. Uganda is now on its way to establishing a system of universal primary education, which should be high on the priority list for other countries as well. Whether education should actually be compulsory is debatable, but it seems that this may not be appropriate, at least initially. In the longer term, I would not mind such a law.

During the period of structural adjustment, attempts to revive education have meant that fees have been introduced (also referred to as 'cost sharing'). This is unfortunate, but still preferable to no education at all. Notwithstanding this, primary education should be a basic right and thus be made available to all. It is also the most effective way to bring about a measure of egalitarianism in Africa. It would seem appropriate to phase out some other programs in order to realize this aim. It is better to do a few things well than to spread efforts in too many directions. Governments in Africa should stick to the basics.

There has been debate in the Nordic region about whether the welfare state has hindered or facilitated structural changes. The argument that it has helped change has been based on the notion that if people have basic security they are willing to accept change, since they know it will not leave them destitute. Rather, the system ensures that they manage reasonably well when they transfer to a new firm or a new sector where they again will be earning approximately the same salary. Whether this effect outweighs the negative incentive effects is not at all obvious, but African countries cannot afford a solid safety net anyway. Some faith in the government and some confidence in the future would make it easier for labor to accept structural changes, and since those would normally increase growth they would also help increase real earnings among the population. However, political confidence building has to be done on the basis of the local political process, and this may of course be quite different between African countries and the Nordics.

3.5   A conducive environment for private enterprise development: Property rights and regulatory institutions

By 1910 some Swedish manufacturing firms had become world leading. Firms such as AGA, ASEA, LM Ericsson, Separator and SKF were all based on unique Swedish innovations. However, heavy industries such as pulp and paper were also important, and with access to cheap electrical power they were able to introduce new technologies. Sweden at this time was not just applying foreign technology but actually helping shift the technological frontier.

The Nordic governments have generally been supportive of private enterprise. I have noted that property rights were clearly defined at an early stage, which helped pave the way for the private enterprise economy. The state has not been a major factor in primary or secondary production, although it has had a large role in recent decades in the provision of health and education services as well as a range of other social services. The experiences of African parastatals do suggest that African governments should follow the Nordic countries and not involve themselves in directly productive activities.

I also noted that goods markets were liberalized early on, although there have been continued interventions in housing and food markets. In the 1970s some African countries tried to use price controls to manage inflation. With the exceptions just mentioned, price controls have been used only in emergencies in the Nordic countries, and the experiences of the attempts do not suggest that this is an efficient tool for either supporting growth or creating justice. Instead the systems generated inefficiencies and a lack of competitive pressure, which means the price levels in those areas are much higher in, for example, Sweden than in Europe generally.

The judiciary has been independent and during the whole period of industrialization it has been able to deal effectively and largely impartially with legal conflicts between enterprises. Contractual enforcement is absolutely essential for a market economy to function. Effective bankruptcy legislation is also a very important ingredient in a system that needs structural change, and in which firms will inevitably die and (sometimes) be resurrected.

The Swedish government early on took responsibility for the creation of an effective transport infrastructure. It borrowed heavily abroad to finance this, not unlike many less developed countries of late, but the growth response was good and events favored Sweden, which made it possible to repay the debt. African countries have been less fortunate in this respect. With the introduction of the Heavily Indebted Poor Countries (HIPC) deals, the debt burden of many countries will be reduced, but it may also mean that they will find it harder to go to the international capital market to get more investment resources. In the Nordic countries the infrastructure was largely built and run by the government, though there has been some movement in the privatization direction recently.

It has been the intention in African states too to provide an effective infrastructure, but given the weakening of government finances this has been less feasible, and more private initiatives have been forthcoming. Still, on my list of priorities for African governments, the provision of infrastructure is a top priority along with education. A major concern in the infrastructure area is that few African governments have been able to develop effective systems of maintenance, which means that a lot of investments go to waste. What they can learn from the Nordic countries here is not quite clear, but basically it will depend on the ability to create an honest and working government system with the appropriate incentives for the people engaged in it. Public sector activities in Africa have been run into the ground, and the restoration of viable government institutions is a top priority. One thing of major importance in the Nordic case is that government institutions are essentially non-corrupt and relatively efficient. The general public does not condone government bureaucrats enriching themselves on tax revenues, and even small transgressions can lead to trials and/or dismissals. In Africa, voters seem to be more forgiving, particularly if culprits share the loot with their constituents.

The Nordics have been among the countries most open to foreign trade, and the institutions supporting the system were in place early on. The Nordics started out as raw material and agricultural exporters while learning the trade, but once this had been done they could use the institutions and the knowledge to export more sophisticated goods such as industrial goods. The same pattern was evident in Africa when countries started to export copper, cocoa or coffee, but African countries have had great problems in moving beyond this pattern of specialization into industrial production. In Sweden, the trading houses that initially sold raw materials were able to use their knowledge and their trade channels to sell industrial goods too. It seems fair to say that openness has been a crucial ingredient in the Nordic development model. The introverted pattern of development that emerged in Africa in the 1960s and 1970s was certainly not appropriate for the tiny economies of Africa. It precluded the exploitation of scale advantages and it created domestic monopolies that needed to be controlled. This then opened the way for harmful and ineffective (often cost-plus) price control arrangements. Free trade is an effective way of controlling domestic market power without forcing producers to produce on an unnecessarily small scale. We may also note that, to the present day, Sweden and Finland rely on the export of raw materials and products based on forestry and mineral resources, and Denmark is a major agricultural exporter. It is thus not the case that these sectors have been abandoned, although they are less important in relative terms than they were in the nineteenth century.

The Nordic countries rapidly reached the global technological frontier when they started to industrialize, even if they also relied extensively on copying and borrowing foreign technologies. Few African countries today are in a position to move to the international technological frontier on any significant scale. It is also the case that the gap between subsistence agriculture and the global technology frontier is much larger today than a century ago, which means that it has become harder to join the innovation club. This means that, in terms of technology policy, there are certain limits to what Africa can effectively do. For the time being it seems reasonable to concentrate on learning how to adapt and use existing technologies rather than to try to move to the frontier – even this requires a good technological education, which is largely absent in Africa. Interest in technology has always been high in the Nordic countries and post-secondary education has always provided good technical education. This should be the priority in Africa as well. The problem here again of course is that this type of education, if it is to be good, is much more costly than the humanities or the social sciences.

One example of how adaptive use of existing structures may facilitate growth is the role of energy production in Sweden. The country has an abundance of rivers that were exploited for energy production. At the same time, the process industry was building generators and other forms of equipment. These two sides were thus mutually supportive and helped create demand for the technology and the knowledge of how to provide it. These industries were also very successful in export markets. Sweden thus became very efficient in producing power-generating equipment at the same time as it got cheap energy for the rest of the economy. This is one example of several where there was a complementarity between the state as a buyer and private firms as suppliers of equipment. With the state as a stable long-term buyer and a partner that was willing to discuss and develop the relevant knowledge, the private firms were able to grow into major multinationals (for example, ABB). Other examples of this type are the links between Swedish Telecom and Ericsson or the Swedish health system and the pharmaceutical industry (present-day Astra-Zeneka and Pharmacia Corporation). It should be noted, though, that there has for a very long time been a regulation about public tenders that has forced even firms with a long-established relationship to tender in competition with domestic and foreign buyers. That honesty and transparency are vital for such a mechanism is clear to anyone who has seen its extensive misuse in countries such as Kenya.

It is not quite clear how the emergence of the so-called new economy is going to change the scenario for Africa, but potentially it could shorten the route to the frontier. Information is much more easily available and the disadvantages of a peripheral location may be reduced. The latter is not self-evident, though, because even IT firms in the North tend to cluster.

The Nordic labor movement has generally been positive about structural change and a liberal trading regime. This is a reflection of its experience of the positive effects on living standards of that type of policy. However, the economic changes associated with, for example, the recent phase of structural adjustment in Africa have often not been translated into increasing real wages, which has meant that both the labor movement and the general public have been lukewarm in their support for the new policies. This is a significant problem and it can be overcome only through the success of the policy. Preaching will probably not do the trick. So the real issue is whether a reform policy can be kept in place for long enough for it to start delivering increasing real wages. This has happened in the case of Uganda, for example, but there are cases where it has not happened. This may then lead to policy reversals that further undermine the confidence of investors and there will in the end be a vicious circle driving real incomes further down. The policy or its implementation may of course be wrong, but it is not clear that more sensible policies are what, for example, African trade union bosses generally advocate.

African economies are dualistic or at least far from homogeneous. This means that factor rewards such as wages may vary a lot between sectors or activities, and this has an efficiency cost. Swedish trade unions did try to avoid this by actively squeezing wage differentials that were unrelated to the type of job that the worker was doing. This increased the rate of structural change and real income growth. Whether this would be a feasible strategy in Africa is debatable, and there is actually now a debate in Sweden about whether this is the right strategy for today. Maybe some regions should accept lower wages in order to reduce their unemployment problems? Still, it does not seem like a top priority for African economies to drive bad firms out of business, when the alternative for labor is either unemployment or the informal sector.

The stringent levels of firm taxation that were pursued in Nordic countries do not seem appropriate for Africa either. Retained earnings finance most investments in African manufacturing, and as long as there is little in terms of alternative sources of finance it is a high-risk strategy to tax firms heavily. It is very important to remember that state ownership was always limited in the Nordic countries. This needs to be contrasted with the role of parastatal firms in many African economies, which has been very detrimental to efficiency and growth. The basis for the Nordic welfare state was a functioning private sector, and this is a lesson that African economies would be well advised to heed.

4   Concluding remarks

The first and most obvious limitation on the application of the Nordic model in Africa is the large differences in income levels. At present the Nordic countries have per capita incomes in the range of US$25,000–30,000, whereas African countries often have per capita incomes below US$500. Even if we correct for differences in purchasing power, there remains a huge gap. It is important to remember that the welfare state in the Nordic countries provided a very limited safety net when their economic standard was comparable to that of African economies today. There are thus choices to be made with regard to where to start. The African tax base is not such that it can enable governments to have everything at once – although Nyerere's Tanzania did attempt something of the sort. With limited resources it seems sensible to me to put top priority on the provision of public services, such as education and health, on a broad scale plus the basic infrastructures necessary for a functioning economy, rather than, for example, generous social insurance to formal sector employees. Transfer systems cannot be comprehensive in the African economies of today, whereas universal primary education could benefit vast segments of the population. It seems reasonable to pursue egalitarianism via the provision of public goods or the public provision of private goods such as education and health services rather than trying to achieve equality through an elaborate transfer system of the Nordic type. That can come much later. There may still be some cases where there will be a need for some form of safety net, such as care for orphans, but often this is taken up by the extended family system and it would be better to leave it there for now.

I also noted that, during the industrial breakthrough period, the Nordic countries were not too dissimilar from the leading economies of the world, albeit a bit poorer. This meant that domestically they catered for a similar pattern of demand to that dominating the world market. The situation in Africa is at least partially different. The middle class and the elite do have a consumption pattern that is relatively similar to that of the North, but the bulk of the population does not. This means that in the case of Africa it is even more harmful to focus on trying to produce only for the domestic population, since this may mean that firms are locked into a pattern of production that is out of step with what the world market demands. It will therefore not be a route to creating a competitive edge for the supply of, for example, cheap consumer goods for the global market.

I noted that Sweden was able to change its capital–labor ratio considerably through labor emigration and capital immigration. In the current situation it seems hard to expect the North to open up significantly to African labor emigration. There is, however, an abundance of internationally mobile capital available, but to attract this to Africa the environment has to be seen to be economically and politically stable. At present this is not the case. Thus, although factor mobility would be helpful, to bring it about demands that African states put their houses in order to a degree that is acceptable to domestic and foreign profit-maximizing investors. In the meantime, they have to rely on what they can get in the form of foreign aid, although this type of capital is not a perfect substitute for private capital. Direct investment resources often come with technology attached, which can then spill over, affecting the productivity of other firms.

The political institutions determining how a country is run are very important. In a formal sense, the Nordic set of institutions is not that dissimilar to what exists in Africa after the recent political reforms. What is different, however, is how the political process works and the scope for and acceptance of effective debate and opposition. Here most countries in Africa have a long way to go before they reach the Nordic level of political tolerance.

Generally one may conclude that there are lessons to be learnt for Africa from the many aspects of the Nordic model, as indeed there are lessons to be learnt from other regions. What makes the Nordic countries stand out, though, is the extent of social peace and the comprehensiveness of the welfare state that they have achieved. However, the foundations of peace are often country specific and must evolve out of the local social setting. It is thus not obvious what Africa can learn from the Nordic countries about how to replicate this important ingredient of their development over the past century. What is more certain is that, although a welfare state may be a long-term aim for Africa, in the short to medium term African countries need to focus on the core ingredients of development in order to ensure maximum impact on their societies.

Another important issue is what drives institutional and policy change. Recent changes in the Swedish structures were undertaken after the country had run into a severe economic crisis. Until that happens, people tend to take a wait-and-see attitude, expecting things to return to normal. The same attitude existed in Africa in the 1970s, but in the 1980s there was finally a realization that structures needed to change. The structural adjustment packages have grappled with this, but some institutional changes that are needed do not follow immediately out of those programs. For example, dimensions such as honest and transparent government and politics are not easily changed either from above or from the outside. Nevertheless, sensible reform of policies and organizations may help pave the way for change.

Notes

1. The pattern of development and the social and institutional structure of the Nordic countries are very similar, but most of the examples in this chapter will be taken from Sweden. Hence, references to the Nordic model in the text will in many ways also be to the Swedish model.

2. Three Scandinavian countries – Sweden (Eklund, 2000; Schön, 2000a,b; Södersten, 1991), Denmark (Paldam, 1991) and Norway (Hveem, 1991) – had a rather similar pattern of development and their growth acceleration started at the same time, that is in the mid to late nineteenth century. Finland was slower to take off, but has since gone through a very similar growth process and has now caught up with the rest (Haavisto and Kokko, 1991). Iceland, being sustained by fisheries, is a special case.
3. Note, however, that Denmark saw rapid income convergence with much less emigration than Sweden.
4. There still is a Swedish-speaking minority in Finland.

REFERENCES

Bigsten, A. and Moene, K.-O. (1996) 'Growth and Rent Dissipation: The Case of Kenya,' *Journal of African Economies* 5(2):177–98.

Eklund, K. (2000) 'Svensk ekonomisk tillväxt: Rekordår, stagnation och nya möjligheter,' in B. Södersten (ed.) *Marknad och politik*, 5th ed., SNS förlag: Stockholm.

Haavisto, T. and A. Kokko (1991) 'Politics as a Determinant of Economic Performance: The Case of Finland,' in M. Blomström and P. Mellor, *Diverging Paths. Comparing a Century of Scandinavian and Latin American Economic Development*, Inter-American Development Bank with Johns Hopkins University Press: Washington, DC, and Baltimore, MD.

Hjalmarsson, L. (1991) 'The Scandinavian Model of Industrial Policy,' in M. Blomström and P. Mellor, *Diverging Paths. Comparing a Century of Scandinavian and Latin American Economic Development*, Inter-American Development Bank with Johns Hopkins University Press: Washington, DC, and Baltimore, MD.

Hveem, H. (1991) 'Developing an Open Economy: Norway's Transformation 1845–1975,' in M. Blomström and P. Mellor, *Diverging Paths. Comparing a Century of Scandinavian and Latin American Economic Development*, Inter-American Development Bank with Johns Hopkins University Press: Washington, DC, and Baltimore, MD.

Meidner, R. and G. Rehn (1951) *Fackföreningsrörelsen och den fulla sysselsättningen*, LO: Stockholm.

O'Rourke, K. and J. G. Williamson (1999) *Globalization and History. An Evaluation of Nineteenth Century Atlantic Economy*, MIT Press: Cambridge, MA.

Paldam, M. (1991) 'The Development of the Rich Welfare State of Denmark,' in M. Blomström and P. Mellor, *Diverging Paths. Comparing a Century of Scandinavian and Latin American Economic Development*, Inter-American Development Bank with Johns Hopkins University Press: Washington, DC, and Baltimore, MD.

Schön, L. (2000a) *En modern svensk historia. Tillväxt och omvandling under två sekel*, SNS: Stockholm.

——— (2000b) 'Tillväxt och omvandling i svensk ekonomi,' in B. Södersten (ed.) *Marknad och politik*, 5th ed., SNS förlag: Stockholm.

Södersten, B. (1991) 'One Hundred Years of Swedish Economic Development,' in M. Blomström and P. Mellor, *Diverging Paths. Comparing a Century of Scandinavian and Latin American Economic Development*, Inter-American Development Bank with Johns Hopkins University Press: Washington, DC, and Baltimore, MD.

Concluding remarks

Steve Kayizzi-Mugerwa

The studies presented in this book touch on the subjects of institutional capabilities, reform ownership and development in sub-Saharan Africa. The focus was elicited by three important changes during the past decade in the general perception of the role of the public sector in economic development in Africa.

First, there has been a slow but unmistakable quantitative shift to smaller and less intrusive government. There is not a single African government that has not attempted some reform measures for the public sector, including retrenchment, in the past decade. Decentralization is back on the agenda, with attempts being made to bring about genuine devolution. However, in spite of the related recent moves toward more democratic forms of governance, African leadership has been more willing to open up economic rather than political space.

Second, and partly as a result of the quantitative changes mentioned above, some countries have seen improvements in the delivery of services. Their governments no longer see themselves as sole suppliers of social services and have either opted for partnerships within the private sector or proffered specialized agency autonomy. Efficiency and choice have entered the language of the planning and implementation units of the line ministries, and privatization is no longer the controversial subject it was a decade ago. Inevitably, complex agency problems have arisen in the public sphere, especially since the new thinking has superseded the much slower attempts at establishing effective regulatory mechanisms.

342

The civil service itself is on the verge of transition: the old ways of doing government business are now clearly inadequate, but training and skills upgrading for the 'new' civil service have only just started.

Third, poverty reduction has been designated the raison d'être of the public sector. There is general agreement among donors that governments that demonstrate genuine ownership of policies for poverty reduction should be rewarded with more aid or given preference in Heavily Indebted Poor Countries (HIPC) arrangements. However, ownership remains a fuzzy concept that has generated much confusion, notably when donor and recipient countries fail to agree on how to measure the progress made towards its attainment. Cynicism and the taking of shortcuts have resulted on both sides. With regard to conditionality, some African countries have complained at being singled out by donors for more stringent treatment when, in their view, their neighbors have been treated lightly.

In discussing public sector reforms, it is relatively easy with the benefit of hindsight to criticize governments for poor implementation strategies and for lack of commitment. However, in light of the reform tasks, African countries were probably more overwhelmed than uncommitted. Thus, although the failure of reforms to improve policy implementation and generate growth has been blamed on the intransigence of African governments, the donor community shares some of the blame. In the area of institution building, for example, both sides lacked the farsightedness and patience required for success. African governments, partly for lack of precedent, were prepared or forced to revamp their public sectors in a matter of years, while donors conditioned their support on the success of this rather unprecedented experiment. Both sides clearly underestimated the serious lack of capacities in individual countries as well as the time required for completing the reform process.

In these concluding remarks, I reflect on the African experience with institutional reforms as portrayed by studies in this volume, especially focusing on issues of ownership and the enhancement of institutional capabilities. I shall begin with the important question of reform ownership.

Public sector reforms in Africa have been complex. This was not only for lack of finances and human resources but also because the civil service, identified in many reviews as the weakest link in the reform process, was assigned the task of reforming the public sector, including itself. The agency problems implied by this peculiar role explain in part the recalcitrant nature of and the confusion related to public sector reforms. In practice, reforms were easier to draft, especially with donor assistance, than to implement or internalize. In many countries, situations arose in which different groups were engaged in reorganizing the same entities but with little or no cooperation between them. Often, competing interventions were suggested and implemented without considering the implications for the program as a whole. This has been especially true in decentralization efforts. Reforms at the center have sometimes failed to take into account the implications of decentralization, which implies that capacities need to be shifted from the center to the locality.

Another problem relates to external financing and its implications for ownership. Donor assistance has been a precondition for the success of public sector reforms in Africa. Many of the interventions – including retrenchment of the civil service, the creation of agencies for revenue collection, privatization and utility regulation – have been very capital intensive and few governments would have been able to undertake them without external support. However, financial dependence and domestic ownership are not compatible. Few countries can establish real ownership when donors finance the bulk of their budgets. Thus, engaging in far-reaching reforms without sufficient of their own resources risks subordinating the governments' political agenda to that of the donor community. African governments learn quickly that they are not in the driver's seat when technical and other disruptions to aid disbursements delay domestic programs, including those for poverty reduction.

Reform ownership is sometimes mentioned in the same context as partnerships for development. 'Partnership' is a much more appropriate expression, because it allows for various levels of collaboration. What is required for partnership is a similarity of goals or ambition; it does not have the confusing implication that recipient countries can 'own' their policies. The latter contention is ironical in a situation in which such countries continue to depend heavily on the donor community for funding and policy advice. However, even a partnership demands that minimum conditions be met. Thus, for a true partnership to emerge, both sides need to let go of the old conceptions and focus on strengthening institutions that enable a more transparent recipient–donor relationship. Both sides are aware that financial independence will not be achieved in the near future. Nevertheless, efforts at improving capacities in the public sector in general, and in the civil service in particular, could ensure that future reforms will be driven from within.

Broad participation and democratization are also important for policy ownership, even in the narrower sense of partnerships for development that I am suggesting. The idea that populations must be involved in the formulation of policies that affect them is very attractive. This, in turn, demands the devolution of power to increase the proximity of local populations to policymakers and to make it possible for citizens to monitor the performance of their leaders. However, mere proximity is not enough. Local democracy must be encouraged in order to strengthen local governments in their dealings with the center. On the other hand, central governments must also learn when to let go. Many have held onto the purse strings, claiming that this is the only way of ensuring account-ability at the local level. Decentralization without local responsibility, in-cluding over finances, is bound to fail.

With regard to developing institutional capacities in the public sector, a major issue relates to making the civil service an attractive place to work, with good career prospects and remuneration. The strategy of turning the civil service into an employer of last resort must end if the sector's pro-ductivity is to increase. Furthermore, studies in this volume raised the possibility of a mismatch between the current skills of employees in the civil services and the skills needed to accomplish the ambitious reforms embraced by the governments in the 1990s. The mission of the public sector in Africa has been declared to be that of poverty reduction. Pri-vate sector development has also been mentioned as a key goal, espe-cially in the broad sense of incorporating peasants into the market econ-omy. To accomplish these tasks it will be necessary to undertake more holistic measures. Thus, to ensure that civil servants are facilitators and not impediments to reform will demand the improvement of their remu-neration as well as creation of facilities for their training and skills up-grading. It is important to remember that a professional civil service will not thrive on exhortation alone.

These issues also relate to those of transparency and accountability. The lack of both has been blamed on poor remuneration in the civil services. However, since corruption continues to be a problem even in the new agencies, where wages and other benefits are far superior to those in the normal public sector, the causes of corruption and malfea-sance are much more deep-seated. First there is a general paucity of control mechanisms based on transparent procedures to ensure checks and balances in public sector operations. Notably, financial controls within the public sector remain weak. The security sectors continue to be financial black holes in many countries. Although the military accounts for the bulk of budgetary resources, military spending is hardly subjected to official auditing procedures. Parliamentary committees for public ex-penditure are often ineffective; their reports, made public long after the events referred to occurred, have little impact. The offices of the auditors general are poorly funded in many African countries.

Perhaps even more serious is the lack of a relevant body of law to en-sure that corrupt officials are punished in a manner bound to be a deter-rent. It is not uncommon for corrupt officers' cases to be adjudicated under statutes from the 1960s. Thus, besides the modernization of the financial and accounting systems, and raising the technical capacities for budgeting and financial analysis, the upgrading of laws relating to public sector employees will also be necessary.

Second, governments have weak budgeting systems. In recent years, some attempts have been made to relate budgeting procedures to program targets. Much hope currently rests on the donor-supported medium-term expenditure framework, which it is hoped will help countries to target their resources on poverty reduction.

The current state of African institutions is thus conflict ridden, and predictions about the future must be guarded. However, the studies presented here have not suggested in any way that the challenges are insurmountable. Examples, though few, were given of countries that have overcome financial and human resource strictures to restructure their institutions, rejuvenate their economies and begin to address poverty. The irony for Africa is that the countries that seem to be making progress in their reforms are not necessarily those that were well endowed in earlier decades or those that had a capitalist base. It is often countries that suffered serious setbacks in earlier decades – caused by civil war and natural catastrophes – that have made the most impressive institutional and economic turnaround.

Finally, reforms demand strong political leadership. However, where influential bureaucrats remain largely indifferent or even cynical, reforms will make little headway. Successful institutional reforms are characterized by enthusiasm across the board and not just at the top.

Index

Catalogue Request

Name: _____

Address: _____

_____

Tel: _____

Fax: _____

E-mail: _____

To receive a catalogue of UNU Press publications kindly photocopy this form and send or fax it back to us with your details. You can also e-mail us this information. Please put "Mailing List" in the subject line.

 **United Nations University Press**
53-70, Jingumae 5-chome
Shibuya-ku, Tokyo 150-8925, Japan
Tel: +81-3-3499-2811 Fax: +81-3-3406-7345
E-mail: sales@hq.unu.edu http://www.unu.edu